Great Betrayal

Volume 2

Vyacheslav G. Naumenko

William Dritschilo
Translator

Created using OpenOffice Writer 4.1.3

Translation and added notes: William Dritschilo

Cover design: Jamie Dritschilo

2018

Printed by CreateSpace, an Amazon.com Company

© Copyright held by William Dritschilo, Proctor, Vermont. No re-publication, dissemination in any form, or other re-use, in part or in whole, is allowed without permission from the author.

Gen. V. Naumenko

Great Betrayal

Repatriation of Cossacks at Lienz and Other Places
(1945-1947)

Collected Documents

Volume II

All Slavic Publishing House
New York
1970

All books by the All-Slavic Publishers are published thanks to the efforts and support of Count S. S. Beloselsko-Belozersko.

From the Publisher

In bringing the second volume of V. G. Naumenko's book, *The Great Betrayal*, to the light of day, we have completed the public exposure of documents and exhibits, arriving in the presence of heavy discussions by former allies and the enlightened West, of the to-this-time unprecedented massive betrayal of honest Russian people to punishment by the Red Moloch.

There is much that is still secret in the archives of the former Western Allies, and there have yet to be answers to many questions, but what is presented on the pages of these two volumes puts a shameful mark of betrayal before the face of humanity that can never be cleansed. (We will not even speak about Russia. What of Russia! …)

Below, we give room for the words of the famous Polish writer, Josef Maczkiewicz, in excerpts from his book on this question, in which he so colorfully, aptly, and precisely puts everything in its place and names all and everyone in his own words:

"The turnover of Cossacks by the Allies in 1945 to the Bolsheviks should, it would seem, have shaken the conscience of the free world. Nonetheless, this did not happen. To the contrary, few even knew about it and those who did were inclined to quickly justify the actions of the Allies, at best not even willing to give much significance to the events: 'This alleged episode of war, in truth, rather ugly, is something that happens often in war, but … compared to Hitler's crimes …,' etc. …"

"… Over the course of six years, all the countries in the world that call themselves free democracies carried on one of the bloodiest of wars; one for which the general slogan and moral principle was not one of life, but of death, ostensibly tied to their love of freedom and their attempt to overthrow tyranny and free the enslaved. In a political sense, the issue was not the liberation of a certain country, but of all the people of Europe. Subsequently, the blame was placed on tyranny rather than on the political violations of the sovereignty of other nations and such, but more directly: for crimes against humanity. In the face of this global moral arousal, it logically seems that the fighters for the freedom of humanity should first have bowed before those who, not just in the course of six years, but for twenty-eight years now did not make peace with slavery, did not lose hope, but waited or, without putting down their arms, fought to free people against a not yet revealed, but fuller, more total, more shackling tyranny.

"Thus it would seem when based on noble ideals of justice and conscience. But it turned out to be the opposite. When the war ended, those who suffered in bondage more than others, who fought for freedom incomparably longer than others, were the ones who were herded behind barbed wire, then given into the hands of executioners to their deaths, to imprisonment in concentration camps …!"

"… Someone once said: 'It is not a problem when the killer turns out to be a professional criminal. It is much worse when the professional judge turns out to be a cheap pickpocket..'

"Nonetheless, even this juxtaposition does not fit here, because at the very same time, as came out in the Nuremberg trials … Things were very much the opposite: rather than a minor thief caught there, it was an accursed criminal, by orders of magnitude worse than those put on trial. In one instance, the Katyn Massacre, he blamed those on trial for the evil deed that had been done entirely with his own hands. Those in court knew well that it was so, that killers were brought to court but not charged. Nevertheless, the Tribunal considered it proper to sit in comradeship with professional killers and even to call the entire vulgar masquerade 'Tribunals of International Law…'"

"… The future establishment of a free world depends on whether this false facade is destroyed in the near future to show the truth.

"General Naumenko, to my mind, belongs to those few who, as much as they are able, attempt to break through the curtain of lies …"

From the Publisher

On this, we will end our words, making note of our disappointment that the author, after submitting his words to print, did not heed our repeated insistence, but found a need to cut his own excellent material on the "Russian Corps" and Colonel Rogozhin's note, "On the turnover of the wounded in hospitals."

Foreword

Foreword

In 1945, toward the end of the 2nd World War, up to 110,000 Cossacks were present on the orders of the Main Command of Cossack Forces in the territories of Germany and Austria, and also at times in France, Italy, Czechoslovakia, and several other countries in western Europe.

Of them, more than 20,000, mainly elderly, invalids, women and children, were found in the Cossachi Stan in southern Austria on the shores of the Drau River at Lienz.

Up to 45,000 men[*] in units of the 15th Cossack Cavalry Corps were also gathered in southern Austria, north of the city of Klagenfurt.

Many Cossacks, in the form of separate platoons, squads, regiments, formations, and commands, were found in various German military units.

Thousands of Cossacks were spread over the territories of Germany and Austria in various military units, in factories of the Todt, as farm laborers under peasants, etc.

There were Cossacks in units of the Russian Liberation Army (ROA); although in what numbers has to this time not been established and probably never will be, because they were not separated out into special Cossack units, but marched as part of various units designated for the ROA.

In volume 1 of *Great Betrayal*, a large number of pages have material about forced repatriation of the inhabitants of the Cossachi Stan. They are especially frightening, not only because of the ferocity of the users of force, but because these were British soldiers, "armed to the teeth," against non-resisting, unarmed women, children, and the elderly.

But much material intended for volume 1 never made it into print and is now given in this volume.

---

[*] Incorrectly given as 15,000 in volume 1.

The same applies to the mountain people of the North Caucasus, whose camp was located in the immediate vicinity of the Cossachi Stan* on the Drau River.

This volume presents a continuation of material about the repatriation of Cossacks and mountain people of the North Caucasus on the Drau River, the forced turnover of the 15th Cossack Cavalry, and forced turn overs in other places: Italy, France, and England.

The collection of information on forced repatriations continues.

A large number of pages in this volume come from observations of victims en route from their place of betrayal to concentrations camps in Siberia and life in prison. Some also were given on the return to Europe by those released from incarceration.

Here also are printed several documents from Yalta, along with debates in the English Parliament about bloody events in Italy before the betrayal.

After volume 1 of *Great Betrayal* came out in print in 1962, we received questions from several readers concerning why we printed material only on the betrayal of Cossacks, even though the same fate was falling on many others of our compatriots at that same time.

The collection of materials and documents about forced repatriations is so complex and grave that it is beyond the powers of any one person to complete the task in total.

Besides that, it is clear that several escapees from the betrayals are collecting materials about this tragedy and have published small parts.

At this time, three volumes titled *For Stalin's Pleasure* [translator's note, as are all bracketed notes that follow: *В угоду Сталину*] by B. M. Kuznets consisted of exquisitely well-gathered material.

---

* The first fully accurate and detailed account of the destruction of the Cossachi Stan was given by Ivan Constantinovich Zubenko, a Cossack of the Beysugskoy Stanitsa.

Such material was put into print, too, by M. V. Shatov, who has published two volumes: the 1st under the title, *Bibliography of Liberation Movements of the Peoples of Russia in the Years of the Second World War (1941-1945)*; the 2nd, *Material and Documents of the ODNR* [Liberation (O in Russian) Movements (M) of the Peoples (N) of Russia (R)] *in the Years of the 2nd World War."*

It is expected that both authors will continue to gather and publish evidence.

Still, it falls to us in several instances to bring up occurrences of forceful repatriations of several groups and individuals who were not Cossacks, but who were found in the immediate vicinity of Cossacks.

Among such cases, we put repatriations by Tito of Serbian Chetniks under Generals Mushitsky and Rupnik.

Likewise, we bring up several occurrences characterized as "technical" repatriations. One such instance happened in Italy with the "Varyag" Regiment commanded by the now-deceased Colonel M. A. Semenov.

It should be mentioned that there were Cossacks in the ranks of this regiment.

Likewise, we bring up similarly characterized instances in Italy of repatriations by Americans of people who, in the words of those who gave them over to the Soviets, convinced the Americans that they were "invaluable servants." This instance occurred with the Turkestani, Tinio, and his small unit.

Following are characteristic instances of handovers of individuals who had escaped to the Western Allies from the Bolsheviks.

A certain young man escaped to Berlin from the Bolsheviks to the Americans. No amount of persuasion by Soviets and Americans could break his unswerving decision not to return. Then Soviet Commander-in-chief Zhukov wrote to his "wartime buddy" Eisenhower, and the unfortunate youth was given over to the Reds.

Another, no less characteristic, instance took place in Italy. A young man, born in America and still a minor, fled there from Berlin and was taken off to his parents. He requested refugee status, but the American powers in Italy, "in order not to harm relations" with Stalin, gave away the unfortunate youth to certain death. He attempted to jump from an airplane en route to the USSR, but failed.

And those who have read the book by A. I. Delianitch, *Wolfsburg 397*, know that the commander of this camp, the English Captain Hyam Hillman [spelling could not be verified], had handed over Kennedy "wholesale and retail" into the hands of Tito, according to notes received from Titoists, in exchange for "raki" ["ракию"] and various items of provisions that were under lock in this camp of Serbian volunteers.

They were all transported in camp trucks to be turned over to Titoists and executed there in place.

We call the reader's attention to documents reproduced in this volume from the Yalta Conference, from which it can be seen that there was no provision made for forced repatriation.

There is an idea that these forced repatriations did not take place until the Yalta Conference, which took place February 4-11, 1945, had ended. As the reader can see from these documents, however, forced repatriations began before then.

The documents demonstrate that, even before the conference, there were handovers of prisoners of war by way of Mediterranean ports by both Americans and the English.

These documents report the handing over by Americans of 1,100 of our prisoners of war, while the English sent 10,000 people from England by way of Mediterranean ports and 7,500 from France.

As concerns the Yalta Conference, itself, on the exchange of prisoners of war, it did not envision forced repatriation. Little more is said in it beyond that agreeing sides MUST USE ALL PRACTICABLE MEANS to ENSURE THE EVACUATION TO THE REAR OF THESE LIBERATED CITIZENS. [The exact words of the agreement are given here, rather than a translation of the author's translation.]

The governments of the Western Allies and the Commands of their armed forces included among "PRACTICABLE MEANS" the

APPLICATION OF CLUBS, WEAPONS, and TANKS to force the unwilling to "return to their homelands." [But for those enclosed by quotation marks, the capitalized words are not found in the form given in the Yalta Agreement.]

From the Yalta documents, we can see that speedy turnover of prisoners of war to the Soviets was an especially firm requirement that was energetically supported by the English government.

Americans in general were opposed to the use of force. At the same time that leaders of the United States expressed the same view, their actions to prevent forced handovers fell apart under the firm decision of President Roosevelt, the Commander of the General Staff under him, and USA Secretary of State Stettinius.

Without looking at the rationale being presented from Washington, American forces in Europe judged the question in favor of Stalin's convenience, and millions of people were given over by them to certain death.

Neither does it follow to lose sight of the fact that several representatives of parliaments in the USA and England made inquiries about illegal forced repatriations in their parliaments, but to no avail.

These were the sorts posing the questions: Congressman Albert Bosch in Washington and Lord Kriby in London, but their questions to this time "remain tabled" ["*лежат под сукном*"] by the responsible law-making organizations of the USA and England.

After the bloody events of 1947 in Italy, Senator Stokes requested an explanation about them from representatives of the English government, Minister Bevin and Prime Minister Eden, but he never received a satisfactory answer.

Attempts were made to obtain explanations from those guilty of the glaring crimes, including by several writers, the Polish writer J. A. Maczkiewicz and the English writer Peter Huxley-Blythe, for example, but without success.

***

Regardless of the passing of almost 30 years since the time of the bloody events of forced repatriation, certain facts tied to them remain unexplained to this day.

For example, there is no doubt that massive executions of Cossacks took place in the vicinity of Graz in Austria, but to this day we do not have supporting evidence to establish the Bolshevik crimes.

Below, we print the testimony of a Kuban Cossack, who on passing through the camp in Graz, at which he stayed for several days, watched how Cossacks were taken away at night and how the same trucks that took them away returned empty. This Cossack succeeded in learning from one of the drivers that those taken from the camp were executed.

Likewise, we obtained a map of the city of Graz and vicinity on which several places where Cossacks had been executed were marked.

In volume one of *Great Betrayal*, we mentioned that there was a film made by one of the American officers at a quarry in which Cossacks were executed.

This film was sent to me in America, along with several documents. There is evidence that it was received in America and hidden in a safe place, but to this day, I have not succeeded in obtaining it.

Similarly, we also have not succeeded in receiving materials on the handover of several regiments of the 15th Cossack Cavalry Corps.

It should be noted that for some reason or other, the majority of Russian interpreters are evasive and abstain from confirming information given in testimony about forceful repatriations which, since they were in the center of the events, should have been well known to them.

In this matter, I gratefully acknowledge one of the interpreters in the Cossachi Stan, O. D. Rotova, who provided us with many valuable accounts.

Likewise, it must also be noted that Austrian railroad workers at those stations at which loading into train cars bound for the USSR was carried out and on which trains passed to the east, to this time have refused to give any testimony in regard to the removal of people and in general what has to be known by them.

They are motivated to do so because, in due course, they have accepted the words of the leaders of the Western Allies and kept their mouths shut.

Almost 30 years have passed since the tragic forced turnovers.

By this time, Russian and other presses have published tens of books and hundreds of separate memoirs, sketches, stories, and such in periodicals and other collections.

This speaks for the conscience of humanity not being able to reconcile itself to what took place in 1945-7 until measures are taken to prevent the future subjection of ordinary individuals to the use of illegal force.

V. Naumenko

Cossachi Stan

How the Turnover of the Cossachi Stan was Carried Out by the English Military Command

What concerns how the turnover of the Cossachi Stan was carried out by the English military command (leading to a tragic end), the entire procedure of the handover and communications, beginning at Tolmezzo and ending at Kötschach (Austria), was recorded almost stenographically by the translator at the events, O. D. Rotova.

Her diary reveals another page in the sad tragedy of a remnant of Cossacks torn from Soviet hell.

For negotiations with representatives of the English command, the following were sent from Kötschach as emissaries: General Vassiliev, assistant to the Field Marshall, Captain [*подъесаул*] N. N. Krasnov the younger, and O. D. Rotova, interpreter.

The cordial reception given them by representatives of the English command, along with an atmosphere that was more than friendly, inspired our emissaries with hope for an optimistic perspective for the Cossacks' future. Further talks with the staff of the Field Ataman strengthened these hopes even more.

O. D. Rotova lived through all the disturbing events of that time and remembered them well. Her knowledge of English gave her the ability of being present in the course of these secret discussions.

Reading her diary brings back memories of living through those times for us and affronts us even more by knowledge that the plan to betray the Cossacks to punishment by Stalin had already been prepared by the English.

There is no sense that, having greeted our emissaries so warmly and affectionately, the English staff already had in its hands that noose which in time would tighten around Cossack necks.

For us, as former officers of the Imperial Russian Army, trained in the noble traditions of Suvorov, Kutuzov, and Skobelev, we will never understand such a crime from the side of brothers in arms, our former allies in the First World War.

From the Diary of Translator, O. D. Rotova

During Passion Week [Russian Orthodox Easter Holy Week] (at the end of April, 1945), the situation on the Italian front was such that Field Ataman General Domanov decided to leave northern Italy and move north, into Austria.

After prolonged and heated discussions with Italian partisans, the Cossachi Stan moved north to cross an Alpine pass.

The Field Ataman answered the Italian demand to disarm and remain in Italy with a strenuous refusal, informing them that if they chose to hinder the Cossacks, they would force a breakthrough in strength.

The Italians backed down, but at the same time, General Globocnik, commander of German forces in northern Italy, ordered Domanov to remain in the region of Tolmezzo so that the Cossacks could cover the retreat of German units.

Domanov could not obey this command, for the poorly armed Cossacks were already in retreat to the north.

In heavy rain, then rain with snow, on roads covered over by drifting snow, the Cossachi Stan moved on, making a frightening, difficult trek over the pass and stopping at the Austrian town of Kötschach. There, the Cossacks celebrated Easter, performing Easter morning services in an Austrian cathedral.

The staffs of Generals Krasnov and Domanov took accommodations in its only hotel, reserving its dining room for the families of the staff. I found myself there, too.

Due to not having followed General Globocnik's orders, General Domanov had placed on house arrest there in Kötschach.

On the second day of Easter, it became clear that either the English or Americans had reached the pass.

Something had to be undertaken. The initiative for this was taken by an assistant to General P. N. Krasnov, Major General S. N. Krasnov, who was still in the situation of "honorary guest" of the Cossachi Stan, as was the entire staff of the Cossack leader.

I sat on some sort of chest in the front of the hotel and waited for the chance to join once more with the Free Stanitsa, which had what was left of my things.

Unexpectedly, an agitated Colonel A. S. M. arrived with General Vassiliev. Seeing me, they quickly headed in my direction.

"Mrs. Rotova here can come with us as interpreter," Colonel M. said to General Vassiliev.

"Olga Dmitireva, allow me to present General Vassiliev to you, with whom I ask that you come in the role of interpreter for negotiations with the English or Americans."

"But I cannot go. Look at what I am like after such a nightmare crossing on foot over the pass. I have neither the physical or moral capacity."

Knowing me well over long years and soon to be the future brother-soldier to my husband, Colonel M., took me by the hand with these words:

"Well, you must definitely and without procrastination come. Don't waste a single minute."

General Vassiliev excitedly seconded his request.

We almost ran to the auto, where Captain Krasnov was already present as General Krasnov was also quickly running up to it.

"Olga Dmitrievna, sit down quickly. You must hurry! General Vassiliev will explain everything to you on the way." With these words, he and Colonel M. literally shoved me into the auto.

Noting that we had no white flag, Captain Krasnov asked for white material of some kind. They ripped up some bed sheets or pillow cases, tied them to a stick, and attached them to the auto.

"Well, go with God!" S. Krasnov shouted and we took off in the direction of the pass.

General Vassiliev, standing in for the Field Ataman, was in a highly agitated state. Captain Krasnov was silent.

All the way, we tensely stared into the distance as we moved toward the unknown. What was ahead waiting for us was known only to God.

But we had little chance to ponder it. No sooner had we left the village of Kötschach, than a cry of "Halt!" from an English tank stopped us.

We stood still.

A lieutenant came toward us from the tank.

Through me, General Vassiliev conveyed to him that we had been sent by the Cossack Group, which was not at war with the Allies, to negotiate with the English Command.

The lieutenant suggested that we follow him to their captain up in the pass. He sat down with us and we followed the tank.

A radio transmission about us was sent to the pass and before we could reach it, an English captain and two war correspondents from English papers with photo cameras came out to us.

General Vassiliev briefly explained his mission to the captain and gave the correspondents an interview.

At that time at the post, two German SS officers were there to negotiate the surrender of their units. One of them, who spoke Russian well and knew General Vassiliev, came over and said:

"Behold, General. This is excellent! We will go together and, of course, we will not leave you."

Taking the SS officers with him in the tank, the captain escorted us to a major, the major to a colonel. The latter was in Polluzo [English spelling could not be verified].

After listening to General Vassiliev's statement, he said that he could decide nothing himself and had to deliver us to Tolmezzo, to the staff of the English Command.

Here was thrown before our eyes the different attitudes the English had toward us and the SS officers. The latter they put in a tank under guard; we rode in back by ourselves.

In this way, we came back once more to the place we had left a few days before. Once more, we found ourselves among Italians with hostile attitudes towards us. It was not only unpleasant, but dangerous, even with the tank guarding us.

On our entering populated areas, we were met with hostile shouts and threats. General Vassiliev and Captain Krasnov wore Cossack uniforms and there was fear that they had been taken prisoner.

"Barbarian Cossacks!" the Italians shouted, waving their arms and threatening us.

We stopped at the English staff building in Tolmezzo which, at one time, it seemed, was where the staff of the Field Ataman had been.

There, we were met by an English general to whom General Vassiliev conveyed through me that he wished to speak to him in strict confidence.

"Yes, of course, please!" the general answered and invited us into his office, where he identified himself as General Arbuthnott, shook our hands, and asked us to be seated.

General Vassiliev started to set forth the purpose of his visit. It must be said that General Vassiliev, an officer of the Cossack Life Guards regiment in the Imperial Army, brightly educated, with worldly manners, conducted himself with great dignity.

This had to have been noticed by any English officer who had the chance to observe his mannerisms and speak with him.

He briefly and clearly spelled out to the general that the

Cossachi Stan did not consider itself to be at war with the Allies and their aims. Cossacks did not see themselves as the enemy of the Western Allies.

As to any sort of surrender, there was no such discussion from General Vassiliev's side, as has been implied subsequently.

"The goal of the Cossacks, led by Field Ataman Domanov," he emphasized, "is to continue their interrupted one-time fight against Bolsheviks to free their homeland. In the name of the Field Ataman, I, as his assistant, ask that the Cossack group be given the opportunity to join the army of General Vlasov."

Having listened to all this, the general asked with amazement:

"But who is this General Vlasov?"

General Vassiliev explained the creation of the Vlasov Army and its aims: "Armed battle against Communists."

"You mean your goal is the rigorous continuation of war against Bolsheviks?"

"Yes," General Vassiliev distinctly and decisively pronounced.

"Before anything, the Cossacks must turn in their weapons," said General Arbuthnott.

On hearing this, General Vassiliev posed the following question:

"Are you considering this group of Cossacks as prisoners of war?"

No, we consider prisoners of war as those who we took in battle with weapons in their hands. I count you only as having **voluntarily surrendered** [bold print and lack of any kind of quotation marks in original].

At this time, another English general, who had apparently been told about us, arrived.

General Arbuthnott introduced us to him and asked Vassiliev to repeat once more what he had said to him.

Having listened to this with great interest, this general, who turned out to be Brigade Commander Musson, repeated what General Arbuthnott had said earlier:

"The Cossacks should immediately disarm."

General Vassiliev announced that he, not being the actual Field Ataman, was not able to give an answer to that demand.

Obviously, General Vassiliev's announcement resulted in both English generals not pressing for an immediate answer.

We were politely asked to go into another room, since they had things to discuss.

After a short time, we were again invited in. Their decision had been that tomorrow, at 9 in the morning, both generals would go to Kötschach to negotiate with the Field Ataman and his staff. General Musson also asked that Cossack supplies and patrols be removed to avoid misunderstandings with English patrols that might not yet have been informed of our discussions.

"The question of disarmament," he said, "we will put off until meeting with the Cossack staff."

The talks concluded, we rose to start on our return.

The brigade general asked that we wait a short time until he gave orders for a tank to accompany us.

"It is not without danger," he said, "in this location." Then he left.

General Arbuthnott turned toward us to kindly offer us a cup of tea.

General Vassiliev politely refused, motivated to do so because the staff of the Field Command must have been very worried, having waited for so long.

"No, no! Everything is ready and we will not let you go," said the general. Orderlies entered leaving trays loaded with sandwiches, cookies, jams, etc. Everything was presented so well and appetizingly, something to which we had long ago grown unaccustomed.

It was obvious that N. N. Krasnov interested General Arbuthnott, since the latter turned to him with several questions meant for him especially. Nikolai Nikolaevich told him in short that he was an old emigrant; had lived in Yugoslavia, where he had completed military school; served on the front in the army of the

King of Yugoslavia; and fell prisoner to the Germans. When he was released from prison, the Germans offered to let him become an officer-volunteer in their units in Africa, but he, not wishing to bear arms against his former allies in the 1st World War, refused.

General Vassiliev was very nervous and strove to leave to return quickly.

General Musson came back.

"Everything is ready," he said, "and you can depart."

At the same time, a soldier appeared with a large package. The general took it, tied it up himself, and gave it to me with these words:

"This is for you, madame."

I politely declined it, thanking him.

"No madame!" he continued. "I ask you not to refuse it; it is only tea, sugar, and chocolates."

Both generals saw us off to our automobile. General Musson, already out on the street giving us his farewell, went over to the SS officers found there.

General Arbuthnott came all the way to our auto and, as we waited for the tank, spoke with us about extraneous things and offered us cigarettes.

Amazed Italians stood on the street:

"How can it be? We thought they were bringing prisoners, and here are two generals accompanying them, smiling sweetly, shaking hands, etc."

During the conversation in the auto, I asked the general what his attitude was toward the Bolsheviks.

"Negative!" he said, emphasizing the word. "But at this time, they come as our allies."

"But how can you trust them," I asked, "knowing their disruptive actions, at least in your India in this war?"

"Yes." he answered laconically. "Still, for the time being, they are our allies, even if not our friends."

"But General, there will come a time when you yourselves will regret this union."

"Everything is possible," he answered.

A tank arrived and we set off.

The general waved to us affably until we were out of sight and shouted, "Until tomorrow!"

The Italians were so stunned by all they saw that, as soon as our auto started off after the tank, they started to yell enthusiastically: "Vivat! Vivat!"

One girl out of a group of youths waving their hands in welcome, dropped a large bouquet of lilies in my lap.

Those flowers I gave to Lydia Fyodorovna Krasnova on our return.

Even General Vassiliev, with his closed and morose attitude easily came to life for a brief time.

It must be noted that in discussions with the generals, he was dryly official, reticent, and not once smiled.

We returned to Kötschach at 9:30 in the evening, having left the Cossack Staff at 11:00 in the morning.

We had been awaited with great patience and worry. We went quickly to General Domanov's. General Vassiliev briefly apprised him of the course of the discussion and said that I would describe it in more detail.

I informed the Ataman of every detail and answered his questions.

After my report, we went out into the hallway, where Lydia Fyodorovna Krasnova awaited us at the door to her room.

"Peter Nikolaevich asked that you go in to see him," she said.

Once more, we had to tell our story in detail and answer questions posed to us.

It was obvious from everything with how much impatience he had waited to hear the results of our trip. Having listened attentively without interrupting me, he then began to pose questions that it seemed to us were, maybe, of little substance. He asked about everything down to the smallest detail, obviously giving them more than a little meaning. At times I could note traces of some sort on his face of what I would have described as worry and concern. Still, what I saw with my own eyes there convinced me that it was a substantial person with great government experience in and knowledge of his own business who was questioning me.

But this is what struck me then the most—why did Field Ataman Domanov, in the room almost next to General Krasnov's, consider it unnecessary at such an important moment in the history of the Cossachi Stan, not only to go in with his representatives to the Head of the Chief Administration of the Cossack Forces [this was the title authorized for Krasnov by the SS], but to even have the disposition to go see General Krasnov.

As they promised, the generals came to us on the next day. They were met formally, but not the way expected, for they arrived a half hour too early. (We wanted to greet them with an orchestra and an honor guard of cadets, along with the regimental guard of the Field Ataman.)

Discussions were carried out in the hotel dining room. I was invited to interpret. After introductions were made with handshakes, General Musson turned to me and asked that I convey the following to the Field Ataman:

"The Cossacks will not be disarmed, but will rather be used to guard German supplies and the road from Oberdrauburg to Lienz."

He asked for a map, which was spread on the table for him, and discussion began in an atmosphere of friendship. Major points were presented and the smallest of questions were considered on how all this was to come about.

There were joyful expressions on the face of the Field Ataman and members of his staff, although all were very restrained. This time, General Vassiliev was in good spirits. Everything spoke of the Cossacks not being counted in any way as foes or prisoners, but as if allies.

At this time, an English captain arrived who spoke French and, since General Vassiliev was fluent in the language, there was no longer a need for me. Still, General Domanov asked me to be ready for any circumstance and not to leave the hotel. I left and waited with Domanov's wife for the conference to end.

After it ended, General Domanov asked me and his wife to act as hosts to our guests.

When I entered the meeting room, General Arbuthnott came over to me and thanked me for translating, as he had in Tolmezzo.

The atmosphere was more than friendly. Lively discussions were carried on, hors d'oeuvres were eaten, wine was drunk, and glasses were raised in toasts to one another.

The entire event took 2 ½ hours, the entertainment being brief, for the generals were in a hurry.

During the day, correspondents from the British newspapers, *The Times*, *Daily Mail*, and one other whose name I have forgotten arrived.

They were interested in how this group of Cossacks found itself in Italy with their wives, elders, and children, as well as the origin of the Cossack Forces.

Through me, General Domanov explained everything about Coassackdom on a map of Russia: how the Bolsheviks behaved with Cossacks and their stanitsas and how, at the first chance, Cossacks rose up against the evils of the Soviet regime and had to leave their homeland because of it, taking everything that they could, partly by carts and wagons, partly on foot, to complete a long and difficult journey, not knowing what would await them, knowing only that they were escaping from Stalin's tyranny.

On the next day, the staff of the Field Ataman was moved to Lienz, there to join with the staff of P. N. Krasnov.

O. D. Rotova

From "The History of the 8th Argyll Sutherland Scottish Battalion. 1939-1947". — A. D. Malcolm.[*]

The Occupation of Eastern Tyrol

---

[*] A. D. Malcolm in the introduction to his book writes that the 10th Chapter is G. I. Malcolm's and that its information "was from a primary source.")

(Chapter X, written by Lieutenant Colonel G. I. Malcolm*)

[The original is still available, although not readily so, under the title, *History of the Argyll and Sutherland Highlanders 8th Battalion. 1939-1947*. What follows is a translation into English of Olga Rotova's translation to Russian.]

Several days after the capitulation of hostile units in Italy and Austria, the 78th Division was sent to carry out the disarmament of units found in Carpathia and East Tyrol. For that reason, the battalion moved north from Tolmezzo, prepared for resistance in a tactical formation. This move acquainted us with the history of an interesting political movement.

When the Germans in 1942 penetrated the Caucasus and the Ukraine, they accepted a large number of Russian Cossacks who, previously staunch anti-Soviets, chose to abandon their own country and follow the Germans west. This horde consisted of entire communities of households with all their belongings. The Germans, with their genius for organization, quickly formed the men into "divisions" to do guard duty near Udine and northern Italy, allowing the women, children, and small livestock to stay in temporary barracks.

We expected resistance from these divisions, given that the surrender of their allies (to whom they were in fact hirelings) meant their transport back to Russia and eventual death. For this reason, the 73rd Division made a tactical advance—but, in reality, there was no resistance of any kind to be encountered.

This was a very pleasant campaign, because the road wound through green valleys, beside clean, fast streams, beneath the spine of the Alps, and, of course, over the Grossglockner [*Сан Грос* in Rotova's translation] pass to Austria. This was the kind of country we had not seen in the course of many years, a country unaffected by

---

* From this chapter are given portions concerning Cossacks and their handover. Translation from English was done by the former interpreter of Camp Peggetz.

war and almost totally untouched by civilization. This was indeed "The Promised Land"—the incarnation of ir in the world.

Colonel Malcolm walked with his unit considerably in advance of his battalion, meeting up with Brigadier Musson, who ordered the 8th Argyll Battalion to occupy Lienz, where he would be "responsible for disarming the Cossack division which had moved into this zone, as well as all German units found there." Such an order would have been an overly board directive at any other time, but being two hours in advance of the battalion, the order seemed beyond the possible.

On arrival, Lienz appeared to have been an important military center, having entire rows of barracks and camps. Units would have to clear out those already occupying them before settling the battalion into them before dark. Major Lisk, with his dynamism, stepped up to the task, which was completed in a very short time. But this was only the first in a long sequence of problems requiring permission. Most of them became clear on the next day.

There were freed prisoners, refugees, compulsory laborers, resident civilians, and, finally, an entire Cossack division, which needed to be governed.

First of all, a transit camp was needed for all the released personnel and in a very short time. It takes little imagination to realize that this was a polyglot task, and Lieutenant Monroe, with an entire command of interpreters, was busy solving this international problem.

Take how many people came to the camp on May 12: Belgian —1, British—3, Dutch—2, French—108, Italian—77, Yugoslav—8, Rumanian—3, Russian—105.

It can be seen from the list that this was a problem beyond the ability of any ordinary soldier.

Surrendered enemy personnel presented an easier task, since there was a large military depot in Lienz and several infirmaries. The depot had capable administrative personnel and a large store of provisions. Major Charters [exact spelling could not be confirmed], in charge of all enemy surrendered personnel, found the task posing a huge hurdles.

But without doubt, the most serious problem presented was the unfortunate Cossack Division, which approximately numbered:

Men—15,000
Women—4,000
Children—2,500
Horses—5,000
And can you believe?
Camels—12.

The men were scattered over their units, living in tents along the length of the Drau River Valley, stretching 15 miles, from Lienz to Oberdrauburg, while women and children found places in the barracks of camps around Lienz.

Major Davies was named the officer who was the intermediary to the Cossack staff, and his duties consisted of making the Cossacks obey British commands—not an easy task, for, although their officers tried to help, discipline in the division was decidedly absent.

They were left in this situation until June, when the order came to send the Cossacks back to Russia. The Cossacks feared this fate greatly, and there was subsequently much unrest and many escapes. Since the camps were not enclosed in barbed wire, nor under guard, their residents could easily run off into the hills (as many did); **but time did not simplify the obligation to load the remainder onto trains. After several unpleasant days, this obligation was fulfilled: the camp was freed of these residents** (Emphasis ours. Editor), but 5,000 horses were left in place and Captain McHale [this name could not be verified; Rotova had it as Mack Hale] had to use great initiative in finding pasture for this herd. In the end, the horses were spread all over Austria, but not before he chose horses for the 8th Argyll Battalion.

… One horse chosen by Captain McHale is worthy of mention, for it became famous in S. M. F. racing circles. This was a bay mare which was called Katenka. She was imputed to be pure-blooded, but the Viennese Jockey Club could not protect their complete documents from fire during Russian bombing attacks. Nevertheless, at races organized by the 46th and 78th Divisions, she showed herself to be a real thoroughbred and brought the battalion 10 victories during the years 1945-6.

She always kept her place and carried her rider, beautifully— Captain Evato in1945 and Captain John de Burg in1946. [Neither the spelling of the names nor the fractured syntax could be verified.]

She is now (March, 1948) found in Poltalloch, Argyllshire, for breeding purposes.

Major [as given in original] A. D. Malcolm's book has a series of illustrations, among which are of 2 groups of battalion officers with their ranks and family names; the battalion on parade in Lienz on April 23 1946; and photographs of Lieutenant Colonel A. D. Malcolm with Lieutenant Colonel Tayer [spelling could not be verified] and an image of Katenka with her trainer, Vsevolod Nebo [spelling could not be verified] and Captain John de Burg.

Which Military Units of the Western Allies Carried Out the Forced Repatriation of Cossachi Stan?

With the aim of establishing which units of the English army took part in the forced repatriations of Cossacks and their families in southern Austria, from the banks of the Drau River on its flow from Lienz to Oberdrauburg in the spring of 1945, and if the Palestinian Brigade was involved in the matter, I sent a letter to English Lieutenant Colonel A. D. Malcolm, who was at the time the commander of the 8th Argyll Sutherland Scottish Battalion that carried out the forcible removal from Camp Peggetz on June 1, 1945, asking for his help in understanding this matter.

I received an answer from him which to some degree answers the question I posed.

Here are the texts of these documents, translated into Russian [and translated back into English].

June 29, 1956

Dear Lieutenant Colonel Malcolm,

As you well know, a significant number of Cossack anti-Communists were given up by the English to the Soviets during the course of May and June of 1945, in agreement with the Yalta Conference, in the region of Lienz and in camps along the length of both banks of the Drau between Lienz and Oberdrauburg.

I have taken upon myself the task of gathering material concerning the circumstances of these handovers and, during the course of the last 10 years, have collected an impressive number.

From your book, *History of the 8th Argyll Battalion, 1939-1947*, I learned that the responsibility of conducting repatriations in the region of Lienz was given to the aforementioned battalion.

Besides them, testimony of witnesses indicates that ranks of the Palestinian Brigade also took part in repatriations at Lienz, Peggetz, and other places along the Drau.

It is known to me that squads from the Palestinian Brigade were at that time sent from Italy to southern Austria with the assignment of finding Jews in this region and redirecting them to the location of the Brigade in Italy.

In the interests of historical accuracy, I now address you, as a historian and author, with a request that inform me of what you know regarding these aspects (points)—that is—what units of the British Army took part in these operations, and did the Palestinian Brigade or any other sorts of Jewish nationalists, either from the Soviet Army or local residents, take part?

I will be very grateful for whatever information you might be able to let me know on this question.

Yours Vyacheslav Naumenko

17 July 1956

Dear General Naumenko.

I have received your letter of June 29.

As far I know, the only military units taking part in the repatriations of Cossacks located in camps between Lienz and Oberdrauburg were units consisting of the 36th Brigade, that is, the 8th Argyll and Sutherland Battalion, the 5th Royal West Kent Battalion and the 5th East Surrey Battalion, although I do not think the last-mentioned took part.*

I never saw any units of the Palestinian Brigade in this region nor any units from it taking part in the repatriations, nor any Jewish nationalists of any kind taking part, wherever they might have been.

I hope that this information is of help to you.

Sincerely Yours, A. D. Malcolm

Concerning Chekists Among Scottish Soldiers in Camp Peggetz on the Day of June 1st 1945

(Excerpts from letters)

… Evidently, there were hidden Chekists in the ranks of English soldiers. My wife witnessed this.

For some reason, on the days of the handovers, a group of hospital employees from lower ranking personnel gathered on the threshold of the kitchen that exited directly onto the street of the village of Nußdorf, at which, from time to time, transport vehicles carrying English soldiers passed through. At the time, there was an 18-year-old-girl dishwasher hoping to remain "here." Being acquainted with English guards, she took rides with the soldiers on Cossack horses in the emptied camps and back to the hospital.

With evident fervor, she told us these observations:

---

* We managed to obtain the history of the Royal West Kent Battalion, from which it could be seen that this battalion did not take part in forced repatriations. It was at this time found in another region. We could not get the History of the 5th East Surrey Battalion. Editor.

"... and there were Russians among those Herods. The soldiers were dressed in English uniforms. They shot right at people. They were Chekist, have no worry!"

"Here they were, firing at defenseless people. Everywhere, they were darting around."

Convinced that they were there, she indicated to the group in the doorway, "And here they are, with those riding past."

"Why are you staring?" she shouted at someone in an English uniform, seated in a cart. "What are you looking at? Do you understand what I'm saying? Answer me at once!"

The one she addressed smiled and shook his head negatively.

"Don't understand?" she said in outrage. "You're lying!"

The soldier laughed while the English soldiers with him looked around, not understanding a single word.

My wife saw this scene from a close distance.

Second occurrence: While impressions were still fresh, one woman in camp asserted on oath that English soldiers (during the carnage on the square in Camp Peggetz) attacking her with a rubber club, striking her with all their strength, added the condemnation: "So I've caught up with you, have I, damn your soul! You won't get away!" and struck her so that she wound up in the hospital.

When we told about this later in camp, many women confirmed that "English soldiers" very often spoke to each other in Russian.

"We will all swear to it," they said. "Let them just ask!"

But for all I know, no one officially asked about it.

Th. V.

Churchill-Davies

Churchill-Alexander-Arbuthnott-Musson-Malcolm-Davies

Of those named above, most are not known to us, but they all took part in one way or another in the Cossack tragedy that took place along the Drau River in 1945 in the town of Lienz.

Some of them were involved through the Yalta Conference, on the basis of which Cossacks and their families were turned over to the Bolsheviks, others gave orders for the handovers, a third group appeared in the instances of transfer of these orders, a fourth directly executed the orders.

CHURCHILL, WINSTON—Prime Minister of Great Britain. Along with Stalin and Roosevelt, he signed the agreement at Yalta on the basis of which followed forced repatriations and reprisals of those not wishing to voluntarily return to the USSR.

ALEXANDER, English Lord, Field Marshall (at that time general in command of the 8th British Army in the region to which Cossacks came.) To him, General P. N. Krasnov applied in vain by letter: he received no answer and was one of the first to be turned over to the Bolsheviks.

ARBUTHNOTT, P. K.—Major General, leader of the 78th British Division in which were the 1st Guard, and 2nd and 36th Infantry Brigades. This division was given the responsibility of disarming units found in Carinthia and the western Tyrol.

This division had a distinctive arm insignia—a battleaxe without handle, yellow on a black background. In battalion history, it is written about this insignia: "This was a finely drawn symbol which had earned fame from Algiers to Cairo and from Syracuse to Klagenfurt." It is not known to us whether it found glory in other places, but we know that in the region of Klagenfurt, it earned infamy for violence against defenseless people in Lienz.

MUSSON, George—commander of the 36th Infantry Brigade, which included: the 8th Argyll Sutherland Battalion, the 5th Royal West Kent Battalion, and the 5th Surrey Battalion. He gave the order to the commander of the 8th Argyll Sutherland Battalion that made it responsible for disarming the Cossack division, that is, Field Ataman Domanov's Group, controlled by the English in the region of Lienz-Oberdrauburg.

MALCOM, A. R., Lieutenant Commander of the 8th Argyll Sutherland Scottish Battalion, ranks of which used force on the unarmed and defenseless settlement of Cossachi Stan in Lienz.

The distinguishing emblem of the battalion—a narrow transverse stripe with white and red squares arranged in a checkerboard of two rows.

DAVIES, V. R.—Major, an officer in the 8th Argyll Battalion, designated as the liaison to the staff of the Field Ataman.

On him was laid the responsibility to "attempt to make the Cossacks obey British commands." He was directly responsible for implementing the order to remove the officers of the Stan on May 28 "for a conference" and the use of force and beatings in following days at camps on the river Drau.

It should be noted that he fulfilled fervently and with zeal "the duty of a British officer," something which is worthy of being put to use in a better way.

Those who survived the tragedy of June 1st in 1945 in Camp Peggetz relate that on several instances he turned to his own direct superior, battalion commander Malcolm, who on the evening and day of the tragedy in Peggetz, came there several times in person.

About the above, it must be added that from the history of the 5th Argyll Battalion, we see not only that the forcible handover in Lienz was carried out by ranks of this battalion, but that they knew that they were handing over people to CERTAIN DEATH. Lieutenant Malcolm gives witness to this on p. 252 of his work: "Their handover to our allies meant their transportation to Russia and, subsequently, DEATH."

V. Naumenko

Major Davies

It is said that there are as many Davies in England as there are Ivanovs in Russia.

But the name, Davies, who sent off 2,000 officers of the Cossachi Stan into the hands of the Bolsheviks through the pretext of a "conference," who led the bloody carnage on the 1st of June of the same year, and who forcibly repatriated Cossacks and their families from the region of Lienz in the days that followed—is famous to all

Cossacks and all those who are interested in the question of forced repatriations of anti-bolsheviks by the Western Allies to behind the "Iron Curtain."

Many incorrectly call this major the commandant of the city of Lienz.

This he never was; he was rather the English liaison officer to the staff of the Cossachi Stan.

He was an officer in the Argyll Sutherland Scottish Battalion, whose commander, Lieutenant Colonel Malcolm, wrote:

"Major Davies was named liaison officer to the Cossack staff and his responsibility was to try to make Cossacks obey British orders. This was no easy task …"

At this time, the question of handing over the Cossacks to the Soviets had already been decided by the High Command of the Western Allies! Subsequently, Davies's assignment included the attempt to force Cossacks to repatriate.

He was the immediate executor of orders sending the officers of the Cossachi Stan "to a conference" on the 28th of May, violent attacks on Cossacks and their families, for the carnage on the square of Peggetz, and for their later removals from camps in the Drau River Valley.

V. Naumenko

Letter to the Prime Minister of the Kingdom of Great Britain, Winston Churchill, and Its Answer

26 November 1953

Your Excellency
Sir Winston Churchill
Prime Minister of the Kingdom of
Great Britain and Ireland
London
Sir:

In February 1945, in Yalta, you, F. D. Roosevelt, and Joseph Stalin signed an agreement, on which basis were repatriated former soldiers of the Red Army and former citizens of the USSR driven off with them by the Germans or voluntarily having left their homeland.

Perhaps you do not know how zealously this decree of yours has been carried out in life by the immediate executors of your will or what the repercussions of this were to those who did not want to return to their homeland, which is why I permit myself to forward to you three of the first issues of "Collection of Materials on the Handover of Cossacks in 1945 in Lienz and Other Places," in which what took place then in Austria on the banks of the Drau River is very clearly described.

The three issues are being sent to you by parcel post simultaneously with this letter.

Further materials being collected for an impartial history will recompense by their merit each of the former principals of the fate of nations.

If you would like to get further issues of the collections of such material, then I ask you to send me a note and they will be sent to you in the order that they come into print.

I ask you to forgive these documents being sent to you in Russian, but I expect that if you are interested in their content, you will find the means to read them in English.

Always Respectfully Yours,
Vyacheslav V. Naumenko
Kuban Cossack Ataman

British Embassy
Washington
March 19, 1954

Dear Mr. Naumenko,

I have been asked to thank you for sharing what is expressed in the package to the Prime Minister on the three issues of the journal entitled "Collection of Materials on the Handover of Cossacks in Lienz and Other Places in 1945."

Cossachi Stan

Your action in this matter has been highly valuable.

Sincerely yours,
Peter Marshall
Personal Secretary to Her Majesty

Preparation for Betrayal

Letter of Colonel of the Almighty Don Host
M. Buguraev, author of the above book

In materials issued by you on the handover of Cossacks in Lienz and other places, you write that many are interested in the question—Why did the officers of the Cossachi Stan so easily let themselves be tricked and go almost to a man to the imaginary conference?

You tentatively identified as main reasons:

1. The meticulous preparation by the English command on the Cossack leadership and the ability to carry it out in the person of Major Davies.

2. Russian officers were accustomed to trusting the word of an officer and never allowed even the idea of possible betrayal by an English officer,

With these reasons, of course, I am in agreement. But ... let me explain my hypothesis.

Cossacks and their officers were irreconcilable foes of communists. They fought for and hoped to bring about a Great Russian Nation and a rebirth of Cossackdom. All their efforts, all their thoughts were directed at this. The special situation in Cossack military units at the end of 1944 is necessary to take into account. In step with unending battle, they started organizing Cossacks units into a Cossack Corps.

I served in the Russian Corps, and at that time among us there was determined talk that the 1st Cossack Regiment was soon to be taken off its position and joined to the Cossack Division.* Plans were

---

* This account concerns the Cossack Division under the command of General

made. I even know of plans for officers to take over command duties, since there were very many senior officers with battle experience within the ranks of the regiments. Supposedly on this basis, the assistant to the commander of the regiment, Colonel V. I. M., asked for my agreement to a transfer to the Cossack Division to command an artillery battery, and maybe even to command an artillery division. In the regiment, I commanded an artillery platoon. He told me that soon it would be possible to transfer the entire regiment to the Cossack Division. This discussion took place at the end of July.

Subsequently, several officers of the regiment actually received the designation and left for the named division.

Already by the beginning of 1945, we began to talk about how peace would soon be concluded, but that the allies, along with the Germans, would carry on battle against the Communists.

I am convinced that such talk took place not only in our regiment, but everywhere, in all Russian units.

This created special circumstances to contact with and an unconditional belief in the Allied Command.

This, by my reckoning is the main reason for "belief in a conference" and belief in the English command.

And, when they were given the command, "to the conference:"

1—All thought of continuing battle with communism;

2—All the older, highly disciplined officers considered it necessary and even mandatory to follow the order;

3—Many of the officers who had doubts (there were, of course, such) went off out of a feeling of camaraderie. The basis to support this is served by conversations with the wives of my friends who were taken away.

Don Artillery Colonel **M. Buguraev**

On the question of betrayal by the Western Allies, much has been said and written; still, one cannot remain silent on it, but must speak out continuously, so that mankind can come to know and never

---

von Pannwitz.

forget about the glaring injustice and savagery perpetrated after the end of the 2nd World War on anti-Bolsheviks, among whom were Cossacks, who only aspired to help their people free themselves from the hateful yoke of the Bolsheviks, who were already decades into destroying the people of Russia and their belief in God, trampling both on the laws of God and man to devastate our heritage, all in the name of a bloody internationalism.

After the end of the war, hundreds of thousands of Russian people, Cossack men, women, and children, in the main, were betrayed to torture and suffering in Red dungeons.

To bring about this betrayal, leaders of the "civilized world" prepared gradually, wanting to lull vigilance in those designated for sacrifice in order to make it easier to deliver them into the hands of Stalin's executioners.

In the letter from Colonel Buguraev above, he barely touches on the reasons for the belief by Cossack officers in the word of an English officer that resulted in over two thousand Cossack officers, headed by General Krasnov, finding themselves in a deftly-placed trap at a camp in Spittal.

But this was just one of the elements quietly prepared and in good time worked out in the plan of betrayal.

One thoughtful and cultured person who lived the dark days of 1945 in Lienz, says:

"Undoubtedly, the whole plan for this tragedy in its entirety belongs to the Bolsheviks. It was obscenely developed by specialists behind the walls of the NKVD! ... It is too brutal to have been credited to the English; from it wafts a deep knowledge of the psychology of Russian people, so alien to cold Brits.

"The turnover would not have been easy even for Satan. The question posed was on the life or death of thousands of Cossacks, who, as is well known, are capable of exacting a high price for their lives. From the other side, it is clear that Satan does not like to waste the blood of his favorite servants. There was one other condition—among the Cossacks there were not a few who unavoidably had to be taken alive in order to sweeten their suffering, or maybe at the price of superhuman torture, squeezing from them needed confessions.

"In addition, completion of this plan achieved another aim—that of not disappointing their British allies, future conflict with which at that time seemed unavoidable ...

"And, what else?—A need for as much vileness and meanness as possible and to write all this down as 'actually on the account of' the English—right off killing two rabbits: achievement of aims and driving a wedge between the English and Russian people ... And if by this the uniform of an English officer will be dirtied and dishonored, why that then will just be unexpected 'interest' on invested 'capital.'

"The Satanic plan ready and, thanks to the nearsightedness of the 'farsighted' English, everything ran as if well oiled."

The author of these lines writes only about Cossacks, with whom he lived through those dark days, but his words are generally true of the Russian tragedy in the spring of 1945 in its entirety.

It has been more than 20 years since this sad time and what happened, which was not clear then, now has become very clear.

Preparations for the betrayal took place in good time over the course of several years.

Strong proof of this is provided by examples from camps of the ROA.

Two huge camps, Menzingen and Heuberg, their location totally in the open, existed for quite some time. There is no doubt that they were specifically known to the Allied Command. Massive formations of allied power flew over them almost daily. Nonetheless, they never once bombed these camps.

If it only took 48 minutes to destroy the large city of Dresden, then the destruction of ten thousand-odd soldiers of the ROA in the two camps had more than ample time available for it.

Nonetheless, they were untouched. Apparently, destroying them did not fit into any plan—they were marked to be taken alive ...

In connection with flights by allied aviation over these camps, there are firm memories of rumors being spread by word of mouth about English aircraft flying over close to Menzingen and dropping bundles with the insignia of the ROA woven on them.

Another example of how well-thought-out and finely conducted preparations were was the suggestion to Russian people that all anti-Communists struggling on the side of the Germans against Bolsheviks would be needed afterwards when the Western Allies, having finished with the Germans, turned their weapons against their current allies, the Bolsheviks.

This rumor cycled through with such certainty and so finely that even the staff of the ROA and Vlasov believed it and helped to spread it.

An officer in the Russian Corps, N. Besskaravayny, turning up after the end of the war in the region of the XV Cossack Cavalry Corps, who later succeeded in escaping from Siberia, published his memoirs in the journals, ***Archival Gazette*** and ***Our News*** [*Епархильные Ведомости* and *Наши Вести*], apropos of this writes:

"The head of the propaganda section of the staff of A. A. Vavilo positively convinced me that General Vlasov had a connection with Churchill, who promised him help in fighting the Reds at the end of the World War."

General Vlasov told me personally before one of our last meetings that he had an arrangement with the allies and if I or the Cossacks, on their arrival, found ourselves in a difficult situation, we should say that we belonged to units to Vlasov's organization.

Not only that, but he indicated to me the region of Austria, as the place which, toward the end of the war, units of the ROA, the Russian Corps, Cossacks of the XV Cossack Cavalry, and the Cossach Stan should bear in mind.

Actual movement in this direction by the ROA and the escape from Italy of the Cossachi Stan gave this support.

In this way, finely carried-out psychological preparation lulled the vigilance of the Russian people and filled them with hope of being able to continue their fight to free their homeland from the

Bolsheviks.

This preparation went on all in due time. It continued to the last days before the betrayal.

The trick on the officers of an invitation "to a conference" by which 2,000 officers were ensnared is obvious to us all, but to a few, the more classic example is the betrayal of the XV Cossack Cavalry Corps.

In his article, "The Last Days of the 1st Cossack Division of the XV Corps," A. Sukalo, court chairman of the 1st Cossack Division, wrote of this betrayal: "… Even a day later (May 24) **on the initiative of the English, in the presence of a prominent officer of the 34th Infantry Division—a colonel**—an election was carried out for the Field Ataman of the Cossack Host."

N. Besskaravayny, whom we have earlier mentioned, writes in detail of this event:

"We came out onto a huge field where representatives of all the Cossack regiments were standing. 'At attention!' was commanded. The general gave us his greeting and announced that the convention was in session. The election of a Field Ataman commenced …"

Besskaravayny writes further of the actual election. General von Pannwitz was chosen.

"… In his own brief words, in which he gave thanks for the election, General von Pannwitz said:

"'Here is the representative of the British Army. **He came here to pass on the decision of the British leadership.** He does not know how to speak Russian, so I will be the translator.'

"All that time, I stood next to him," Besskaravayny writes, "and kept my eye on that mute representative. It appeared to me that he understood Russian very well and listened to everything very attentively.

"'My dear Cossacks,' the general began his translation.'**The British leadership takes you under its protection. Let no one worry about or believe the rumors that you will be sent to Australia or Canada.** For now, until we get to know you better, we ask that you maintain discipline and obey your officers. Maintaining discipline will disprove the accusation that is thrown at you by the Soviets that you are not an Army, but a gang!'

"A loud 'Hoorah' from Cossack voices for the British leadership deafened Althofen.

"Cossack representatives stepped out and turned their attention to the English officer with the question: 'We thank the English leadership and ask that wherever we are sent, we be kept together and that our Cossack traditions not be disturbed.'

"'Good,' the representative answered. 'I will convey your request to my leadership and ask you once again to remain disciplined, so that we don't have to blush because of you.'"

Another long. loud "Hoorah" was the answer to these words. [It cannot be determined from the author's punctuation whether he was still quoting from text by Besskaravayny at this point, or had lapsed into his own words.]

This took place May 24, 1945, while on the evening before in Vienna, that is, May 23, representatives of the English commander, General Alexander, and representatives of the Soviet Command signed an agreement which **obligated the English to turn the Cossacks over to the Soviets.**

From then on, everything went "smoothly."

A day later, that is, May 26, the just-elected Field Ataman, General von Pannwitz, was arrested. May 28, officers were separated out from the Cossacks and given over on the next day to the Soviets. Then the rest of the Cossacks were turned over.

How artfully this comedy was played out through the "election" of the Field Ataman can be seen from how Pannwitz, himself, believed the English, for on the eve of his arrest, he toured the Cossack regiments of the Corps and conveyed to them the words of the representative of His Highness, the King of England.

To end this brief overview of the leisurely prepared betrayal, one needs to linger on the coincidence of units of the Cossack Corps, Cossachi Stan, and the mountain people of the Caucasus all coming together in Carinthia in southern Austria to be left leaderless **on one**

and the same day—May 28, 1945—when the officers of the Stan were invited "to a conference," while the mountain people were "presented to" the English High Command, and the officers of the Cossack Corps were simply locked up behind barbed wire in Camp Weitensfeld.

Already, this circumstance alone shows how meticulous was the subterfuge and plan prepared for the betrayal and how artfully it was put into practice.

And, along with this, it speaks to what low moral levels those who carried the plan out to completion had fallen.

V. Naumenko

The Psychological Preparation of Major Davies

All the deepest evil of Camp Peggetz, all the low and Satanic shiftiness under the preparation for handover in Lienz, shown by Davies, a major in the British Army, is hard to imagine even in a professional criminal, for his actions did not just flow linearly with orders from higher up the chain of command, but were arrived at through the meanness of a trick that counted on the mental preparation of the suicides of Peggetz and Lienz in order to fool them into the snare of the British Command.

Having completed his Cain-like act, Major Davies, apparently like Pilate, announced after the 1st of June:

"I am a soldier and must carry out my orders ..."

Among the duties of a soldier, as Major Davies must have understood them, must be attributed even the mental preparation for his deceit, which he carried out ahead of time, according to plan.

Here is yet another example, which has until now not been disclosed, of the ethical and moral unfitness of Major Davies.

On May 20, 1945, commanders of barracks in Camp Peggetz very attentively read the proposal by Major Davies that all journalists and representatives of Cossack presses be gathered together in Lienz on May 21st for discussions to be held in the building where the staff of Ataman Domanov was housed, the Lienz "Employment Office."

On the appointed day, we journalists, twelve people, gathered in one room on the top floor of the "Employment Office" building.

One of the officer staff read Major Davies's address to the journalists. It asked for the organization of an editorial office for newspapers that would be assigned social-informational duties for **"larger and better ties with the English Command in the interest of the Cossacks."**

Davies's appeal promised full support for Cossack journalists, both morally and materially, but it especially underscored Davies's desire to establish editorial colleagues, by naming an editor, secretary, and even staffers for the new paper …

Now, of course, the perfidious role in this proposal to work with the English Command is clear: Major Davies wanted to create the mental preparation that might lead gullible Cossacks to look for the goodwill in English commands, while they were at the same time giving over into the hands of executioners those people who, pen in hand, ideologically wrestled with and spiritually brought Cossackdom to irreconcilability with Bolshevism …

But at the time it seemed to us that Major Davies, the military representative of cultured England, was only calling us on a path to similarly cultured collaboration.

Our conference of journalists had to have served the same purpose as the "conference" of officers of the Cossack Host.

And we journalists passionately took up the matter: outlining in general the publication of the future newspapers, distributing roles and tasks, and choosing an editorial board, headed by E. Tarussky, as its editor (ending in suicide after the betrayal.)

The list of all the cooperators in the editorial offices, designated by which barracks they lived in, was presented to our staff officer, Major Davies, and we happily dispersed, having received in advance the promise from Davies of a quick acceptance for and release of the desired newspaper …

By getting the desired list of Cossack journalists, Major Davies in this way fulfilled his duty as an English soldier, to be certified in blood by the pogrom of June 1st and the Golgotha for 30,000 Cossacks handed over to the Bolsheviks ...

But let Major Davies not forget that, for this type of understanding and fulfillment of a "soldier's duty," in Nuremberg, German generals were hung.

Peter Mar

More on the English Psychological Preparation for the Lienz Slaughter

Having read the piece by Peter Mar about the methods resorted to by representatives of the English Command to lull the vigilance of the victims of the betrayal, I can add what I myself witnessed.

The English comported themselves as if preparing all manner of assistance to the residents of the camps and creating real improvements in them.

For example, Major Davies comes into the camp one day with his engineer and some large sketches. Over the course of two hours, he tells me that he intends to replace the outdoor cookfires on which Cossacks prepared their food with stoves that are sheltered from the rain. They estimated one such stove for every 5 families and even brought bricks for their construction.

The second of their actions, as they called them, appears to be the construction of privies, to the point of even starting to build them, although they were to be only temporary, on the edge at the end of one field. They showed sketches for substantial toilets with hermetically sealed covers and rubber seats [кольцами]; gave directions for how deep holes should be dug; brought shovels, saws, hammers, nails, and boards; and asked the district atamans to designate people for this work. In the evenings, all the materials were stored in a room in Davies's office. The wooden benches [сидения] were almost ready. All these boards were laid together in a pile and when the June 1st crowd burst out from pressure by English soldiers, many, of whom I was one, fell over them.

Within two days of disarming the officers, Major Davies suggested that we hold concerts and that I, with several performers, should go to Lienz to check out a hall that the Englishmen could repair. Truly, on the 25th of May, several of us searched Lienz for an appropriate hall, about which I let Davies know. He wrote down the address and said that he would order that it be repaired.

Then, chocolates and oranges were given out to children.

I and translator L.S., on demand by the English, spent our evenings translating into English the training program of the cadet corps and the military school.

I also remember that, for some reason, several English officers were in the camp as the cadet orchestra, in their presence, played several waltzes, marches, and songs. One of the officers asked me about Cossacks, and when I told him how they had traveled more than three-and-a-half thousand kilometers in carts with their children, elderly, women, and invalids, all in order to escape the hard yoke of the Bolsheviks, he said with great sorrow in his eyes while gazing at a cadet:

"Yes. God help them!"

At that time, nobody had the thought come into their head that something horrible was being prepared. Quite the contrary—all were filled with hope.

And even after that, when on May 27, weapons were taken away from officers, everyone still believed the English.

As if it was today, I can see the smiling face of a Terek district ataman, M. I. Zimin, as he stood waving to me from the transport he was already in.

One old former ataman, who perpetually went about in civilian clothes, urged his wife to get his military uniform, which she cleaned and ironed. He dressed, put on his medals, and left … never to return.

Translator **R.**

Concerning the Article by Translator R., "More on the English Psychological Preparation for the Lienz Slaughter"

One Kuban Cossack described for me his mood on the day that the officers were taken off to a "conference."

The possibility of a trap and betrayal never entered his head.

The matter took place in Camp Peggetz.

Following the order that officers be ready to be driven to a "conference," he too dressed and prepared for departure.

The officers and officials were assembled according to their Cossack host. Don Cossacks were on the right flank, beyond them were Kuban Cossacks, while Terek and Stavropol Cossacks were on the left flank.

The English vehicles were waiting not within the camp, but on the road by its gate.

It was a hot day. My companion having already reached the gate, where there was a large back up, decided to run into an adjoining barrack for a drink of water.

Coming out of formation, he asked the officer and official standing in front of and behind him to save his place.

From the window of the barrack into which he went, he spotted two officers that he knew. When he stepped out of the barrack, they threw themselves at him and started to talk him out of going, pointing to an armed English soldier. But this was not what convinced him. He remained adamant in his decision to go to the "conference." He did not go only because the two officers physically held him back.

V. Naumenko

More on the Tragic Days at Lienz

Cossachi Stan

There has appeared in print under the name of "Kubanets" an account entitled, "The Final Days of Cossachi Stan."*

Everything revealed in it is factually and historically true. But of course, he could not, being inside a crowd of several thousand, from that one place see and watch all that was happening in other places. For this reason, I would like to describe several incidents that were not revealed by "Kubanets" that took place within my sight and that of my family.

The English started to surround and press on the crowd at the moment that those Cossack men and women who wanted it were receiving holy communion. My wife was the next to last to come up for communion. Having taken it, she stepped aside for another communicant just as the crowd, disturbed by gunfire, suddenly pressed toward the platform upon which the clergy stood, squeezing against her and knocking her over, so that her body lay on the platform while her legs were pushed under it. Nevertheless, she did not panic, but firmly grasped the huge, booted leg of someone who was standing on the platform. The leg, as became known later, belong to archdeacon V. T., who hurriedly accepted the holy offering from the chalice which he held in his hand, so as not to spill it. Then, realizing that someone was holding onto his leg, he pulled my wife up to her feet. Along with the crowd, she then retreated from the advancing soldiers. Stepping around the platform, she noticed a woman with a child lying on the ground, trampled to death.

My eleven-year-old nephew was at this time in a different part of the crowd, and this is what he saw: one soldier ran up to the crowd and grabbed a six-year-old boy in his arms, quickly carried him to a truck, and threw him into its cargo hold [кузов]. The boy's mother took off after him, and when she ran up to the truck, the soldier grabbed her and threw her inside, too. Seeing this sad scene, the woman's husband ran up to try to get them out and was also grabbed and thrown into the vehicle. The father and mother of this woman and their 9-year-old son were in a different part of the crowd and knew nothing about what had happened. Those thrown into

---
* Article in Volume 1 of *Great Betrayal*, page 219 [221 of translation].

trucks were taken away the same day by train, but my nephew described what he saw to those who were left. Remaining were an old man and woman, their twenty-year-old son, and the nine-year-old nephew. The old man was a Yugoslavian emigrant, a Cossack of the Bessergenevskoy Stanitsa, Don Region, V. Pavel Mikhailovich, father-in-law of L., who was taken away.

It is of interest to note here that in 1947, in Camp St. Martin, near Villach, Pavel Mikhailovich received a letter from the daughter who was taken off by truck. It was sent from Siberia to Yugoslavia in the name of a second daughter who had been left in Serbia. The daughter who was taken away writes that on being handed over to the Soviets, guides began a sorting out. Men were separated into one group, women in another, and children, a third. They never saw each other again. And she wrote that she was still wearing the same dress and underclothing in which she was thrown into the vehicle in 1945.

My daughter, having seen her husband off on May 28 to the "conference," also was in the crowd of worshipers on June 1st. The motion of the crowd somehow caused her to wind up at its edge with her six-year-old son in her arms. An Englishman ran up to her and grabbed her by the arm, pulling her from the crowd. Out of fright, not knowing what to do, she yelled to her son: "Pray Borya! Pray Borya!"

Borya started to cross himself repeatedly. The soldier stopped. Then, waving his arm at the boy, walked away. My daughter and grandson stayed together and alive to this day.

To this mourning liturgy similarly came Lydia P., also having seen her husband off to the "conference." Impending motherhood was upon her. She wanted to take communion, but did not get the chance. The sideways-moving crowd so pressed against her that her labor pains began. "Good-hearted" Englishmen sent her to the hospital in Lienz, where she gave birth to two boys, one of whom died at once, the other—Anatoly, survived and lives today in Argentina. But the mother's melancholy over the loss of his father on May 28th is reflected in the child's face—he rarely smiles.

Soldiers here and there pulled Cossack men and women who

were stunned by clubs or gunstocks from the crowd. As the crowd was pushed away from the site of the religious service under their onslaught, it reached the camp's lattice wood gate, which collapsed under their pressure. People began to emerge onto a field with deep gullies and boulders. Along the way, Father Alexey F. (now in Australia) fell into one, still wearing his vestments. How many Cossacks jumped over him is not known, but when someone came along who noticed him and began to help him up, he said: "Brothers! Do not touch me. I am fine here." Still, they raised him to his feet.

When the crowd came out onto the field, even there it was surrounded by tanks. Several aimed quick runs at them. The entire crowd, as if one, fell to it's knees and sang a song calling to the Holy Mother of God: "Holy Mother of God save us!" Particularly memorable was the prayer of a boy of 8 or 9. Crossing his arms and raising them to the heavens, in a hysteric, soul-wrenching voice, he shouted: "Lord! Why are you punishing us? Lord have mercy on us! Save us!"

This prayer of his, even now, I can't remember without tears.

And there was a Cossack woman whose nerves did not hold up. She rose from the crowd with her two children and headed for the bridge across the Drau. Thinking that she wanted to cross it, a soldier chased after her, but on reaching the bridge, she threw one child after the other into the Drau, then followed them into it herself.

The soldier chasing after her was dumbfounded.

At the same time that Father Anatoly Batenko conducted his discussions with whichever higher-up was speaking through a bullhorn, Sergeant-major K. (a Cossack of the Kochetovoskoy Stanitsa, Don Region) was running, half dressed and covered in blood, from the camp to the crowd. It turned out that he had been caught in the camp by soldiers, but broke away from them, leaving his jacket behind. A soldier caught him on the run and stunned him with a blow to the head from a club. K. fell down from the blow, but quickly got up again. The soldiers again grabbed him by the arms. Struggling strongly, K. left them his shirt and ran out from the camp onto the field. There, close to the crowd, an English medic wanted to bandage his battered head, but he, cursing him and the entire English Command, took his own handkerchief out of his trouser pocket and bound his head with it.

He survived the day, as did the remainder of the crowd, but where he is today is unknown.

On the 2nd of June, as Kubanets writes, I performed a service in the morning among the conifers on the right bank of the Drau. I gave farewells, communion, and blessed those departing for the hills. On the morning of the 3rd, all the clergy on the right bank of the river had to cross over to the left bank on the agenda [*по повестке*] of Dean Father Vassily G.

And here we witnessed a frightful drama. Terrible screams were heard from the bank of the river. We ran up to the bank and saw bodies floating swiftly by.

In front was a young woman with an infant tied to her breast. The child was gasping for breath in the water and waving his arms about. The mother still had the strength to lift her head and look (she swam on her back, head upstream) forward—across herself [*против себя*]—were they still behind her, those who had jumped in after she had? And truly, two more bodies were swimming and choking. An English soldier with a long pole ran along the bank, obviously trying to save them, but they were too far from shore for the soldier's pole to reach them. All the same, he ran along the bank and did not fall back from the swimmers. His hopes met with success. Farther along, the current brought the mother and infant close enough to shore to allow the soldier to pull them out of the water. The child was dead, but the mother was still alive and taken to a hospital. There, she announced that they had struggled in vain to save her, for she had already taken a large dose of morphine and had given similar doses to all her companions. She died in the hospital.

These victims were a Kuban Cossack woman-doctor of Voskoboynikova, her child, mother, and 14-year-old sister,

Thus, some preferred death in Austria over return to the Soviets.

Archpriest Timothy Soin

Cossachi Stan

From the Past of Camp Peggetz

The camp of the death, tears, and suffering of the many thousand in it, Camp Peggetz, near Lienz, will go down in the history of Cossacks in foreign lands, and for that reason interest in it is no less for the days that followed its existence after the drama of June 1, 1945.

Following a brief period of command by Father Anatoly Batenko, the English designated an old emigrant from Yugoslavia, a certain Constantine Shelikhov, to replace him. It must be said that his dignity did not do honor to Russians, for he continued the politics of Major Davies in the capture of new emigrants, known as "Soviet subjects."

How many invisible tears, damned and deserved odium, how much terror, and how many escapes under compulsion by these unfortunate Russian people lay on the dark soul of Constantine Shelikhov for the lentil soup [чечевичную похлебку] of command that he exchanged for these renegades he named "Soviets?"

Having peace neither day or night, and knowing that the English made nocturnal round-ups in the barracks in search of "Soviet citizens" on Shelikhov's orders, people left at night for the woods.

Only in the camp church, where Father Timothy Soin, who lived through the entire horror of June 1st, was the superior, applying his general love and kindness to his true-pastoral service and strengthening the will of the Cossacks with his inspired sermons, did the men and women find soothing calm in his fervid prayers …

Nevertheless, Major Davies ordered that a list of all barrack residents be prepared, with their citizenship noted. Here, Shelikhov, knowing that almost all the new emigrants obtained either legal or counterfeit documents from Poland, Yugoslavia, etc., in order to pass as "old emigrants," he, Shelikhov, zealously began to expose those individuals, taking away from them their life-saving documents and putting them on the list as "Soviet." Toward himself, Shelikhov was always self serving, passing himself off at first as a colonel, but when that threatened him with the danger of being called with the officers to the "conference," he, surprising all, started to call himself an "engineer," even though he had been an ordinary draftsman in a geodesic bureau in Belgrade.

Having put to use his powers of betrayal in the theft of English goods from camp stores, to general contempt and hatred, Shelikhov was in the end expelled from the camp by the English at the end of 1945, after first being relieving of any commandant duties.

After him, Serbian Captain Lakic, who had fled from Tito's Yugoslavia, was named commandant.

Lakic, a former Serb, a stranger, unlike the Russian Shelikhov, was nevertheless a great friend to the Russian residents of the camp, which was filling up at the time with Slovenes and Croats emigrating from Yugoslavia.

Aside from the camp having been declared as a camp for old emigrants by the English after June 1, 1945, Lakic tried with all means and powers available to him to hide old emigrants who had not yet been captured and sent off by Shelikhov, even knowing that the documents of these new "Yugoslavians" were, as was then said, "limey."

And after all, everyone knew of the sad fate of those sent off under Shelikhov. Unless they had managed to run off into the woods and surrounding villages in time, all were all sent to the "Soviet camp" on a field near the settlement of Dölsach (within 4 kilometers of Peggetz in the direction of Oberdrauburg.)

At this time, a red Soviet flag was flown from it. At night, it was lit up by searchlights and protected by armed English guards.

The fate of that unfortunate camp, of Shelikhov's victims, was the same as that of those given up on June 1.

Captain Lakic, knowing all this, showed no fear before Major Davies in insisting that all Russians in Camp Peggetz were old emigrants.

Personal patriotism, love for his enslaved Yugoslavia, meant that Captain Lakic did not stay for long as commandant of the camp, to general regret, and left, as he promised, for the long fight against Tito "in the noise," that is—into the woods …

After Captain Lakic, commandants changed fairly often, since the English conducted an election system for the duties of commandant.

But the roundups and searches by the English, with the aim of catching new emigrants and those officers who failed to arrive at the "conference," continued to the middle of 1946.

By the middle of 1946, talk began about turning over Camp Peggetz to be administered by the city of Lienz as part of its construction industry. And in December, before St. Nicolas Day [*под Николин день*], in 20 degree weather, Russian residents were loaded into livestock cars, without heat or food, and taken to a camp in Spittal. The distance to the camp was only some 40 kilometers in all, but it took **ten hours** to deliver the unfortunate refugees, hungry and half frozen. Along the way, two children froze to death.

None of the remaining residents of Camp Peggetz—all Slovenes and Croats—were sent out of Peggetz so cruelly into the winter cold. All were left in place until spring.

Here was the hated Major Davies and his "soldierly duty" expressed in inhumanity and terror against defenseless Russians in Camp Peggetz.

As of December 1946, there was no longer a Russian population left, but a little later, several Russian and Cossack families were settled into half-empty barracks there as part of the workforce of the timber firm of the new proprietors of the camp—the Austrians.

Thus ended my own sad days at tragic Peggetz. All that remains of it now is the Cossack cemetery that serves as a rebuke of the executioners for the evil done by them.

Former Commandant, 10th Barrack

***

The accusations in the above item against the former commandant of Camp Peggetz, Mr. Constantine Shelikhov are a bit severe, for betrayal stands alone among the worst of human sins.

But sadly, the testimony given of his actions is supported by other residents of the camp.

The one plus for Mr. Shelikhov's impact during the time he was commandant was in the form of a large white cross on a tall pedestal that the residents of Peggetz put up in his presence for its first memorial marker.

The Death of E.V. Tarrusky (E.V. Rishkov)

(Excerpt from the item by V. Orekhov. published in the journal, *The Hourly* [*Часовой*] *No.* 275/6.

I met Eugene Victorovich Tarrussky in Italy in April 1945.

He was in one of the "Cossack stanitsas" and took little part in the unfamiliar-to-him life of Cossacks in those troubled times. He told me that he had left Berlin in February, and in answer to a question on his future plans, he said that he wanted to share the "general fate."

However, he held no illusions regarding this fate, convinced only of a tragic outcome.

Two months after our meeting and almost a month after surrender, I again saw Eugene Victorovich, in Austria, in the city of Lienz, at the gathering of Cossack officers to attend the notorious "meeting with units of Marshall Alexander."

Even then, there were already clear ideas about this ploy, but people reluctantly—all those not yet having disobeyed the order—forced themselves and others to believe the English. The order read that all officers must go to the meeting, exclusive of the ill and elderly.

Before boarding the bus, I said to Eugene Victorovich:
"Why are you going?"
He smiled at me and asked:

"What? Do you count me among those discharged as 'elderly and ill?' Or do you not consider me an officer?"

Thus, we went to this fatal meeting. The elderly and ill did, too. Even two priests were among those taken away.

Two hours later, we were in a camp behind three rows of barbed wire, surrounded by machine guns and tanks.

When darkness fell, it was announced that we all would be sent to our "homeland."

Someone suggested writing a protest, sending a telegram to the leaders of America and England, and of the Red Cross. Someone hysterically shouted that he had a Nansen passport and for that reason could not be given over to the Bolsheviks.

I stood at a barrack window and gazed at the machine guns set on high points, at the tanks at the gates, at the brightly lit yard, and the dark mass of the nearby forest.

Eugene Victorovich approached me.

"This is the end," he said quietly, as if addressing no one in particular.

For some reason this made me feel unbearable sympathy for this gray and quiet man, alone and tired.

I wanted to somehow cheer him up. He did not believe in the success of any petition or telegram that was noisily being drawn up in the next room.

Perhaps because of this, I began to nervously and, I think, unintelligibly, flap my mouth on, say, not all being lost yet, that it might be possible to escape on the journey, that perhaps the English may yet have mercy on us, etc.

"This is not yet the end!" I finished my tirade.

Not having heard me, Eugene Victorovich asked again, using the well known gesture of his hand to his ear.

I repeated. He shook his head and said with certainty that this was—the end.

"May God grant you luck. You are young and healthy."

Eugene Victorovich ended his life at dawn. I saw him dead, already cold.

A doctor was called—an Englishman. The doctor never came. Why should he have for an outcast! Then we carried the dead man to the gate, where a tank was standing and Englishmen were crowding around. None of them paid any attention to this.

... The sun set. All stood for a prayer before being sent to certain death.

But at the gate, left lying in the dirt of the road was the corpse of an honorable officer and fighter for Russian Honor.

Yu. T.

Clarification: Tarrusky was the name used as a journalist and writer by the deceased. His real name was Rishkov He was the son of the famous Russian dramatist Victor Rishkov.

Lienz

Reprinted from the newspaper, *Our Times*, *No.* 22/127, June 13, 1957. [There was no possible way for me to maintain the author's clever rhyme scheme in translation.]

On the banks of the Drau
Where the lush grass was,
Where were so many worn out places,
Washed by rain,
There stands a forgotten,
Simple, rickety cross.

At times only birds
Sit on the cross
And a tired wind circles
And cries feebly
At the very grave
Where a Cossack quietly lies.

The ground has not forgotten

Cossachi Stan

What happened here
But will remember for centuries of ages
How a horrible force slyly slayed
A brave handful of Cossacks.

Then, in front of the tanks
Flashed a Kuban woman
With curls beneath her shoulders.
"Have mercy on us, Lord,"
She said without a shudder,
"It is time for my bones to rest."

We with the sun's aim [к солнечной цели]
Could not come in time
And will drink a cup dry ...
Caught in a trap,
They take us for a fly ...
We all, like heroes, will die.

Shoot us in the heart!
We will perish in Lienz.
A rifle butt to a Cossack woman ... do not dare!
Better soon in the Drau
Than to you for punishment
Behind prison walls to a savage death.

Not so easily will it be forgiven ...
She flashed up like a bird,
Her arms—two white wings.
Into the cold Drau
To eternal glory,
As if to a holiday, she went ...

On the banks of the Drau
Where the lush grass was,

> Where the wind rages around
> Writhing flowers,
> Washed by rain,
> Stands a rickety cross.
>
> **B. Burdarm**

By Reason Inconceivable

Excerpt from the book by Professor F.V. Verbitsky

In this deep box, stretched over several tens of kilometers, someone's malicious hand, already tangled up with top leadership, placed the Cossack "camp." Stanitsas were located through the camps fringing the Drau's meadows within close distance to the scattered settlements pasted at the foot of forest-covered hills, while the staff and "leadership" settled in the small city of Lienz, sheltered as if in a locked box by transverse mountain crests.[*]

Unharnessed horses happily took to the juicy grass; campfires spread around created a fantastically beautiful scene at night out of what were to that time drab places.

Everyone was cheerful and, as it is with Russian people of optimistic stock, rosy hopes and unbeatable thoughts arose. Word was passed that the winning allies, already at that time having entered into contact with our "representatives," had conducted themselves very graciously toward Cossacks and, keeping in mind their bravery in battle, promised various possibilities: if not all being sent overseas to places in need of robust guards, then being including "with all rights" in their own military units, or promising "an honorable peace without annexation or indemnities." Only individual old men, keeping their thoughts to themselves, looked fearfully at the brick wall of mountain ranges encircling us. Several of them went missing in the mornings, heading for the cover of hills or thick

---

[*] The Professor writes about the valley of the Drau River as it stretches from Lienz to Oberdrauburg where, on the direction of the English Command, the Cossachi Stan was located after it left Italy in May of 1945.

woods, carefully looking over suitable paths and searching out secluded corners.

Then came the fatal day—May 28, 1945.

From that morning, a special stirring was felt ...

The Cossack staff churned with life; taut leadership figures flashed about everywhere; not infrequently, Cossacks were taken from the staff to be sent somewhere; having just with unbelievable difficulties established our hospital, the sick for some reason were moved to different places.

We were ordered to remain in place. The hospital was positioned high enough on the foothills to have a wide view that opened up onto the valley, where the barracks looked like palms spaced closely around a large camp. Drill exercises were fit into a nearby meadow.

Close to midday, news reached us from the staff that the head of an English division had invited all gentlemen [2.] officers to a meeting in their General Headquarters, some tens of kilometers from Lienz. As someone not in uniform nor being part of the officer contingent, I asked, "Does this include doctors?" I received the answer that "the order pertained only to those in Cossack uniform."

Until all were done fussing about, grooming themselves and putting on the best dress uniforms they had, I decided to go home for lunch ... I never had the chance—a messenger from the hospital: "You need to go, too." It turned out that our well-meaning head of the medical unit, D., allowed the command to apply to physicians. Someone's malicious hand, whose remained unexplained, widened the impact of the order to even non-combatants and to all the former officers who had long since not been in service and were now in civilian dress. This way "they caught" both those capable and incapable of bearing arms, all the very elderly with gray beards to their waists, the half-ill, and invalids ...

When my eyes befell the sight of the "Cossack Host" at the gathering point, they teared up at the sorry picture, the variegation and poverty of the uniforms, the unremitting sadness and anxiety on faces.

Along with this, "someone" was constantly rousing the assembled ranks, firmly trying to instill a belief that we were being called for our own interests and there awaited us some sort of "flattering offers." An order was an order, and all of us, old, accustomed to discipline, boarded one truck after another at the assembly point without a murmur. The official notification held that the meeting would only take several hours, so that we did not need to take anything with us.

If there was a single skeptical individual who might have shaken some doubt into heads, a large majority (in whose number I belonged) piously believed the staff and the word of an English officer. I left without a hat, toothbrush, or towel, dressed as I had been; without a morsel of bread. That the latter was really thought to be unnecessary, for they fed us "for slaughter," changed the perspective on everything else from a totally unpleasant complication into a devastating situation.

The general look of those leaving was little congruent with "guests of the King of England," and the provision [предоставленные] of amenities for our trip did not approach the comfort which surrounds those traveling to the "staff." Our truck was packed so full that we all had to stand, which made the highway's potholes perceptible in their abundance. When those isolated skeptics brought attention to this, all said, in one voice, shrugging their shoulders: "As if there were a place for such ideas there where the orders come from the leaders and the English military command."

Never-give-up Russians, not under any circumstances, good moods and humor appeared even here in no small measure, although shyly and not without disbelief, it is true. They even tried singing a song, but it fell apart on the middle of a word, not having helped raised the mood at all.

The center of attention for us had just been on the promotion to sergeant-major [в старшини] for bravery and diligence in battle with Italian Bolsheviks who were attacking the position of his regiment, the mountain man of the Caucasus, Naz-ov. Also memorialized was the always stalwart *sotnik*—with the simple pockmarked face and rakish manners.

At the twentieth kilometer, our convoy of trucks was stopped by some sort of barrier which had not been present there earlier. Some sort of inscrutable "strategic" rearrangement of vehicles began. In the first row, next to us, went vehicles holding staff and a light automobile with the venerable P. N. Krasnov in it. All eyes were captured by the close presence of large English battle units. When exchanging impressions, the phrase, "Jewish Brigade" was voiced several times. This did not foreshadow anything good. That became completely clear as the English tanks fanned out to encircle our column.

Two soldiers, "armed to the teeth," appeared at each vehicle. From this moment, there was no longer any doubt that "guests of the King of England" had been transformed into the status of prisoners … But whose? … The more tolerant continued to keep themselves calm by holding that it was obviously still the "English," since no one could in any way allow any such crude trick on the part of individuals wearing military uniforms. Isolated skeptics shook their heads in doubt … Spirits dropped sharply. We rode on in silence. If any phrases passed between us, they were whispered.

We rode on for another three hours. We passed some sort of barracks full of soldiers along the streets of a small city … Before us, heavily guarded, was a large camp. Its front consisted of a row of dark, gray, three-story buildings. Farther back were unending barracks. The entire facility was fenced in by three rows of high barbed wire. In the middle, between barracks on both side, was a narrow drive, also bordered by barbed wire. Barely a few days later, I learned that this camp was "Spittal." The column of autos stopped in the center of camp on a large field that was there and reformed into several rows.

Unloading began.

Here, I looked upon the faces of many acquaintances and friends for the last time. All were bewildered and visibly tried to find the strength to maintain their outer calm.

First, the staff was unloaded and surrounded by heavily armed guards, even the staff officials. They were led through a narrow corridor into the depths of the camp.

Here, before general courteous silence and heavy sighs, the venerable P. N. Krasnov was among the first to go through, led by the arm by S. N. Krasnov and surrounded by the aura of his previous grandeur and great literary talent.

After staff, medical personnel were ordered to unload. Among us were 14 physicians and 7 orderlies ["paramedics" in today's jargon]. The younger 4 physicians and the 7 orderlies were separated out and taken inside. There was a doctor in charge, wearing the uniform of an English major, who spoke Russian flawlessly. Later, he remained for a long time as the head of the medical units distributed through the division's area. He was reserved and even polite.

When my turn came, he said to me in a tone more like a request than an order, "One of the generals has had a heart attack. I want you to take a look at him." Calling an armed soldier, he gave him some sort of instruction in English. I understood that I was to go with the soldier and he led me to one of the gray buildings.

We went to the first floor. On the door opening, I went into a large room in the middle of which I noticed a large group in Cossack uniforms, some 15-20 men. Straw had been thrown about on the floor along the walls. There were no beds. Everyone had a haggard face, as if from not enough sleep, and concern in their eyes. Half-way across from me, my old acquaintance from Belgrade, General Shkuro, came out of the group. He was in the unbuttoned uniform coat of a German general; conspicuous in his neglect of his uniform and grooming.*

---

* On the specific question of how General Shkuro was dressed, there followed this answer from Professor Verbitsky: "I can categorically confirm that Shkuro at that moment was in a German uniform, since he was fairly disheveled, with his coat unbuttoned from top to bottom, but since I could not at that time nor now determine what constitutes various ranks in uniforms, I do not feel myself truly able to confirm that the uniform was that of a general. What kind of shoulder boards he had, I do not remember, but because before then I had seen him in a German general's uniform (even in Lienz, where he visited for a short

He walked toward me with quick footsteps and, looking to the side at the English soldier, whispered a short question:

"Who is here and where are they taking us?"

In his expressive eyes, with their peasant cunning, I read alarm and bewilderment.

When the soldier either felt that his presence was interfering or maybe there was some hypnotic influence directed at his eyes, he went out and we were left alone ... I clearly understood that the matter did not have to do with any heart attack, but I nevertheless asked him to unbutton his shirt and put an ear to his chest. In such a pose, we continued our conversation.

When I said that they had taken all the officers of the Cossachi Stan, with P. N. Krasnov in the lead, he turned pale and waved his arm hopelessly. Even I could find no soothing words, and we, lost in our own thoughts, could not find anything to discuss for those few minutes.

The minutes passed quickly. The soldier reappeared and it became clear that it was time for me to leave.

We kissed each other's cheeks in goodbye. This was our last farewell, and when later the executioners' radio publicized to the soulless world about bringing "the sentences to completion," I remembered this last meeting as if I was still there.

I walked away with a heavy soul that even now makes my skin crawl to remember. I gave myself a clear account of what Shkuro was thinking. Those same thoughts owned my very being. They were so horrible that we decided not to voice them to one another. We could not admit them to ourselves.

I beg the reader's forgiveness for burdening him with these minor details. In those days, when a wide river was always flowing with human blood, when from all sides came wails of desperation and deafening groans, when it was difficult to find one house without a bottomless abyss of their own grief—these individual events, affecting even prominent people, needed to be drowned in a sea of

---

while), there remains to this time a firm belief that he was then in the uniform of a German general.

general grief. I write about this because the business carried on, after all, to several tens of thousands of Russian people, among them thousands of officers and Cossacks hardened in the struggle with Bolsheviks, who after a few months were able to ascertain their weight in gold in **general** affairs of betrayed and betrayer ... I fear that this might have its own meaning in the subsequent lives of two great nations.

Coming out from the gray building accompanied by the soldier, I quickly saw that on the field where the physicians had been assembled, none were left. The doctor-major told me that they were taken from the camp's limits to another place and that I had to go with them. Finding myself "without a tongue" and not knowing where to go, I went almost at a trot to the exit. The guard there directed my soldier to the left. Within two hundred paces, I saw the backs of my acquaintances in a line bending around the camp. And they were surrounded by guards.

When I rejoined them, we followed our escort around a corner and went lengthwise along the barbed wire fence of the camp. On the other side was a row of barracks, also guarded by armed sentries. When we reached a turn, our eyes caught sight of a sign on a post, "Kriegsverbrecher" [German for war criminals]. Now, when I remember all this in a quiet moment, I find it comic how anxiety seized me from the dread that I would not get into this "paradise." One thought only pressed me on—not to fall behind the others and be left by myself. Beside us, individual groups of Germans were led in this direction. All of them were distributed among separate barracks. We found ourselves in the fifth by number. This was a large, empty barrack, apparently for horses. A floor had been laid in the front, where it looked like grain had been stored and the grooms had lived. Stalls for horses were farther in. It was dirty everywhere and unpleasant. Wicker baskets, in which grain had been kept, were strewn around on the floor, along with the sorry remnants of grain and straw.

Many cut-off Cossack shoulder straps [*погон*] lay about the floor, as did several uniform caps, separate jackets, and underwear.

One of the younger doctors found an entire shaving kit and a silver neck cross and chain in the middle of other things. It was clear that people for whom it had been necessary to hide their actual positions and who no longer attached any meaning to earthly connections had been sent off to somewhere from here.*

Unexpectedly, a loud gong was heard and people began to pour out of neighboring barracks. We decided to go out, too. What was to that time an empty passageway to keep us off the barbed wire, came alive and changed into a noisy street. We heard many different tongues, among them Serbian. In a minute, I was surrounded by a group of Yugoslavs, among whom happened to be several who were my patients and acquaintances. At the "barracks at the entrance," where Nazi Germans were held, the German envoy to Zagreb stood out among them in his short sport pants.

Many of them were later shot. According to stories from Croats who had long been held there, one could conclude that what awaited all of us was no better than the chance to be imprisoned in a camp, whether treated as state criminals or war criminals. [I believe this to be the sense of this passage, if not its exact translation, as is also true for the following paragraph. The professor's prose can sometimes be quite dense.]

Hour by hour, it became no easier ... Nonetheless, when we saw that among the barracks closest to us, there were those similarly full of Cossack officers behind barbed wire, but who were still not allowed to go out, it became clear to us all that we had the greater freedom. In these hours, they only had doors opened wide and they crowded together near them like herring in a barrel, masses of people

---

* On the question put to Professor Verbitsky what was found in the barrack-stables in which the doctors were held, such as items of military uniforms, he categorically confirmed that such was found there and of hearing a suggestion that they belonged to the mountain people of the Caucasus, who also had been taken that day of May 28.
But what was found among the items lying about, uniform caps and crosses, seem to contradict this suggestion. [People of the Caucasus found with Cossacks were rarely Christian or wore Cossack uniforms.]

greedily gulping for fresh air, apparently studying their new situation. Don caps prevailed in the alley [алеы].

An hour later, the sound of the gong ordered us back inside. Food was brought—many varieties of canned goods which we had long since not not seen in our lives. Night fell; time to think about bedding. We bunched up something beneath our heads from what remained of the dirty straw and, pressing against each other, for it was cold, tried to fall asleep. Changing swarms of the most grim thoughts interfered with sleep and we forgot ourselves only for moments. Single shots were heard within the camp; we counted eleven of them.

At 7 or 8 in the morning, we were again let out for fresh air. Here awaited our first surprise: all the barracks behind barbed wire were empty. Even more surprising, none of us had heard any kind of noise during that sleepless night. Our hearts fell ... Possibilities spread, one grimmer than the other.* A Croat from an adjoining barrack, who was led across the camp early in the morning to the dentist, described what he saw deep in the camp on his way: several naked and half-dressed corpses in the barbed wire besides the woods ... He did not want to believe, did not want to think.*

Hot coffee was brought and a fresh pile of "treats" with it. The coffee was drunk, but the treats were left untouched.

---

* A Kuban Cossack officer taken from Lienz to Spittal May 28, who succeeded in escaping during transfer to Judenburg, attested that officers were removed from Spittal May 29 at 8 o'clock in the morning, which does not fit in with Professor Verbitsky's details. It needs to be assumed that either their removal took place earlier than 8 o'clock in the morning or the professor and others were let out for their walk after 8 o'clock.
* That about the shots and the corpses seen by the Croat in Spittal, the professor supported it by a special letter, in which he wrote: "I personally counted eleven gunshots in the night. Others, too, heard them, but their actual number was not discussed. The young Croat, with whom I also met here in Buenos Aires, although I had not been long in contact with him, having been made anxious by their fresh impressions, told only about what he saw of the dead with his own eyes on returning from the dentist, who had a dispensary at the very end of the camp. As can be judged by his description, he saw them at the barbed wire fence. They had to have been attempting to escape."

About midday, a Croatian interpreter in the uniform of a German officer arrived and ordered us to be ready to leave in 10 minutes. All of us became very agitated, exchanging whispered suppositions. Most looked at the change with gloom; in others, some faint hopes were stirring.

After this, we were led to a truck. The motor was running, and we were ordered to take seats. We followed the order without a murmur. Time went slowly, seeming like eternity to us, while the motor kept running and the truck did not move. Finally, the driver put the truck in motion and, in a half-whisper, said a single word: "Lienz." None of us could believe it and breathed freely only after going out to the highway and turning left, in the direction from which we had come. Our spirits calmed even more when we passed familiar barracks and it became clear to us that we were going back.

After some wandering, we were brought back to our hospital ... I feverishly searched among the eyes of those spilling out of it for those of my wife. She was in a tent, where she had been put to work in order to ensure her presence there. In her meek eyes and her pale, tired face, I read the usual acquiescence with fate.

Instead of being in freedom, we found ourselves in the role of prisoners, We were put in one of the houses close to the hospital. A substantial sentry of soldiers with a Scottish sergeant occupied the room neighboring ours. Some more new faces were added to ours and we were organized by threes: a doctor, nurse, and orderly. In my trio, my wife was allowed to be counted as the nurse; for an orderly, I took an elderly man from the hospital. Daily, in the mornings and at midday, trucks drove up to our house and each time a trio of us was required to go off somewhere ... None returned from there. Munich and Vienna were bandied about, but no one could say the terrible truth. We knew it ... but all the same, people left submissively in the company of armed guards. Our situation was involuntary, reminding me of a pen with sheep from which every day one or two were taken away for slaughter. And all along, there was never even a thought of resistance, but we so often wondered about animals going to the slaughterhouse.

We were allowed to continue working in the hospital and attend the Catholic church that stood only a few paces away.

In those days, a frightening drama took place before my eyes that left an indelible scar on my soul for the rest of my life. Even if things followed from an individual misfortune with us, there were still floods of tears and thousands of lives destroyed.

From our first days, everywhere there was the Cossack diaspora, flags of mourning came out bearing the inscription, "better famine here and death than return to Sov. Russia." Such flags flew in front of the hospital, too. When the English brought food, they had to take it away again. Even though emaciated from a long-standing lack of food, people still chose to starve and rejected the rations.

Everywhere, church services continued without interruption, and from the windows of the hospital we could easily see processions with choirs and kneeling Cossacks. Being acquainted with these people, patients sobbed and nurses cried, unable to keep back tears. It underlined our helplessness and lack of strength even more.

In my wife's words, as she tried to share her own suffering with me, our unexpected departure called up indescribable mental turmoil and desperation in those remaining, particularly in the women's realm. All understood that it had been something frightening that had happened that could not be fixed. But side by side with the burning eyes and true grief, there were also people found who fully preserved their tranquility. It seems that they had prepared earlier for it, and maybe even had taken some part in it. There was no doubt that all the foul mystification in the staff itself had its own helpful directors, who, like Judas, turned their own brothers over to death for a few pieces of silver. Not for nothing did a lost, but honest Burtsev cry out against a tide of evil: "Damn you Bolsheviks! What have you done to the Russian people?" In place of Alyosh Karamazovs, he had given birth to Cains.

I must point out this one small, but very characteristic note. People were found in those days who "washed their hands" at the expense of the unfortunate families who remained. On the day after our departure there appeared an announcement that purported it was possible to send all the things they required over to the departed. It need not be said that the best of all their poor belongings began to be brought from all sides. All this drifted off into obscurity along with the wittiest of this author's works.

But the image of what was going on in these days in various ends of Cossack settlements forgotten by God is never to be forgotten. Mute, but constant witnesses to these events are the many graves left by suicides and those who met innocent deaths. The suicide of the woman physician, Voskoboynikova, who threw herself into the raging Drau with her child and left our world in order to tell the Lord God of her earthly suffering, stands out from the others in its degree of tragedy. And how many are not marked by crosses still? And for how long, too, were individuals still hanging from trees with peaceful and calm expressions on their faces in the more forest-covered hills? They were buried wherever they were found; there was no time to put up a cross and their names, "only You, o Lord, knowest."

Great was the suffering of people; immeasurable terrors produced dreamless nights in these pale, emaciated beings and faces with voluntary hunger; bottomless grief was written in those eyes gone somewhere deep and far away …

But an even deeper impression, indelible for the rest of life, was left on my soul by Cossack horses. Even in those days I involuntarily remember eerie and stunning scenes from the world of animals as expertly written about by Shmelev in his unrivaled tragedy, "Son of the Dead" … Even now, after many years have passed, in my not-yet-weakened memory, rows of horses without their masters clearly stand out. As if some sort of foreign apparitions appearing in front of the hospital, thin and dull, they passed through a broad meadow which, not so long ago, was boiling with life: where cooking fires burned; where horse carts stood, near which children once swarmed; and where, among others, they saw the familiar-to-them figures of their owners. Back then, they pastured in that same meadow, part of a cheerful, friendly herd … Now the juicy grass beneath their legs no longer attracted them; their restless gaze searched out those that they would never again see; as they trotted past abandoned, empty carts, an insecure sadness emanated from their yes ... Without black flags, without words, it seemed that their horse souls merged with that of their masters: through a conscious hunger strike, they protested against arbitrariness and the corrected laws of God and man on the use of force on people. It is as if they still somehow could not believe, could not understand and embrace what happened, and kept searching for a place for themselves.

Never as in these days of horror and death has a Cossack family felt as strong as when a man grows together with a horse and the horse merges with the family.

Involuntarily, too, scenes from being left far behind in Novorossiysk which forever are cut into my memory come to me.

Pressed against the sea, Cossack regiments agonized ...

There was not enough room for people, over whom hung death, on the fragile boats, so for every Cossack, life posed a cruel dilemma: either inquisition and death by executioners or safety ... and maybe, just maybe, more new feats in the Russian business ...

I personally came to see how stern-faced, gray Cossacks, illuminated with boundlessly warm love for their horses, with which so much had been lived through in the last years, bid them farewell forever ... More than once, they look at their horse's face, lovingly pat its neck, caress its mane; impetuously kiss its forehead ...and ... taking out a revolver, press it to its temple ... Hot tears, so uncommon with them, fall on the snow-covered ground from faces having become deeply creased, more than anything [*ярче*] telling what this last shot cost ... Burning into the snow were tears that went into native soil to be left as perpetual symbols of the love Cossacks have for their horses.

Days and nights went by ... like a pack of hungry wolves in the form of soldiers of the royal army, the English gathered together with Austrian residents; with a lasso or a tempting piece of sugar, they tried to appropriate "war booty." But the booty did not come to their hands ... For quite some more time, one saw horses searching for their masters.

And there were, in truth, miracles happening. Our entire camp knew about one of them. Horses were treated as if they belonged to all those living in the camp. One family in those frightful days had to hide in an inaccessible place high in the hills, apparently forgotten by God and man. One can imagine its amazement when on a cold morning it nevertheless saw "Gnedka" before them, escaped from the camp ... How he [although the name would seem to refer to a bay mare, the author uses *он*] could find them, how he managed to get through those thickets to where they could not be found by the "fearless hunters of unarmed people"—English soldiers—will forever remain a secret.

I cannot help but remember here another touching event that took place before my eyes. We lived with a German woman, affable and sensitive to the sorrow of others because she had her own: her husband had not returned from the war and she was in a difficult situation with two young daughters and their grandmother.

Nevertheless, near evening on the day before one of the "voluntary" returns to their homeland, a nondescript old Cossack appeared at our house leading a similarly nondescript dark cow. He started to tell the German woman something, but we could see through a window that neither understood the other. I went out to help, and, at the request of the Cossack, translated that this was his family's "beloved" cow ... That all of them had prepared for death and that ... Since he saw that the woman had two small children, he asked that she accept his cow from him with only the condition that she "guard and take pity on her."

The German woman kept trying to find out how much he was asking for the cow and could in no way understand that it was a gift from him ... One needs to have seen the joy of the children and the happiness of the mother and grandmother when, from the following day, the meadow in front of our house in the camp became empty and they really did believe that the cow had truly become their property.

I now remember and can clearly see, lost in the impending darkness of night, the figure of that Cossack ... His name remains unknown to me ... This was one of those simple, dark Russians by whom Russia had once been kept well-fed and strong.

A second, third, fourth "troika" left ... We were the eighth ... I do not know why eighth ... Could it have been because the cold-looking sergeant executing his orders felt sympathy for my gray head? Could it have been that, having had an English governess in her childhood, my wife "miraculously" remembered some English words and through their power succeeded in explaining that I was a physician and a professor, doing more than just a little good for people? ... But ... with his authority in this predetermined slaughter of "sheep," he left me for one of the last. Undoubtedly, it had been his doing ...

I must confess that, ignoring their indifference to our fate, even these "cold-blooded" people obviously felt some sort of concern at times ... and even embarrassment and awkwardness reminiscent of a conscience. Not knowing the language, we could not exchange views, nor was there enough time and enough strength to do so, given everything that was going on before our eyes.

If, in normal times, some sort of killing sometimes remains for months perennially dark to discussion and commentary, then in those days, when hundreds of the worst crimes against laws and morals were committed every minute, my own small fate seemed small change.

But still, when they took away the 6th and 7th "troikas" and the Sword of Damocles hung directly over my head, my heart began to contract and my skin crawl ...

Totally unexpectedly, a new "troika," consisting of a doctor from the Kuban, his wife as nurse, and his brother as orderly—the 9th—arrived the evening before our day was to come. They spent the entire evening reading the Gospels they had with them until late at night.

Every day, on the small field near the hospital, early in the morning, my wife and I stood for the akathist to the Mother of God, "The Bright Abode of Homeless Wanderers," which in that situation brought tender feelings to us all and infused us with courage.

Typically, the automobile came at 9 o'clock in the morning. Having taken a rarely published prayer book with me that my wife had, I slipped a note into it requesting that it be given to the mistress of our room. When we went into the Catholic church, I left the book on one of its communion tables.

At such times, we naturally began to speak about suicide, which I considered to be the only way out of our situation … Even now, I remember sharply, how not too long before, grabbing at life, I suffered so through bombardments and fearfully took measures to remain whole—passionately and sincerely praying to Lord God to send me an unexpected death … What luck a "peaceful and painless" end beneath bombs falling from the sky then seemed to me. What an easy, simple, and natural answer to the question that tortured me at the time: "Was suicide in these moments, when torture and death awaited, a sin or not a sin?"

Strengthened by the Holy Word, my wife energetically opposed it, insisting that it was forbidden by the church and that, in any event, the moment for it had not yet come … We parted after leaving the church.

My wife went to the hospital.

A holy father sat in one of the vestibules, Father Theodore. Pressed down by matters, elbows on the table, he hid his face in his hands.

"Father," my wife turned to him in a teary voice, "can it really be that, even in this situation, suicide is a sin?"

He revealed his face and, gazing past her, without any emphasis, answered simply:

"Do not even think of it."

"How can I not think of it? You certainly must know what awaits us!"

"This is how it is … Do not think of it and do not speak of it …"

At that same time, on the way to the hospital, I met our deacon. He was a simple and uneducated man, but everyone loved him for his good heart and deep faith. We greeted each other and walked together in silence for a while.

Totally unexpectedly, he took me by the hand and said with great emotion: "For God's sake, professor, do not destroy before the Lord all the good that you have done in the course of your life …"

Interestingly, much later, when we remembered those days together, he could not remember those words—I remembered them exactly—that he had spoken.

My wife and I returned to our dwelling with heavy feelings. My entire, vain life passed before my eyes, full of tumult and minor suffering: with and without hope; falls and recoveries … And all this seemed to me now so insignificant, so unnecessary. I lamented on having had great opportunities to do so, but never having done anything for the church … And I so wanted, had fate allowed it, to take part in establishing a shrine. My wife spoke up. She said:

"Among Russian people, the habit in case of illness or misfortune is to make a vow of fasting, a prayer to God, construction of a shrine … Let's promise something like that and piously fulfill it, if the Lord saves us. Right away, our spirits will be lighter …"

We went up the stairs. The truck was to come any minute and not much time actually passed in truth before we heard the noise of it's engine. A sergeant came into our room and, addressing those from the Kuban without looking at us, said: "Get ready to leave!"

I froze in wonder … also, I will not hide, from muted animal joy. I had an abundance of sympathy for those from the Kuban who were obediently gathering their things together in silence. There was a moment when I even wanted to point out that not they, but I was next in line according to the sequence, but something held me back … I said nothing.

He went off … For a long time, I tried to find an explanation for why the sergeant changed the order … but I could not find the sergeant … My belief is that there was a higher order involved here … but how and for whom to this day remains a secret for me.

Professor F. V. Verbitsky

Cossachi Stan

More "On the Spittal Tragedy"

In the 1st volume of *Great Betrayal*, on pp 273-276 [pp 275-8 in my English version], due to my oversight, there was an article entitled, "On the Spittal Tragedy," written under the signature, "Stepnoy" ["Of the Steppe," which, in my English version of Volume 1, I translated as "Steppenoy" to emphasize that this was a pseudonym], which was reprinted in the paper, *Russian Thought, No 546*, April 17, 1953.

This article, for which the author's identity is hidden behind the pseudonym of "Stepnoy," is full of malicious attacks against Professor F. V. Verbitsky, blaming Professor Verbitsky of having given an incorrect account to Professor Grondis of events in Lienz that he could not have witnessed.

In his article, Mr. Stepnoy writes:

"In what possible way could Professor Verbitsky have simultaneously been with the high staff and not have been a combatant? Something singular.

"But this is not so important. Much more important is what Professor Verbitsky claims to have witnessed. It turns out that Professor Verbitsky was everywhere and knew everything.

"In actuality, Professor Verbitsky appears to be no more than a transmitter of those words and explanations, if not to say worse, with which Lienz was then full, especially the refugee camp in which Professor Vebitsky had lived ..."

Before anything else, it must be noted that Professor F. V. Verbitsky, even if not a "combatant," was in that number of other officers, military officials, and physicians who were taken off "to a conference" on May 28, 1945, in Spittal and only on the next day, as were most of the physicians, returned to Lienz (see [см.] Vol. 1 *Great Betrayal* pp 175-176 [pp 174-5 in my English version].)

Faulting Professor Verbitsky for omniscience, Mr. Stepnoy resorted to a common narrow-minded device, asking the question: in what way could the professor have knowledge about events that took place concurrently in different places and affecting different individuals in the tragic situation of those days? But of this, he, freely or not, missed that Professor Verbitsky was in the Cossachi Stan not as an ordinary person, but was in the thick of the life and existence of the Cossachi Stan from which hung the fate and life of many thousands of people, including himself and his family and many individuals close to him.

Naturally, Professor Verbitsky, like many others who lived through the Cossack tragedy at Lienz, could not have witnessed all the facts about which he informed Professor Grondis. It appears, though, that there was an instructor of hygiene at the Cossachi Stan's military school who lived alongside those serving there and found himself in the same situation as his son-in-law, N. N. Krasnov, the younger, who was in long-standing, close communication with his grandfather, General P. N. Krasnov, and uncle, S. N. Krasnov. In anddition, Professor F. V. Verbitsky, as a physician, was in contact with a heterogeneous group of people and suffered with them through fateful events. Even if he did not personally taking part in the events, he learned about them from credible sources.

Mr. Stepnoy also missed the circumstance that Professor Grondis's article was written several years after the dramatic year of 1945 and that much has since been established through the testimony of individual participants in the events who managed to avoid the bitter, general event of betrayal.

Even conceding the possibility that there may have been inaccuracies and untruths in the evidence received by Professor Grondis, as Mr. Stepnoy, in his own complaints, states: "Errors are always possible." Yes, and he, too, makes a mistake, suggesting that no one escaped on the way from Lienz and that "all arrived in Camp Spittal."

We have a completely credible account that Sotnik Alexander Shparengo succeeded in jumping off the truck on its way to Spittal, about which he writes in detail in his own essay, "On the Banks of the Drau," published in Volume I of *Great Betrayal*, pp 159-165 [pp 158-64 in my English version]. One cannot eliminate the possibility of other escapes.

We also know that Y. T. G. of the Kuban, who told us what took place in Spittal on May 28 and the morning of May 29, succeeded in escaping.

To our regret, the individual who heaps such venom on Professor Verbitsky is well hidden behind a pseudonym.

V. Naumenko

More on the 1st Cossack Regiment of Cossachi Stan and on Cossack Horses

The fate of this regiment is written about in Volume I of this book in the article by M. Alexeevich, in which, on p 214 [p 215 in my English version], he wrote that, having left the regiment's position in the evening of the day before, he watched from the forest as the regiment was surrounded by the English and taken away without any resistance. [Based on my translation, it would have been June 4. An incorrect date given in it on the page before is obviously a typographical mistake and not relevant to this point.]

The same author writes in the following article with complete certainty, having stayed behind near the regiment's camp, that the 1st Cossack Cavalry Regiment got away into the woods in plenty of time, so that it was only the families of a few Cossacks who were not part of the regiment, but were only found in the area, who were taken away on June 3.

Asked about the matter, M. Alexeevich answered that, as he was in the woods some distance from the camp, he might have erred in saying that the 1st Cavalry Regiment was taken away by the English without any resistance.

An English officer and female interpreter in a light vehicle drove into the location of our regiment on the evening of the 2nd of June.

Since the commander of the regiment had been taken away on May 28, along with all of the officers, the English officer was met by the regiment's Cossack master-sergeant [*подхорунжий*], a Don Cossack who was filling in for the commander.

The interpreter passed on an order from the officer that the regiment should prepare to be sent to the USSR the next morning.

The Cossack master-sergeant temporarily in command of the regiment asked that the the following be translated for the officer:

"There will not be a single one of us here tomorrow morning, and it would be better not to bother with coming."

The interpreter translated this to the Major, who replied:

"I am giving the order, but the matter is theirs after that." And he left.

Toward evening, all the Cossacks broke up into groups, and, after abandoning horses, carts, and tents, glanced back for a final farewell to the camp.

They regretted having to part with their horses, and, as long as there was still light enough to see, they kept an eye on the camp, intent on bidding farewell to them.

By evening, only I and two other Cossacks were left.

We watched an English auto approach. It reached the staff location and the officer in it, seeing that there was no one in the camp, dropped some provisions and left.

After their departure, we came out from our cover, went up to the provisions and took what we needed.

With the coming of darkness, we noticed shadows in the forest—Cossacks who had left were preparing themselves for the evening.

It felt eerie, but all the same, we decided to spend the night in camp, taking note in advance of the large wheat field next to us for a place in which to lay low once morning came.

After it became dark, a German interpreter drove up to our staff location. My stanichnik [transliterated term meaning "fellow Cossack villager" or "fellow of the same stanitsa"], Theodore P., walked up to him and asked what he wanted.

He answered that the English needed about twenty people to herd horses. Theodore answered that herding horses did require that number of Cossacks and signed up all of his stanichniks. There were 26 of us, so six, me among them, happened not to get signed up.

After the departure of the interpreter, we decided against going into the forest, but to gather up our stanichniks from there in the morning.

I went into my tent, but I slept—fearful of sleeping past dawn and being captured.

That night, I could hear the conversations of our escapee Cossack men and women. They were also deciding what to do: several intended to hide in the woods, others—to go to the USSR.

In the morning, I woke my acquaintance, who was sleeping in the barn [*стодоле*, a transliteration of a German and Czech term for barn, "stodola"], and we went to where our fellows [*ребятям*] had gathered in a neighboring barn. In all, there were 26 of us. But come what may!—Everyone decided to start herding horses together.

The sun came out and we watched fearfully in the direction from which vehicles had to come to get people, worrying that we might somehow get tossed into them.

Soon, a column of trucks appeared, some twenty in number, at the front of which was an officer. In all, they held some 100 armed English soldiers.

Finding the camp empty and littered with carts, saddles, clothing, and such, the soldiers climbed down from their vehicles, which stood at the edge of the camp, and began to poke through the junk, turning it over with rifle butts, then began to look into the escapee's carts.

We watched from afar. We heard ourselves being called. We rode up on our horses. There, we were read the names of the Cossacks who had signed up to herd horses, now not 20, but 46, among whom we 6 had been added, too.

By evening, we had gathered up almost 1,000 horses, along with cattle and camels.

People were also gathered up. Instead of 46 men, it was now closer to a hundred.

The English separated out 60 of us to take to a different herd that was lower down toward the river.

Vehicles arrived. We boarded them, but feared that instead of to a herd, we might be loaded into rail cars and sent to the "father of the people."

Four vehicles took us down to the railroad tracks. There were no guards. We were taken to some other barn and unloaded. Provisions had already been brought there.

It turned out that 2,000 of the mountain people's horses had been gathered there, guarded by 40 men of the Don. Ostakhov was their leader. They found a place for themselves in a different barn on the same meadow.

Our group took the herd from them as ordered by the English. They stayed there for another 3 days. I don't know what became of them.

In the evening of their last day, they were told that they would be taken to guard a different herd.

Sure enough, on the morning of the 4th day, a vehicle arrived. The men of the Don boarded it. They were taken onto a highway, then turned off onto a railroad line, near some freight cars. It was obvious to them that they were about to be sent to the USSR, and they began to leap off of the vehicle and run away. The English did not shoot at them. Still, a part of the group of Cossacks wound up in the freight cars. The English loaded the things the runaways had left behind into the railroad cars.

Those who had been loaded into the cars were sent to the USSR.

The interpreter behaved very well toward us. He saw that there were some people who had joined us from the forests and warned us to be careful and not let the lieutenant set eyes upon the new arrivals.

Lieutenant Thomson was left in charge of the horses after the herds were all combined. He gave part of the herd to the local residents for their use, and left the herd leaders to separate out weak or ill horses, which was done.

Then an excavating machine was brought and dug a trench some 3 meters in depth and 9 meters in width and very long.

At first, we had no idea what it was being dug for, and only realized what it was for when the English ordered us to bring all those horses, numbering some thousand or so and all the camels.

They shot them all. Then the machine filled the trench and leveled the ground over it.

All the remaining Cossack cows were slaughtered.

On the 9th of July, a lieutenant came to us and asked if there was among us a good saddler and if he would be willing to take care of saddles for the English under their command.

I knew the business very well and agreed.

It happened that the English already had one saddler, a Kabardin, working for them, along with a veteran medic. Besides them, there were 6 men seeing after 8 of the better horses taken away by the lieutenant.

On the 17th of July, all of us, along with the horses, were transferred to Klagenfurt, where the 4th Royal Hussar Regiment was stationed.

There turned out to be 23 more of the best Cossack horses with this regiment, a total of 41 in all including those added. They, too, were cared for by Cossacks. Besides those, there were 11 Cossacks working in the kitchen for this regiment.

Our lieutenant returned to the herds and, as we later learned, the horses were sent off somewhere accompanied by English soldiers, while the Cossacks were released to find work—some with farmers, some on the railroad, some as loggers.

The Hussar regiment (and us with it) changed where it was stationed several times and wound up in Trieste on October 30.

All of us Cossacks who were working for the regiment were offered a contract to sign for a one-year term. They gave out English clothes to us and warned that when we left the regimental grounds to go into the city, we should not speak any Russian, since there were Soviet officers and soldiers present who need not know that we were with the English regiment.

In March of 1946, we were given forms to fill out. Our kindhearted interpreter warned us not for any reason to write that we were military, but to say that we were civilians. We did so.

The evening of April 2nd, all the Cossacks were told that we would be sent to tend to the horses of another regiment.

Some doubt about that arose among us: "Are they taking us to be turned over to the Soviets?"

Truly, on the morning of April 3rd, we were seated in a truck. An officer and an interpreter were with us.

Our worries became worse when, as we exited the gate, two British officers threw packs of cigarettes into the truck for us.

When we were some 70-80 km from Trieste, the truck stopped at an empty field. Some 130 cigars, soap, toothbrushes, combs were passed out to us.

We went on. We were fed on the way, in Venice. We moved on, but more slowly. We could see that the English were in no hurry. We had no clue what the deal was until around 10 o'clock in the evening, when our truck drove up to the gate of a tent camp encircled in barbed wire.

Apparently the English thought that, had we caught sight of the camp from afar in the daytime, we would have run away.

We were taken to a camp in Rimini that later became famous for a bloody betrayal from it of Russian anti-Bolsheviks.

The following morning, we saw that we were in a huge camp in which thousands of tents had been erected. They were divided by barbed wire into separate squares [клетки], each marked with its own number.

In the first square were 13,000 from Galicia, in the second, Germans, among whom SS officers were held separately.

Some three days later, we were transferred from the transit tents into National Square *No* 7, in which people of various nationalities were found.

The camp was guarded by Poles. Everywhere, there were elevated sentry posts. Flood lights lit up the camp at night.

S. E. B. (Cossack of the 1st Cavalry Regiment)

Note: These Cossacks witnessed handovers while escaping that bitter fate themselves thanks to the good advice they got from the German interpreter when they were still in Trieste, who warned them to enter that they were civilians in the form given them.

The Lessons of Lienz

Do not think that I want once more to repeat what in past years has been said and written about the Russian tragedy at Lienz. As a former member of the Cossack Committee created by refugees at Lienz, I consider that not all of the truth about Lienz has yet been told. This does not mean that there is in general no truth in what has been said and written about Lienz, but the memories of individual witnesses to the Lienz betrayals do not uncover and have not the ability to uncover what is uppermost: WHO, AFTER ALL, IS TO BLAME FOR THIS NATIONAL TRAGEDY? **(emphasis added by the editor.)** Who prepared it and who bears the main responsibility for it before history and our nations?

I answer this question within a framework of actual observations, confining myself only to evidence based upon facts that are capable of answering it. However, before doing so, we must remind ourselves about so-called "German mistakes." Within the German military organization there were individuals who tried in every possible way to patronize former officials of the Communist Party, justifying their policy by saying that former Soviet Party administrative officials, Komsomol and others up to NKVD-ists [энкаведистов], better understood Soviet reality and had experience in supervising "labor." It needs to be underlined that local leaders in the fight for freedom did not object to those who honestly repented their previous sins and wanted to become fighters to free their country of Bolshevism, rather than having it subjected to unnecessarily repression, but they categorically rejected a basic-utilitarian approach in valuing former Soviet people and allowing them to manage work. There were more than just a few skirmishes with German administrators in places based on this.

Unfortunately, the higher positions were taken by German administrators. So, the city of Nalchik (Kabardia) had Party professors, refugees from Leningrad, among their burgomeisters. The city police were headed by a Party member chosen literally on the road by Germans. It is no surprise that such people led a fight not against Bolshevism, but against anti-Communists. The Nalchik administrative organ was entirely turned into a Bolshevik underground, which later, fearing the threat of arrest, ran off. I can supply hundreds of such examples. The Germans naively supposed that they were "using" former Soviet administrative organs and their leaders for their own interests, but, in fact, those fifth columnists used them for their own aims. The Soviet underground unfurled its net ever wider, spreading turncoats everywhere—on the staff, or in duties of interpreter, cook, or secretary, who used all manner of diversions in order to provoke mass arrests of peasants and "partisans." In the village of Chikola (Ossetia), the "secretary" one night ordered the arrest of 300 peasants who had with great difficulty so recently managed to free themselves. Soviet infiltrators [лазутчики] penetrated the German military staff and its units, frequently provoking conflict between residents and the army. There was one such conflict provoked by them between German tank units and residents in the village of Surkh-Digora that almost ended in its destruction. Guard duty in prisoner-of-war camps was almost completely in the hands of "repentant" NKVD-ists who took fierce vengeance on the prisoners. In Camp Georgyevksy (N. Caucasus), there was an "officer's barrack." Although made up by the Germans from "prisoner-of-war volunteer" officers, it considered itself an arm of the NKVD.

It is fully natural that organs of the NKVD did not miss out on "work" inside those masses retreating from their homelands alongside the German Army. Evidence shows that the leadership of several national groups of refugees was already in the hands of Soviet agents as early as Simferopol. Lists of refugees were sent to

NKVD organs from there and then from Belarus.

Here is where individuals of those organizations from the Caucasus that surrounded the "Ostministry" first stepped out on the stage in the role of so-called separatism.

The point is that the mountain people had rejected the "representatives" of separatism who had arrived in the N. Caucasus with the German army as "consultants and intermediaries" between the Germans and local population. Having listened in one meeting to such a "representative" of the North-Caucasus Committee lay out his "program" for the future, the mountain people let the Germans know that they should not send any more such "liberators" to them. And that made the Germans deal with the wishes of the people. Representatives of the "Berlin Committee," in particular Germans on the North-Caucasus Committee, stayed on the sidelines from the people. It was rare for one of them to be included as a guest of the local population ("for a banquet.")

Relations between the army and local inhabitants were regulated by local leaders in the fight for freedom. Seeing this, "separatists" started to link up with Soviet elements appearing in their field of view along the way and began, together with them and with the help of the German administration and its ties with the "Ostministry," to fight against local anti-Communists, their organizations, and leadership.

So, into the leadership of the refugee masses, who had similarly rejected separatist "representatives [*фертреторов*, a transliteration of the German *vertreter*]," the Berlin "Committee," with the help of the "Ostministry," began to plant individuals useful to them from among those German and Soviet elements the refugees had become conditioned to. In actual fact, the refugees, including those who were put in the "Italian bag," turned out to be squeezed by the fist of their own "liberators." The political leadership turned out to be held by Nazi "liberals" among the Germans. The military and administrative leadership was in the hands of Soviet agencies through being in the hands of Soviet infiltrators, of whom several were even kindly introduced into the North Caucasus Committee to head its propaganda organ.

In this way, even up to their own meeting with the English at Lienz, refugees turned out to be in the hands of Bolsheviks who, speaking of which, created "class" attitudes in the private lives of refugees, set up their own "platform," putting it on the basis of rules of Soviet cooperating organizations, already having "named" people for posts in their own future "North-Caucasus government," and such. In a word, an unbridled NKVD-ist cynically amused himself by mocking his own sacrifices. There was even an attempt made to "select" the political leadership only from the Berlin Committees.

Do we need to speak of the Soviet Leadership of the refugees not being organized only along legal methods in war? Almost the entire refugee regiment, created for self-protection, was given over to Tito in the most dangerous moment for the refugees, when the refugees really did need to be protected. But it was not only that the refugees were left without protection. Within the refugees there were active, so-called "youth organization" soviets which had ties with the Reds, headed by a certain Major Ivanov, in the mountains. When this underground organization was exposed by an individual of their own group, that exposure began to confirm that they had "gone over to Badoglio, but accidentally wound up with Major Ivanov." Several of these infiltrators were brought to trial by refugees in their own courts, but the majority of them avoided trial.

The situation after Germany's surrender did not allow a chance to carry on in due measure the fight against the Soviet fifth columnists among the refugees. The leadership of the refugees was changed after the German surrender, but it was already too late. It merely led to Soviet infiltrators removing their masks and acting openly. One Balkar announced openly: "I am a hero of the Soviet Union sent to work among the refugees." Separatists also openly told the English: "We have no special ties to these people," and separated themselves from the refugees. Their leaders never considered it necessary in so dramatic a moment to show themselves to refugees. The Soviet fifth column tossed at the refugees its Komsomol propaganda group, consisting of young, beautiful as if so selected, girls, who crawled into almost every refugee hut. Soon there appeared alongside the refugees within their camp territories a camp of returnees, over which a Soviet flag was raised and from which came Soviet songs. The remnants of Ulagay's divisions were disarmed by these girls and moved to the Soviet camp. Leaders and officials of the "Youth Organization," which was hardly made up only of youths, began to prepare people for the means with which to make refugees return to their homeland. Leaders in the fight for freedom, in their turn, were prepared to overcome obstacles by force and carry off all the refugees in the Free World.

But even in this anti-Communist leadership, there again turned up "disagreements," sparked by separatist elements who "met" with leaders of the Soviet agents in charge of refugees and tried to orchestrate the newly elected replacement for the detached leadership of the refugees, called the Caucasus Committee of Refugees, accepting into it one of the officials of the North Caucasus Committee (Berlin)—General Khan-Kelitch-Ghirey. **(Editor's Correction:** Instead of Khan-Kelitch-Ghirey, it should be Sultan Kelitch-Ghirey)

At one of the first meetings of the Caucasus Committee, at which a draft of an appeal to the allied Anglo-American command was under consideration, this General Khan-Kelitch-Ghirey suggested changing the name of the Caucasus Committee to the North-Caucasus Committee, but his suggestion brought such derision from the others that the general hurriedly dissociated himself from the "North-Caucasus Committee." After this, on meeting with the English staff, the general tried to have himself designated as the sole leader of refugees from various national groups, some 10 thousand men in number.

All this caused a split in the Caucasus Committee on Refugees, from which even Colonel Ulagay withdrew.

An extraordinary meeting of most of the officials of the Caucasus Committee who had parted ways with the general was called at Colonel Ulagay's apartment, They quickly decided to make contact with the Cossacks, which they did.

But the Soviet "leadership" was far from asleep within the refugees. While still in Italy, it showed its potency with weapons in its hands. Thus, just before the retreat from Italy, headquarters was raided by "Badoglists" (partisans), although they were disarmed. Then there appeared an armed North-Caucasus fifth column that tried to sever the ties between Cossacks and the mountain people by placing a barrier in the gorge at the moment of departure. At the same time as that skirmish, though, Cossacks (cavalry) went around the rear of the Soviet position, destroyed it, and took 8 prisoners.

These situations prevented further attacks planned by partisans against refugees, but at the moment of betrayal at Lienz, the "Youth Organization" soviet attempted once more to use force to keep refugees from escaping from the camp. Soviet propagandists spread rumors among the refugees that the English were capturing all escapees and taking reprisals on them. However, it was afterwards seen that the English soldiers were themselves helping escapees in the woods to the north. This situation does not remove the English leadership from responsibility for the tragedy of the refugees, but to lay all of the blame for the "Lienz Tragedy" only on the Anglo-American allies is to distort reality. The Yalta and Potsdam agreements cannot be justified, but they were not carried out solely under the initiative of the Western powers.

In conclusion, it should be strongly emphasized that, 12 years after Lienz, refugees are now prepared to meet new "Lienzes."

There is enough of a basis now to say that the "Youth Organization" left Lienz with the refugees and continued its subversive "work" of betrayal. Conditions for this are now no less favorable than under the Germans.

The forces for liberation abroad weakened very visibly after the blow of Lienz. Never in their entire history have they carried such losses as at Lienz and in the period that followed. The problem was not just the betrayal at Lienz. No less of a heavy blow to liberation forces in the Caucasus was the betrayal of armed legions in northern Europe. In this, too, separatists played their role. Anyone interested in the detailed facts about Lienz and of the "work" of Soviet fifth columnists within emigrés from the Caucasus can find them in my pamphlet, released by the "Kosti Foundation [*Фондом им. Кости*]." In it, the facts are given about that "work" carried out by fifth columnists in the Caucasus after Lienz up to this time,

Akube Kubati

("Informational Bulletin of the Office of Representatives of Russian Emigrants in America." [*Информационный бюллетень Представительства Российских эмигрантов в Америке.*] *No 3.* June 1958.)

A few words about the article by A. Kubati:

This article refers exclusively to mountain people of the northern Caucasus who traveled from Italy to Austria at the same time as the Cossacks, settling near them on the banks of the Drau in the area of Nickelsdorf-Oberdrauburg.

The removal of the mountain people was carried out at the same time as the people of the Cossachi Stan were removed.

The author of this piece writes that during the removal and handover to the Soviets, the organizers of the repatriation not only did not prevent, but even "helped escapees going into the woods."

Possibly! But such relations with the English authorities, as can be seen, for example, in the forced repatriation of the people of Cossachi Stan, had to have been the exception. To everyone who lived through June 2, 1945, on the field at Camp Peggetz, it is very clear that not just Cossacks, but even women who attempted to break out of the encirclement perished from the bullets of British soldiers.

That having to do with infiltration by Bolshevik provocateurs into the refugee groups, in particular, parachutists, also had its place in the Cossachi Stan.

We must trust that future chroniclers of the life of the Stan in

Northern Italy and Austria will note not just one occurrence of this deplorable appearance.

V. Naumenko

Betrayed Beliefs

There has been much said about the unprecedented conduct by the British in the Tyrol. The blood of unarmed Cossacks, their wives and children, cry out and will cry out to heaven.

There is no justification whatever and cannot be!

The civilized leaders of the leading countries agreed without reservation to the betrayal of thousands of defenseless people to their enemies —to deliberate torture and death ...

Leaders of the armies of "Christian" nations trampled various laws of God in Lienz and its surroundings when they beat mobs of worshipers at prayer, who in their last hour awaited God's salvation but were given up to the despotism of the godless.

The English command, officers seemingly educated in military honor, trampled forever this honor of theirs in the dirt, **knowingly** deceiving gullible officers and luring them into a trap set up in advance.

Can we even attempt to find any kind of mitigating circumstances for this breach of faith?

But still, there are people who try to bring in legal paragraphs to support glaring lawlessness! For example, the English officer, Oswald Stein, admitting that he was "one of the officers primarily responsible to the British High Command in Austria in 1945-6 in fulfilling the orders of what was formerly His Majesty's Government on the repatriation of prisoners of war." In an open letter to *The Times*, he gives his assurance (which, after all, on the word of a British officer, should be reliable) that Soviet citizens not coming under the listed categories were not subject to being turned over and had the right to remain in the British zone if they wished.

What bald cynicism!

Oswald Stein's arguments on the correctness of repatriations of individuals who were Soviet citizens on September 3, 1939, is completely refuted by the open letter of Count Bennigsen in the same newspaper, *The Times*. But I want to make one more addition.

If repatriation was not required even of Soviet citizens not coming under three of Stein's specific categories, doesn't that obviously mean that individuals **never having been Soviet citizens** but who were "in opposition" to Soviet authority and had lived many years **outside of** Soviet territory inviolably had **the full legal right** to remain in in the British zone? This seems unarguable, but the reality was the opposite.

Let us consider just one example, but one that is so logically convincing—an example for which **nothing could justify** betrayal: the turn over of General Krasnov.

This remarkable individual was well known to the English government, He was **never** a Soviet citizen, lived outside its borders as an emigré for 25 years—and all that time fought unstintingly by means of the written word against Communism. His works were widely known throughout the world. They were translated into every European language. The English reading public was especially familiar with them. And, apart from General Krasnov's final campaign against Bolshevism, just the fact that he was the author of books that revealed the ture nature of Bolshevism was quite enough to make an agreement on his death with the Soviet government.

The English knew all of this very well and still gave him up.

General Krasnov was totally unprepared for this ending: he believed in the honor of the British command.

Toward the end of May, 1945, he was already retired and, subsequently, as an old emigré, could consider himself totally safe under the protection of the British government. He was acquainted with influential Englishmen. In particular, that is clear from his being on good terms with Field Marshall Alexander, to whom he addressed two letters from Lienz concerning the further fate of the Cossacks.

About his own, personal fate, he was calm …

The circumstances surrounding the betrayal of the Cossack officers to the Bolsheviks is known for certain. It now seems unbelievable to us with what gullibility almost every officer allowed himself to be fooled by a deliberately placed trap. We may asses it now as gullibility, but under those conditions, it was nothing but **unquestioning trust**: Russian officers measured British officers **by their own yardstick!** A huge majority simply did not have the thought of betrayal come into their heads.

Neither did the thought occur to General Krasnov when he received his invitation to the "conference." Excerpts from the letters of the general's widow, Lydia, Fyodorovna Krasnova, now deceased, from November 6, 1957, in which she shared her suffering with her close acquaintance are good evidence for this.

If General Krasnov had even the least bit of suspicion of how events were to develop, he would naturally not have been in a mood to start planning a new literary work, would not have pondered a quiet life at the end of his days in a quiet and picturesque corner of the Tyrol, or leave for a "conference" and indicate with near exactitude the hour for his return.

But let us leave this commentary in good time to his letters: many of his lines speak for themselves.

M. V.

The Number of Inhabitants of Cossachi Stan
(the Group of Field Ataman Domanov)
Forcibly Turned Over from Lienz and Its Surroundings

Popular rumor varies on this, in most instances overestimating the number of victims of betrayal.

I visited the Cossachi Stan for the last time after its move from Belarus to Italy, in the area of Gemona in October of 1944, that is, seven months before its tragic betrayal in Austria on the banks of the Drau.

At that time, I made a detailed list of the number of people present in the Stan based on official statements and lists kept by the staff of the Field Ataman.

In all, there were 15,590 men, women, and children.

This number was made up of the following hosts: Don—7,254, Kuban—5,422, Terek-Stavropol—2,503, others—411.

Of the over-all number of 15,590, there were 7,155 in the military, the rest were what was called the civilian population, that is, the aged, total invalids, women, and children—8,435.

The active military were distributed as follows:

Guard Division—386, 1st Cavalry Regiment (Cossacks from all hosts)—962, 1st Don Regiment—1,277, 3rd Kuban—1,136, Terek-Stavropol—780, reserves (various hosts)—376, 9th Regiment (then being disbanded)—803. The remaining staff and administrative staff —334.

The civilian population by host consisted of: Don—3,774, Kuban—3,071, Terek-Stavropol—1,281, others—309.

This gives a total of 15,590 of both sexes in the group of the Field Ataman (in the Cossachi Stan).

But then, apart from the indicated units, the 8th and 10th Regiments were on their way to Italy, as was the Bondarenko Regiment from Warsaw.

After this, when the German collapse began to be known, many Cossacks and Cossack families headed for northern Italy (where the Cossachi Stan was moved from Gemona) and to the Drau River Valley after the move of the Stan from Italy to the vicinity of Lienz in southern Austria. Several groups of Cossacks headed there along with small Cossack units of the Cossack Host of the High Command [*Главным Управлением*], found in Berlin.

In this way, the total population of the Cossachi Stan in the tragic spring days of 1945 increased by many thousands, and it must be allowed that there were close to 21,500 people, as noted in the *History of the 8th Argyll Sutherland Scottish Battalion*, units of which carried out the forced repatriation of Cossacks and their families from the Drau Valley in the vicinity of Lienz.

V. Naumenko

The Final Housewarming

> Dedicated to the memory of the mountain people of the Caucasus, their women and children, victims of betrayal by the "cultured" West.

If the tragedy of the Polish officers at Katyn Forest goes down in history as incontrovertible proof of the frightening reality of Stalin's tyranny, then the tragedy of the "Valley of Death" opens a new page in this history in which an "honorary" place will be devoted to the "Cultured West." When a future historian, with the help of the labors of General Naumenko, arrives at a full and unbiased spelling out of the events of those days, he will not forget about those mountain people of the Causcasus, whose blood the western democracies so lavishly spent on the account presented to them by their "true" ally, the bandit Dzhugashvili, professional executioner of the people of Russia, on whose "conscience" there already were millions of lives. "One can bargain with cannibals," but can one bargain over human blood is a question to be answered by the future Russian spawn of the honorable sir, author of such frankness. If all the surviving Cossacks affirmed that the foul tragedy was carried out entirely by the hands of the English, my task would be to strengthen this declaration, even though it would have been naive to believe that this role, to their great disgrace, they might have fulfilled without the presence of an agreement, even such a closed-mouthed one on that side that by rights belongs to the European High Command.

Will our future generations forgive those guilty of monstrous evil, we cannot know, but our debt to the survivors is to leave them the written truth about the events of these difficult and unforgettable days, when the English command in Austria, themselves using the methods of Stalinist dungeons, tested their abilities in practice, using unarmed people for their subject. (Emphasis added by the editor.)

Thus, I alone of the few mountain people who managed to remain on the short list of those left alive and well and, apparently, to recount for our offspring the sad picture of those sad days of May of 1945 on the banks of the River Drau, far from our homeland—in Austria.

Here, I let down a curtain, but not the "iron" one, which the deaf West so uselessly attempts to raise, and, "by notes" and a little imagination, bring my readers to that place where my mountain people left their last housewarming and there raised it again.

Paluzza… This name can be found only on a detailed map of this part of Italy. Here, in Paluzza was found the staff of the Caucasus Division. It consisted of the regiments: North Caucasus and Georgian.[*]

The duties of the to-be-named [вр. и.] head of the division were held by Colonel Törman [Тоерман], a former officer in the Russian Imperial Army, German by blood, born in the Baltics, subsequently a German citizen. Under him was a German adjutant captain (hauptmann).

This division was supposed to have General Bicherakhov, but illness held him up and he never arrived (which saved him from certain death). The North Caucasus Regiment was commanded by Colonel Kuchuk Ulagay, his close assistant and commander of the 1st squad was the writer of these lines.[**]

The Georgian Regiment was commanded by Prince P. Ts. The Polish squad was stationed there in Poland, commanded by a former major in the Soviet Army, Ossetian by origin, T. This squad was formed in 1942 in the territory of the Northern Caucasus, mainly from Ossetians. They answered directly to a German officer, Major Tör [Тоеру], and was part of our division as an independent entity.

What touches on the refugee masses of the mountains, is that they were quartered in three villages close to Paluzza, the Italian

---

[*] Former mountain legions fought on various parts of the Soviet front within the ranks of the German Army. They consisted exclusively of former Soviet citizens in the Red Army. In April of 1945, numbering some 500 men, they came to Paluzza by way of Berlin and began to form the Mountain Division, at the head of which was to be General Bicherakhov [Бичерахов].

[**] General Bicherakhov lived in Germany after the war and died in an old people's home. The author of this piece also died in Germany.

inhabitants of which fled with the partisans into the hills at the first arrival of our units in the area. I note in passing that the entire place, starting from Tolmezzo and stretching beyond the valley to the Austrian border, was a cradle for Red partisans, but the energetic joint measures taken by mountain people and Cossacks cleared the entire road of partisans so that they no longer came down off the hills, for they knew that "neither mounted nor foot soldiers would pass through alive."

I will not stop to spend time on those operations of clearly military character that we employed against partisan bands, but I do note here that these bands very quickly understood their weakness in battle with us in the hills, situations more familiar to us than to them.

Time passed. One alarming thing followed another. Always the circle around the once mighty German Army was tightening stronger and stronger. Things became depressing for the Germans and they became depressing for us. They understood the mistakes committed by their political leaders. They understood that we had been right and that they should have followed our suggestions. Now it was too late to speak or think about mistakes. The 9th wave approached ...

We did not have long to wait and when the first Cossack transport vehicles appeared in the early days of May, we understood that we had to leave also.

Ignoring our situation, our German authorities continued to wait for an appropriate marching order, which was completely pointless, given that military actions on the Italian front had already concluded.

Those days in Paluzza there was a special stirring up brought about by mountain people coming from surrounding villages to find out what was happening.

If the center of the Cossack settlements in Italy was the city of Tolmezzo, then a similar center for the mountain people of the Caucasus had to have been the village of Paluzza, since that was where the staff of our division, headed by General Sultan Kelitch-Ghirey, was located, its office providing supplies and such. Here the

"Gazette" of mountain-separatist people was printed, the appearance of which we explained to ourselves as a consequence necessitated by the powerlessness of the political deal-dodgers. There was a cafe-restaurant with billiards and several drinking establishments, wine for which was supplied from the city of Udine.

In a word, it was a "Mountain Republic" in Italy, but without a president, since suitable candidates were taking in their own time to make their way from Berlin to Switzerland, leaving their people to the arbitrariness of fate and the "kindness" of the English Command.

On the eve of departure, there was a joint meeting at the staff of all officers, at which officers of the Georgian Regiment were also present. The commander of this regiment was Colonel Prince Ts., who, after greeting all the officers, turned to Colonel Törman to announce that he was leaving with his regiment for the hills to continue operations against Red partisans, asking that he (Törman) release him from the pledge by which he was still tied.

Suggesting that such formality obviously no longer had any meaning, but since in the case of his refusal, the Prince would still not alter his decision, Colonel Törman, acceded to his wishes.

When the Prince, after giving his farewell to all, left, I caught up with him and asked what all that meant and what his plans were.

He answered as follows:

"A meeting with the Red Italian Partisans awaits me, but for you and all the others—Red Army Bolsheviks. So I choose the lesser evil."

The words of the Prince turned out to be prophetic and I remembered them for the entire road.

It must be noted that Georgian refugees were in very small numbers in the mountain people's camp—individuals, so that the situation required the Prince to make independent decisions.

The next day, the transports of the mountain people spread out, merging with the endless flow of Cossack carts, their path passing through Paluzza.

The Georgians left for the hills. I later learned that they were surrounded there by Italian partisans, disarmed and interred, but then, after all that, released. Many of them remained in Italy. Others moved to various countries. All remained alive and unscathed.

Colonel Törman and Major Tör did not go with the mountain people. They vanished from their location and General Sultan Kelitch-Ghirey became head of the mountain people.

Many have already written about the journey from Tolmezzo to the banks of the Drau and in so much detail that there is no need for me to repeat it all.

At the moment of the hill people's departure from Italy, they generally numbered (not counting Georgians) probably about 5,000, of whom about 40-50 were officers. Some of the mountain people and all of the Georgian refugees stayed in place.

Moving through were Cossacks, mountain people, Germans, Cossacks, again, and it seemed that there was no end to their carts and wagons. Many were on foot. Most did not understand what danger it was they needed to flee, where the road on which they were going went, and what uncertainty it was that gave them such alarm.

I stopped along the road, greeting with my glances those riding and walking past, checking their transports in hope of finding one on which I might get a place. It was a long wait and it seemed hopeless, Suddenly, a truck approached with a German soldier at the wheel and a non-commissioned officer beside him. I gave a hand sign. The vehicle stopped. The non-commissioned officer gave me his place, going himself atop some crates, with which the truck was full.

Still, I could not manage to make my journey to the end by motor vehicle. It failed later and came to a stop, so I continued on foot.

Night fell. I could see Austrian houses ahead on the road. I went to the first one, asking the women there if I could spend the night. Getting a positive answer, I stayed, but I could not fall asleep, even though exhausted. The Prince's words had bored into my mind.

In the morning, going to the kitchen and acquainting myself with the hostess, I asked if she could let me have some civilian clothes, since changing from my uniform was a must.

Apparently suspicious of something bad in my intent, she answered that there were no such clothes for me, and that I should instead go to a small house visible at the edge of the forest and wait there.

I thanked her and did go there. It turned out to be a small wooden shed such as is found in gardens. Two to three hours later, a girl came with some clothes, trousers that were admittedly too short, shoes, and a kepi [flat-topped cap]. After changing, I put any items I no longer needed into a sack and gave it to the girl. I kept my revolver, binoculars, a sleeping bag, and some small change.

In this state, I went farther.

When there were approximately 10 kilometers left on my journey, I saw the Cossack officer of one of the regiments sitting beside the road. Greeting him, I sat down. We talked. I learned that he was an old emigrant, a "Parisian" like myself.

While we were discussing things, we saw a couple, apparently husband and wife, making a great effort to pull their overloaded cart from a meadow onto the road. We decided to help. As we approached, it became apparent to us that he was a Cossack. We asked where his horse was. He waved an arm hopelessly and said it was lying motionless on the ground. We helped to pull the cart onto the road and push it a kilometer or two to a nearby house where we spent the night.

Now better acquainted with my co-traveler, I suggested that he follow my example and change into civilian clothes. He turned out to be more far-seeing than I and already had civilian clothes among his things, into which he did change. He gave his military uniform to our gracious hosts.

In the morning, we two set off again, but the Cossack did not want to part with his wife and remained.

We came to a bridge over the Drau. After crossing it, we walked along the bank of the river. Having gone some distance, we decided to stop, and, climbing up a tree, I looked the terrain over with my binoculars. In the distance, I could see the camp of the mountain people. Thus, I had found my way back to my people.

After sleeping there on the bank, we headed for a railroad hut, and, telling the sentry that we were French, stayed with him. He suggested we could use the hayloft in the barn. The hayloft became our dwelling. It was an excellent vantage point, useful to us in all respects.

We needed to take action vigorously and quickly. We went out on the road and stopped an American auto with a Negro at the wheel. The English, we did not see yet. My co-traveler asked the Negro where we could find an American officer. He suggested we take seats in the auto. He took us where we needed to go.

We went into a building where an American officer met us. To his questions—who we were and what we needed—we answered that we were French and needed a pass.

The American knew no French, but he believed our declarations and immediately wrote out an individual pass for each of us without asking us to present any documents. We wrote our names without changing them on scraps of paper.

The passes we received signified: Commander 4th Buffer Distribution [*буферного распределительного*] Point, with his signature. Each was dated May 13, 1945.

Having such a pass, I could now go to the camp, since I could not be held up while holding it.

On the Twentieth of May, I came to the camp for supplies as always, but at the moment that I found myself in a group of officers and was telling them of my adventures, open-top trucks with Englishmen behind the steering wheels drove into the very center point of the camp at the same time as a small auto in which sat: an officer, two sergeants, and a driver who was also their interpreter. All were English.

The auto stopped near us and the interpreter, addressing himself to the group I was in, asked in perfect Russian:

"The major [*Господин майор*] wants to speak with the general in command of the camp." He apparently meant General Sultan Kelitch Ghirey.

I noticed several tanks along the highway.

The general was in the same building as the staff.

After a little while, with quiet steps and head held high, General Sultan Kelitch Ghirey walked up. He wore his white tunic under his black cherkesska, the waist tightened to its limit. There was gold gilt over the entire outfit, the same gold gilt on his cartridge pouches.

[My apologies for not knowing how the various items of the Caucasus mountain people's uniform, from which all Cossack uniforms were derived, translate into English or Russian. The full Russian text was: *Белый бешмет под черною черкской, на всем наборе золотая насечка, такая же насечка на рукоятке парабеллума, талия перетянута до отказу.* "Cartridge pouches" might better have been left as "parabella handles."]

The arrival of the "commander" in such dress obviously made a great impression on our "hosts."

The General wore the epaulets of the Russian Imperial Army.

The interpreter passed on the words of the officers, saying that by order of the English High Command, all arms in the hands of the mountain people had to be turned in at the trucks. Officers could keep their personal weapons.

Not a single muscle twitched on the General's face as he walked back and forth in front of the English vehicles while giving this order to all present.

Weapons were turned in. The trucks left. The tanks disappeared.

The next day, I learned officers were being registered at the staff. When I went there, one of the officers addressed me, saying that all officers, without exception, were required to go to "present themselves" to the English High Command, for which I was already entered on their list.

The word, "conference," had been changed to "presentation." I approach A., who was preparing the list and, seeing my name on it, asked if I could be crossed off, announcing at the same time that I was not about to go present myself to whomever it might be, because I no longer had an officer's uniform.

I told the General that it looked to me like a "trap," or else how could one explain why all of the officers had to be present without exception.

Apparently, even General Sultan Kelitch Ghirey felt great suspicion of such a trip, but, not wanting to show that, he himself perished with the group of officers he headed.

Colonel Kuchuk Ulagay was taken separately, but was not given over to the Bolsheviks, because he carried documents on him that showed that he was an Albanian citizen.

In his time, Kuchuk and his group of Russian officers had helped Zogu take the Albanian throne [as King Zog I]. In gratitude, Kuchuk was named by King Zog to be head of the military school in Albania.

Kuchuk Ulagay's life ended on April 1st, 1953, in Santiago, Chile, several years after the tragedy on the Drau.

On the next day after registration, that is, May 16, weapons were taken from officers according to the previously prepared list, but even after this, many of them continued to believe the assurances of the English, considering all of these actions to be normal.

I did not believe it. I did not believe them, and Sultan Kelitch Ghirey, who, if he had told the soldiers what he thought, would have had to leave the camp and hide with them in the woods.

Why then did he continue to hide from his officers his misgivings about the English, whose conduct raised such great concern in him?

To this question I offer a precise and considered answer:

It was only on the Drau that Sultan Kelitch Ghirey understood the great moral responsibility he had taken upon himself as the leader of the entire mass of mountain refugees, even though totally voluntarily, as he had not been named as their leader by anybody. He was not just a general for the mountain people, but what was a part of the mountain people's tradition of elder, or "starets," whose word was law for all. His exceptional understanding of their defeated situation and his own lack of power to help every single one to the end, made him choose the only path acceptable to him—to remain with the people that he led.

General Sultan Kelitch Ghirey perished in the name of noble feelings of love for Russia on the whole and his own mountain people in particular.

As always, I visited camp on May 27, where I learned from the officer that the next day, May 28, all officers without exception were going to be "presented" to the staff of the English Command, but where, this no one knew.

To one officer's question, why I did not want to go, I had to answer that my name did not appear on the list presented to the English, which as far as it concerns my reasons, was known to the general.

On this day, I visited the camp for the last time, nevertheless managing to go around the entire camp and share my thoughts with many.

The events of the following day unwound according to plan for the English.

May 28, Major [*esaul*] N. (my co-traveler) set off for a reconnaissance of our camp, at which, by the way, none of the mountain people knew him, while I took up a position on the haystack, where, removing some shingles on the roof and using binoculars, I could watch what was taking place in the camp and along the road from the hole I made.

It was a clear, sunny day. Vision was excellent.

Trucks and an open car with three English soldiers sitting in it arrived. I assumed that an officer was among them, or several officers. The mountain officers took places in the two covered trucks, while Sultan Kelitch Ghirey took a seat in the auto.

The auto went off in the direction of Spittal. At a short distance from those three, another open automobile followed, in which there were three English soldiers. I did not notice any tanks, machine guns, or automatic weapons whatever, but one must assume that they had weapons.

When N. returned from the camp, he told me that they were searching for me while the officers were boarding the trucks, since he heard my name announced several times to the mountain people. This news finally convinced me that my misgivings had not been in vain and that the officers had been fooled. N. held the same ideas.

On that same day and in the same direction, 2-3 dozen [I took the liberty of changing *"десятка"* to "dozen'] trucks drove past, but even with them, we could not recognize any kind of special convoy.

They were transporting Cossack officers, I learned the next day from N., who had made contacts in the Cossachi Stan.

If there had still been any kind of hope for a better future among the mountain people, it dissipated as the camp learned that their officers had been handed over to the Bolsheviks.

That was when I again remembered the words of the Prince, whose prediction had come true with striking exactitude.

Further events unfolded with complete correspondence to what happened in the Cossachi Stan (in Lienz). Since the English were not dealing individually with Cossacks, Russians, or mountain people, but with the single mass of refugees that the Kremlin bandits required of their "true" and diligent ally, synchronized action was necessary for the handover.

I am acquainted with material already published about the handover of the Cossacks, so for me to try to draw a picture of the removal of the hill people by the English to give them over to the Bolsheviks would only repeat what was already well known to readers.

I will only say that, as was true for the officers, the rest of the refugees suffered the same horrible fate as the Cossacks. The one difference was that victims of the English in the Cossachi Stan numbered in the tens of thousands, while at the mountain camp, there were only some five thousand.

Were there many mountain people who escaped?

Not counting Georgians, about whom I have written above, there were left from the officer contingent only: the regiment of Colonel Kuchuk Ulagay, Staff Captain S. T., and the writer of these lines.

With respect to the crowds of mountain refugees, some 200 of their general number of 5,000 hid in the woods, while all of the rest were handed over to the Bolshevik criminals.

Those who hid in the woods were hunted. Individual gunshots were heard from the woods. This was a "gentlemanly" hunt for unarmed, unaided people. The wounded were taken to Spittal. The dead were abandoned in the woods.

I and my faithful companion went back to Italy, but this time to the south, where, on a hot August day, we shook hands for possibly the last time.

He went to Argentina, while I, to where I am now found.

Ossetian Cavalry Regiment Captain
G. Tuaev

Note: It needs to be mentioned that the Cossacks of Cossachi Stan and the mountain people were concentrated some twenty kilometers from each other in the vicinity of the Drau River from Lienz to Oberdrauburg.

On the left bank of the Drau, parallel to its flow, lay railroad tracks and a highway to Spittal, to which Cossacks and mountain people were taken for later handover to the Bolsheviks.

On the part of the river specified, the Cossachi Stan occupied the region of Lienz and farther down on both sides of the Drau to the city of Nickelsdorf. The mountain people were still farther down the river at Oberdrauburg along a distance of 5-6 kilometers.

Letter from Captain Tuaev

Allow me, as one of the officers for whom the Lienz tragedy is an event of historical significance, to answer the letter written by the English officer, Oswald Stein, that was published in *The Times* on May 14, 1952. In this letter, the author, answering the Duchess of Athol, had in mind the English reader of the paper. To that target I aim, too, for details of this monstrous evil were well known to the Russian readership long ago.

Here is my answer, the answer of an officer who suffered through and survived the tragedy, to Mr. Stein:

—As an officer trained in the glorious traditions of the Greater Russian Army, I, nonetheless, at first did not believe the word of an officer and my "tactlessness" saved me from the "conference."

Whether Oswald Stein convinced the Duchess of Athol that she was definitely mistaken is not clear to me, but at least, he convinced me that not only is he wrong himself, but, even more—bears full responsibility for actions that are customarily called **betrayal**.

In the British Zone of Austria, Mr. Stein, individuals who were not subjected to compulsory repatriation, myself among them, were those who saw through to the core of the foul plan for betrayal and found the means to keep themselves out of the trip to the "conference," or who, hiding in the hills, made their way to the American Zone.

This English officer assures the Duchess of Athol that former **Soviet citizens could remain in the English Zone if they wished.**

Wouldn't it be interesting to know where, when, and who interviewed these unfortunate people being beaten with rifle butts?

Or later, before the victims were loaded into trains and were already in the bloody paws of Stalinist heroes?

In reality, Oswald Stein confuses events when he speaks of the wishes of prisoners of war, because such a question did come up, not in Austria, but rather far away in Korea, and the interrogation was not made of Russian prisoners of war, but Koreans and Chinese. Apparently, he does not know that this had not been in a British Zone, but to the luck of the prisoners, American.

Right here was born the general rule for voluntary repatriation. It appeared subsequent to that miraculous use of force by the English Command in Austria, responsibility for some of which is borne by Mr. Oswald Stein.

But what category of compulsory repatriation listed by the letters "a," "b," and "c" did this officer attribute to us? We, for whom

Soviet authority always appeared as a gang of international criminals, headed by a self-appointed "Generalissimo?" Our attitude toward his gangs calling themselves a government was well known even to the government of his Royal Highness.

Maybe the article is not confined to the letters given, but continues to the final letters of the alphabet?

Those three letters of the alphabet used to characterize former Soviet citizens, and whatever letters applied to those of us who were never Soviet citizens, were what invited us to a "conference" where many, very many, were herded with bayonets into train cars and sent off to our "homeland."

Oswald Stein knows all about this, but is silent about it for now, although there may come a day when he will have to reveal the secret of this "alphabet" …

And he knows that the time has come when not just the defeated, but the victors will be judged.

Betrayal is a great crime.

Captain **Tuaev**

Note: Oswald Stein's letter is printed in the 1st volume of *Great Betrayal* on p. 218 [p 219 in my translation].

Victims of Forcible Repatriation, Their Graves, Monuments, and the Group Cemetery in Camp Peggetz Near Lienz

I — The Victims Who were Given Over.

The first victims were Pavel Sergeevich Galushkin, a Cossack of the Umanskoy Stanitsa and Captain Peter Vassilich Golovinsky, a Cossack of the Akhmetovskoy Stanitsa.

Both were precursors of the future tragedy.

Having no doubt in their forthcoming turnover to the Soviets, both took their own lives before it began.

Their names are worthy of note, since by their death they warned Cossacks of the coming tragic days.

Colonel Galushkin was an old emigré who had lived in France. Taking part in Cossack movements during the withdrawal of the Cossachi Stan from Italy to the vicinity of Lienz, he was in one of the stanitsa without having taken on any specific duties in it.

Winding up along with the rest near Lienz, he settled temporarily with several other Cossack families under a bridge that crossed a dry channel near the settlement of Dölsach.

Finding himself in the region of Austria occupied by the English, he did not believe them in any way and prophetically predicted the inevitability of being handed over. He always insisted to those who lived with him under the bridge that the turnover was forthcoming and said that something had to be done so as not to fall into the hands of the Soviets.

At dawn on his third day in the Drau Valley, he took the carbine of a major (later given over to the Bolsheviks) and shot himself through the mouth.

About the death of Captain Golovinsky, who was at the time an adjutant in the 1st Cavalry Regiment, a person close to him said:

"In the anxious days before the turnover in Lienz he understood in which direction English 'politics' inclined and did not believe their intentions with the Cossacks. He warned Cossacks to go into the hills and stay there.

[As punctuated in the original, it is not clear if the paragraph above is a direct quote, nor if it extends to the paragraphs that follow it. Where I have it ending is my guesswork.]

"When the English ordered that weapons be turned in, he did not give up his pistol and warned that the 'final hour' was near.

"When the directive for the officers' trip to the 'conference' followed, he did not go. He spoke of this step by the English as being an artfully placed trap, of English treachery, and he called on Cossacks one last time to disperse into the hills. Then he shot himself.

"This gunshot was his final warning to the Cossacks of the Cavalry Regiment."

When the English vehicles came to his camp to gather them to be loaded into wagons, the camp was empty. Following the advice of the deceased, the Cossacks had scattered into the nearby hills and woods in plenty of time.

The bodies of both of these officers rested first in the cemetery in Dölsach, in the woods, then were moved to the group [*браткое*, as in the title of the chapter, which can as easily be translated as "mass"] cemetery in Lienz.

How many Cossacks and members of their families perished during the handovers can hardly ever be established with any exactitude by anyone.

Some perished on the 1st of June on the field at Peggetz; some perished on this and following days from the bullets of English soldiers who followed them in the hills and woods; some died of their wounds; some committed suicide. Instances were known of mothers throwing their children into the Drau, then following them. Several jumped into the river with their babies tied onto them. There was the well-known occurrence of the woman doctor, Praskovia Voskoboynikova, who jumped into the river with her own infant, mother, and sister. A Don Cossack of the Novocherkesskoy Stanitsa, Peter Mordvikin, having used his revolver on his wife, Irina, 12-year-old son, Yura, and one-yer-old daughter, Vera, then turned it on himself. And these were not just isolated instances.

Those who survived the day of June 1, 1945, in Camp Peggetz remember how toward the evening of that day, when things were settling down and calmer, gunfire from rifles and automatic weapons could be heard. These were by English soldiers "hunting" for those who had broken free of their encirclement. They shot into overgrown meadows and wheat fields, their bullets finding those who could not be seen by eye.

One Cossack woman hidden in the thickets on the edge of a farmstead, was given away by a barking dog. An English machine-gunner headed in her direction, found the woman, and shot her.

At that time, more than a single dozen [again, the exact term was ten] found death in the waters of the Drau or its banks near Lienz and its nearby villages.

Perishing from English bullets in the turbulent Drau were several who sought safety by swimming to the right bank of the river.

One Cossack jumped while mounted on his horse from a steep bank. Both perished in the river's waves.

Cossacks perished even while being driven to be handed over to the Soviets. Several found death on the way by jumping from vehicles onto hard pavement, others jumped out when crossing bridges ...

The wounded died during forced repatriation in the hospitals and abandoned farm buildings where the sought safety.

Many, many dozen [see above] of the inhabitants of the Cossachi Stan perished during the forcible betrayal, but an exact number was never established and cannot be established.

This becomes understandable when taking into account the situation at that time and the mood of those who suffered through the tragedy:

1. In those days, when thousands of people were taken away to be turned over to the Soviets, there was no register kept of them, and if one had been kept by the English, we have to this day been unable to obtain any of its data. After calmness did return, they began to investigate who was missing, but to establish who was turned over, who perished, and who succeeded in escaping and went into the hills was impossible.

2. Those still remaining after others had been turned over had very low morale due to all they had suffered through. The menace of being handed over by a single order hung over them. There were perpetual fly-overs and drive-throughs made by the Soviet Repatriation Committee, whose base was in Klagenfurt and which "hunted" people who had formerly been under the Soviets, keeping those left in continual tension. All of this forced people to avoid being seen by English eyes, while those who decided to leave the vicinity of Lienz did so hurriedly, in most cases at night.

3. To this has to be added that for a prolonged time, the hours of free movement were restricted.

4. The English strove as quickly as possible to hide traces of their bloody reprisals and hurriedly buried the victims of their violence. If this attracted the attention of certain residents and the spiritual ministry, they were all told to keep silent on the number of burials and not do anything that might be interpreted as a demonstration.

5. Bodies of those who were killed or took their own lives outside the boundaries of the camp were buried by local residents where they died.

6. Relative freedom of movement wasn't established until the fall of 1945, after victims were buried in a group grave, and the majority of graves in the surroundings of Lienz began to be covered with grass and had their soil settle.

These were the main reasons preventing a count of the victims of the forced repatriations of the Cossachi Stan.

Only after the passage of several years was there a committee organized under the auspices of the Austrian Archbishop, Vladiki Stefan, to look after the cemetery in Lienz. He took upon himself the task of transporting bodies from its outskirts to the city of Lienz.

The bodies were brought to the group cemetery in Peggetz. The bodies of Captain Golovinsky and the woman, Dr. Voskoboynikova, were brought there, as was Colonel Galushkin, from the village cemetery of Dölsach.

This question of graves being spread about in the fields and woods requires us to pause at several cases that bear witness to how depressed the hunted people were:

A Cossack woman detailed how, soon after the 1st of June, she was walking from camp to a nearby village and noticed a wooden cross erected from branches among the bushes. Coming closer, she made out the inscription scratched on it. It was the first letter of a given name and the full family name of the person lying beneath it. The woman was dumbfounded. It was the same as her husband's, who had been taken away on May 28 to the "conference." Over the next few days, she returned to this grave, wishing to dig it up and confirm whether the body in it really was his, "but I didn't know how to manage that," she said, "and I was afraid to talk about it with anyone." It later became known that this was not her husband, but a member of his family.

And there was an occurrence about which an eyewitness only told after the passage of much time. — On the 2nd or 3rd of June, 1945, he saw many corpses in the cellar of one of the barracks in Camp Peggetz—several dozen [tens again].

This evidence is believable in all respects. The number of corpses might have been exaggerated, but we cannot eliminate the possibility that the English, striving to hide the number of victims of their carnage, temporarily stored corpses in this cellar before graves for them could be dug. That others living in this barrack did not notice anything can also be explained. All their attention was focused on saving themselves.

Returning to the question of how many people of the Cossachi Stan died through forced repatriation on the 1st of June, 1945, and in the days that followed, we find in one document about that alarming time that there were as many as 100. That figure was given in a report from October, 1949, of the commission designated by Colonel Rogozhnim, Head of the White Camp in Kellerberg, to oversee work on the construction of grave markers for the cemetery in Peggetz. That same number is given by Father Alexander Vladimirsky, who, on orders from Major Davies, buried several of those who perished on the 1st of June.

In this number he included Voskoboynikova and her family, the solitary grave in the cemetery at Dölsach, those buried in the municipal cemetery of Lienz, and one overgrown grave on the bank of the Drau.

The figure of 100 cannot be considered to be exaggerated. To it needs to be added the bodies of several victims carried away by the Drau River, those still lying in lost graves, and those taken away along with the living by the English without a full count having been made before they were handed over to the Bolsheviks.

2—The Graves.

Even before the tragic days of the handovers, there were several residents of the camp buried where the Group Cemetery in Peggetz is now found, but when victims turned up after the bloody violence of June 1, 1945, the English prepared several mass graves into which those who bodies were put.

At present, 28 graves are found in the cemetery, of which 18 are group graves.

Among those buried there also rest those who died of natural causes, such as Veroshka Khovanskaya, who died May 26, 1945, Nikolai Gordienko, born in July of the same year and dying in the hospital, along with several others.

Victims handed over, with the exception of Peter Golovinsky (grave *No 26*), Paraskova Voskoboynikova (grave *No 27*), and Pavel Galushkin (grave *No 28*), are buried in group graves.

Looking at a photograph of the cemetery and its arrangement, the following might be questioned by the reader: the individual graves and the group graves are the same size.

On this point, a member of the former Permanent Committee for the oversight of our cemetery writes:

"Concerning the graves in our cemetery: they were made for their external appearance and uniformity. The exact positions of mass graves were lost over time and all that remained was to lock up the area. The names on graves refer to those known, while the rest fell under the group rubric, because several men were buried in the pits. That is, in the remaining area of the cemetery, aside from individual graves, graves were dug where they are now independently of where the group graves were, their mounds made and crosses placed on them, and the concrete frames put in last."

That same member of the committee said that it was very difficult to establish the number buried in our cemetery, because the English, noting that they were absolute signs of evil being done, hurried to bury them as quickly as possible.

Almost all of the graves in the cemetery are identical: they are enclosed in a concrete casing and a reinforced concrete cross is placed on them. Aluminum tablets with stamped inscriptions that were painted black are on them. The group graves is inscribed: "Their names, Thou, Lord, knowest. I. VI. 1945." For individual graves, the first and last names of the deceased are given. On several of them, monuments or crosses of a different kind have been placed.

Besides the graves in the Group Cemetery in Peggetz, there is a group grave in a cemetery in the village of Nickelsdorf, in which 3 bodies were buried—Cossacks who perished during the forced repatriations and a child who was crushed by a tank. Their names remain unknown. The grave is encased in a frame made of granite stone and a metal cross was placed on the granite base.

In the middle of the military cemetery in the city of Lienz, within the 19th grave, in which are buried those who died within the hospital in 1945, and in the 10th grave, lie the bodies of several who perished on June 1 and those who died afterwards, apparently from wounds suffered on that day.

In writing this brief essay on the graves, I need to note that in the fall of 1945, under the direction of the Austrian Black Cross, graves scattered about the fields and woods had their bodies moved to the cemetery in Peggetz or to those villages on whose soil the graves were found.

To this must be attributed the grave of P. Novikov, which was seen by many in the summer and fall of 1945 on their way from the village of Nußdorf-Debant [*Нюсдорф*] to Camp Peggetz.

According to the community of this settlement, Novikov was in a building of the village school in which the hospital had been. He jumped out a window and was smashed to death. His body was wrapped in a blanket by one of the local farmers with help from two women and taken by stretcher to be buried by the road close to a brook. He cut off a branch and fashioned a cross from it for the grave. Those women carved out the last name of the deceased on it on the following day. Later, through the disposition of the Black Cross, this body was moved to the Group Cemetery in Peggetz and must have been buried in one of the group graves, since there is no individual grave for him.

One Cossack who survived the tragedy on the field at Peggetz on June 1st, reports:

"I saw a grave near the bridge across from Dölsach on the opposite bank of the Drau. The cross on it was made of branches tied together with white scraps of fabric. During the summer of 1945, someone brought a tin food can filled with water and fresh flowers and put it on the grave. The summer was rainy, so toward autumn its hillock collapsed and its location was marked by a small depression."

The further fate of this grave is not known.

From what is noted in a confirmatory letter from the rural village of Nickelsdorf, it is apparent that bodies of 3 Cossacks and a crushed child now resting in their village cemetery had also been dug up from graves close to the village by its residents and brought there.

One Terek Cossack living in Judenburg, wrote:

"Several Cossacks managed to escape torture at the very factory at which the Soviets locked up the Cossacks who were turned over to them. Before crossing over the bridge from which it could be seen that NKB soldiers were on its other side, several Cossacks jumped into the river. These unfortunates merely escaped torture at the hands of the Bolsheviks. They could not save their own lives, for the bridge at Judenburg was very high and the Mur River, like all mountain streams, was fast, but shallow. Those who jumped smashed themselves on its rocks. The Soviets fished out all of the corpses and took them into their own zone. Only one washed up in the English zone without being noticed by them. The English decided not to give over the dead man and allowed Austria to give him a funeral. His body was buried by the highway and the inscription on its cross read: 'Unknown Cossack Soldier.' It was in English. A German helmet was put on it. Russian DPs living not far from it performed funeral services over it. When, after the rains, they returned to the grave to refurbish it, they always found it in perfect order. This was done by the Austrians of a nearby village."

3 — The Monuments.

The idea of placing a monument on the Group Cemetery in Peggetz arose in the first month after the tragedy among survivors of the handover, when their emotions over what they lived through had eased somewhat and, in the fall of 1945, with funds gathered together by them, the first monument was put up in the form of a white, cement cross, erected on a pedestal with its top corners cut off.

Toward the day of the monument's placement, the cemetery's square was spruced up. The mounds of the 14 graves found there of various heights were made level and the path through it was cleared of grass and filled with sand.

Here, I'd like to note one touching event that took place prior to the service on the occasion of the placement of the foundation.

On the night before this solemn event, the father of one of the pious families and his 11-year-old daughter brought a clod of soil to the cemetery that had been brought from Russia. With his help, the daughter made her way down into the recess dug for the foundation, dug a small hole using her hands, and filled it with this clump of native soil,

This monument was blessed on October 15, 1945 by Archpriest Father Timothy Soin, in a combined service with Archpriest Father Fyodor Vlassenkov and the priest, Father Vladimir Tchekanovsky.

Father Timothy said the following words before the memorial service which were later placed on the monument:

> Every country, every nation, has its own famous leaders, war heroes, men of science, and people of all branches of human knowledge and creativity. We had many such glorious individuals in our homeland. Epics and songs were composed in their honor. Monuments were erected on the graves of these famous predecessors.
>
> Before us is this humble, cement cross put up at the group graves of Cossacks perishing on the 1st of June of

this year at the hands of the English Command. These Cossacks were heroes of the spirit, unselfishly loving their Mother Russia and born in their regions of the Don, Kuban, and Terek.

Many of them were in the White Movement of 1918-20 and were left on the shores of the Black Sea due to an insufficient number of the transports that were to have kept them from falling against their will under the Satanic regime of the Soviet government to face all of its miseries: NKVD, prison, and concentration camps.

Then came 1941. The Germans broke through the Soviet Iron Curtain, quickly reaching Petrograd, Moscow, Tsaritsyn, and the Northern Caucasus. But at the end of 1942, failing to hold Tsaritsyn, they had to retreat quickly.

With them went all those who hated the Soviet government, who had suffered tyranny for more than 20 years. Both old and young went. Families went and individuals went. They went off into unknown distances, rather than remain beneath the iron heel of the Bolsheviks. They went with unwavering hope that nothing could be worse than the Soviet Union: after all, they were going west into the civilized countries, the democratic countries.

And so, they came to northern Italy in the area of Gemona and Tolmezzo. There, they formed the Cossachi Stan. At the end of April, 1945, the move to the western Tyrol under the patronage of the English Command was announced by the leadership of the Stan. "Cossackdom is expected to be entrusted with some kid of honorable mission," is what they told us.

When on May 28, all the officers were taken away to a "conference" of betrayal, only then did we all understand what the "patronage" of the English Command meant for Cossackdom.

The 1st of June was named as the day for the repatriation of the entire Cossachi Stan.

So as to paralyze it somewhat, it was decided to hold a general prayer service on the 1st of June in Camp Peggetz, with the entire Stan coming together there in hope that people in prayer would not be touched—for the English where Christians. But that hope was never realized.

When the liturgy came to the moment for communion, the multi-thousand mass of people was trapped in a circle of tanks with machine guns and soldiers with clubs and bayonets. They began to beat the unarmed Cossacks with clubs and stuck those who resisted with bayonets, They even shot some.

And this was the result of the "patronage of the English Command"—a common grave and 14 separate mounds.

As long as this cement cross still stands here on this common grave to symbolize the Cossack Golgotha, it will serve as a rebuke to the English Command.

Up there, from a high mountain peak, watches the immortal commander, Generalissimo Suvorov. (On that sheer cliff someone's noble hand traced out Suvorov's silhouette, while on the very peak of the mountain there stands an iron cross named after him.) He watches and is amazed that armed English soldiers are beating unarmed Cossack men, women, and children. Suvorov also once fought here and lost 26,000 of his miraculous bogatyrs, but he lost them in a fair fight, and he won the battle. From that day forth, this valley was called "The Valley of Death." Now in this Valley of Death, there have been another 26,000 valiant Cossacks, betrayed by force and cunning to certain anguished deaths, the descendants of those former Cossacks whose bravery was admired even above that majestic spirit to which the entire world bows.

By placing this monument in the form of a cross on the graves of the Cossacks, though, we are unable to fulfill another Cossack request, one voiced in the song: "A Cossack Rode Out to a Foreign Land Far Away."

In this song, it is told how the soldier died in that foreign land of his wounds or of some fatal malaise, but a difficult death in a foreign land, with neither his own mother, nor his lifelong friends, nor his children by his death bed. The Cossack asked his brother-soldiers to pile a big mound up to the height of their heads and on it to plant a bush of native guelder rose with the intention that, when a little bird flying by rests on it and chirps that here is buried a Don Cossack, it will then fly to his native land and there tell his mother, young wife, and dear children that they should not await the return of their breadwinner. "The good Cossack will no longer fly home." Although we are not able to plant that native guelder rose, we will hope that a flying bird will sit on this cross and chirp that in this grave lie, beaten by a betraying hand, heroic Cossacks who preferred death in a foreign land over return to live under the Soviet yoke. Then the bird will spread the story of this evil, never before seen in history, over the world.

Those present at the blessing of the monument were the dwellers of the camp and Cossacks gathered from nearby surroundings. Also there was the English Major, A. E. Richards, then commander of the camp, who listened attentively through an interpreter to everything said by Father Timothy.

Time passed. The camp was disbanded. Few still lived in it.

Church services were performed by Father Alexander Vladimirsky from Camp Spittal. The cemetery was tended to by surviving Cossack men and women. As much as their means allowed, they kept it in good order.

Services were conducted at the monument in the cemetery on the memorial day of June 1st and on commemoration days, for which men and women from nearby areas gathered.

An inscription was placed on the monument: "To Those Who Perished I. VI. 1945 yr."

Soon, the stucco on the pedestal began to fall off, as did the inscription. After that, someone carved "I. VI. 1945" on it.

Cossacks began to consider erecting a new, more substantial monument and, on the advice of Father Alexander, decided to put up a memorial plaque with an appropriate inscription on it.

A committee was formed to erect the monument. It proceeded to raise funds within the English Zone of Occupation. The engineer, Margushin, was chosen to oversee the project to completion.

In view of having raised only a very humble sum of money, it was decided to remove the cross from the first monument and to make an inscription appropriate for its pedestal.

Such a plaque was made and attached to the pedestal.

But just like the monument, so did the plaque not satisfy Cossacks, so it was decided to erect a new monument on a new foundation and contact all Cossacks found in emigration, particularly those living in the USA, with requests for donations.

Soon, close to $8000 was collected, which was enough to proceed with erecting a monument according to the design of the artist, Lieutenant Polovinkin.

The Committee on the Erection of the Monument was headed by Colonel Rogozhin, while direct oversight of the work was given to the secretary of the committee, Major Vertopov.

The work was completed over the course of two months. A large obelisk-type monument, having a height of 5.5 m, was erected. It had a gold-gilded cross and a marble plaque on which was inscribed in both Russian and German: "Cossack Victims I. VI, 1945."

The monument was blessed on August 15, 1951. Archbishop Stefan officiated over its consecration at the head of an assembly of clergy. A Russian choir from the DP camp in Klagenfut sang. Wreaths were laid. About 200 people were present at the blessing of the monument. The locals were Cossacks mostly, as were those who came from Salzburg.

4 — The Fence Around the Cemetery.

The group cemetery in Peggetz grew from several group graves, some of them for residents of the camp who died before the tragedy of June 1, 1945.

The English returned on the night after the tragedy to bury the victims of their atrocities in a hole that they dug.

Around the time of the placement of the first monument in the fall of 1945, there was not any kind of fence around the cemetery. Later, barbed wire was stretched around it on wooden stakes, and, still later, the stakes were replaced with concrete posts.

After this, when in 1951, the obelisk monument was erected, the simple fencing was seen as an eyesore by everyone, and the idea of replacing it with something more solid arose.

A call went out to collect money for it, and in a short period, a sum was gathered that was more the estimate for the cost of putting in a fence. Even the "Austrian Black Cross" helped.

A solid metal fence was put in under the auspices of the Standing Committee for the Welfare of the Cemetery, which was also charged with the responsibility of decorating and maintaining the cemetery in the future.

Soon after, a metal arch was put up at its entrance, the small tablets on the crosses were replaced, and other small tasks kept being seen to.

A substantial number of shillings remained. They were used from that time forward for general maintenance expenses.

Along the fence, inside it, was planted a row of arborvitae.

V. Naumenko

The Painting, "Lienz Massacre, June 1, 1945"

In 1957, through the initiative of the All-Cossack Stanitsas in New York, the talented painter-sculptor Sergey Grigoryevich Korolkoff, a Don Cossack of the Konstantinovsky Stanitsa, painted a picture depicting the beating by British soldiers of Cossack men, women, and children on June 1, 1945, on the square of Camp Peggets, near the city of Lienz in southern Austria.

The painting measures 6×12 feet.

The impetus to create this painting arose in 1955 when, in one of its meetings, one of its members, the Don Cossack, V. I. Babustov, presented a written proposal for the aforementioned painting and supported it with a contribution of $25, which served to start a fund toward the goal.

The Stanitsas' Board of Directors had a lively response to this proposal and requested the artist, S. G. Korolkoff, to do the painting.

At that same meeting, a call was made for contributions, and the members of the Board of Directors themselves contributed $50 toward the goal. They also made an appeal at the same time for all who had any kind of materials related to the Lienz Tragedy to send them to help S. G. Korolkoff.

There was a broad response not only from Cossacks, but even some other individuals, and the necessary funds were raised.

The artist completed the work by the spring.

One thousand three hundred dollars were spent on the production of the picture, plus $140 for its frame.

The blessing and "opening" of the painting was held on the day of the 12th anniversary of the Cossack tragedy at Lienz, the 1st of June, in the Russian Club at the Shrine of Christ the Savior in New York in the presence of the Board of Directors and the Cossacks of the All-Cossack Stanitsas of New York. Representatives of other Cossack organizations and guests gathered in great numbers for this solemn occasion.

Currently, this painting is kept at the Cossack Home in the State of New Jersey and is available for viewing to all who may wish to see it.

V. Naumenko

Memorial

Victims of the Cossack Tragedy in Lienz in 1945

In southern California, not far from the city of Los Angeles, there is a small city up against the hills called Glendora. It once was drowning in orange groves and lemon trees.

There, with the help and support of American friends, a Cossack hamlet was gradually built up on two streets: Vladmir and Cossack. Included in it are the Church of the Apostle Andrew and a Community House.

Memorial services for the victims of the turnover of Cossacks at Lienz began to be conducted almost immediately on their arrival in the USA, starting in 1950.

That all of America says prayers on May 30 for its veterans who gave their lives to free other nations—Memorial Day—only made our own memorial more solemn.

In 1954, on the initiative of Don Cossack, V. G. Ulitin, a group of American students built a commemorative cross.

When a substantial church monument was built in the hamlet, the cross was moved to the site of the church and is now found at its entrance.

Every year, on the Sunday closest to the day of betrayal, memorial services are conducted in front of a large group of people by the Bishop himself.

The inscription on the monument is in both English and Russian.

Not only Russians visit it, but also Americans.

Old Cossack, **Gr. A. Ulitin**

Victims of the Cossack Tragedy in Lienz in 1945

(A Cossack creative work from recent years.)

Where the cold Drau rages
From the snow melting above,
Every stone will remember
The bloody sacrifices forever.

    Where shaggy mountains rise,
    Grazing the smooth sky above,
    The wind tells of the sin and disgrace
    That will not stop, circles, and repeats.

But there is a heart—colder than snow
And the unfeeling, gloomy cliffs;
How many dark, natural villains
The devil found in his servants!

> What can these weak lines tell of it?
> Mouths fall silent, not breathing …
> Before the horror of a new Golgotha
> To this time my souls stiffens.

They fooled laws and defenders
And entreaties could not move them …
People's blood, of unseen dead,
Scream, scream, from the ground!

> The Drau fights back unstoppable tears
> Around its tortuous banks:
> How many Cossack lives were here
> Vilely betrayed into the hands of the foe!

Struggling unarmed, exhausted,
Taken off to a savage death,
Senseless cries and groans
Shook the azure expanse …

> But with chains the monster tanks
> Dragged and tore flesh …
> Who, with what words can describe
> The triumph of broken faith and evil?

Cossack men, women, and children—
The flowering of the last Cossack land—
In the most frightful and violent century
Fell forever in the west …

Cossachi Stan

Where the Drau cascades from the mountains,
With its own unquenchable song
Of the the sacrifices of the Cossacks
Every stone will remember and feel shame.

15th Cossack Cavalry Corps

On the 15th Cossack Cavalry Corps and Its Commander, General von Pannwitz

In 1952, a book written in German, *Wen Sie Verderben Wollen* [*Whom the Gods Wish to Destroy*] by Jürgen Thorwald came to light.

In it, much attention is given to General von Pannwitz and the 15th Cossack Cavalry Corps, which he commanded.

Several details about them from that book are given below.

[Here I would be translating into English a Russian translation of a German document. Although the original book is not available to me in English, the passages below have been reprinted in Thorwald's, *The Illusion*, pp. 306-10. For ease of translation, I have followed this English language version, which is one language closer to the original, while making changes necessary to make it consistent with Naumenko's version, which, after all, was based on an earlier version of Thorwald's text and may include material that was deleted from the later version (which itself holds material that may have been added.) The reader might find it interesting to compare Thorwald's text with my translation of Naumenko's version.]

While Vlasov was meeting his inescapable fate, Pannwitz with his Cossack Corps was embroiled in the chaos of the German retreat from Yugoslavia. Pressed by the superiority of the Soviet forces, by Bulgarians, and by Tito's partisans, the remnants of the German Southeast Army fought to keep the road northward open for troops that were coming from Greece, and at the same time to retreat into Austria themselves.

Behind their front and among their columns rolled the dreary lines of the refugee *Volkesdeutsche* (Germans of foreign citizenship) who were fleeing their homes and heading north and northwest. There were ambushes on every mountain road. Nobody knew who was a friend and who a foe.

In the midst of this retreat, with the soldiers inadequately supplied and almost without ammunition, the Cossacks also moved north and northwest, fighting off attacks here and there. Near Varazdin at the end of February, they succeeded at another exploit: they won a river crossing from Soviet units and Bulgarian troops and had mounted a cavalry attack in the old style that overran the enemy. Completing that task, they continued to provide cover for retreating German units. At the beginning of May, they secured the area north of Celje along the Drau River. Pannwitz no longer had any illusions about the immanence of the end. He had cherished hopes for a long time and a belief in new weapons. Still, in the end, as the March days had the front falling apart even more, he recognized the whole bitterness of inevitable doom. Early in April, in the midst of battles on various fronts, he held a general Cossack Congress in Virovitica. There, he once more felt himself to be the true Cossack leader, their general, who they trusted and believed and held more hope for than many of their actual leaders. Neither Pannwitz nor any of the other Cossacks knew anything about the "southeastern plan" that Meandrov was advocating at this same time. The Cossacks were more familiar with the turmoil in the Yugoslav region and therefore were trying to reach Austria or Czechoslovakia more quickly.

After the election of General von Pannwitz as the Cossack Field Ataman in Virovitica, Brigade Commander Kononov was sent to see Vlasov with an ulterior motive. His boundless ambition in the course of the last months grew ever larger and it seemed that he no longer recognized any borders. He undermined himself in the rear and in this way threatened the goal of unification.

At the end of April, Kononov was with Vlasov on the outskirts of Prague ...

He used the chance of the meeting above all to influence Vlasov to name him as the commander of the 15th Cossack Cavalry Corps and by this to become the Field Ataman of all Cossacks, which is what happened on May 5th after many professions of loyalty.*

At that time, Pannwitz was fighting for the future of the corps. During April, he sent four officers, including Prince Schwarzenberg, with orders to get in touch with the British. The instructions he gave them were short and simple: "The struggle against Bolshevism is not yet over. The Cossack Corps must be preserved as it exists. Even if it is to take refuge in Africa or Australia or some such place." But he waited in vain for news of results. Nonetheless, he did not altogether abandon hope.

On the evening of May 8, the corps, still fighting delaying actions, reached the areas around Gradac in Slovenia and Western Varazdin. There the operations officer of the First Cossack Division received a telephone call—the lines were still intact—from a colonel in Tito's Eighth Partisan Army. Such telephone communications were nothing unusual in the partisan fighting. What was unusual was that the officer informed the Germans that Germany had capitulated and that from eleven o'clock on no marching movements were permitted on the German side. Half an hour later confirmation came from the German side.

---

* Corps Commander General von Pannwitz was chosen as Field Ataman by the Cossacks at a congress on March 29, 1945 in Virovitica and, as such, in the most difficult of times, brought the Cossack Corps out of the chaos in Yugoslavia into Austrian territory, remaining as their leader to the end.

At that time, Kononov, having left the corps ranks immediately after the congress in Virovitica, remained behind in the rear over the course of almost two months, regardless of having full capability of returning to the corps. But he chose to the end to remain deep in the rear, having no interest at all in the fate of the Cossacks and by this never served a single day as Field Ataman. **V. Naumenko.**

Pannwitz's small, stocky figure shook with agitation. If he obeyed the conditions on marching, it meant that he would have to unconditionally surrender his entire corps to the partisans and the nearby Soviet tank troops.

HOWEVER, AT ELEVEN O'CLOCK THAT NIGHT HE HAD ALL HIS COSSACK TROOPS DRAWN UP IN MARCHING ORDER. HIS ORDERS WERE CLEAR AND SIMPLE: MAKE YOUR WAY THROUGH TO THE AUSTRAIN BORDER AND TO FIELD MARSHALL ALEXANDER'S ENGLISH ARMY.

WHAT AWAITED HIM AND HIS MEN THERE, HE DID NOT KNOW YET. HE KNEW ONLY ONE THING: AT NO PRICE TO SURRENDER VOLUNTARITY. (Emphasis is ours **V. N.**)

All night long, the Cossacks marched, passing German, Croat, and Hungarian troops, supply trains, and refugees. The partisans who tried to block the highway were driven off. The Second Cossack Division fought its way laboriously northwest from the vicinity of Varazdin. It suffered great losses. Many times the disposition by Titoist partisans of those surrendered could be heard from the hills. Those Cossacks who lost touch with the main highway were cut down by partisans.

Early in the morning of May 9 the worst was overcome. Toward ten o'clock in the morning, two Cossacks officers made contact with advanced units of the Eleventh British Armored Division.

Pannwitz headed forward—to the English.

While the Second Cossack Division was partly broken up in severe battle, so that its regiments had to fight their way through the mountains north of the main line of retreat, the First Division closed ranks around the area of Griffen. It took a brief rest. Then the regiments rode on, past more scenes of flight and general dissolution.

On the morning of May 10, the First Cossack Division was marching along the road from Lavamund to Volkermarkt when it suddenly came upon a column of cars approaching from the opposite direction beyond the crowds of retreating refugees. In the front car stood Pannwitz. Behind him rode several English officers. The

Cossacks believed that this was their salvation.

Sharp commands suddenly rang out. It was as if all the terrible marches of the past few days and nights, and all the fighting of the past week, had never been. The regiments turned from the highway, formed in lines, and dismounted. Convoys arrived.

The English officers approached. Suddenly, from regiment to regiment Pannwitz's command was passed on: "First Cavalry Diivision. Form up by regiments. March past in line."

It was a fantastic scene: amid a terrible collapse, amid misfortune, amid escape, amid a hundred thousand people in fear of their lives …

The bugle corps wheeled opposite Pannwitz and the British officers. Then the first squadron came riding up: regimental commander and squadron chiefs in the van, the cavalry of the First Don Cossack Regiment, the Second Siberian Cossack Regiment, the Fourth Kuban Cossack Regiment, and the Mounted Military Battery. There was no trace of unreliability, no sign of a beaten army. At the end of the march, the regiments reformed into columns and continued along the road to Griffen-Volkermarkt.

Pannwitz's broad face twitched.

There, alongside the road lay the weapons that German units had thrown away, and his Cossacks, who had become the mission and meaning of his life, had marched past him not in that frivolous horde they were usually seen in, but in proud and orderly ranks.

He looked silently at the English. Did they now understand what he had told them? Did they understand that these Cossacks need not perish nor be turned into the hands of their mortal enemy?

That afternoon, east of Volkermarkt, the division laid down its arms. Then the First Division marched into the Klagenfurt-St. Veit area. The remnants of the Second Division followed two days later. They had seen dozens of slain comrades caught in the weirs of the Drau. For them there was no doubt about the fate that awaited them in the east. Their lives were now in the hands of the British, who on the afternoon of May 12 assigned them camping grounds in one of the valleys further to the west.

The commander of the Eleventh British Army Division and his men were distant but courteous. They showed almost comradely feelings. They left the leadership of the Cossack formations to Pannwitz and the division commanders, Colonels Wagner and von Schulz, and they spoke of "internment" rather than "imprisonment." All the Germans and Cossacks were allowed to travel within specified boundaries and do whatever they pleased. Colonel Hills, the commander of the British, displayed a generosity beneath which one could have sensed pity for men hopelessly lost.

Several weeks passed in almost total isolation. Hopes almost became realities.

When on May 26, Colonel Wagner went to Neumarkt to see Pannwitz, he did not anticipate that the shadow of a cruel death hung over Pannwitz. The Cossack general said nothing about the possibility of being handed over to the Russians. The fair treatment he and his men were getting from the British had given him a sense of security. He was almost certain that it arose as a consequence of his having sent emissaries to the English in April.

In fact, three days earlier in Vienna, a special agreement had been signed between representatives of Field Marshall Alexander and the Soviet High Command in the Balkans in which Alexander had undertaken to hand over all Cossacks to the Soviet detachments, beginning May 28. In the agreement, the Cossacks were defined as "special units of the German SS partisans" and "counterrevolutionary White gangs who were in the pay of the Germans." The belated naming of Pannwitz's corps as the 15th SS Cossack Cavalry Corps made it easier for the Soviet negotiators to win consent from the British. This argument was one of many.

In less than 24 hours, on May 27, Pannwitz was arrested and taken to Graz, where representatives of the Soviet Union were waiting for him. In Graz he found Generals Krasnov and Shkuro, the two old men who had been handed over the same day. Even by the terms of the Yalta Agreement, the extradition of these three would not have been required. At the same time, a British general came to the headquarters of the First Cossack Division in Sirnits. [For the second time here, as is true later in the text, this general is identified as "*Эйчер*," a name that does not appear in any recognizable form in the Thorwald book from which I am getting this text nor in any listing available to me of British generals.] He told Colonel Wagner little that would not lead to suspicion of his order: "Tomorrow you are to march all of your units to the camp at Weitensfeld, Germans separate from Cossacks. When can you fall in?"

His face returned to a mask. Wagner found it difficult to keep his composure. For a moment he thought of Pannwitz. This would be a mortal blow to him.

He gave the general the necessary information while his mind raced over what could be done to save the Cossacks. He felt this in the general's words. As soon as the British general had left, Wagner sent one of his officers to Weitensfeld to look over the terrain. The officer returned after a few hours with the report that high barbed-wire fences were being set up, also guard towers with searchlights.

Wagner did not put things off for long. Surreptitiously, he had the entire division informed that contrary to expectations the internment was about to be changed to imprisonment, and that this would probably be followed by the surrender of the men to the Soviet authorities. He left it to every individual to act as he saw fit. He hoped that he was understood by all. He told the seven officers of his staff that he would personally try to get them to Germany.

Two hours later, the British general returned. He looked hard at the scene of frantic activity, as though surprised that preparations for departure were actually going forward.

"Have you any questions?" he asked Wagner.

"With regard to the transfer of the First Cossack Division—no," Wagner answered. "Still, am I allowed to ask you several other questions?"

The general nodded his head. "Please."

"In this case," Wagner said, "the first step is prison camp, the second being handed over to the Soviet Union, the third the long ride to the Siberian mines. That's it, isn't it?"

The general bowed his head. "We're both soldiers."

"Exactly," Wagner answered.

"You must understand," the general said, "there are ... political considerations."

He abruptly turned on his heel and headed for his car.

That evening, British cordons were formed around the camp, evidently to prevent the Cossacks or the German cadres from fleeing into the mountains. Nevertheless, Wagner and sizable numbers of the Germans and Cossacks (division staff) managed to escape during that night. A British lieutenant helped them.

The majority, who could not make up their minds to undertake the flight through the Alps, were transported to Weitensfeld on May 28.

Jurgen Thorvald

Bezkaravayny's Memoir

Former officer in the Russian Corps, N. I. Bezkaravayny broke away from his own unit at the end of the war, and the surrender of the German Army left him in southern Austria, in the vicinity of Klagenfurt. There he found himself within the position of the 15th Cossack Cavalry Corps and was commandeered into the 4th Kuban Regiment, with which he was turned over by the English to the Bolsheviks.

He wound up in a concentration camp in Siberia, fled from it to the city of Baghdad in Mesopotamia.

Bezkaravayny's memoir is interesting on its own. Apparently a very observant man, over the background of all he had lived through, he lingers at several details, sometimes goes off on a tangent in his memories of the past, and prognosticates into the future.

His memoir, entitled, *Sufferings of Modern Martyrs*, was printed in New York in *Diocesan Statements* and the journal of the Russia Corps, *Our News* [respectively, *Страданья Современных Страстотерпцев*, *Епархиальных Ведомостях*, and *Наши Вести*].

Regrettably, he never submitted the ending to his memoir: he does not write how he escaped from the concentration camp and how he wound up in Baghdad.

At the beginning of his work, he records some rather interesting information about the Cossack Congress on May 24, 1945, in the town of Althofen, which took place with the permission and maybe on the initiative of the English Command.

> At the Congress in which General Pannwitz was reelected the Field Ataman,* a representative of the English Command announced to the Cossacks that the British government decided to transfer the Cossacks to Australia or Canada.
>
> The Cossacks did not know that that evening, that is, May 23, representatives of the English and Soviet Commands signed the Vienna Agreement, by which the English were obligated to turn the Cossacks over to the Soviets.
>
> The Cossacks and General Pannwitz could not have known of this, but the representatives of the British Command knew that the fate of the Cossacks had been decided, and they lied with complete understanding that they were, which as we all learned later, was standard practice among English officers, but at that time no one knew, so Cossacks applauded the words of the English representative with a loud, "Hurrah!"
>
> On the evening of the same day, the corps's remaining three tanks were taken by the English.
>
> "We no longer need them. We are going to Canada!" is how the Cossacks reacted.
>
> On the next day, General von Pannwitz reviewed the corps's regiments in formation and conveyed to them the words of the British Command.
>
> But the next morning, the general was arrested by the English.

---

* It is difficult to decide why the English needed the election of General Pannwitz as Field Ataman, since he had already been elected to the post on March 29 by the Cossacks in Virovitica.

Cossacks were concerned on learning of this and demanded that the English reveal where he was.

Knowing that the Cossacks had been living in conditions of near starvation, the English answered that he was diverting 50 trucks full of provisions meant for the Cossacks to the SS partisans instead. This was an outright lie.

"Don't believe it!" Cossacks shouted. "Our general would never do that."

"If he doesn't do that, then he will return tomorrow," the Englishman answered.

The Cossacks dispersed in silence. They never saw their commander again.

N. Bezkaravayny

The Arrest by the English Command of the 15th Cossack Cavalry Corps's General Helmuth von Pannwitz, His Staff, and Cossacks Found with Them

General von Pannwitz, after the withdrawal from Croatia to southern Austria (Kärten), in the region occupied by the English, and still remaining the head of the corps, reviewed his units in formation, but on on May 24, with the blessings of the English Command, in the presence of their representative, was elected the Cossack Corps's Field Ataman. A day later, he was arrested by the English.

Approximately a week before his arrest, General Pannwitz, with his staff and the Cossacks found with them, moved from the settlement of Althofen to the small village of Mühlen, in which he and his staff settled into a school.

The corps commander's Cossack convoy and Command staff were housed in small, nearby villages: Hämmerle, Sank Veit, and Muhl[z]dorf [*Мюльудорф* did not match any likely village names in Austria, so that the "z" or "*у*" is in error].

In the summer of 1947, a Kuban officer was commandeered to go to the village of Mühlen on the task of finding out under what circumstances General von Pannwitz, his staff, and Cossacks found with them were arrested.

He questioned a number of residents who witnessed the proceedings and established the following:

— On May 26, around 9 or 10 o'clock in the morning, two light English vehicles and two trucks arrived at Mühlen.

In the first was an English colonel who walked into the building and stayed for about an hour.

At that time, a tankette came and the loading of officers and Cossacks into trucks began.

On coming out of the school, General von Pannwitz, his chief of staff, and the English colonel boarded one of the light vehicles. Staff officers were apparently placed in the second, while Cossacks went into the trucks.

As soon as loading was completed, all the light vehicles were surrounded by tankettes and motorcyclists armed with automatic weapons. The small column went in the direction of Neumarkt, then farther on to Unzmarkt, occupied by Soviet troops, and from there to Judenburg.

More details could not be obtained from the residents, since two years had already passed and many details were forgotten, not to mention that the Austrians were not eager to remember that time. They said that the "picture was frightening."

V. Naumenko

On the fate of Lieutenant-General von Pannwitz

The commander of the 15th Cossack Cavalry Corps, Lieutenant-General von Pannwitz, was arrested by the English on May 26, 1945, in the small Austrian village of Mühlen, in which he had been with his staff.

Apparently, on that same day, he was turned over by the English to the Bolsheviks in the city of Judenburg. It is now known that on May 29, the English also handed over two thousand officers, led by General P. N. Krasnov. The officers of the Cossack Corps and their commander, General von Pannwitz, were already there.

On the next day, May 30, von Pannwitz, along with General P. N. Krasnov and several other officers of the Cossack Central Administration [historians have this obscure Berlin organization variously named using the words general, office and directorate in addition, although usually without any translation of "*войск*," as Naumenko (who was one of its members) has done—or with any kind of standard capitalization] and the Cossachi Stan, were taken to Graz, and, on the next day, to Baden, near Vienna.

From Baden, General Krasnov and all Cossack generals and officers present with him were sent to Moscow on the 3rd or 4th of June.

From unverified evidence that we have, he again appeared in the hands of the English. It must be assumed that this occurred because he had been taken prisoner on territory occupied by the English and was a prisoner of war of the English army.

It is known that he was questioned in Trieste and other places; that he was questioned by investigators on matters having to do with war crimes by a major of the forces [*войск*] of the MVD, Serov-Serin-Meshcheryakov (being one and the same person). At one time, he was even questioned by a Yugoslavian (Titoist) investigator.

It is also known that from June 5 to 8 he was, as were several corps staff officers, questioned by investigators of the Commission on War Crimes at the Headquarters of the British Zone of Occupation. From June 8 to 9 he spent the night in Steyr, in the quarters of the CIC in the area ["*CIC*," which, given that there is no "I" in the Russian alphabet, leaves a mild doubt that the initials are for the Counter Intelligence Corps of the US Army], while on June 10 a group of English officers and soldiers was brought by car to Enns in the company of American officers. At its station, he was put on a train which was taking Cossacks and German soldiers who had been found at the moment that the truce was signed in territory of Soviet occupation and who were for that reason moved west into the

American Zone of Occupation in the area of Innsbruch-Salzburg by order of Field Marshall Schörner and Colonel General Rendulic.

On the basis of the terms of the truce, all those Germans and Cossacks were given over to the Bolsheviks, including Field Marshall Schörner and Colonel General Rendulic.

Furthermore, we point out the article published in Linz in the Austrian Newspaper *Weekly Echo* [*Вохен Ехо*], on August 9, 1953.

The article is entitled:

VOLUNTEERED IN ORDER NOT TO LEAVE HIS SOLDIERS TO CERTAIN DEATH.

As a preface to the article, a special box contained the following:

"Death of a German General. In order not to be a traitor to himself, Helmuth von Pannwitz in 1945 voluntarily accepted a sacrificial trip to Moscow. He could have stayed in the West. No one forced him into taking this step. Nonetheless, he set out to share the fate of his Cossack Corps. We announce here, based on the account of a survivor of that tragic episode days after surrender, when thousands of Cossacks who fought on the side of the Germans were turned over to the Soviets. We want only to remember the general who in the midst of death, panic, and general demoralization showed an example of human greatness."

The article continues. We reproduce only these excerpts from it:

> It was the 10th of June, 1945. At about 9 o'clock, a train made up of approximately 30 freight cars enclosed in barbed wire arrived at the Enns station. It was met on both sides of the railroad tracks by a hundred Soviet NKVD soldiers with machine guns at the ready. This cordon had as its goal the prevention of attempts at escape by the two thousand one hundred Cossacks who two weeks before had been given over to the Soviets.
>
> Within the NKVD cordon on the platform, encircled by several English and Soviet officers, stood the commander of the Cossack Corps that fought to the end of

the war on the German side, Lieutenant-General Helmuth von Pannwitz, a 47-year-old officer who wore, besides a German uniform, the fur papakha of a Kuban Cossack.

Fixing his gaze on the barbed-wire-enclosed freight cars which had come to a halt in front of him with a screech, General von Pannwitz could see through the windows of the freight car to the pale faces of Cossacks who had been in his corps.

There were exactly 2146 of them. After momentarily being shocked by their surprise, they suddenly shouted the news:

"Father [Батько] Pannwitz is standing there at the station!" But after spontaneous, stormy jubilation, a bitter silence fell over them.

Those Cossacks who took such delight in seeing Pannwitz had the thought immediately flash through them that the German general, knowing full well what awaited him with the Soviets, had decided to share the fate of the Cossacks being turned over to the Soviets, who knew full well that what awaited them there was a miserable death or lifelong compulsory labor.

The quiet in the Enns station, broken only by commands and the scrape of steel, lasted no longer than a minute before a Cossack song suddenly arose from one of the freight cars—it was a song about General von Pannwitz.

The singing drowned out the threatening commands voiced by a Soviet officer over the station's loudspeaker.

Pannwitz had tears in his eyes. He raised an arm in a call for prudence.

Pannwitz had been separated from the Cossacks after his arrest by the English on May 26, 1945.

After the passage of two days, the British commandant informed him what had happened to them. He was astonished. He aged several years.

When he inquired whether there was a possibility that he, too, could be given over to the Soviets, they answered that he, Pannwitz, was fortunate that, as a German officer, he did not come under the agreement on hand overs. As it was, he could take off his Cossack uniform and remain a British prisoner of war.

But Pannwitz said curtly:

"No!"

He wished that he too could be handed over. Then he explained:

"I shared the good times with the Cossacks. Now I want to share the bad with them. I locked my friendship to them for life or death. Maybe I can make their terrible plight easier for them by taking part of the guilt ascribed to them upon myself."

This is what happened. On June 10, 1945, as we have said above, Pannwitz stepped onto the transport train leaving for the USSR. In that car, in which he set off on his own journey to death, he met once more with those he had been with during the war …

… The final information: on that train in which von Pannwitz undertook his journey from the Enns station to death, he vanished in the same way as his Cossack Corps.

Survivors speak of him even today, of how in the face of death, he showed the kind of nobility that is rarely seen today …

V. Naumenko

A German with a Russian Heart

Fond Memories of General Helmuth von Pannwitz

Helmuth von Pannwitz considered it his great fortune and honor to have the right to command the Cossack Corps in the Balkans in the days when all of our fates—and his—had already been decided at the Yalta Conference. By then, there was already no hope, or, to put it less harshly, hopes for the victory of sanity over a mad conqueror evaporated when hope and belief for a victory by the white idea over a red nightmare vanished. That was when General von Pannwitz was with us, was one of us. He loved and valued every person, Cossack, and fighter, gave an oath, stayed true to it and did not leave, refusing his right as a German to abandon his post and his people. He chose to instead protect, if not freedom, then, in any case, life.

He preferred to keep the honor of a soldier and his own name bright in the memory of all those who lived through the catastrophe of being handed over in Austria in 1945, all those who fought against Communism under his command, all those even that he may have only met just once.

A. Delianich
(Excerpts from the article in the journal,
Russian Life, No. 342, August, 1956)

The Last Days of the 15th Cossack Cavalry Corps

1 — First Cossack Division

… The Easter holidays (May 1) found us in a group in a Croatian settlement. A dinner for the officer staff arranged by our division leader, Colonel Wagner, despite an abundance of wine, could not enliven those awaiting a fatal predetermined decision.

A general funereal depression hung over Colonel Wagner's reading of the reports by German operatives that announced Admiral Dönitz's acceptance of the duties of Supreme Commander in the wake of the Fuhrer's recent suicide and that an order had been given by Dönitz to cease military action against the Allies and turn all forces against the world's common foe—totalitarian Communism.

This announcement raised our mood somewhat. We held hope —in truth, very weakly—that joining forces with the Germans and Allies would allow us to knock over the monstrous Bolshevik regime. However, harsh reality did not let us realize our hopes, for the Allies did not cease war on the Germans, but the opposite, dealing crushing blows to the German Army, which had directed all of its strength against the Soviet Army. Because of this, from the second day of Easter, our units began rapid retreats under cover provided by the fairly well battered regiments of the 1st Don and 2nd Siberian Divisions.

The wide and spacious highway soon filled up with several rows of carts and trucks. The congestion in one place brought entire columns unexpectedly to a halt.

The announcement of surrender had created a great panic. Everything got mixed up.

Of some sort of discipline, there is nothing to tell. All ambitions and hopes were on the fastest way to break out of the sphere of Soviet influence so that weapons could be surrendered to the English.

Bottlenecks became more severe. We traveled day and night, almost without sleep or food. In the end, the fatal border was escaped. Passing through Slovenia and descending into Austrian territory, those in retreat surged through any road in which bottlenecks had been permanently eliminated. It became possible to organize rest days.

Day and night, without interruption, we heard the chatter of machine guns and rifles shooting reserve ammunition, no longer needed and now slowing retreat. Constantly, generally at night, there were aimless rocket signals. In some places grenade explosions and the deafening sound of antitank weapons being fired were heard. Personal belongings we either destroyed or left along the sides of roads to be quickly carried off by local residents. Germans set fire to the most beautiful light autos and convoy vehicles. Here and there lay perfectly adequate weapons, sometimes whole, often disabled. New military radios were thrown away in great numbers. Quartermaster's supplies and stores of new uniforms and government blankets and such were abandoned.

Around the bags of canned goods, biscuits, tobacco, and cigarettes lying by the roadside, there were soldiers and local residents, including women and children, going over the piles in search of provisions.

In the end, we got to Austrian territory. There took place the first meeting with the English Military Command, who told us to quickly disarm.

Several days later, we received an order from General von Pannwitz about our surrender terms. The general briefly informed us of the progress of his negotiations with the English on the words of the surrender, announcing to us that he was taking whatever measures he could to change the English intent to turn the corps over to the Soviets. The order was given in extremely vague, nonspecific terms and did not give any hope for a successful outcome to the negotiations.

All this reinforced the depressing mood we already had even without it, which had not left us for even a minute since we heard the reports of the decision by the Germans to give themselves up to the mercy of the victorious Allies. Vague forebodings pressed at our chests. Soldiers were dejected. Happy Cossacks songs were no longer sung. Every doomed one of us tried to sleep more to get away from ourselves, from our grim thoughts.

On one of our rest days, not far from the city of Feldkirchen, the English ordered that Cossacks be separated from Germans. The division leader, Colonel Wagner, was left in his post. As the senior officer in terms of service, I was named to the post of head of division staff.

Even without considering my having been charged with control over the proper distribution of property to us and the Germans, I was driven by our situation as prisoners of war to almost indifference to the bickering involved with it, figuring that these arguments were all worthless pettiness.

It is with some interest, though, to note that the English, in order to properly orient themselves in an unfamiliar place—or due to some other reason—gave their own staff several offices, in which only imprisoned German officers could work. These offices took up two front (from the entrance) rooms and kept strict control over visitors to bar elements unwanted by the English.

The division was quickly reorganized under the direction of the English: the entire thing was divided into 5 blocks, of which former staff were attributed to the 4th block, with me designated as the Chief of Staff for the 5 blocks and Quartermaster Telyakov, the leader of the blocks.

Further developments first showed benevolence toward us by the English. Then, on another day of division reorganization, an order came from the head of the 34th English Division on the return of pistols to the officer staff and 10 percent of Cossack rifles. A day later—May 24—on the initiative of the English and in the presence of one of the prominent officers of the 34th Division—a colonel—an election took place for the Field Ataman of the Cossack Hosts. Only one candidate was nominated at this congress of delegates, General von Pannwitz, who, even though of German origin, was loved by the Cossacks for his bravery, fairness, and good relations with them.

The passage of these events not only foreshadowed the tragic unfolding that followed several days later, but it also did the opposite. It infused us with a strong belief that the Allies would decide to fight together with the Cossacks to once and forever end the totalitarian regime in Russia.

On May 25th, all heads of blocks were ordered by the English Military Command to prepare a list of the names of officers and rank and file within twenty-four hours.

This requirement made my mood drop precipitately.

I intuitively felt the approach of something terrible, inevitable.

Officers and Cossacks asked me why I was in such a mood, but I could not explain it to myself.

The division was located in the mountains in almost unpopulated places. It required making do on my own abilities and skill.

Having kept with me the unit's tent cloths gave me the means to construct collective coverings from rain and wind. Not having beds, or even mats, we cut boughs and made floor mats that served at night as improvised beds.

May nights in Austria, especially in the mountains, were so cold that many Cossacks, having no blankets, shivering and cold, spent their nights sleeplessly and caught up on sleep in the daytime.

Horses grazed attentively on the areas of heavy growth of moist, green grass on the hillsides, turning them into bare, black desert, lacking even a single trace of growth, in the course of two or three days.

We were grateful for anything that came our way. Mostly it was the meager ration that the English provided. The chief attendant turned out to be an officer of the propaganda office, Major Bogush. He had a truck with which he continually rode around getting produce from storehouses and giving it out to an agreed-upon number of people, being particular to supply every authorized unit.

Time trickled by under heavy, agonizing idleness.

We were not able to embrace all the inexplicable beauty and charm of that mountainous, wooded part of Austria that was so admired by rich tourists. We looked at it indifferently due to the uncertainties of our situation.

Disturbing thoughts about the falsity of our situation crept stubbornly into our heads, since as nationless prisoners of war, the normal principles of international law cannot apply, especially to legal protection as agreed upon in the Hague Convention of the International Red Cross.

We were terrified by the thought that we might possibly be turned over to the Soviets. Their lasting and friendly ties with the Western Allies, in the absence of any relevant political and military information, seemed to us unshakable and for this reason fraught with fully unwanted consequences.

May 27, at 11 o'clock in the morning, our block received written orders from the English Command, given to us by Colonel Wagner, to descend from the hills to the highway at 8 o'clock the next morning, that is, May 28, where the English would direct us to our stay in a special camp for prisoners of war.

The order brought feelings of depression on us all. Officers and Cossacks were very well aware of what awaited them in connection with this order.

Quartermaster Telyakov and I quickly went to Wagner's staff office, which was about 3 kilometers away, to try to get more complete information. Arriving there, we found Cossacks from Colonel Wagner's personal guard wandering the streets. They told us that he had called them to him that morning and told them the following:

"My friends! The way the situation is unfolding, I must leave here without wasting a second. You are completely free and can leave while there is still time."

Following this, they gave the colonel a loaded pack horse.

Giving his farewells to his guard and the Germans close to him, the Colonel went off to hide in a nearby forest. Following his example, the other Germans went off in various directions.

Even though we never did get complete information, nevertheless the decision by the English to transfer us to a prisoner-of-war camp did not call forth thoughts of preparing ourselves for any intolerable events.

Gloomy and depressed, we returned to where we were bivouacked. What could we say to the Cossacks patiently waiting for us?

Bringing all the blocks out into formation, I briefly described a picture for them of our visit to Wagner's staff and, without hiding any of its dangers, put forth to the Cossacks that, with the coming of darkness, they should go into the hills to find safety. To those who would remain, I pleaded that they try to preserve full order and tranquility, maintain their self-control, and prepare themselves thoroughly for a loss of personal freedom.

Suffering greatly from what was happening, I lay down to sleep while the sun was still high overhead. Heavy feelings pressed my chest. Turning from side to side, I could not fall asleep for a long time.

Three staff officers arrived at 8 o'clock in the evening. They gave us their decision to head for the woods that night to escape from being locked up in a prisoner-of-war camp. They asked me to go with them.

Thanking them for their concern, I categorically refused to flee, for I considered that I could not allow myself to leave to the mercy of fate the Cossacks who trusted me.

On the morning of May 28, at 6 o'clock, checking on the cash situation of the staff and the military composition assigned to it, I convinced myself with some bitterness that not one Cossack had fled. All were there to a man, on their way to meet an inexorable fate. There were also three officers left and who came to me.

Bringing my detachment to order, I gave the command to descend the hill onto the asphalt highway.

There, the picture that presented itself was one of meticulous preparation for battle with well-armed enemy forces.

Stretched along the length of the highway for several kilometers, one up against another, stood brand-new English tanks, menacingly bristling with cannon barrels. Their cannons were directed straight at us unarmed Cossacks. It is hard to convey the feeling of despondency and bitterness that this precaution for battle had on us.

With the tanks as escorts, we went slowly on the last trip of our lives, half-way to terrible, doom-harboring, suffering, and uncertainty. We did not travel for long, since Camp Veitensfeld, to which we were assigned, was only some 8 kilometers away.

On nearing the camp, we were met by a lean, taller-than-average-height, English major of the Kings Guard. He quickly separated officers from Cossacks, first allowing them the right to keep their orderlies with them. My orderly, a Cossack of the Novoshcherbinovskoy Stanitsa, Karo Nebovsya, paying no attention to my arguments, for a long time refused to be separated from me. It was only after I categorically forbade him from staying with me that we kissed each other on the cheeks in farewell and, with tears in his eyes, he left with the other Cossacks.

I was the first to enter the camp, in preparation to which I was subjected to a humiliating search and the theft of my "Omega" wristwatch, flashlight, and razor.

Camp Weitensfeld presented itself as a rather small square of land fenced in by several rows of barbed wire. On its right side was a hilly brook, bordered by a small pine forest. The other three sides were edged by fields. With the exception of one incomplete barrack, several tall double tents served as our living quarters in the camp. The camp was guarded by a squad of up to 10 English soldiers armed with automatic weapons. Machine gun stations encircled the camp, with 9-10 machine guns aimed at it.

I settled into the first tent I came to. Following me, one after another, were the staff officers, doctors, the division priest, Father A., and several sisters of mercy. Then came the officers of the division's regiments. By evening, the camp consisted of 190 men in number.

We had a meeting of the staff in the tent of the commander of the 1st Don Regiment, Major Ostrovsky, coming to a unanimous conclusion on the inevitability of being given over to the Soviets, since having the English taking such extraordinary precautions against us unarmed people did not bode well for their intentions with us.

In full accord with this, we were given a memorandum in the name of the British Command. Putting aside the essence of our White idea of fighting Communism, which started back in 1917, and having no antagonistic feelings toward the Western Allies, we asked only not to be given over to our accursed enemy—Communism. In case such a handover had already been decided upon, we demanded that we be executed by the English.

By the way, it turned out that I was not the only one robbed. So were all the other officers. The main objects of the offense appeared to be wristwatches.

Upon hearing this grievance, the major immediately directed himself to the quick return of everything that was stolen. After half an hour, a sergeant brought in a carton with a jumble of every possible manner of time piece in it. All who had had watches taken from them took immediately to searching for them, but they quickly recoiled with disenchantment: all the watches turned out to be worthless junk. Where they could have found such a pile of broken watches, it is hard to guess.

The camp became so highly well lit by the strong beams of searchlights that as soon as it became dark, staying outside became positively unbearable—their bright, unbearable light totally blinded us. Everyone went into their tents, where the light did not reach.

Having somehow settled ourselves down on bare ground, none of us could fall asleep for a long time, and only at dawn could we lose ourselves in some anxious sleep.

At 6 o'clock in the morning, we were awakened by an English sergeant who, threatening us with a weighty cudgel he held in his hands, suggested we quickly get up and prepare to leave.

To our question, "Where?" the sergeant answered, "I don't know!"

We then asked the sergeant to let the major know that, until they let us know where we are going, we were not moving from our place.

After some time, the major came to tell us that he did not know any more than did the sergeant and urged us over our protests to follow the order quickly.

We fell into bickering: neither side wanted to give an inch. Finally, the major left, ostensibly to find out about it from the division staff.

On returning, he told us that it had been decided to deport us, that is, send us to the Soviet Union.

You had to see what kind of storm this announcement evoked in us.

Noise, shouts, exclamations of protests: "We are not going. Better shoot us." We did not allow the major to speak. Desperate from having failed to bring us to order, the major left and came back with an English general who must have been the Chief of Staff of the 34th Rifle Division. The general's assurances and reasons met with the same attitude as those of the major. Neither assurances nor threats of being shot as mutineers had any effect on us whatever. All 190 men were unanimous in their preference for death over being sent to Stalin's dungeons. The general then tried to make us believe that it was known to him that the Soviet government had decided on a broad amnesty for all their political opponents—nationals from the Soviet Union. Since most of our group had earlier been Soviet citizens and knew Communist promises very well from their own bitter experience, the general's assurances did not hit their mark, They seemed simply ridiculous.

In the end, the general decided to resort to psychological-scare techniques. In the middle of debate on the humanism of Soviet power, he abruptly changed themes and loudly commanded: "Those who wish to face a swift execution, stand over on the left side. The rest of you, on the right."

Confusion ensued. The division's priest was caused to go to the right. Following him, after some cleaving, were 130 men. The rest of us stood on the left.

My close friend from way back on the Kolchak front, Major Bush, had been the best officer in the valiant Votkinskoy Division, at which he was commanded by General Molchanov, famous for his bravery. Under the influence of some sort of moral shock, Bush joined the 130. Then he quickly ran over to our group and hotly began to urge us to join the group that had decided to follow the general's request.

"Gentlemen!" Bush howled. "Let's go! Let's show the Bolsheviks that we Cossack officers do not fear death!"

In answer, angry shouts arose from our group: "There, there! …"

Meanwhile, red in the face from shame about my friend, I quickly turned my back to him without saying a word of rebuke, for, like us, they were also going to certain death.

After the 130 men said farewell to one another and came over to be blessed by our senior clergyman, Archpriest Father Fyodor Vlassenko (Don Cossack), they took seats in the trucks. We formed up in a single line after that and froze in expectation of being shot.

Father Fyodor offered the proposition that meeting death from a sitting position made it more likely to be hit than in a standing position.

A group of English riflemen arrived under the command of an officer. They formed up across from us. They went through almost the entire command ritual that is given for an execution. Automatic weapons were aimed at us. Another blink and goodbye to life!

The agony connected with the approach of a violent death was not new to me. Back in 1918, I had been taken out by the Cheka to be executed seven times. It would seem that you would fall into habituation to similar situations. In reality, that is far from the case. Each successive instance remains unique Each time, my entire life passed before my eyes in a flash. Each time the perception of an inner peace was lost, seeming mere phantasmagoria at the time, something contrived and unreal.

I glanced momentarily over our row of suicides. All of the doomed, without exception, held themselves stiffly. Brows were furrowed, faces pale, but cold and determined. Major Ostrovsky stood with an arm around his orderly. A contemptuous smile wandered over his face. Father Goergii Trunov, a priest and former officer, stood leaning against his 17-year-old daughter, Zhenya, who did not want—as did the other sisters of mercy—to accept the English general's offer of a transfer to another camp to serve under the Red Cross. The other sisters of mercy, mother and daughter Rayutsky [*Реуцкие*], agreed to the general's offer on the advice of Major Ostrovsky, so that they would be able to tell the others about the Cossacks' last minutes.

None of us gave much thought to the approach of our ends. Suddenly, though, a messenger comes running, head down, from the English staff to the place of our execution, and gives something to the officer in charge of the execution ceremony. The officer withdraws his platoon [*взвод*]. A sigh of relief comes from us. But our joy was only momentary. A flamethrower rolls up and stands across from us at about 20 paces. We were completely dumbfounded. The first river of fire flew over our heads and landed not far from us, scorching the grass and trees on the spot. An awful sight! ... First Lieutenant Popov, an emigrant from Zagreb, fell to the ground with an inhuman scream in a fit of momentary insanity. He was quickly taken away. After firing three more times in the same way as the first, the Englishmen left.

A minute later, the general appeared once more to say, "I changed my mind about executing you. I've given an order to have you tied up as soon as possible and to be sent in that bound condition to the Soviet Union."

It was as if we were struck by lightning. By being prepared for death at the hands of the English, we had demonstrated that, for us, being sent to the USSR was a fate worse than death.

The general had barely had time to tell us of his new decision before a group of soldiers with clubs appeared in order to encircle us and take us by force. At the same time, three trucks loaded with rope, leather straps, and electrical wires drove up.

Major Ostrovsky, enraged by the monstroucity planned us of force, stepped out of line and began to hurl selective Russian curse words at the general, up to the most obscene [*"мата"*], accusing the English of the sale of people, of destroying any belief in English politics, of the tradition of raking hot coals [*загребании жара*] with the hands of others, of holding commercial gains above the need for basic human morality, and so on.

A Croatian interpreter stood next to the general, translating word for word for him what Ostrovsky was saying.

The general's face took on red patches and foam appeared in the corners of his mouth.

"Shoot them!" he shouted in a rage.

Several hefty soldiers ran up to Ostrovsky, shoved him into a nearby car, and took him into the woods to carry out the order to shoot him.

Since further resistance seemed impossible or ineffective, I brought forth the following suggestion in search of an exit from the current situation:

"Gentlemen! As you can see, we lack the physical ability to interfere with the Englishmen carrying out their general's orders. Once we are tied up, we will no doubt, without any hope of being saved, fall into the hands of the NKVD. I suggest that we seat ourselves in the trucks without resisting but with the intention to try to escape along the road. Those who do not succeed can use potassium cyanide, which almost every one of us has."

There were no objections to my idea. We began to load without our things, leaving them behind in camp. All 60 of us fit into 8 trucks.

Vehicles with the 130 officers that were loaded earlier stood awaiting us. I was in the first truck with 8 other officers, directly behind the last truck of the first group.

Taking into account that the British felt compelled to take such precautionary measures for us 190 unarmed men made it seem as if the English considered us equal to a heavily armed regiment.

Still, our fallen spirits did not interfere with sharpening our mental faculties. All possible schemes either faded away or flared up anew for us.

We had no doubt that jumping from a fast-moving vehicle was almost rational suicide. But such a death, for us, was a better end to our situation.

I began to watch our guards. Three English soldiers—still almost youths. In outward appearance they seemed exceptionally good-natured. Let me try to talk to them. Luckily, they turned out to be familiar with German, with which I addressed them.

At first our conversation revolved around questions about their names and families. Then I subtly changed the subject to international politics. As a preliminary to that, I offered them cigarettes and gave each 10,000 Croatian kuna.

Mention of Stalin brought forth the approving remark, "Stalin goot." But when I objected and called Stalin a bandit, they not only showed dissatisfaction, but also smiled and shook their heads approvingly, as they had at first.

To my direct question of how to avoid repatriation, the soldiers suggested fleeing while on the road. At the 10th kilometer, the approach to the hills is so steep that autos had to go in the lowest gear. There, on that approach, would be the easiest of all for escape, according to them. They would shoot at us, of course, but they would aim above our heads.

A signal is given for the approach. The sorry cortege of the doomed moves on. My heart misses a beat. Still, the thought of possible escape brought on irresistible cheerfulness.

We barely go two kilometers before the column stops. Why is not clear. Thirty minutes of anxious waiting go by. In the end, a group of soldiers with an English major at its head appears at the tail of the column. A pleasant surprise for us is the smiling face of Major Ostrovsky, who had earlier been taken away to be shot on the general's orders.

The group approaches every truck and conducts some sort of questioning of its officers. In the end, they reach us.

They ask where we were from 1920 to the beginning of the Second World War, that is, the commission was interested in whether the person questioned belong to the old emigration or came to it after leaving the Soviet Union.

Major Ostrovsky nods his head as if urging us to answer that we belonged to the old emigration, which, its seems is what saves us.

All of us, with the exceptions of Sotnik Ivanov, Major Pismenksy, and Lieutenant Khimin, call ourselves old emigrants.

My entreaties that the above-named three officers be changed to the same category so that the worst does not happen have no effect. The basis for it is that their ignorance of foreign languages, if carefully checked, would put them in a false position.

Here it is appropriate to note that the Serbian translator knew Russian very poorly, but he had Sister Rayutksaya (daughter) to help him translate from Russian to English. This translator had asked her why most of the people in the vehicles said they were from Serbia, although they could not speak Serbian. She assured him that if he did not tell them that, the English would not notice. In this way, she managed to wrest the priest, Father A., from the vehicle and move him into one for those not slated to be sent to the Soviet Union.

Having been established as Soviet citizens, the above-named three officers, who would not take my advice to call themselves old emigrants, were ordered to be placed with the 130 men. This latter group, regardless of its having a fair number of old emigrants, was not questioned by the commission.

After all this, our trucks returned to the camp at which we had spent the night, while the first group was sent to Graz, beyond which the Soviet zone began.

We did not find our things in Camp Veitensfeld. They had been picked up either by the English or by those living in nearby villages. This situation did not embitter us too much, but the joy of having been saved was strongly overshadowed by the thought of having lost our comrades-in arms and by less-than-total belief in the reality of our own safety.

About two hours after our arrival in the camp, guards were taken off, machine guns were removed, and the gates were opened wide.

We are told that we are free. It is met with great disbelief. A reaction sets in for us. After having lived with our nerves so tightly wound, we felt unbelievable fatigue, as if after heavy physical work. We still did not feel ourselves fully calm; we all awaited new surprises.

An hour later, one after another, trucks drive into camp to toss out to us every kind of provision in huge quantities (flour, sugar, galettes, fat, and such.)

At 5 o'clock in the evening, a light automobile drives up with English officers and two ladies in Serbian uniforms. One of them was an old emigrant from Belgrade named Ara, the other was a Serb. Ara had acquaintances in Belgrade in common with us. A lively conversation ensued.

Ara wrote down our ranks and family names and promised to find a permanent (relatively) place to live.

Convinced that the danger of threats of being given over to the Soviets had lessened for us, we quickly decided to hold a prayer service on our miraculous recovery.

We held the prayer service in the still-unfinished barrack. Father Adam, a monk with a long, flowing beard, a former major in the Kuban Host, led the service. We had quickly gathered together an improvised choir, in which three additional priests took part: Father Fyodor Vlassenko, Father Georgii Trunov, and the former division chaplain, Father A.

Many eyes had tears streaming quietly from them during the service.

We slept peacefully that night. In the morning, we were brought even more provisions, which we did not know what to do with.

At 12 o'clock, an English major arrived and announced that, by order of the English Military Command, they would remove us from this camp at 4 o'clock and take us west to join "our White Guard friends." In order that we remain calm and not think we are being sent to the Soviets, the automobiles will not have any kind of escort and the driver will not be armed.

When the trucks were brought for us at 4 o'clock, we seated ourselves in them, but it was not without some misgivings. We figured that in case we went off to the east, we would throw the driver out and continue west on our own.

We drove off. A sigh of relief—we were going west. Soon our column was stopped by some kind of English officer who handed the driver some sort of papers.

At 5 o'clock, we approached a populated Austrian point. A group of Russian officers in German uniforms with the letters, "ROA," sewed on their shirts came out to meet us. It turned out that we had come to the staff headquarters of the Russian Corps where it was staying in Klein St. Veit.

Colonel Rogozhin, the corps commander, and officials of his staff greeted us with extraordinary friendliness. They asked about our imprisonment. In their turn, they let us know that that day, May 30, they had seen great numbers of Cossack officers being sent off en masse in an eastern direction, among whom were Generals P. N. Krasnov, S. N. Krasnov, Shkuro, Solamakhin, and others. These were, as we later found out, the officers (2,500 men) of what Cossacks called the Domanov Division (**Editor:** officers of the Cossachi Stan), who had been tricked by the English into carrying out the pretext of going to a conference, but in reality, to the Soviet Union.

Thus came to a tragic end the heroic epic of this famous stretch of Cossack history, when a group of patriots, on fire with love for their homeland and their native Cossack stanitsas, stood up to defend Russia and the whole cultured world from hated Communist aggression, the cause of famine, death, slavery, and a net of countless concentration camps.

The Yalta Agreement forever will leave on the banners of freedom-loving democracies the shameful stain of the loss of brave soldiers and put moral responsibility on the conscience of Europe and America for the unforgivable mistake allowed by the leaders of their governments.

22 June 1946
Camp Kellerberg, Austria

A. Sukalo

2 — More on the First Cossack Division

Excerpts are presented below from the memoirs of the former commander of the 1st Don Regiment, B. V. Ostrovsky. They describe circumstances concerning the betrayal by the English of the officers of the division and their actual handover. There are repetitions of what has already been presented in the article by A. Sukalo; but so as not to break up complete memories that have so many details on the day of May 25 that Sukalo makes no mention of, and also keeping in mind that there are several discrepancies in the accounts of these prominent participants in the events, such as the moment of Ovstrovsky's appearance, entailing his being ordered to be shot by the English general, these remembrances are printed here almost in full.

There are also discrepancies in the accounts describing the extreme nervous tension of all those who had to live through the day of May 28, 1945, in Camp Veitensfeld.

V. N.

On the eve of betrayal, that is, May 27, 1945, I came down from the hills, where I was staying with the 1st Regiment to visit division staff, along with the Siberian and Kalmyk Regiments, which had been put under my command.

On arrival at staff headquarters, I met with its commander, Colonel Wagner. He told me what the leader of the reconnaissance unit, Major Trisch [*Трич*], reported with absolute exactitude after having driven around the area where units were being gathered together behind barbed wire, after which they faced being sent without exception to the Soviet Union.

Colonel Wagner asked me what I was thinking of doing. I simply did not know what to answer him. Wagner suggested that I go to where the Russian Corps was. Consisting of emigrants, it was not subject to being handed over. (This Major Trisch learned.) He gave me a pass for the trip and requisitioned a considerable amount of gasoline for the automobile. Personally, he was going to release all those under him and advise them to leave Sirnitz (where the staff was staying.)

To my question on what he personally recommended doing, Wagner answered that his orderly had already prepared a pack horse and that they were going into the hills and following mountain paths into Germany. He hugged me and, hiding tears, said farewell. This capable person now looked just terrible. I knew him well as my former commander. He was never at a loss, always calm, brave, and sober. Now he was totally beaten down by all that had happened.

However, even I was not myself, as I was lost in my own thoughts and helplessness.

After saying my farewells to Colonel Wagner, I once more listened to his advice to go to the Russian Corps, stay with it, and under no circumstances risk my head. He also asked me to tell the regiment of the coming turnover—betrayal—to the USSR and to give the officers and Cossacks freedom to act. I assured him that I would go to the Corps in order to familiarize myself with that situation and also confirm to its commander the verity of the coming betrayal. After that, I returned, since I could never accept a decision not to inform the regiment of what awaited them.

On my arrival in the area in which the Corps was staying, I went to its commander, Colonel Rogozhin and told him of the coming turn over of the Cossack Corps.

Colonel Rogozhin was upset by my announcement, since on the eve, he had received an order from the English to prepare a list of all Cossacks and present it to their staff.

As I understood Colonel Rogozhin, he and Wagner knew each other. He also knew Major Trisch well from their service together in the Russian Corps, where he was liked and valued.

Returning from Colonel Rogozhin, I drove to where the German staff of our regiment was put after it was separated from us by the English. It was already late, about 9 o'clock at night. I had been held up some at the Russian Corps, not only by its commander, but also my younger artillery lieutenant brother, with whom I had served in the same battery in the Corps.

I told the Germans what Wagner had asked me to tell them. They had gathered at Major Divientall's [Дивиенталя]. They decided to also leave.

Along the road, I met automobiles loaded with German staff from our division. There were many among them that I knew. They shouted to me that they were going to Klagenfurt, and farther, to who-knew-where.

I arrived at the 1st Don Regiment after 10 o'clock in the evening and immediately ordered that all officers gather for a meeting.

I saw several tanks in front of the hotel at which I lived, and my assistant (the former Lieutenant Colonel and Assistant Commander of the 12th Kaledin Regiment) told me that the English had gathered together there on tanks and automobiles. They were very friendly, even to the point of almost hugging Cossacks, photographing general groups, and riding horses. Three officers, from whom an order to drop down to the highway tomorrow morning to change sites, were staying in the hotel.

I explained to him about "changing sites" and asked for his impressions.

Major D. (Zhora) told me straight out that we needed to leave, that it was a sound decision, but an officer's honor does not allow taking such a step, that all the officers should be asked their opinion and take steps accordingly.

I was in full agreement with him. By then, all the officers had gathered together in the hotel's dining room. I familiarized them with the given situation, hiding nothing.

They were stunned. All sat with heads held down, lost in complete silence.

I started sounding them out by asking the opinion of the junior officer. He stood up and firmly stated that he considered himself duty-bound to stay with the Cossacks. The same opinion was offered by the others, including the most senior one.

In principle, I was against the decision. Yet, still full of feelings of duty and solidarity, I said that I agreed with their advice and ordered them to inform the Cossacks what awaited them, setting them free to choose whether to leave the regiment. I also stressed that this freedom of action applied to each officer.

Dismissing them, I ordered the regimental adjutant, Sotnik M,. Lieutenant G,, whose father was an old emigrant killed in battle at Bjelovar, and Major D. that they ride in the front automobile with me tomorrow, while the regiment would be led by the commander of the 3rd Company, Sotnik M.

In spite of my exhaustion and trepidation, I fell asleep for at least two hours before morning. Then I went down to the hotel's restaurant, where the English officers were already having breakfast in one of the rooms. One of them was Russian, from a very famous aristocratic family, Prince ... Here I do not remember. It was Golitsyn, Trubetskoy, or some such other.

He told me that he was not at all certain of a handover, but that we would lose our freedom and be put behind barbed wire was certain. He expressed his sympathy and said:

"If I did not live in England, where I grew up and went to school, I would be on your side, fully, sharing your view of Bolshevism, but I am an English officer, with all that that entails."

The Cossacks were to the side, on the meadow where the convoy stood, saddling their horses for the last time.

Sitting in the car with the higher officers I have indicated, I descended from the hills onto the highway and there saw the columns of the 2nd Regiment and the Kalmyks, along with the reserve units, standing in wait for their turn to be sent to death.

English pickets and outposts stood here and there at intersections along the hilly road, sometimes even tanks. On the highway, there were tanks and machine guns.

Arriving at the staff's "new site" near some sawmills, I found the colonel of the Royal Welsh Guard, who after being introduced to the officers with me, suggested that I move to our allotted "site," which was a relatively small, square place surrounded by barbed wire and machine-gun nests with reflectors standing by them. A barrack, latrines, and a number of tents placed in a single row could be seen inside the fencing.

The colonel told me that the Cossacks were being separated from the officers, but that each could keep his own orderly with him. He announced that of our further fate, he knew nothing certain.

We spoke to each other in a mixture of French and German with the help of a Croatian Ustashi who had been born in America. To my question, given to him in Croatian (which I owned completely, as a former Yugoslavian officer):

"What will be done with us? And is it true that we will be turned over to the Soviets?"

15th Cossack Cavalry Corps

He answered: "Yes, Mr. Major, that is what I have heard, while our people will be turned over to Tito."

I asked for the colonel's permission to go meet with the regiment, with the aim of suggesting that all who wished to should head for the woods.

He gave his permission but with the proviso that D. and M. remain with him.

Lieutenant T. took the wheel and I was preparing to sit down in the car when Major D. came up to me to say:

"Volodya! You are leaving us here?"

"No Zhora," I answered, "I will not leave you. I'll return. Believe me!"

I have to admit that not coming back had been on my mind, but after such a question and the sorry looks of the two officers, along with that of my best friend, D., I was ready to take a bullet.

We went back. A column of reserve officers and division staff stood by the side. They were being searched and their belongings checked.

Meeting up with the regiment, who were still on the hilly road, I told all the officers who were riding in front what I had just seen and ordered them to drive into the middle of the formation, from which I suggested to the Cossacks that they leave any way that they could manage.

The order was followed. I myself saw a group of Cossacks from the 1st Company, with the Quartermaster in their number, approximately a platoon or two detachments, turn off on a side path, where there were no English outposts. Individual Cossacks turned and hurried off, but the majority continued rolling on, for turning off was not possible for all so ordered. Besides the regiment's 9th Company, 3rd Kuban mounted battery, and supplies, there were also the staff battery, the ROA tank group, and about 50 Ukrainians of the SS Ukrainian Battalion (not Galician, but Russian).

My mood was desperate. I was not myself as I looked with horror at the column going away ... Stopping was prohibited. Light tanks and automobiles rode along with the column, pressing them forward.

I came down, got out of the car, and stood waiting. My two friends who had been left there met me with joy—I hadn't trick them.

The regiment came down to the highway. The officers and their orderlies were ordered to step away from the Cossacks. They went to the camp set aside for staff, while Cossacks with horses went forward in a different, huge block. There, they were hurried along. Grooms were designated to take the horses out to pasture in the meadow.

Supply carts were in disarray and were left not far from us.

Then there began a humiliating search procedure. I was ordered to give up my revolver, which I threw into the car.

Why I didn't shoot myself then, I have no idea, but there was probably not even the thought of it in my head. Truly, this was under the influence of mass psychosis, for all of the officer's eyes were fixed on me. A spark of hope to live always flares up. I experienced this personally in Yugoslavia during the beginning of the war when I was sentenced to death by the Ustashi after being captured through trickery in the city of Shibenik.

The search was rudely overseen by a sergeant with a club in his hands. I repeat that this was a unit of the Royal Welsh Guards.

They made the officers raise their arms to be searched. Protests were of no help, but the club in the hands of the sergeant was always waving back and forth as if threatening a beating. He was rude, cursed, and yelled. The English officers stood on the sides,

I decided I would rather die than raise my arms. Luckily for me, they did not search me, and I was the last to go through the fence gate, which slammed shut.

My orderly, Ivan N., and the wounded Quartermaster I., who was also with me, improvised some bedding on the ground for me and started to entreat me to eat and lie down to rest. But it was not to be.

I walked all over the entire block and saw many familiar faces. How many men there were all together, I don't know. Certainly 150-180 men.

I also do not remember what occupied my time until evening: certainly I walked around the fenced-in field. I remember that the colonel was called several times, some sort of orders were given, a request was made that officers be allowed to chose horses and saddles, provisions were brought, and such.

Then this happened: Lieutenant T. lost his orderly and asked me to assign Cossack C. from one of the companies to him. Through the Croat, the colonel ordered that the request be fulfilled. After some time, a Cossack arrived with a satchel [*саквами*] and by all signs he appeared to have come according to orders. The lieutenant could see that this was certainly not C., but then, having given it some thought, he told him that he could stay if he wished. The Cossack not only happily agreed, but also asked to remain with the officers. This later saved him. Some thirty years old, he was an exemplary orderly, taking care of the lieutenant like a nanny. He was not even from the 1st Don Regiment, but from the Siberian. It seems that he remains inseparable from the lieutenant, even now.

In the evening, we were informed that we were in a temporary location. Night came.

The camp in which we were locked up was called Veitensfeld.

We were also given an order in the evening to be ready to leave in the morning of May 29.

That morning, awakening from an anxious sleep, we saw trucks approaching. An English general came to us at the camp with a group of officers. Among them was Colonel Hills, commander of the Horse Guard-Artillery Regiment, with whom I was acquainted from the first place that the regiment stayed. He was very demanding with regard to order and discipline, but treated us with goodwill and met us halfway on requests. Greeting me, he shrugged his shoulders and indicated the general with his eyes.

Right then, from the very first, we were told openly that, whether we wished it or not, we were being transferred to a location under Soviet command. It was announced to us that the order had to be followed, even if it required force.

A column of English soldiers stood in formation, ready for orders.

Trucks came and the command was given to board them, but no one moved. The general and some of those accompanying him began to shout, wave their arms about, and demand that I give the order to load.

I, personally and in the name of the group, refused to board, and addressing him, told him that we outright refused to board and that I suggested that each man proceed as he found necessary.

Even though we were unarmed and herded into an enclosure, tanks standing nearby aimed their weapons at us and machine guns were prepared for firing at us. Several soldiers got their automatic weapons and rifles ready.

It was announced to us that, no matter, living or dead, we would be taken away. Then he told those wishing to remain among the living to step to the right side and those who wished to be shot right there—to the left.

Most could not stand it, nerves gave out, "hearts were lost," even though many among them had been good, brave officers under my command.

One of the first to step out was the priest, Father Evgeny, and he dragged several others along by so doing. The widow of the military doctor, Morozov, who was killed in battle in Croatia, a young woman, laughing hysterically, shouted:

"To the homeland! To the homeland! We can't live anywhere. Damn you!"

She threw her things about and kicked a gramophone, Then she ran to a car.

Many came up to me to say their farewells. I advised a few to stay, but after all, to persuade and somehow convince anyone under conditions of complete uncertainty as to what awaits us was not possible. I, myself, became somewhat dull headed, and only inside me did resentment and rage boil and fight powerlessly to break out, but not against the English—against fate.

Our entire group bunched up and Major Bogosh came up to us with the words:

"Let's go! It's better to die from Russian bullets than English …"

He was shouted down and driven away with curses.

He left, and the entire group of 120-150 men in agreement with him loaded themselves into the trucks. They went off in the direction of the main road and stopped about 800 meters from where they were loaded.

Those of us choosing death remained. Again, discussions began, followed by threats from the English side. Lieutenant Merkulov went up to the general and asked if he could hand out bullets to those choosing suicide, so that they could do it right there in front of his eyes and other Englishmen. They listened attentively to him (however, they listened to everyone seriously and attentively), but bullets were not passed out. Although, as if in response, a command was given to the flamethrowers standing on the tanks. A flame rose up from them and burnt some grass.

Someone—maybe it was me—said that it would be better to spread out and sit on the ground, The bunches dispersed into individuals. I sat down with my orderly, Ivan Unremembered, and Sergeant-major Ivanov, neither wanting to leave me for a minute.

My thoughts were confused. A kind of indifference arose in me, but I did very much want to live.

I started saying a prayer to myself that I remembered. In plain words, I asked God and St. Nicholas the Miracle Maker to help me and not to spare his mercy.

Plumes of fire were released several times. No one paid attention to them. A priest recited a prayer loudly. We all awaited death and delivery to eternal life.

Suddenly, the soldiers stacked their weapons (in the English system, right on the ground). Some of them ran off to somewhere and came back right away. Ropes and electrical cords were delivered.

Attacking the first Cossack they happened on, they started to tie him up.

This caused me to blow up completely. I ran up to the general and his officers and started to curse them in every language I knew, Italian among them, which most would have known from having been in Italy. At the same time, someone yelled out that it was better to go freely than tied up. I picked up that idea, realizing that it was easier to escape if one was not tied up. and asked the general to stop it, announcing that we would go if he did.

"Cancel that order!" the general said.

I explained that we could in no way either escape or kill ourselves if tied up and thrown into the vehicles, but we could do so if untied, so I suggested to everyone that we take seats in the trucks.

Abandoning their things, we all straggled to the trucks.

Seeing that threats met with success and brought us to obedience better than tanks, machine guns, or other weapons except for rope, an English major came up to me and, taking me under the canopy, said that I was to go in my own car, which he had already arranged to be brought over. My "volkswagen" really did drive up. Treskin asked to be the driver. The Cossack driver moved to the back. My first Ivan took the trunk with travel necessities, put it in the car and climbed in with my dog, "Karlo Ivanovich"—a dachshund having been with me through the war. He did not want to give him to the "lords" who had asked about him.

I asked those with me if they really wanted to go to the Soviets. All of them answered in the negative, and the driver added that it would be better to die than wind up in Soviet hands. We decided to turn off into the river from a hill on the road to Judenburg. The decision was accepted unanimously.

But here, something happened that might be called a miracle. It saved our entire group from being driven over to the Bolsheviks.

It seemed as if God had heard our prayers and protected us from torture and humiliation.

The engine of my car would not start. The magneto was not working properly. It was giving off sparks.

Huge guards began to cheerfully push the car back and forth without results.

We were ordered to move to a truck, while I was told that I was to go with the major in his car. My fellow travelers left; I remained. The major and the colonel graciously asked me to go with them. Indicating the ribbons on my chest, they suggested that I take them off and go without them. (I had all levels of eastern ribbons, two iron crosses, and a silver Italian medal for bravery.)

I tore my ribbons off and threw them on the ground. The colonel bent down, picked them up, blew the dust off them, and carefully wrapping them in cellophane, put them in his wallet, saying:

"These will make excellent souvenirs of you and your behavior."

That was the point at which I became overcome with rage. I decided I would not go. My jacket collar was choking me, so I tore off the hook and threw my papakha to the ground, proclaiming:

"As of now I am no longer obeying you and will go nowhere!" and, addressing the "gentlemen," I added several insulting epithets to this.

Shouts were made, along with the order:

"Shoot him!"

I was grabbed by the arms and pushed in the side and back by automatic weapons and led over a bridge across a stream. They then brought me back, put me into the front seat of a "jeep," and, pointing automatic weapons at my head and spine, drove me out on the road.

My compatriots had already driven off and waited close to the tail of of the previously departed column.

The jeep raced along the main road. I sat still, as if made of stone. My outrage had settled down. I became indifferent to everything. I once more mentally recited prayers and thought of my mother, who at that time was in Germany.

Suddenly, sirens were heard from behind, shouts and whistles, too. The jeep slowed to a stop. A totally dust-covered motorcyclist caught up to us, said something, then returned to the

English camp, the entrance of which was mobbed by excitedly shouting soldiers. We drove in toward the staff's tent. My escort hid, as did the driver.

An officer came up, bringing me a cup of tea, biscuits, and a pack of cigarettes, set everything down, and told me that I had to strengthen up. I understood that I was to be executed.

I tried to drink the tea, but the metal cup burnt my lips, I lit a cigarette and, as if in a film, my entire life flashed through my head, beginning with my youngest years. How simple it all was, how clear and easily understood! I had found complete peace. Death no longer frightened me.

Those same officers and the motorcyclist, came back. There was also an officer in a short-sleeved shirt with sheets of paper attached to a carton with rubber bands. Something had been typed on the papers. I figured out from the words addressed to me that I had to sign the papers.

Thinking that it was some sort of formality that had to be filled out before an execution, I, of course, did not refuse to sign it, but informed them that, since my pen had been stolen by soldiers of the Royal Guard of His Majesty the King of Great Britain, I requested that I be given a pencil or a pen.

Confusion reigned until one of the officers present explained that I did not understand what was wanted from me.

Then he explained the following to me:

"You have been rescued and need to give us all of your information."

To this, I said:

"But what about the rest of my friends?"

Again, confusion among the group of officers. All of them were talking and gesticulating in eager argument over something.

The senior of them said something. Then, turning to me in complete silence, he said:

"You White Russians are all our friends. Having not been within the boundaries of the Soviet Union until 1938, you are not subject to repatriation. So, let's go and sign up all of your friends."

Only then did I understand that we had been saved.

Getting out of the auto, I went with the colonel and the whole group of officers to the row of trucks that stood facing the highway along the barbed wire.

Coming up to the first truck, I said to the officers looking out of it:

"Gentlemen! All of you came out of the borders of Russia at the same time that I did."

I could not tell them straight out, because I had been told to keep quiet about what I knew, since they were still looking for those who wished to leave.

At first, no one seemed to have understood what I had said, so I repeated myself, ignoring the stern prohibition typed on the page.

As I later found out, the colonel knew Russian, for he could repeat Russian names very well and wrote them down accurately right away.

After my words had been addressed to those sitting in the vehicles, I tried to encourage them with gestures and mimicry.

The first one out, in truth climbing out from under a tarp, was the artillery major, Captain Yu. Antonov of the Kuban Artillery, an old emigrant from Paris, who gave his name, the place beyond Russia's borders where he had lived, and the year (1920) that he had left Russia. Others followed him, such as Major G. Druzhakin and one of the former, as we now call them, Soviet or new emigrants. Several of them became confused, so I tried to help them. Again, I was cautioned, but on the whole, the first truck was signed up.

When we went to the second, I was told:

"Mr. Major, Sotnik Popov has lost his mind."

Looking inside, I saw the pale, leathery face of the sotnik. He was an old emigrant, an officer in the Nizhegorodsky Dragoon Regiment. He had previous spent 20 years under contract to the Foreign Legion.

Popov shouted and fought as he was held by Lieutenant Treskin and some other person. I ordered them to turn him over to me, took him still fighting and yelling and carried him in my arms right up to the colonel, stretching his arms out with our officers underpinning them as I approached, before stooping down and putting him right on the ground.

He said that it was all useless.

It was a terrible experience. It was obvious that all the Englishmen were affected by it.

I returned to the trucks to continue my walk around them. No one interfered with me now. I just called off the names myself of those who were sitting in a truck and said where they were from.

For the younger ones, I simply said, "Born outside of the borders, of course, mainly in Yugoslavia."

After having gone through all the vehicles, the colonel came to me and asked:

"Did you also list the two Cossacks who had stood with their arms around you?" He did not even ask who they were and where they were born.

After this, a command was given to get out of the trucks and go back to the camp.

Shouts then went up from the other trucks.

"But what about us? They will take us away. Help us!"

As I started off toward them, someone's arms grabbed me ...

A signal was given and the column started off.

Whether the priest, Father O., had been saved, I do not know.

Coming back into the camp, we were met with a total mess. The guards stole whatever had not already been stolen. But we were not interested in all that junk. Although Cossacks, we were tidy people, so we put that single barrack back into some kind of order and held a prayer service inside it to give thanks. All of us stunned survivors were truly grateful to the Lord God for deliverance from a savage death.

Major V. Ostrovsky

The End of the 360th Cossack Regiment

This regiment, called the Rendell [*Рентельна*] Regiment had been transferred to the Balkans from France on March 29, 1945, and entered into the makeup of the 1st Cossack Division in the Corps of General von Pannwitz.

Colonel Rendell was recalled by Pannwitz and designated as the commander of the 3rd Cossack Division. Stepping up to command the 360th Regiment was Captain Kullgavo [Кульгаво].

On their arrival in the Balkans, the regiment took a week to rest, then it took up a position on the left bank of the Drau River.

At dusk on the night of May 7-8, all the German officers abandoned the regiment during a battle with Red Bulgrarians, as did the sergeants and junior officers. Captain Kullgavo put Sotnik Sh. in command of them, as the sole Cossack officer remaining with the regiment.

Sotnik Sh. understood that to extricate the regiment from the battle without great losses was impossible, but after waiting for the battle to quiet down, he took his regiment out of its position at about 12 o'clock, and they set off using an alternating gait to the north.

The regiment withdrew quietly until 10 o'clock in the morning, when Bulgarian armored units caught up with it.

Seeing no other way out, Sotnik Sh. turned the regiment around and gave battle to the Bulgarians, ending with the Bulgars in retreat.

The regiment continued to withdraw and soon ran up against retreating convoys of German gendarmes and police. At this time, the Bulgars cut off their route anew. Their obvious intent was to take the Cossacks as prisoners.

Stumbling again upon Sotnik Sh., the Bulgarian officer was told that Cossacks do not surrender and suggested that the regiment be allowed to pass.

The Bulgarian agreed.

During its long trek, the regiment was fired at by Titoists after it had gone some 30 kilometers. Once more, it had to turn around, and, after a battle lasting approximately 20 minutes, proceeded farther.

On the night of May 9-10, they continued without sleep. On the 10th, Titoists again blocked their path. Again, they had to return to battle formation to clear the path. During it, 10 to 15 supply wagons fell into enemy hands.

During the battle, 4 Cossacks were killed, including Sotnik Sh.'s brother, with whom he had been reunited only a month before after a separation of 20 years. There were also 5 wounded.

He broke through. They went on some 6 kilometers and ran into English tanks that let the regiment pass. Going another 15 kilometers, they spent the night.

They walked the entire day of May 11, but on the 12th, about 30 kilometers east of the city of Klagenfurt, they lay down their arms in the city of Völkermarkt. From there, they went to Feldkirchen (about 20 kilometers northwest of Klagenfurt). After spending the night there, they went another kilometer-and-a-half to two kilometers to bivouac on the morning of May 13. They remained there until May 19, when, seeing that there was no longer enough food for the pastured horses, the regiment went another 15 versts or so to the north in the direction of the village of Sirnitz and stayed there until May 28.

There were about 800 in the regiment.

Being in the English Zone of Occupation, the regiment was given provisions by the English and from German stockpiles.

On May 27, Sotnik Sh. received an order from the head of the 1st Cossack Division, Colonel Wagner, that was given to him by the English. The next day, May 18, at 7 o'clock in the morning, the regiment was to go some 11 kilometers to a prisoner of war camp in the village of Weitensfeld.

Having passed the command on, Colonel Wagner himself headed for the woods after warning Major Ostrovsky about it.

On receiving the command to move to Weitensfeld, Sotnik Sh. gathered the regiment together and warned them of the forthcoming betrayal. He advised Cossacks to break into small groups and head for the woods or hills. Counting on history, he told the Cossacks that such a situation could not be permanent and better days would come.

In the morning, it became clear that no one from the regiment had left. Sotnik Sh. stayed with them, considering it not possible to abandon them.

From the evening of May 27, English tanks were stopped for the night near to the regiment's position.

On the morning of May 28, the 360th Regiment left its night's lodgings first and after descending onto the highway from the hills, continued on. The English tanks that had spent the night near them went alongside the column.

After 11 kilometers, the regiment was stopped near the settlement of Weitensfeld. Removing Sotnik Sh. from the regiment, the English put him in an automobile and took him through the barbed wire into the camp which was along the highway close to the settlement. There, they took away his watch, knife, shaving kit. soap, cigarettes, edibles, and the pistol that had been left him when the Cossacks were disarmed.

The Cossacks were led 2 kilometers even farther. Hurried along and left with only 3 horses for each convoy, they were imprisoned in the same kind of camp as Sotnik Sh. The horses and supply carts were sent 1 kilometer farther to a third camp.

None of the three camps could be seen from any of the others.

Farther down, Sotnik Sh. tells of the approach of the Schools of the 5th Reserve Regiment, 2nd Siberian and Kalmyk Regiments, Caucasus Division, and the 1st Don Regiment.

Further, Sotink Sh. gives details about how the units named above were locked up that have already been included in the excerpts by Lieutenant Colonel Sukalo and Major Ostrovsky.

Sotnik Sh. describes how on the morning of May 29, the English informed the Cossacks, imprisoned as they were behind barbed wire, that they would be taken by railroad to Italy to be reformed to fight the Bolsheviks.

The entire multi-thousand group spent May 30 being ostensibly loaded onto that railroad. There were only two English soldiers with them. They went freely—those who wished to leave could leave—but no one left. All believed the English. All thought they were being led to that railroad.

To the question of why they had been separated from their officers, the English answered that there were Titoists and Bolsheviks not far away, so that, in order that officers not be killed, they were taken away separately under heavy guard to Italy. This answer satisfied the Cossacks.

What happened to this huge group of Cossacks was told by 3 Cossacks who, after going 15 kilometers, had been held up in one of the settlements. They saw from a distance how the entire group of Cossacks was suddenly surrounded on their journey by Bolsheviks who had set up an ambush. Not one of them got away.

Taken from the words of Sotnik Sh.

V. N.

From the Memoir of an Officer on the Staff of General von Pannwitz's Corps

In his memoir entitled "Ten Years Behind the Iron Curtain," an officer on the staff of the 15th Cossack Cavalry Corps, B. K. G., tells mainly about his experiences in various places of imprisonment.

With his kind permission, excerpts are reproduced below.

The spring of 1945 was unusually warm and pleasant. Succulent, fresh greenery covered the hills and mountain spurs. It seemed as if nature was celebrating the end of the war which, having long before lost its initial purpose, had turned into just mass killing. Many rejoiced along with nature and prepared to return, finally, to a peaceful life of rest.

The English showed neither any special administrative need, nor desire to convert our situation into one of prisoners of war behind barbed wire, nor to release us and give us the chance to somehow be responsible for our own well being. Then again, we could not stay long at one and the same place the way we were doing. Some ten thousand of our horses, coming into Austria in excellent condition, ate all the grass like locusts, forcing us like a migrating Tatar horde to seek out a new place. The victors looked on rather indifferently as our contingent of horses died of dysentery and our leadership perhaps took more care for our war horses, than Cossacks.

The last place my units were quartered was Klein St. Paul, a small settlement close to Sirnitz and Weitensfeld.

The officers of the English division serving there often came to visit us. They were very friendly toward us, drank our *"шливовицу"*—a Yugoslavian plum vodka—and red wine, and ate with pleasure the dried meat we had brought with us in the carts of our supply trains. They particularly liked to ask to go for horseback rides on our horses, most often the pure blooded ones.

Among these victor-guests were a number who had been in Russia, in the north or in the south, at the time of the Civil War. They always unambiguously alluded to the possibility of continuing our war against the Reds, but this time side by side with them. With what joy we responded to these hints. They were even the main reason that obedience and discipline were so well maintained, especially in units made up in great part of those formerly under the Soviets, who had already been believing for a long time in that sort of promise.

It cannot be described through what an impossible mix of German-French-Russian we and the English communicated, but good wine and good relations untied our tongues, allowing for mutual respect and friendly ties. It seemed to all of us that life was once more smiling on us, that not all was lost, and that the time was approaching …

On May 28, the commander of our brigade, Lieutenant Colonel Borisov, was given an order by the English Command to prepare all officers at 8 o'clock in the morning for a … change in location!

"The situation has changed somewhat, so we are transporting all of you to a single special officer's camp in northern Italy, where you will be allowed to determine your own fate: either to move to an overseas country or to join voluntarily with units of our occupying forces or … to return to your homeland—to the USSR. Do not bring any personal things. They will be provided. In order for you not to have to make the decision—German uniforms have been deemed inappropriate. Also, as many are found with your units, do not bring any women and children. They will be sent on a separate train."

One dark feeling or another pressed against our hearts. Something was wrong. It all seemed smooth and logical, but within those words were hidden falsehoods and trickery.

Having listened the Englishman, we asked him straight out, without equivocation, if he thought we might be given over to the Communists.

The Englishman swore to us on his personal honor as an English officer:

"Do not even think about that! What betrayal? Of someone we count as English and allied with the west? That would be barbaric or worse!"

But all the same, we did not believe his vow. Those of us who spoke a little English said so right to his face.

The officer went away, but he soon brought his own chaplain, who **swore to us that England could never carry out such a disgraceful act.**

This calmed us down.

Does this chaplain remember those words of his today? Does it gnaw at his conscience at times? Did he then know the truth, or had he been tricked and committed a sin out of ignorance?

Vehicles rolled up to our location on the morning of May 29. Cossacks watched morosely and suspiciously as their officers were separated from them. We tried as well as we could to calm them down, all the more so because we had been told by the same Englishmen that those who resisted would be sent on after us, followed by "children and family."

They seated us comfortably, along with our things, without crowding us too much together in the trucks. We noticed nothing suspicious. Still, we began to feel ill at ease when an English captain came up to each of us in order and, politely taking us under the canvas, repeated in a very natural tone of voice: "Misters officers, you no longer have need for your weapons. Would you care to give up your revolvers?"

My heart almost stopped when I unholstered my trusty, never failing "O. 8" and gave it into the hands of the Englishman. I remembered the words General A. Shkuro not so long ago said to our Cossacks:

"Mates! Do not let your weapons out of your hands! ... For then ... they will be cut off."

When they finished collecting weapons, an officer gave a terse command and English soldiers threw themselves into the trucks, holding rifles and automatic weapons at the ready, two hopping aboard each vehicle.

The trucks jolted off and rushed at full speed, raising heavy dust over the narrow, hilly roads there, making our breathing difficult from being unaccustomed to it.

Along the entire road, for over a distance of 200 kilometers, two Englishmen with automatic weapons stood every 50 meters, while every 200-300 meters, there was a tank.

The English showed themselves to be masters of betrayal.

After several hours of headlong racing, we finally reached the city of Judenburg ...

I will not attempt to write about what happened in the vehicles at this time. Some were totally paralyzed from shock. Others believed that we were being stolen from under the noses of the Reds in order to be "saved." There were instances of leaps from the vehicles that ended in death (one kind or another) ...

The trucks stopped on the highway near a concrete bridge across the Mur River, where it flowed deep in steep gorges with rocky banks. A mob of soldiers appeared on a square on the other side in front of some sort of factory. We could see them threatening us with their fists. Profanities and curses reached us from the square.

English soldiers ... surrounded our trucks. They held something out to us; shouted something.

At first, we could not understand a thing of their unbelievable mix of Polish and Ukrainian, but it became clear in the end that they wanted to buy our watches from us in exchange for cigarettes.

"All the same! [Here the author gave the Cyrillic transliteration of the Polish *wszystko jedno*.] You no longer need your watches!" the enterprising warriors explained to us, and for further explication, they swiped the edge of their hands across their throats or put their index fingers up to their temples in the well-known gesture with thumb and middle finger to indicate the firing of a gun.

Our stomachs were in our throats. Our officers smashed their watches against the bridge or tried to toss them far into the river.

At this point, the first vehicle surged ahead, crossed the bridge, and turned around. People hurriedly jumped out of it with their things and, surrounded by Soviet guards, went through the factory gates. The truck returned.

Our vehicle lurched and went some ten meters. It stopped. Officers hurriedly tore up their papers, photos, letters. Gusts of wind spread the scraps along the road. Suddenly, there was a terrifying yell. One of the officers had jumped from a vehicle at the moment it was crossing over the bridge, did a swan dive from more than 20 meters high over its railing, and went head first into the river. We distinctly saw how he did two somersaults in the air, then hit flat onto sharp rocks. His body shuddered and ... became still.

That night, when they brought me up to the vehicles (in Graz), I saw an entire group of our officers. None of us spoke. We went silently into the trucks in the established system. Five people were removed from the crowd. They were told to climb into the vehicle and sit on the floor with their backs against the back of the driver's cabin, spreading their legs out in a wide circle. The next group of five was seated between their legs and so forth. Thirty people were accommodated per vehicle. People?—No!—Pitiful fragments of a sunken vessel.

Guards with automatic weapons were on each truck, some in the cabin, some on its roof. The sergeant-major in charge of the convoy of guards recited the following, legally obligatory warning:

"Do not turn your heads. Do not speak. Do not stand up. Any violation of this order will be considered an attempt to escape for which weapons will be used without warning."

Many times later, thousands of times, I heard the words of that warning, which workers in Soviet labor camps scornfully took to calling "the prayer."

It is read in a monotone, from memory, without thought, without expression, as if the words were not hiding insidiousness, bloodthirstiness, ruthlessness, just plain provocation, and beyond that, unavoidable death.

The first auto started off. We were so crowded that not only was movement impossible, but even breathing was difficult. Behind us, the rest of the vehicles swam through clouds of dust.

The leader of our convoy preferred to sit on the roof, feeling it to be his responsibility, in spite of the fact that he could have been in the cabin, where it was quieter and more comfortable. He held his automatic weapon firmly in his red, worker's hands and vigilantly kept his eyes on our every movement.

Judging from his looks, the expression in his eyes, this was a kindhearted, displaced [*рассейский*] little peasant, some 35 years old. He could not keep up for long his role of silent, all-seeing Argus. As if he could! For the first time in his life he saw real "contras [*контриков*]"—Vlasovites, White Guards, "minigrants." Curiosity tortured him. In the end, he could not hold out and turned to me as I sat underneath his huge boots.

"Hey, you!" he pushed me with his toe. "What are you? An officer?"

"Officer," I answered as quietly as I could.

A new jab with his toe after a prolonged pause:

"I bet you shot many of our prisoners?"

"We did not shoot prisoners …"

"Well, you're lying!" Then, after some thought, he added: "Where did you learn Russian?"

"Yes, I am Russian, as Russian as you are."

Another pause. More thought. Then:

"Aha! A landlord. Didn't drink enough blood? Once more you wanted to take our land away and bring back serfdom."

I answered that our aims were, in fact, completely different. So began our long, three-day conversation. (We were traveling from Graz to Rumania.) At every re-boarding, the sergeant-major took care that I wound up in the same vehicle and in the same place. Our conversation continued. I told him why we put on German uniforms, against what and for what we were fighting. I told him about how people lived in free countries …

This senior officer listened to me attentively. He had long before lost all of his sternness. He offered us home grown tobacco and ordered that water be brought to us out of turn. He shoved a spare piece of bread into my hand.

When, half dead from fatigue, lack of sleep, and desire to get to Temishvar (Rumania), we started to get out in front of the prison, he came over to me and said:

"Well, what? Good luck to you!" He sighed heavily then unexpectedly whispered, sadly shaking his head: "Oh, and why did you not conquer us?"

Later in his memoir, B. K. G. tells of his meeting with a Cossack from the 15th Cossack Cavalry Corps on the way to a political isolator [*полит-изолятор*] in June of 1953 in a freight car for prisoners. From his tale, we can learn much about how the 2nd Cossack Division was handed over.

My co-traveler—B. K. G. continues—was in the 3rd Kuban Regiment of our 15th Corps. He was the first rank and file Cossack that I met after the handovers. So, on the way to the Arctic Circle, he told me what happened after they took away the officers.

"You were taken away and we knew nothing. We argued everything, but things seemed somehow calm. English 'agitators' showed up to soothe us."

[B. K. G. uses the first person even though what follows is obviously a reconstructed conversation rather than a verbatim transcription.]

In pursuit of what happened to the officers, they promised that they would be sent to a land overseas.

Then they brought suitable baths and disinfection chambers [*дез камеры*] on vehicles to where our regiment was. Everyone was told to wash and disinfect their clothes. They gave out food for three days and told us to load up. We loaded our own supply wagons and carts, which had been fitted up for us by the English. Their soldiers popped up around us if coming up from the ground. They searched us. They took away weapons, compasses, cards, knives, razors. We set off under guard to the east. We went about 30 kilometers and stopped. It was in a large field, fenced in with barbed wire. Soldiers in Hungarian uniforms appeared from somewhere. They jumped on our carts and made them nothing but a memory [*поминаи как звали*].

We were left without our things or food. Just in what we wore. We looked around. We wanted to run, but there were no longer any English. In their place were Soviet tanks and armor surrounding and guarding us. Everything was done so fast, as if in a theater. So expertly did the dogs arrange things [*обтяпали дело*] that we had no time to think.

They did not stand on ceremony with us. Did not judge. Did not interrogate. There was a railroad out of the camp nearby. They loaded us onto a train with a direct track straight into eastern Siberia. I, with a party of some eight thousand, went straight to Kolyma.

They deployed us "freely." They explained that "our homeland had forgiven us everything" and only for our edification gave us six years of "free exile."

Everything there was "voluntary, but obligatory."

We worked "for hire" in mines. We lived in barracks. Our food was prison food. You know yourself what kind. Neither to live nor die. Everything possible was given us for grub.

A little time passed before "forgiveness" went down the drain. They had found the time. It is wholly understandable that the millions sent back could not be sorted out right away and get through the Chekist machinery. Then the NKVD appeared. At first they started to pull one at a time out of the crowds. Then, every day they sent off from ten to a hundred for questioning. Investigation was brief. There was but one criterion. What was for those under the Soviets was also for the emigrants.

Their machinery ground slowly. But why hurry? We sit and we work and that is that. Everyone was given a "katyusha" (25 years), as if by law. I was recently brought to trial. Without investigation, it must be said, they knocked 7 years off. Right now, it appears that there is no one left to be tried. After trial, they usually sent you to a different camp. I am off to somewhere in Vorkuta.

"What? You weren't shot on the way?"

"Why shoot me? Those who get through trial, that person is already dead. He cannot keep on. There is his road. Sure, he is weak and there will not be much from him in the way of work. But why execute working cattle? He costs nothing, but he does have some use. When he is totally done for—like steam after having done its work—he will himself dissipate."

Horrible things are spoken of in plain words on the way to exile, and in the most tranquil way. No emotions whatever. If they are there, people learn to hide them, not only from others, but also from themselves.

That was the last time that I met a brother-soldier from the same regiment. It was the first exact truth about what the English did with the Cossacks after having separated them from their officers. The Cossacks went off to Vorkuta. After a few months, there was a mutiny and a strike there, crushed to a bloody end by Checkists. Maybe he had laid his head down and it will lie there, a frozen icicle in the permafrost, until the Second Coming.

B. K. G.

Total Number Turned Over from the Ranks of the 15th Cossack Cavalry Corps

At the time of the handovers, the units of the corps found in southern Austria north of the city of Klagenfurt were: 1st Cossack Division, in the area of Feldkirchen, the rest were in the region of Althofen-Heumarkt.

The handover was carried out at the same time for units of the 1st Division concentrated in the area of Weitensfeld. The others were removed from where they were quartered

In total, 40,000 men were turned over.

Corrections in the forward to Volume I of *Great Betrayal*, on p. 7 [p. 6 in the translation], it is erroneously printed as "up to fifteen thousand."

V. Naumenko

The Tragic End of the Noble Colonel Kulakov

In the first days of the German surrender in May of 1945, Colonel Nikolai Lazarevich Kulakov of the Terek Host perished tragically.

The biographical details of this famous person are as follows:

He was born in 1880 in Yesentukskoy Stanitsa. His first service was with the 1st Volga Regiment of the Terek Host, which he joined as an ordinary Cossack. He took part in World War I, in which he was awarded all four degrees of the Georgian Cross and reached the rank of sotnik. He took a most important part in the Civil War in southern Russia, at which his service ended at the rank of lieutenant colonel.

During the withdrawal from Novorossisk by South Russian forces at the beginning of 1920, he was wounded severely in both legs by grenade fragments in battle near Kagalnitskoy.

Freezing weather, overcrowded transports, and lack of the necessary medical help caused Nikolai Lazarevich great suffering.

Only after several days had passed after being wounded, in an ambulance en route to Yekaterinograd, was he operated on: both legs were amputated—one below, the other above the knee.

Despite that, N. L. Kulakov did not under any circumstance want to remain and hurried to Novorossisk where there was already a transfer of military forces and refugees to the Crimea taking place. But he had not been fated to get to a boat, and he was left in Novorossisk, where enraged, brutal Bolsheviks killed every officer they could get their hands on.

But Nikolai Lazarevich was saved by his wife. Learning of his serious injuries, she threw herself into finding him. In the chaos of retreating forces, she succeeded in finding him in Novorossisk. Through her resourcefulness, she not only saved him from death, but also managed to bring him back to his old stanitsa.

There, over the course of 12 years, without the most basic medical help and under constant fear for his life and that of his family, he hid in the cellar of his own home. But he could stand it no longer and came out of his hideout. By the next day, Nikolai Lazarevich was questioned by the almighty OGPU.

As he left, the Chekist told him:

"In view of the fact that you will die soon, we will leave you in peace."

Nikolai Lazarevich had to suffer 10 years more under Bolshevik authority, but nonetheless, it was his fate to escape from under it.

With the Germans occupying the northern Caucasus, he felt himself strong enough to give what was left of his life to the great cause of saving Cossackdom and his homeland.

Freed from the yoke of Bolshevism, Cossacks chose him as the ataman of his stanitsa and he started the 1st Terek Company along with his stanishniks, which was later combined with other Terek companies. Lieutenant Colonel Kulakov became their leader and took them west, where he joined the 1st Cossack Division that was being formed under General von Pannwitz.

He was given a prosthesis by the Germans. With the aid of a cane, he was able to walk.

At this time in Berlin there was a Central Administration of Cossack forces formed "for the defense of Cossack interests before the German Command." In performance of his duties as its head, P. N. Krasnov named Nikolai Lazarevich Kulakov to his staff.

But he could not remain an old veteran in the rear. By his own request, he was attached to the 6th Terek Regiment of von Pannwitz's division.

There, among his native Cossacks, Nikolai Lazarevich had an invigorating influence. He was always with the Cossacks, sharing with them the stresses of life in campaigns and battles. Always cheerful, lively, energetic, and protective of the Cossacks, he was loved not only by his Tereks, but even by the Germans, including up to the regimental commander and leader of the division (later—corps commander.) All of them called him Terek Ataman.

For his noble service, Lieutenant Colonel Kulakov was promoted to colonel.

Not too much before the sudden end of the war, Nikolai Lazarevich, along with two other Cossacks, took a short time off to rest in one of the dwellings the corps used for rest in the area of Innsbruck in southern Austria.

In an abandoned small village, he and the Cossacks settled into one of the rooms on the lower floor of the house, while their hostess lived above.

One of the days right after the German surrender, she heard some kind of noise from below, as if of some sort of fight.

When the hostess came down in the morning, she saw the room in which Kulakov was staying in total disarray and traces of blood on the floor. It was obvious that, after a stubborn fight, Kulakov and the Cossacks were captured and taken away by Chekists.

There was soon information received that Colonel Kulakov was being held in the basement of the NKVD in Vienna. His prostheses and cane had been taken away. Every day and even more frequently he was called to answer questions from an investigator on one of the highest floors of the building. He had to go up to the top, then back down to the basement using his arms and the stumps of his legs. It must have caused unbelievable suffering. Only death could save him, which he found in the NKVD's basement.

May his memory remain among Cossacks for all time.

V. Naumenko

Forced Repatriations from France, Italy, and England

This page left deliberately blank

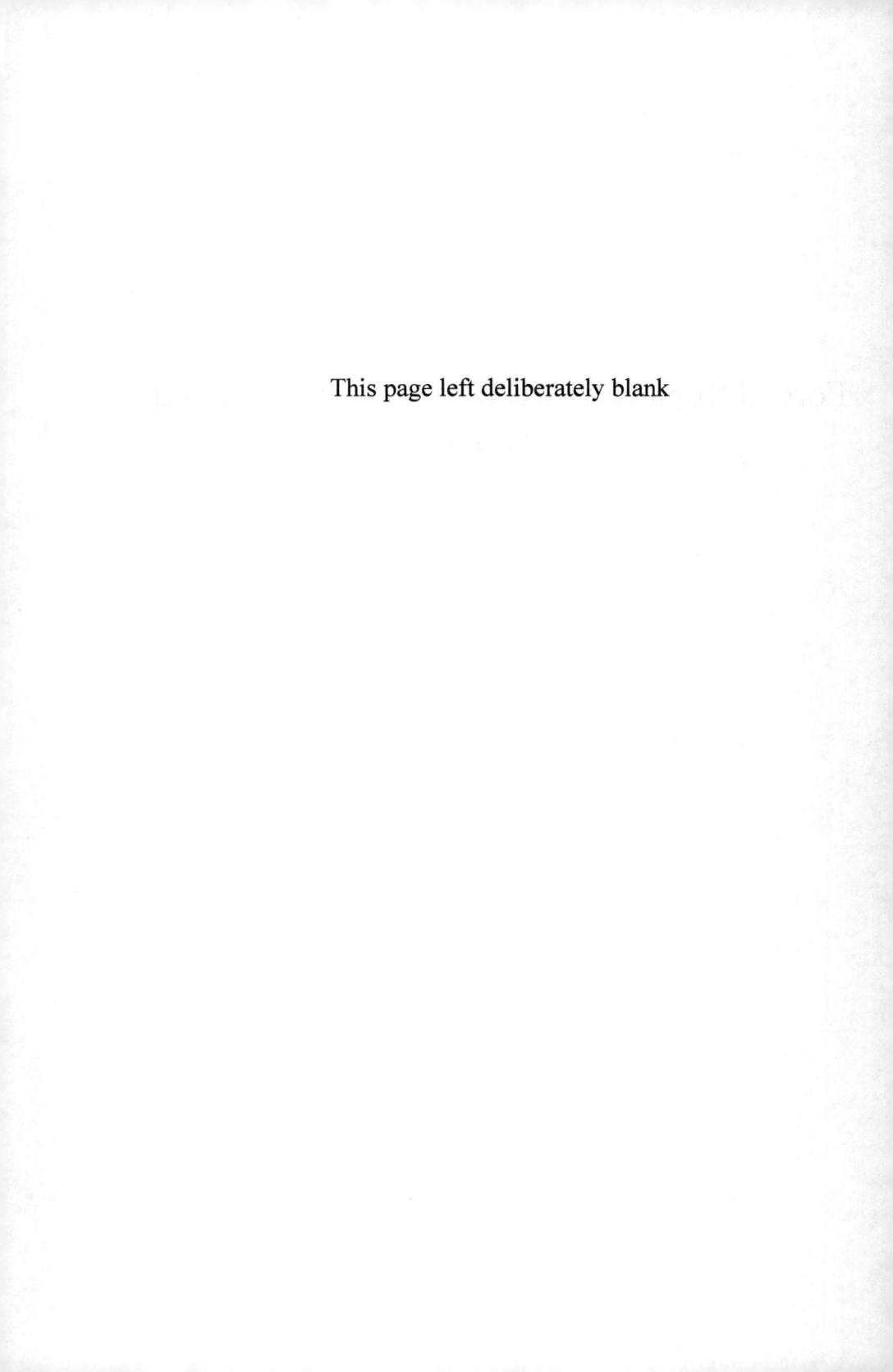

Forced Handovers from France

> Transcribed from the words of a Cossack who was one of the few to manage to escape being handed over from the 2nd camp that is described below.

At the end of the World War II, there was a prisoner-of-war camp in the Pyrenees Mountains of France in the Department of Ariège, near the railroad station, Vernet d'Ariège.

At first it held German prisoners and Magyars [мадьяры], along with many German women.

Then the French began to send ROA members and captured Cossacks who had been captured in the French Zone of Occupation in Germany after having managed to avoid the forced handovers at Lienz and Klagenfurt, where units of the Cossack Corps of General von Pannwitz had been.

Up to two battalions of the ROA and nearly 200 Cossacks, mostly Kuban, were concentrated in this camp.

They were all put in three barracks. The French gave them terrible food: 1 kilogram of bread per day for every 10 prisoners and a liter of hot water. As was later learned, the provisions for these prisoners were taken entirely from American stockpiles by way of the French, who were in charge of the prisoner-of-war camps. This abuse by the French was discovered by the Americans entirely by chance. Provisions then were markedly improved, but unfortunately, only just before their handover to the Soviets, too late for the prisoners.*

---

* **Note:** In connection with the occurrence described here about misappropriation by the leadership of the French Command of provisions released by the American Command for prisoners of war, it is not without some interest to remember a similar occurrence that took place in the years of the First War, when the Serbian Army, under pressure by Austro-Hungary, had to withdraw to the shores of the Adriatic Sea, and then, on the insistence of the Russian Emperor, were conveyed by the Anglo-French to the island of Corfu.

There, the ration allowed the Serbians was taken on by the French and

A Soviet commission made up of two officers came to the Pyrenees camp in August of 1945.

All prisoners of war, included Cossacks, were taken out of their barracks and formed into three columns, the first of which was made up entirely of Cossacks.

The Soviet officers sat at a table. French guards were everywhere. On the other side of the barbed wire, many Soviet soldiers could be seen.

It must be said that when the Cossacks were lined up, they were also moved forward, so that the commission's table turned out to be between them and the second column. When they turned the

---

the English, through whom provisions were released, in alternate months, from the stockpiles of the French and English Commands, but for convenience, the actual task of providing rations to the Serbian Army was completely taken over by the French, to whom the English turned over foodstuffs when it was their month.

And here, completely by chance, as in the Pyrenees camp, it was learned that representatives of the French Command on Corfu did much the same thing as in the Pyrenees. The Serbs were fed poorly—most of the English food never reached them.

And this became known only by accident:

The senior physician of the Russian Red Cross mission with the Serbian Army during World War I, Dr. Sichev [Сычев], told me about his conversation on this question with the Voyevoda (that is, Field Marshall), Stepa Stepanović.

The latter was invited to dine with a representative of the English Command on Corfu.

Ham was served at the dinner. The Voyevoda very much liked this dish and could not keep from remarking that it was the first time that he had it over his entire time on Corfu.

The Englishman was amazed by his words, since ham was part of the rations of English soldiers, and the full rations that English soldiers required were given to the French to feed the Serbs.

After this instance, the provisions that Serbians received from the French did improve, but even still, they did not receive their full portions.

As can be seen by the occurrence in the Pyrenees, the French remained true to themselves over the course of 30 years—to the time of the Second World War.

V. Naumenko

Cossack column around, it made the barracks taken up by Germans right behind their backs, very close to them. This gave some Cossacks the chance to slip into the German barracks. The Germans eagerly accepted and even helped to hide them there, but a large number of Cossacks were caught by the French. Still, 20-30 men succeeded in remaining with the Germans.

After lists of prisoners were prepared, Cossacks were sent to a separate barrack, which had recently held 165 prisoners. Now it was filled to its limit. Five people succeeded to transfer from it as foreign citizens to the Germans and three to the Poles.

After the Cossacks were put into that separate barrack, it was encircled by Negro French guards from Madagascar. Leaving the barracks, even to go to the latrine, was forbidden. A "bucket" was put in the middle of the barrack.

Cossack barracks and those of rank-and-file ROA were visited every day by a Turkestan Soviet lieutenant. He read a lecture, after which he urged people to return to their "homeland," although without success—not one prisoner left.

So it went for several weeks. After that, those in the ROA were taken through the barbed wire and driven by a convoy of guards to the station for boarding.

A week later, the same thing happened to the Cossacks.

In southern France, there was a prisoner-of-war camp not far from Marseilles in the city of Montpellier. In it, besides Germans, there were about 200 prisoners from various nationalities of the USSR who had served in German units. Among them, not counting those who had hid the fact that they were Cossacks, there were about 40 Cossacks, mostly Don.

Cossacks were housed separately from the others.

All the same, in March of 1946, in the time after breakfast when most Cossacks were resting, Soviet officers came to their barracks: one was from the NKVD and wore a burka, the other wore a military uniform. The French commander of the camp and a sergeant came in with them. Both of them soon left.

The Soviet officers sat down at a table. The man from the NKVD was silent, but other Soviet, enlivening things with jokes and humor, spoke on about returning to the "homeland." He prepared a list in which he entered first and last names and the year and place of birth for everyone.

"Well! Go home now and live peacefully," he said on finishing his list.

A week later, the Cossacks were taken away to the USSR. Four managed to remain by announcing that they were Yugoslavs.

This was in mid-March.

It must be noted that every morning after the list was made, Russian Soviet patriots [*сов-патриаты*], a man and a woman who had long been living in France, came to the camp. They urged prisoners, especially Cossacks, to return to their homelands, but no one followed their call.

Besides the Pyrenees camp and the camp in Montpellier, there were other well known handovers from a camp in Toulouse ["*Тупузою*," probably a typographical mistake], from which up to 20 Cossacks were taken, and from a second camp in Marseilles—up to 50 people.

Testimony by Kuban Official, N. P. K., Pertaining to Times of Handovers

… June 22, 1946, I was transferred from a camp for Polish civilians in Barletta (in southern Italy) to the UNRRA camp in Bagnoli. In it, there were about 400 Russians and up to 700 Croats.

I met many acquaintances in that camp with whom I had worked in the past and got to know Major Ivanov, who was the editor of the Russian camp newspaper. There was a list of all the Russians and about half of the Croats in the camp.

On August 14th, at 2 o'clock in the evening, many English military transports came to the camp. No one slept that night. Groups gathered together to try to guess where we would be taken. One decided that it would be to the USSR, others—to some kind of labor. Women were especially worried.

Vehicles came up to the barracks and boarding began, ending at 5 o'clock in the morning.

They gave out food for three days and took us to a railroad station.

At 6:30 in the morning, the commander of the camp, Captain Sanson, arrived.

He was quickly surrounded by people yelling:

"Where are they taking us?"

Captain Sanson answered coldly:

"Go on! It will be better for you."

But his words did not soothe anybody and a cry went out:

"You are sending us to the Soviets!"

Hearing that, Sanson took off his headgear, crossed himself, and said:

"In no way to the Soviets!"

We boarded and the train went off. They went fast, stopping only at those stations where there was a change of personnel. In Rome, the train stopped at a siding for 12 minutes.

On the second day, that is, August 15, at 10 o'clock in the morning, our train began to back up onto a railroad siding that was lined on each side with barbed wire. English gendarmes armed with pistols and clubs stood behind it. There were as many of them, if not more, than there were of us. They had brought us to Rimini.

Where the train stopped, there was a commission of two English officers: an English captain and a lieutenant. They sat at a table.

Gendarmes brought us out one at a time to the table. There, old emigres were given a ticket with the letter "A" on it. For new ones, it was the letter "B." Those who received ticket "A" were taken aside, while those with letter "B" were put in motor vehicles. Every vehicle was surrounded by gendarmes. When it was fully loaded with people, four gendarmes took seats and it set off.

They brought us all to one of the cells that had up to ten rows of barbed wire stretched around it. Later, we learned that this was cell "4B"—for persons under investigation. Families were brought to cell "6," also enclosed in 10 rows of wire.

Before being put into a cell, each of us was searched thoroughly. Knives, razors, and food were taken away. Several pistols were found. After being searched, we were distributed into the cells.

In this way, we became prisoners of war and were treated as such.

Those who received an "A" ticket were that same day transferred to a civilian camp in the small settlement of Riccioni. adjoining Rimini.

Whether the cells were "4B" or "6," they had 10 rows of barbed wire stretched around them, with guards found within and outside them.

Five days later, we began to be called out individually to the English offices, where we were questioned by a Major Hills, who spoke Russian.

When this interrogation began, the younger people with us became upset, started to form groups, and prepared to escape. Even with all the barbed wire and the guards, several people managed to escape each night.

We were fed poorly in camp. People were half-starved.

During this interrogation, Major Hills suggested to everyone that they should return to their homeland, but there were no takers.

The interrogations and investigations continued for three-and-a-half months. During this time interval, we were called to Camp "*No. 3*," which held only Russians, Ukrainians, Kabardin, and a few other nationalities from Russia.

Because Major Ivanov, formerly in Camp "4B," had worked hard at learning Russian and became fairly proficient at it, on being transferred to *No. 3*, he was named the commander of the camp or, more correctly, of the offices of camps and cells.

Every day, he visited the English commandant's office. There, Major Hills promised him that those of us who were counted as civilians should definitely transfer to a military camp, since civilians might be turned over the the Soviets, while military personnel would be sent to work in England.

Every day, during evening roll calls, Major Ivanov urged us to be relisted as military.

I have already mentioned that it was during my presence at the camp in Bagnoli that I became acquainted with Major Ivanov. Here, we became friends. Since I was listed as a civilian, Major Ivanov was quick to advise me to be relisted as military. Our conversations about it rose to the level of major arguments. I remember that one time he chased me out of his office because I said in a discussion that I did not advise that prisoners relist from civilian to military and explained to him that the English were not to be believed, that they said one thing and did another, for which reason I recommended that he switch from military to civilian, but he replied:

"I was military. I am now military. Military I will stay and military I will die."

Colonel Lobisevich was in the camp for families, where his wife and son were also. He lived quietly. I cannot understand why, but 10-15 days before the handovers, Major Hills visited this camp and, through a priest, let Lobisevich know that he should leave the camp, even if only temporarily. Lobisevich did not take his advice. Neither did he listen to Hills's second warning, but on May 8th, he was taken away for handover to the Bolsheviks.

On May 7, the camp commander, Captain Samit, handed Major Ivanov a list of 135 men. He ordered that they be formed up and presented to him.

Returning to the camp, Ivanov gave a signal. People gathered at his office. He began a roll call. Everyone on the list appeared in person.

When they were in formation, a panic began in the camp. Several who were not on the list asked to be placed on it. Others offered to switch. On learning this, Captain Samit said that no changes to the list or substitutions would be allowed.

People stood in formation for over an hour, talking things over with one another. Many of those left off the list looked enviously at those on it, because they were being sent someplace.

I approached Major Ivanov. He was very concerned about not knowing what was going to happen. After calling the roll once more, he went to report to Captain Samit that everyone was ready.

The Captain heard him out. Since it was mealtime, he ordered that they be allowed to eat, but that at 2 o'clock they should be put back into formation.

In talking to the captain, Major Ivanov had said:

"My heart tells me that you are sending us off to the Soviets."

Captain Samit took his cross off, kissed it, and said:

"In no case will we give you to the Soviets."

Ivanov, a very religious man, believed the vow and the kissing of the cross. He returned to the formation in a good mood, stood before them, and happily announced that Captain Samit swore on a cross that no one would be handed over to the Soviets.

"Right now, break for lunch until 2 o'clock, but reform in the same place at 2 o'clock."

People dispersed. A few of us went with Ivanov to his office. When we began to discuss the possibilities of betrayal, the major did not want to listen to us and told us to leave his office.

There were 180 people in formation at 2 o'clock. Major Ivanov did another roll call and, by order of the English commandant, led them out through the camp fence.

Up to 200 English soldiers surrounded them and led them in the direction of cell "4B," in which we had all been earlier and which was close enough to our cell for us hear voices.

When they were in the cell, it was ordered that a list be made up of those who had been in our cell, with the number of their tent identified. The list was prepared and those beds were removed by evening.

This calmed people down. It was thought that they were being taken to England.

At 10 o'clock in the evening, we received an order from Captain Samit that we were to be given coffee at 3 o'clock in the morning. At 4, we would be put into motor vehicles.

Official N. P. K.

The End of the 3rd Reserve Regiment

> This account is by Cossack H., who served with Domanov's Field Ataman Group in Italy in the 3rd Reserve Regiment.

At the end of April, 1945, the 3rd Reserve Regiment, under the command of Colonel Lobisevich, consisted of 8 companies in excess of 2,500 men, mainly Kuban, with three guns. It was located in the city of Gemona, at which one company stayed at a fortress in Osoppo, one close to that one at the stockpiles of reserve ammunition, one along the Tagliamento River in the village of Pione, and half a company at the electrical station near Osoppo—at the village of Tarcento. The remaining companies and the three guns, were in Gemona. There were approximately 30 machine guns with the regiment. The companies in Osoppo and its surroundings were commanded by Captain O. (Stavropol). The companies around Gemona occupied a school in its northern part, on a mountain encompassing it at its north and northwest. In order to leave the city and connect with their stanitsas, some 25 kilometers away near Tolmezzo, a bridge had to be crossed, which required that they first cross the city, before turning to the north,

The brigade staff had been in Gemona, but on April 28, when things became complicated, it was no longer there. Only two officers, from the old emigration, were left: Sotnik V,, from France, and Sotnik K.

The entire staff of the Field Ataman Group was in Tolmezzo. Stanitsas with civilian populations were on its outskirts, while its military units were near the shores of the Adriatic Sea in the Udine-Trieste region.

On April 28th, several Cossacks from the companies staying in Gemona set off to a barbershop in the city, as was their custom. There, they were met by several partisans in red ties who attacked them, killing one of the Cossacks.

When news of this reached the regimental staff, armed Cossacks were sent into the city, but the partisans had already gone into hiding. The night passed peacefully. There were large numbers of bandits around the city, but they were poorly armed and feared Cossacks. It was obvious that they wanted only one thing—for the Cossacks to leave Gemona.

On April 29th, at the location of the companies at the school, two Italian nationals arrived with some person or other in an English uniform who called himself an Englishman. He asked the Cossacks to give up their weapons. Sotnick V. spoke with him in French. Speaking for the Cossacks, he announced that they would not surrender their weapons and that all of them should be allowed to pass though to their families in Covazzo without hindrance.

After more discussion, the Englishman agreed to this.

A heavy rain fell toward evening.

On April 30, the commander of the regiment, Colonel Lobisevich, did not leave Gemona, giving as his reasons the rain and the absence of means of transportation for the women, of whom there were some twenty there, mainly wives of officers. No matter how officers and Cossacks tried to convince Lobisevich that there was no time to lose, he remained inflexible.

The day passed quietly.

There was still a telephone connection to Domanov's staff, where it was obvious what the situation was in Gemona. From there they announced that Cossack artillery was being sent to meet Lobisevich's regiment and give it support.

Individuals coming to Gemona on foot were allowed by the partisans to pass through, but no one was allowed to leave.

That day, Captain O., who was in Osoppo, pulled out the companies at the stockpiles, the electrical station, and Pione and prepared to join up with Lobisevich before leaving Gemona.

However, having waited in vain until evening for Lobisevich, he left Gemona and broke through to Covazzo.

The rain continued on May 1st An Englishman appeared several times that day with propositions that weapons be surrendered. In allowing the Cossacks to leave Gemona, he guaranteed that none of the Cossacks would have anything bad done to them.

On May 2nd, he began to be more forceful, now requiring the surrender of weapons. This can be accounted for by Cossacks already moving north from Tolmezzo at that time, while combat units from the Udine-Trieste region were also leaving in the same direction and along a road that was visible to Cossacks in Gemona.

But the regimental commander, Colonel Lobisevich, still did not want to leave Gemona for some reason. None of his officers and Cossacks saw him. All negotiations were carried out by Sotnik V.

The situation remained unchanged on May 3rd. The companies lived off provisions in the stockpiles, receiving food twice a day.

In addition, the company staying at Tarcento (south of Gemona) under the command of Don Sotnik S., fortified their courtyard and did not let anyone in, firing at those who came near. Their commander did not enter into any kind of negotiations with Italians or Titoists. His order to the Cossacks was "Let no one in." When this became known in Gemona, he was ordered by an officer sent by the Italians to reconnect with the regiment.

On the 3rd or 4th of May, this regiment, in full preparedness, with weapons in their hands, was in Gemona.

Until this time, whenever it was suggested that they give up their weapons, Sotnik V. answered, with full the support of his Cossacks, that weapons would be turned over only to the English, when they reached there.

On May 4th, the same Englishman who had appeared before, once more required them to give up their weapons, making a stronger guarantee of their safety.

This time, after conferring among themselves, the Cossacks decided to give up their weapons, aside from pistols, and it was done.

An entire mountain of rifles, automatic weapons. and machine guns was created. Here, too, were the cannons. Italians and Titoists cheered. After being almost without weapons until then, they now had mass quantities of them,

On May 5th, pistols were turned in,

Searches and thefts began quickly. Baskets were filled with watches that had been appropriated. Announcing that some of the watches were Russian made had no effect—all were taken away. A lot of money was taken, for the officers and Cossacks had just been paid. A silver church utensil was stolen, Some Cossacks were undressed and had their footwear stolen.

Except for one Cossack who was struck on his neck because he did not want to give up his boots, no one was beaten; but all were treated rudely.

The robberies continued on May 6th. Whatever money had not already been taken was taken. Undressing and footwear removal continued.

V. and another officer advised Cossacks not to offer any resistance.

Especially thorough searches were made on May 7th. Officers and Cossacks were searched one at a time. Every last penny they had was removed.

Grain, cheese, and sugar that had been left in stockpiles were given away that day. Everyone received what was approximately a daily ration.

On May 8th, in the morning, everyone was formed up, another thorough search was carried out, and they were marched to the south. A single cart was allowed for the women.

The column was accompanied by 25 Italian nationals on bicycles.

It was a hot walk. After having gone some two kilometers from Tarcento, we stopped to rest.

When we got up from our halt, some 50-70 Titoists appeared. In the presence of the Italian convoy, they jumped the Cossacks and began robbing them, taking away clothes and shoes. The convoy

Forced Repatriations from France, Italy, and England

watched all this in silence. During it, two Cossacks were killed and one wounded.

The regiment's adjutant lost his mind as he watched it all. Some Englishmen who happened to be driving past took him and his wife and child to Udine, saying that he would be put into the hospital.

At the very moment of the Titoist atrocities and killings, a military vehicle appeared from the direction of Udine. It stopped, then left again.

Sotnik V. warned of the possibility that everyone would be turned over to the partisans in Udine: "Brothers. We may perish. Prepare for it!"

Traveling another kilometer and a half from the rest stop, about 18 kilometers still from Udine, the Cossacks saw some 40 English soldiers armed with automatic weapons at a settlement lying along the route. They stopped the column, put the Italian bicyclists in their vehicle and took them off to Udine. Then they surrounded the Cossacks, led them to an empty yard at the edge of the settlement, and fed them. About two hours later, they took them to Udine on civilian vehicles.

There, they unloaded at the large yard of a barrack which was already housing Cossacks and Germans. Knives and razors were taken away, then each man was questioned and put into the barrack.

They stayed in Udine for 5 or 6 days. They were fed very well, three times a day. There were rumors that all of them were to be moved into central Italy.

Either on the 14th or 15th of May, all the Cossacks (1150 men) were loaded into motor vehicles and taken through Venice to the city of Forli, 250-300 kilometers from Udine. There was an overnight stay in Venice. They stayed in Forli for two days.[*]

---

[*] **Note:** As has already been disclosed, the regiment had more than 2,500 men in total, but half of them left under the command of Major O., coming on April 30 from Osoppo to Covazzo in order to combine with the other units and stanitsas of the Cossachi Stan.

This was where Colonel Semyonov was, with the Varyag Regiment, composed of approximately 2000 men. This regiment was created from Russian volunteers.

The next day, they were told that they would be taken from there on the following day, while in the morning of the third day, we were separated into three parts:

Three hundred men with Colonel Lobisevich were taken away in the direction of Rome.

Four hundred men with Sotniks V. and K. and all the old emigrants, 40-50 in number, were taken to Ancona.

The rest—some unknown direction.

There was an immense tent camp in Ancona, holding approximately 50,000 people. There, the Cossacks were met by some sort of Jew in the uniform of an English officer, who asked if they might not be exhausted from being on the road.

The camp held soldiers of varying nationalities divided into separate groups. The Varyag Regiment, arriving in their footsteps, was located not too far in approximate distance to the newly arrived Cossacks.

The Cossacks stayed there several days.

On the third day, an officer in an English uniform who was familiar to them came to see them. He asked if they were not exhausted from being on the road. Then he asked:

"Who are you?"

"Kuban Cossacks."

"What units?"

"Reserve Cossack Regiment."

"Where is your regiment?"

"We don't know, but there are 400 of us here."

"You must go to Russia."

"We will not go to Russia."

After this discussion, he came back in the following days to repeat that the Cossacks had to go back to Russia,

The Cossacks prepared a petition addressed to the English Command. They said that they had fought against the Bolsheviks, had been tortured in Soviet prisons and exiled in that homeland, and in no way would they accept being under the authority of the Bolsheviks.

They read this petition to the officer who was urging them to go to their homeland. He became angry and shouted:

"I will throw you to the Germans!"

"Go ahead," the Cossacks answered.

And truly, he did move them into the German part of the camp and ordered them to line up there. Then, an English major approached in the company of a German commander who turned out to be an interpreter.

The major asked:

"Who are these people?"

"Kuban Cossacks of the Reserve Regiment."

"What do you want?"

"We don't know, but we do not want to go to Russia,"

He ordered that they be fed and once more asked whether they did not wish to return to their homeland.

The answer: "No we do not!"

Two days later, in the morning, all 400 men were ordered to form up. Old emigrants were called out. Some 40-50 men stepped out.

Then they were asked who wanted to go home.

After several hitches, 170 men stepped out. The rest announced that they would not go to Russia. Among them was the Cossacks relating this history.

After that, the old emigrants and those who agreed to go to their homeland were led off somewhere, leaving 196 men behind in the camp.

That very same officer came back on the third day, strongly guarded by about 50 men, to say:

"These are the ones who do not want to leave?"

He was answered, "Yes!"

Then they and 200 Germans were led to a pier in Ancona, about 12 kilometers from camp.

There were ships under foreign flags in the port. No Soviet ones were seen.

On the question of where they were being taken, "not to the Soviets?" the answer was that, no, but to southern Italy.

And so it was. Cossacks boarded one ship, Germans two others, and were taken south. After a day and a half, they arrived in Taranto. They were fed adequately on the way.

They debarked in Taranto and were led to rail cars. Some Jew drove up to them, took off the guards, and ordered that they be fed.

On the question of where they were being taken, he said to a camp.

A group of Titoist partisans were there.

After being loaded into railroad cars, they were held there until 12 o'clock at night. This was the 24th or 25th of May.

At two o'clock in the morning, they were taken to a station in Taranto. They stayed there in rail cars until the morning. At dawn, they disembarked.

Cossacks there who had wound up in the camp earlier told them that it was a Soviet camp. A Soviet flag flew over it. It had no guards of any kind.

The camp was about ten versts from the station.

The Cossacks were met by Major Goncharenko and with music on their arrival there.

Goncharenko told them that "their homeland had forgiven them everything."

On hearing those words, Cossacks asked about the millions who were tortured and perished in concentration camps, prisons, and exile …

There followed in answer the customary remarks of all having been forgiven.

The camp in Taranto held 12,000 men. They were exclusively Russian.

On their very first day there, Cossacks were disinfected and given excellent English outfits. They were given excellent food (lamb, wine). They were given money. Soldiers and Cossacks received 200 lira monthly, while officers got 600. They trained in formation. There were no guards, not even at the entrance.

There were rumors that not long before the arrival of the Cossacks, there was a ship with those being repatriated that was sent to Russia, but many started to jump overboard on the way. The English then turned it back.

They stayed in this camp for about a month.

Toward mid-June, it became clear that everyone would be taken from the camp to their homeland, although not by sea, but by a land route—across Italy and Austria.

That which took place at the end of May and the beginning of June in Lienz, of the trick capture of the officers and use of force against the Cossacks became known from individuals and groups of Cossacks brought there by the English.

Information about land transport across the area where there were many Cossacks left from the Lienz tragedies on the Drau encouraged the Cossacks. They saw hope of leaving along the way to join their own people.

And truly, over the dates of June 15-17, people began to be loaded on trains, 1,000-3,000 daily, and sent to Italy.

From the first train, Cossacks sent their scouts to the station to try to learn what the conditions were where people were being loading and sent off. They learned that there were no guards on the freight cars in which people were being transported, and that the cars were clean and provided with straw. This encouraged the Cossacks.

On June 23rd, with a send-off by Major Goncharenko and a military band, the Cossacks left. With them was a part of the Varyag Regiment.

Where the train could not pass due to tracks having been destroyed, they were switched to motor vehicles. The train was overseen by only 8 Englishmen, who fed the Cossacks very well: giving out dry rations and hot food at the stations. Cossacks were even given wine.

Buoyed by thoughts of the possibility of escape, they were all in good spirits.

They debarked at Forli. There was a camp there of Polish military units who willingly took in the Cossacks. Up to 100 men were received there.

On about the 25th of June, they arrived at Udine. There, they were fed and taken farther—to Gemona, where they were all taken off the train and driven in motor vehicles to the station in Tarvisio [*Тарвиз*], near the Austrian border. There, they were again loaded onto a train.

It was nighttime, but no one slept. They crossed the border and just before the station in Villach, many Cossacks started to jump from the train. No one prevented it.

Before Klagenfurt, my companion left the train, too, with the words of this narrative that I have written about the fate of the 3rd Reserve Regiment. Along with two Don Cossacks, after several days of wandering in unfamiliar places, he wound up in Camp Peggetz in Lienz, and from there reached where the Russian Corps was.

V Naumenko

From the Letter of Kuban Cossack, A. G. Denisenko

I met Lobisevich in a primitive camp near Venice. This took place in the middle of May (1947) when Lobisevich and Cossacks in his regiment were being moved by the English from northern Italy to the south.

The following day, we were put into trucks and taken somewhere. I was in the same truck as Lobisevich and his orderly.

All the men who had families were worrying along the way about what had become of the wives and children from whom they had become separated.

Heat, dusk, stuffiness; no food, no water! There was but one stop over the course of the entire day for 15 minutes in some small settlement point. We spent the night in a field alongside some Serbian volunteers in General Mushitsky's group.

We reached Forli in the morning. There, we met up with Semyonovists ("Varyag" Regiment).

Due to them, or it might have come from Lobisevich himself, thoughts began to arise of joining their regiment.

Colonel Lobisevich gathered the officers of his regiment together and told them more or less the following:

"I want to hear your thoughts about what we should do. Semyonovists are here. Let's ask the English to combine us with them. They are anti-Communists and do not want to return to their homeland, while we have been cut off from our main forces, so that there are few of us."

Lobisevich further explained that the English need not look at us as prisoners of war, since he, in the name of the regiment, had signed liaisons with Italian partisans and English officers before their "truce."

"Our regiments," he said, "could have created many unpleasantries for the English, but, having signed an agreement, we had, in fact, opened up the front for them.

"This is the paper that was signed by the English and Italians —"

If memory serves correctly, "this" document was signed with an indelible pencil [*химическим карандашем*] on a scrap of paper, approximately half a sheet.

"The English must take it seriously," Lobisevich continued. "We will put the question of this 'document' or refer to it and ask to be combined with Varyarg. If it comes to battle, we will present a much stronger force alongside them."

After these words, there were a few voices of approval, but also suggestions to "slap it around their brains [*пошлепать мозгами*]."

After further considering the question, it was established that the Varyag Regiment was an SS formation, which the English looked upon as the Fuehrer's personal guard. For this reason, combining with them might be putting us in a difficult situation.

It was decided that we not ask to be combined with the Semyonovists, but to present the "document" that Lobisevich held to the English, as it might result in some kind of change for the better for us.

A "declaration" addressed to the English Command was prepared. In it, Cossackdom's indigenous democracy was underlined and why we had been with the Germans was explained: because we were anti-Bolsheviks. Referring to that paper which Lobisevich called a "truce," we told of our loyalty and friendship toward the Allies, which went all the way back to 1914 and the Civil War.

We wrote it, read it, signed it, and dispersed to tell the Cossacks about it, naively thinking that we had made a step toward the improvement of our situation.

Among other things, the simple circumstance that we were being given English rations was to many an indication of special attention from the English.

We never got the chance to present out "document" or the "truce," for about an hour after our meeting ended, a group of women arrived at the camp. They turned out to be Cossacks who had been separated from their husbands.

Lobisevich and some others, learning that their wives were in the very same camp, went in a group to the English to ask if they could join them. That "valuable truce document" left along with Lobisevich.

Of the senior officers, only some sotnik was left with us.

Two days later, we were taken to Ancona.

(As has been told in the article, "The End of the 3rd Reserve Regiment," the regiment was divided into three parts at Forli. The article also gave particulars regarding one of those parts, of 400 men, among whom were 40-50 old emigrants. Editor.)

We spent the night in Ancona, but we were formed up in the morning and led out of the camp. An American major addressed us there in Russian and suggested that all those who had lived in various countries outside of the USSR before the war remain there to join the group of nationals from which countries they had lived.

There was a division, the "Eugene Savoysky [*Евгения Савойского*]," in camp that was made up of German volunteer residents of Yugoslavia. There were also small groups of Serbs and Slovenes and a group of Croats.

Twenty of us stayed, including five men who had been under the Soviets, but who could show that they were old emigrants.

I met Lobisevich some nine months later. It was at Camp Bari, to which he had been brought from Riccione for a final breakdown into categories.

A train rolled up behind the barbed wire. We were surrounded by Englishmen with clubs.

An English commission of officers had us pass through one at a time. Depending on what kind of papers one had, all those belonging to letter "B" were kept in the prisoner-of-war camp, while those with letter "A" were sent to the train and taken to a camp for civilians.

Lobisevich stayed at Riccione, while I went to Reggio Emilia, along with my son, for whom I had searched all over Italy for 8 months.

Those left at Riccione (a settlement close to Rimini) were sorted [*сартировали*] in several ways. Not too long before being handed over, Lobisevich was sent to the hospital. He stayed there without any kind of supervision whatever. He could have fled at any time just by simply and quietly walking away, but he made no use of that. Returning to the camp, he explained:

"The English sent me to the hospital on purpose. They wanted one more time to impress on me that I could believe that I would soon receive command of a regiment."

Such thoughts made his young parachutist wife burst out [*разражали*] with expressions [*раздражалась*] of the most obscene profanity.

Some sort of darkness of thought [*затмение*] befell not only Lobisevich, but many others also.

Here, Kuban Cossack, A. G. D., states in an interesting account that several Russian priests who had accepted the primacy of the Pope of Rome (Vatican [*Руссиком*]) knew of the coming betrayal, but did nothing to warn anybody.

In the beginning of May, 1947, he was the senior of a group of Russians in a civilian camp close to Rome. Having a lively interest in the fate of his compatriots, he was often in Rome, where one day a woman who had also accepted the primacy of the Pope, came up to him in the street and said:

"'I know that you are concerned about Russians. For this reason, I want to tell you that today a priest came to the camp in Riccione and said that Russian prisoners would be turned over to the Soviets.'

"'What priest?'

"The woman gave his name, but I can no longer remember it: Vladimir? Vsevolod?

"'Who did he talk to and where?'

"'Father Phillip in the Vatican.'

"'You are not mistaken?'

"'I will swear on the cross to it being true.'

"What was there to do?

"My friends and I had blood ties to the group sitting in Riccione. In case of a need to flee, we had prepared a place of refuge with the Serbs. I personally created instructions for making systematic escapes in groups of three or four people. These instructions had been sent a month to a month-and-a-half before the day of the betrayal of Major Ivanov and others, but they refused to run."

Major Ivanov was a former officer in the Red Army. Ivanov is not his real name. Until the moment of betrayal, he was senior in rank of those sections or cells from which the handover of May 8, 1947, was carried out. He sincerely believed the oath and cross kissing of the English officer, did not allow even a thought of betrayal, and turned out to have been the victim of his own gullibility.

"Having received information that the handover was known by the Jesuits," A. G. D. continues, "I got together with two friends and decided that one of us had to go to Riccione right away. We did so. The meeting with Ivanov and others took place in a settlement in the house of an Armenian."

They took the information on the coming betrayal as being little more than "the imaginings of old ladies" and decisively refused to run.

Blind faith in the oath of an English officer caused their end.

In connection with the Vatican, it remains to mention another fact.

"When the handovers began, that is, May 7, the priest, Father V. Roshkom, living in Camp '6,' was told by English camp authorities that he would be called to the English Staff headquarters in Padua on the morning of May 8th at 9 o'clock. The priest believed this and left the camp on the morning of May 8th. He was detained by the English in Riccione. They kept him in a separate room for as long as it took to carry out the operation needed for the handover. On the morning of May 9th, they apologized for detaining him and released him."

[The original does not make it clear by its punctuation who the speaker of this passage is, but it does not take a leap of faith to assume that A G D and A Denisenko are one and the same, obviating my attempt at proper punctuation.]

This incident brought forth a lot of interpretation and guessing in the camp. Some saw it to be some sort of maneuver by the Vatican, others that the English feared that the presence of a priest in the camp could enable the Russians to embody religious manifestations in their suffering.

In camps Riccione-Rimini at the time of the handovers, Russian groups were composed of 70% Don Cossack, 15% Kuban—the other 15% non-Cossack.

The attitude toward Cossacks, as from the side of the English, so, too, from the Italian, was as with enemies, the reason being the exaggerated and overblown accounts of "Cossack atrocities" during their presence in northern Italy.

A. Denisenko.

Forced Turnovers of Russians to the Soviets

On May 8, 1947, the English military command in Italy carried out a series of orchestrated **forced handovers** from concentration camps in Rimini. On the same day, a handover of Russians was carried out from an American camp in Pisa.

The entire region of concentration camps in Rimini, along with those settlements of Riccione contiguous with it, was cordoned off and patrolled by military forces.

The Italian residents were forbidden all movement along its streets and roads. They were told that major Fascists and war criminal were being handed over to the Soviets.

Still, it its widely and reliably known that there were concentrated within these camps, in various numbers and under various guises, all prior Soviet citizens from neighboring DP camps in Italy. Among them were women, children, the elderly, adolescents, physicians, skilled workers, engineers, an insignificant number of soldiers, and, in total, all of 4-5 officers of middle rank who never held any political views.

In all, 300 men had been prepared for handover over the two camps, of whom only 200 were transported to Bologna before being marched farther. The remaining 100 perished in part by suicide, in part killed by military guards in mass attempts at resistance. Only individuals managed to escape. About 30-40 English and American soldiers and officers were killed or wounded during this capture of 300 unarmed men by an English battalion and American infantry and motorcyclists armed with machine guns and automatic weapons.

The general picture of the handovers was seen from the sidelines by official representatives of four countries: America, England, France, and the Soviet Union.

The people of various nationalities left in camp at Rimini flew black flags over it as a mark of mourning and dedicated a group grave over which the number 197 (the number handed over from that camp) was written. All of them boycotted their camp's English command.

Preparations for the Handovers

Taking into account experiences in Dachau, Plattling, and other forcible actions, the English command went this time for a broad plan of mass deception with strictly calculated details.

Preparation for the handovers took more than year. Italians began endless interrogations, registrations, searches, and such in all the DP camps with the aim of detecting former Soviet citizens during the spring of the last year. To this end, they attracted a suitably wide net of informers. The information received weighed considerably in determining the fate of those who were discovered. Simultaneously, a campaign was launched to calm the refugees and assure them that they were completely safe.

English officers, representing allied commissions (for example, Major Simcock was among that number), often swore in the DP camps on the honor of an English officer that there would be no kind of forced return to homelands.

When their goal was achieved and the English command managed to more or less identify individuals who had been Soviet citizens prior to the war and had concentrated them into a single camp (Bologna), the sequence of prepared steps was unwound.

On August 14, 1946, the entire camp in Bologna was removed under false pretenses and sent to the prisoner-of-war camp, where, using lists prepared in advance, all former Soviet citizens, including women, children, the elderly, and the adolescent were put behind barbed wire that was reinforced by guards. People were put into canvas military tents, where they spent the winter in freezing weather that reached as low as 25° Fahrenheit.

Subsequently, a significant amount of more time was required in order to calm the masses. Outbursts of indignation and desperation were so strong that the English command needed to put into effect a series of measures in justification of their actions. Mainly among them were:

1—People were informed that it was being done with the goal of safeguarding refugees from being harassed by the Soviets. Now found in a prisoner-of-war camp, the refugees were under the protection of the English Army, and no one had a right to interfere with the fate of their contingent.

2—It was likewise announced that there were individual mistakes in the lists of names, so that many of them would be freed as soon as a safe place could be prepared for them in another civilian camp.

This calmed people in several ways, and the command instituted further measures to instill in the refugees a trust in their "protectors." Independent Russian groups along the examples of those of other nationalities were begun. Certain indulgences (passes to individuals to go into town, marks of trust, and others) were allowed. Most importantly, a whole series of individual and general guarantees were given that they would not be turned over to the Soviets and that the emigrants of the camp were first in line because they had greater needs than the others.

After every escape from the camp, Captain Samit made solemn announcements to the entire camp and publicly gave the word of an English officer that no one would ever be turned over.

Major Hills, who began to work in the camp beginning in August, 1946, took on for his task the establishment of personal spiritual contacts* with people (in the main, with those having an influence with the masses) and repeatedly announced to Russian individuals in authority that turnovers would not take place. He even promised to warn the Russians if for some reason things changed for the worse. By this, the Major succeeded in creating trust in him, and he stopped at nothing to reinforce that impression with every day.

---

* **Note:** In one of his letters, Kuban Cossack D. writes: "Regardless of the notorious friendship between Major Hills and Ivanov, about two months before the betrayal, Hills began to avoid meeting with Ivanov and did not visit him. From March 9 to April 8, Ivanov was in the hospital. On the 14th, running into him accidentally, Hills only asked about his health. Such behavior by Hills could only mean that he, knowing of the coming betrayal, wished to save whatever remained of his conscience from excessive torment.

The result—ONLY THOSE WHO BELIEVED MAJOR HILLS DID NOT TRY TO FLEE FROM THE CAMP.

Not long before betrayal, Major Hills made a promise to all the Russians in the camp that they would be taken to Argentina at the first possible chance.

Analogous announcements were made before the entire camp by the commander of the camp, Colonel Myren [*Мэрэн*, possibly Marin?].

In the middle of the month of April in 1947, a spokesperson for the English embassy made an official announcement to the Vatican that no one from Italy would be turned over by Allied forces.

Russian people are gullible. There is no place for lies in their concept of honor. So, it is not surprising that, having such reassurances based on HONOR plus the reassurances out of the broad plan that were made repeatedly by high officials before the world court of public opinion, they turned up in a trap. Russian people did not at first understand all the monstrous lies that put them face-to-face with death.

The Operation Carried Out

On the 7th of May, Captain Samit brought a list of 185 names to the "bachelor" camp and advised those people to prepare to move to a different section for evacuation from Rimini. Clearly wishing to keep people calm, he suggested that they take their things and all available beds and pallets. People calmly moved to the indicated section.

On the night of the 8th, a special exit was prepared in the structure of this section by the English command, a solid chain of guards was put in place, and a search was carried out, during which all possible cutting instruments were taken away, down to bottles and tin cans. At the same time, English clothing was taken away and replaced by German.

Along the entire way, adjoining settlements and train stations were surrounded by English forces and a battalion of Italian carabineers. At stations, there were groups of fifteen men each from a battalion of English shock troops that had earlier earned fame in similar types of operations. With automatic weapons at the ready, they stood in lanes through which people were unloaded from vehicles and led along a street that was alive with automatic weapons to the car in which the arrests were made. Only there did it become clear to people that they had been fooled and were going to be given over to the Soviets.

Loading ended about noon. Only after this were rail cars connected one at a time to the rest of the consist where the guards were, which transported them in its turn in the direction of Bologna.

The following occurrences took place:

1—During loading from motor vehicles to prison cars, Alexander Kristalevsky, 25 years old, broke free, picked up a large rock, and hit an English soldier with it in an attempt to make use of the resulting breach in the chain of men to escape. However, on realizing its impossibility, he struck himself in the temple and ended his life in that way.

2—Paul Rodin, 33 years old, wrested an automatic weapon from an English soldier and attempted to shoot himself with it, but it did not fire, so he then tried to break a path through to freedom with its butt, injuring several English soldiers. He broke through the first chain of guards and was shot there.

3—Bikadorov, father and son, Vladimir, 57 years old, and Nikolai, 22 years old, obviously after having agreed on a plan while in transit in the vehicle, made an attempt together. The father, trying to save the son, jumped from the side of the vehicle onto the chain of British soldiers and knocked several of them off their feet, causing a breach. The son jumped through this breach, but was shot there. The father was thrown unconscious back into the truck.

4—Anatoly Ivanov (in other version, Yemanov), 27 years old, wrested an automatic weapon from a soldier and started firing to make himself a path. He was killed in the ensuing melee.

5—Dr. Kurzakhiya [Курзахия] poisoned himself on hearing of the betrayal.*

---

* **Note:** By other accounts, Dr, Kurzakhiya was never transferred. Learning of the

6—There were 12 men with families among those to be handed over. On being loaded into the rail cars, women and children were forcibly separated from husbands, sons, and brothers. The aged mother of Ivan Korobko, who had accidentally come across her son in Italy after the war, begged that she be permitted to share her son's fate as he was about to be handed over. They tore her away from her son forever.**

After the betrayals, Major Hills bragged that he had managed to save women and children. By this cynical pronouncement he wanted to place a thin candle in front of his own conscience and justify himself before those still remaining among the living.***

The solitary rail cars of the condemned converged on the station in Bologna where about 100 men were added to them from the American camp in Pisa. Exact information or details on what occurred there is not yet available. It was so strongly guarded that not a single extraneous observer could get close enough to see everything. Still, we can establish with full credibility the following:

In that number given over, was the former senior officer in the group of Russians in the camp, a certain Paul Petrovich Ivanov. This person believed up to the final betrayal in the honor of the English officers who guaranteed the safety of those in the camps. Shortly before the betrayal, friends from neighboring camps urged

---

coming betrayal, he simulated an acute attack of appendicitis, was operated upon immediately, and was not turned over.

** According to other accounts—at noon, Samit took the ill Gregory Kalenichenko away from the neighborhood of camp "*No 7*" without allowing him to take his things.

At one o'clock in the afternoon, he arrived at camp "*No 6*" and removed 11 men with their families. Putting them in separate chambers, Major Hills told them that heads of families would not be turned over to the USSR. Soldiers conducted a search, taking away all that could possibly cause death or injury. These 12 men were given over to Bolsheviks.

***A little later, Major Hills called in N. I. and M., to whom he reported: "Your friends were handed over to the USSR. When the Soviet Union requires 400, I cannot send 20. How sad for Ivanov—he was a good commander. His family remains."

him to flee. He refused, announcing that he believed the English Command and would remain honest in his dealings with it.

It is said that it was only at Bologna that he finally understood that he and all the Russians had been fooled. He reacted boldly and decisively. Choosing the moment, he called people to insurrection. The unarmed mass of the condemned attacked their guards, disarmed some of their soldiers and officers, and entered into their final battle for their right to live. About 100 Russians perished in its final spasms. P. P. Ivanov himself, seeing no way out of the situation, committed suicide, cutting his veins, then his throat with a tin can. Those who survived, were transported farther.

It cannot be determined how many people actually were successfully brought to the Soviet butchers. Judging on the strength of the resistance and the conviction of the people—not a single one.

However, no one knows what sorts of things the people involved in the details of transportation were capable of.

The events described were provided by a driver who watched the scene from the side as he waited in his vehicle. There were individuals there, too, who managed to escape, but no details have yet been obtained from them.

Sequential Events

Two days after the turnovers, Lieutenant Colonel Martin appeared in camp in Rimini and made an ambiguous announcement, saying that he had been ORDERED TO CONSIDER those who remained to be civilians, but also twice emphasizing that he CONSIDERED ALL OF THEM TO BE SOVIET CITIZENS.

Major Hills once more guaranteed the safety of those remaining and swore to it in the name of an English officer.

The English Command made soothing announcements in all of the DP camps, saying that the turnover that had been carried out was of major war criminals.[*] Still, the entire Russian population in

---

[*] **Note:** The sketches that follow about several of those turned over in Rimini on May 8, 1947, refute the contention that those turned over were "major war

Italy knew those who were turned over. They again realized that the meaning of WAR CRIMINAL, much like ENEMY OF THE PEOPLE under the Soviets, was nothing more than a sobriquet that could be attached to any individual by the Soviets. It is perfectly clear that all who were Soviet citizens before the war were taken without a word to the Soviets in the category of war criminal. It is also perfectly clear that the English Command that presently controls the fate of Russian refugees fully shares the Soviet point of view.

The population of the camp was alarmed and upset. Mass despair and hopelessness, absolute lack of trust in the administrators of the camps, and a complete absence of support, made life unbearable for the refugees. They were ready to make any kind of sacrifice, even death, just to break away from the camps, leave the constant falsity of their protectors behind, and run off into the sunset. Worse still, the general situation in Italy was such that their last possible escape exit had been deliberately closed.

---

criminals."

Kovalev, Peter Antonovich—Born in 1928. He never served in any army. He was sent to the Soviet Union most likely because his father was on the list for forcible repatriations. (He left Russia when he was a 14-year-old boy.)

Azhnakhin, Ivan—Born in 1927. Due to being under age, he never served in the military.

Podorozhny, Peter—43 years old. He worked his entire life at a railroad depot as a skilled mechanic. When the Germans withdrew from Russia, he was taken under compulsion for similar work in Germany. He was never in the military.

Nikolaenko, Grigory Petrovich—He was never in military service. He was engaged in beekeeping in Russia, serving as a salesman. He was abducted by the Germans as a worker, s.-kh [: *c.-x*] (farm laborer.)

Murzin, Ivan—25 years old. He did not serve in the Red Army because he was in prison at the beginning of the war, sentenced to 10 years for anti-Soviet speech. He never served in the German Army.

This list could have been continued, but enough has been presented to challenge the assertion by the English about having turned over to the Soviet Union only those individuals who undeniably fell under one the categories of the Yalta Agreement.

This is a lie!   *New Russian Word* [*Новое Русское Слово*] June 19, 1947.

At one time during the betrayals, a small contingent of refugees was concentrated in Rome. They usually counted on their proximity to the Vatican and the Pope to protect them in case of danger. Then the Allies began to act in concert with Italian police to capture to a man every refugee not having documents or behaving suspiciously—or who was named by the Soviets. It was perfectly clear that their aim, first off, was to get those individuals who had been spared to that point from being turned over, secondly, to close off any chance for escape by those remaining in the camps, and thirdly, to prepare the next contingent for being handed over.

Bologna, Italy. May 16, 1947 **Fugitive**

After the Rimini Handovers

A.—The visit to the camp by the priest, Father Phillip.

On May 9, in the morning, a priest came to our camp. His name was Father Fillip. He went into the tent where our senior officer had his office. People gathered around. This priest became agitated to the point of almost losing his mind by what the English had done—turned over Russian people. He began to plaintively tell us:

"Know this, brothers! List yourselves somehow as old emigrants, or else they will give you up, for I know how the English are. They will kiss the cross before you, then betray you. How can you believe them? Even if they say so, do not believe them, brothers … !"

The priest said that and went away. We were left with troubled spirits …

From the story by Kuban Cossack L., who lived through the betrayal in Rimini.

B.—Symbolic Grave

On the 9th (May) in 1947, a symbolic grave with a black border around the black numbers, "7-5, 1947," was dug in the camp, with "185" written on its slope. A cross was set up with icons and mourning flags, a St Andrews and a tri-color with the letters "ROA." Passersby stop at the grave. A German lieutenant, with tears in his eyes, raises his hand to his visor in salute. General human sorrow … For several days, Russians do not go out to work and throw almost all of their food away. Every night, there are escapes from camp …

From the article by A. Denisenko, "Inspired by the Lord."

… A sorrowful face of Christ looks out from a small icon, all-knowing, all-seeing there … to the east … He, too, was betrayed …

From the article, "They were 185," Rimini [*Рим.*, possibly Rome] *Russian Life*.

… on the day of the 14th, Major Lynch arrived and ordered that all flags be removed from the grave. He cited an order by the English Command, pursuant to which all emblems but for the English flag were forbidden within the territories of the camps.

But, from the time of the formation of the camp of the Russian group in Rimini, on the "Russian Street," that is, the path along which the tents stretched, at the entrance to the first tent (the group's administration), there had been laid out on the ground a large, double-headed eagle cut from tin and a shield with slanting stripes of white, blue, and red, on which were the letters, "ROA."

From the letter of **A. G. D.**

On Handovers in Italy

(Incidents concerning the Serbian, General Mushitsky, and his regiment, "Varyag.")

1. It has been written above that after the interrogation of the 3rd Reserve Regiment of the Cossachi Stan, during its withdrawal to the south from the city of Gemona, it spent one night with the Serbian volunteers of General Mushitsky. He also became a victim of English betrayal. Below is how one of the Kuban Cossacks describes it.

... Finding General Konstantin [*Косте*] Mushitsky in our camp—Rimini—we proposed to his aide that we organize an escape.

"'Our hosts are so dishonest, that I would have accepted your offer but for the fact that I have received an assurance that there are no threats to me and that I will return to my Sumadians [*шумадийцам*],'" was his answer.

On January 6, Christmas Eve, the general paid us a visit.

Even though we met him daily, we never saw such liveliness in him before.

About 20 minutes after he left us, his roommate, Chetnik Voivode Yevshevich, came to us.

"I was supposed to give you my greetings for our great holiday," he said, "but I must give you some bad news. Russian brothers! Our mutual friend, General Mushitsky, has just been arrested and turned over to Tito. We were celebrating the holiday with our people. Then an officer and soldiers arrived with bayonets at the ready ..."

The general's last words had been:

"Long live the King!"

Leading the arrest was Captain Samit, who two months before had given his word as an English officer that there would be no use of force.

2. The "Varyag" Regiment, having in its complement Russian prisoners of war and Russian volunteers, was moved after the German surrender to a camp in southern Italy in the city of Taranto.

English officers repeatedly assured the commander of the regiment, Colonel Semyonov, that his regiment would not be imprisoned in a Bolshevik camp. The last such assurance was given to him only 8 kilometers from Taranto, where there was a large camp in which Bolsheviks stockpiled former Soviet citizens for repatriation to the USSR.

That is precisely where the English brought the officers and men of the "Varyag."

Colonel Semyonov protested and tried to get them out of that camp. The next morning, he was called on by an English officer who was accompanied by a Soviet commissar. The latter warned the Englishman in a whisper to be careful, because "they" understand English.

Semyonov repeated his request to take the regiment out of the camp.

The Englishman listened to him and agreed, saying that the regiment would be moved to a different camp the next day, but the commissar announced that he needed to remove them quickly, for "Varyag" soldiers spread propaganda among the others in the camp.

The Englishman asked how old emigrants could be separated from the new if they had no documents.

The commissar answered that he could distinguish between them even without documents, He asked that the regiment be put into formation and have its old emigrants called out.

Semyonov did so. About 200 men stepped forward.

The commissar approached and looking intently into the eyes of the man on the right flank, asked where he was from.

He answered confidently that he was from Belgrade.

"Where from?" the commissar repeated, staring directly at the man being questioned.

The latter answered, but less confidently, "From Belgrade."

"Where?" the commissar asked again more intensely.

"From Rostov," was the answer.

Catching two or three others in the same way, the commissar addressed those standing before him, telling the new emigrants to step back.

"All the same, I will figure out who is from where," he added.

After these words, only old immigrants were left standing in formation and even of those, only two or three could withstand the Chekist's stare.

After that, he turned to the Englishman and said:

"As you can see—I don't need no documents!"

Colonel Semyonov notes that under the fierce gaze of the Chekist, people truly were lost.

From the book by **V. N.**

The Cessation of Forcible Handovers from Italy

Thanks to the energy of the more activist Russians who had lived through the tragic days of betrayal in Italy, what took place in Rimini and Bologna was revealed in England in only a few days.

A compatriot of mine who has lived in London since 1920, the Cossack, A. V. Baikalov, a journalist and author who established strong and lasting ties over his life in England, brought his formidable energy to bear on bringing to the attention of the British establishment and society what took place in Italy.

Very soon after receiving the initial accounts of the handovers in Rimini, he gave them prominence in the committees of the Duchess of Atholl and Lord Beveridge, who quickly took steps to prevent the repetition of the events he detailed.

A Labour Party Member of Parliament [Peter] Stokes, posed an enquiry to the Government and Parliament for an explanation of all the circumstances of the events in Italy and a promise that similar occurrences would not be repeated in the future. Like Stokes, so too did several other Members of Parliament. Similarly, the committees of the Duchess of Atholl and Lord Beveridge began a campaign to prevent further handovers from Italy. Similar campaigns to wake the consciences of their countries and prevent their governments from criminal forced repatriations of people to the Soviets were raised by the press in England, America, France, Belgium, and several other countries.

As is demonstrated below, this work was not futile. Handovers ceased.

The Russian press at that time noted only one instance of forcible seizures, that of six old emigrants from a camp in Barletta on the night of July 18, 1947.

After thorough searches and the confiscation of anything that might be used for suicide, those people were sent under heavy guard in an unknown direction. Nothing is known of their further fate.

V. Naumenko

A List of Those Turned Over from Rimini (Riccione) on May 8, 1947

On reporting on the events in Rimini, A. G. Denisenko adds that it was impossible to establish the names of all those turned over.

He only gives the family names for some of the Cossacks, those that he could establish:

From camp (cell) "4B"

Don Cossacks:
Shcherbakov, Peter; Kardaylov; Nosov, Nokolai; Sokolov; Fyodorov; Matveev; Belikov, Alexander; Borodachye, Semyon; Tchebotarev, Grigory; Koldanov, Valdimir; Kovalev, Anton (father); Kovalev, Peter (son); Shapkin, Saveleev; Adov, Alexei; Pikhovkin, I. I.; Bogachev, Ivan; Petrovsky; Govorov, Ivan; Bikadarov, Vladimir (father).

Kuban Cossacks:
Lunev, Dmitry; Sidorets, Stepan; Bereznev, Grigory.

Terek Cossacks:
Podorozhny, Peter Ivanovich.

Given over from the family camp:
Colonel Lobisevich—Don Cossack; Kipa—Kuban Cossack; Godun, Eugene—Kuban Cossack; Korobka, Ivan—Kuban Cossack.

The 20th Century was Horrible

This was first published in the journal, *The Hourly* [*Часовой*] *No 7*, in 1948. It was reprinted in several journals and newspapers.

A search to find its author did not meet with success—he did not respond.

The item is reprinted from the newspaper, *Fires, No 30/393*, February 7, 1948 —Salzburg.

Soviet trucks, tightly enclosed in a circle of small tanks and motorcycles, were waiting at the gates of the huge camp. The inhuman ceremony of forced repatriation "to the homeland" of former prisoners of war had already been completed. About 80 people had been given over, mainly Cossacks, who stood in a tight bunch in the middle of the square, surrounded by English soldiers.

From every direction, steel gleamed, harsh and threatening. The faces of the Englishmen were gloomy and angry. Some were bloodied. They had just been forced to withstand a battle with the most indomitable of Cossacks, who had quickly guessed that the command for "departure to Scotland for work" was a trick and a trap. But their resistance was already broken. To the left of those being handed over, several lifeless figures could be seen covered with canvas on stretchers—corpses of suicides. Groans and wheezes could still be heard from other stretchers—these were those wounded during the resistance and those who preferred cutting into their own veins and throats over a forced return to the Soviet "paradise."

The English were firm. They wanted to turn over all "traitors to their homeland," meaning those who at the beginning of war had not wished to fight for Soviet power and Stalin and had voluntarily surrendered. Now they were being called for by the Soviets based on the precise terms of the Yalta Agreement, and the English turned over to them all those, living, dead, or dying, who were on a predetermined list. An order is an order …

The silent group of almost two thousand Russian "DPs" made a tight circle around those who were doomed. Men looked down at the ground, avoiding the glances of their unfortunate compatriots. Tears flowed down women's cheeks. Children cried quietly.

Those being turned over stood in a silent wall. These were all people in the bloom of their lives, made known to the Soviets based on information from spies as implacable foes of Communism. Each of their wrists were handcuffed. Many of them were severely beaten in the show of force. Several of the wounded leaned weakly on the shoulders of their comrades.

The final minutes before being put into Soviet trucks were passed in being inspected by the party.

A fat, pleased, Soviet colonel with crimson bands, in the MGB forces, began to call out names. No one answered to them. Grim glances sullenly followed his movements. Then the colonel, with a gesture of annoyance, began simply to count everyone—living, dead, or wounded ... In the end, he finished his count. English soldiers began to stir by the gates through the barbed wire.

Then, a Cossack stepped out unexpectedly from the formation. His black beard had thick clots of blood. English bayonets bent threateningly toward him, but he did not pay them any attention.

"Brothers!" he called out loudly, turning to face the formation. His voice carried over the entire silenced square. Thousands of eyes turned on him.

"Brothers ... Let us perform a final memorial service for our souls before we die. No matter what, there is death ahead ..."

"What did he say?" the head of the camp, a polished, dry English major, asked tensely, turning to his interpreter. A young man with a pale face in the uniform of a sergeant answered in a weak voice:

"They wish to perform a memorial service ... a requiem before death ..."

"Requiem?" the major asked. "For whom?"

"For themselves," the interpreter quietly let drop, turning away so as not to look directly at his superior's face.

The major frowned grimly, but signaled to the soldiers not to touch the Cossack who had stepped out of the ranks ... And he crossed himself with difficulty, for both of his hands were cuffed, slowly bowed his disheveled head before his comrades, then looked around the frozen rows of pale faces with his austere gaze.

Everything died down on the square. The Soviet colonel wanted to say something to the major, but he, breaking off his gaze from the Cossack's bloody beard, made a dismissive gesture.

The Cossack straightened and suddenly began with a strengthened voice:

"Blessed art Thou our God ... Always, now, and ever and unto the ages of ages ... Amen."

The entire square answered—an unseen, harmonious choir gasped into life.

"God have mercy."

The Cossack had obviously forgotten the words of the service. Or, possibly, he was too shaken up by what had taken place to remember the solemn, heavy words of farewell of the living with the dead. The he recited "Our Father" and again raising his frightful, bloody, disheveled head, voiced with indescribable sorrow:

"In blissful endeavor, give eternal peace, o Lord, to Thy servant departed ..."

For a second, he faltered, went silent, but then quietly added, again casting his glances over the pale faces of the condemned.

"Our names, You, o Lord, knowest."

As if on command, all of the "traitors to their homeland" and the two thousand people around them fell to their knees along with him. Only the English soldiers uncertainly lowering their bayonets and a group of officers were left standing before the kneeling crowd. Soviet tank crews stuck their heads out through the hatches of their vehicles,

And from the square flowed the mournful music of the final song of the penetrating Russian service:

"With holy peace ..."

The melody grew and broadened. Through that final prayer flowed the spiritual grief of the thousands of Russians. Thousands of faces turned to the heavens, to the bright Italian sky, in a display of faith and hope ...

Chanting rang out even louder and more powerfully. A canvas that had been thrown over one of the stretchers moved and a leathery face showing the sufferings of death appeared at its edge. A bright smile crawled across blue, twisted lips ...

The English major again asked something of the interpreter and, in an unexpected gesture, took of his cap. Several English soldiers, probably unexpectedly to themselves, saluted the kneeling crowd with their rifles,

The sorrowful prayers ended. All arose from their knees and crossed themselves.

The bloodied Cossack proudly raise his head to shout defiantly to the Soviet colonel:

"Well! Do your work of Cain on us now! Lead on! Let's go boys ..."

And, raising his voice, shouted to the crowd:

[There is apparently missing text here] more for our souls. We are all united in Russian truth and will not be drowned in blood ..."

Everyone bared their heads as if before a funeral procession ...

Once more, the major bowed to his interpreter and, turning around on hearing the answer, was heard to mutter:

"Damned dirty politics!"

With a happy face, the Soviet colonel stretched his hand out to him in farewell, but the Englishman made no sign of noticing. His face was grim and stern. His amber tobacco pipe made a noise from being bitten through by his convulsively pressed teeth.

The people condemned to death were surrounded by NKVD forces and went quietly into the trucks. Soviet soldiers, understanding the meaning of what had happened in that scene, tried to avoid their eyes, knowing so well what awaited them.

Depressing silence ruled the camp. The English soldiers stood with heads bowed. The neighboring Polish camp flew mourning flags over its gate.

Motors rumbled and the road emptied after several minutes. But in the air, it seemed that the last melody, "Eternal Memory," had not yet died out, and, with spirits saddened, people tried not to look at one another as they dispersed.

B.S.

Letter from Protopresbyter Father Michael Polsky
June 9, 1959

Much-esteemed and dear
Vyacheslav Grigoriyevich

The administrators of the Russian colony in London, at the request of the English officer-interpreter of the camp, commanded me to the camp to conduct a church service.

The camp was large, having 40 Soviet officers in a separate barrack.*

An English officer led me through the barracks to the kitchen.

I was impressed by the table. They had things and in numbers that the inhabitants of England did not have.

Why such luxury?

The officer told me:

"The administration decided that, before being sent to the Soviet homeland, let them think well of the English."

Mountains of butter, ham carcasses, not to mention the rest. There was no one in the kitchen or in service who was not Russian. They did all the carrying, service, and preparation for the kitchen.

I was surrounded by homesick lads and grown men—soldiers.

The conversation was always the same:

"Will they really send us to Russia?"

I did not know what to say. I suggested that they ask, submit a petition, gave them all sorts of suggestions.

They had practiced before the service. All knew how to sing well. Among the singers was a Soviet officer who was full of yearning and followed me everywhere, telling me over and over—of being saved from repatriation.

Not wanting to disturb the routine of the camp, I started the liturgy early, before the beginning of a typical camp day.

The huge barrack was overflowing. Behind everyone—Soviet officers, obviously out of curiosity.

I quickly heard the confessions of close to seventy men.

The choir sang in tune and with enthusiasm. But later, there took place what was difficult for me, for to a man, all rose for

---

* The piece follows Soviet officers who were prisoners of war.

communion (rather, except the officers) and my officer took communion.

I could not refuse those who had not been confessed, so I decided not to say anything, but to go by the principle of letting people prepare for death in their own way.

The holy offerings were barely enough, disappearing to the last drop.

I had brought several instruments and plenty of books (literary fiction), which had been asked for in advance. They were needed for the homesick camp residents.

It then turned out that the library was examined by officers who were not part of the camp supervision and their henchmen. They removed many "counterrevolutionary" books.

Boarding of the ships then took place under guard by English forces. That same English officer told me this history.

In Odessa, they were put into formation in just their tunics at the docks and taken away. They were never seen again.[*]

In England, there were many attempts at escape and many successes. Those people saved themselves.

Several Russians were with Poles and Ukrainians. They also saved themselves.

In one of the camps, the English did not give the Russians over, but suggested that the Soviets take the group themselves, but without using weapons. They were met by the prisoners of war with curses, and the trucks left.

In another place, Russians were searched for among the Poles. The would-be Soviet officer-detectives were killed while spending the night in camp, and their corpses were nowhere to be found. In the morning, everyone was examined, searched, but not a clue was uncovered.

Were there Cossacks in the English camps? I do not know.

---

[*] The English officer who showed the Protopresbyter around the camp also told him about arriving in Odessa accompanying prisoners of war transported from the area of the Mediterranean Sea.

There were some sorts of complications before the send offs, but what kind in particular, I no longer remember.

Only Russians were turned over to the Soviets. There were Russians in Ukrainian camps, where they endured crowding and insults.

Ukrainians were generally supported by the English administration. I new several Ukrainian intellectuals whose travels to lectures were paid for from government funds.

I also went on business with a certain fellow to another mixed camp. Almost a boy, he was searching for family members and greatly feared being turned over to the Soviets.

With love always, your loyal
Protopresbyter **M. Polsky**

Why the English are Silent (letter from England)

In the muddle of July, 1944, there were several camps organized in England in which there were mixed prisoners of war who had been captured in battle with Allied forces following the landing at Normandy. There was a particularly large group of prisoners taken at Brest, where one of the main centers of the Todt Organization [*Тодтом*], which built the "Atlantic Wall" was located. The labor for this organization was recruited mainly from Russian and Polish prisoners of war and, similarly, from western European countries by the Germans to work in Germany.

The Allied Command took all possible measures to attract these people to their side. Airplanes dropped leaflets in German, Russian, Polish, and Ukrainian on positions occupied by Germany along the Atlantic Coast, while Allied radio continuously broadcast appeals for surrender in these languages, offering all sorts of benefits to those who did. Poles suitable for military service according to their age and health could immediately be taken into the Polish Army, while Russians, Ukrainians, and people of other nationalities were offered special preferential treatment in camps until the end of the war.

Forced Repatriations from France, Italy, and England

Two special camps were created for Russians. Father Michael Polsky, the Abbot of the churches in the Cathedral Parrish of London, went to these camps to perform church services, and G. F. Valnov sent rye bread and barrels of salted herring as supplements to the government rations. In the words of Father Michael, Russian prisoners were maintained in good conditions: clothing, footwear, bedding, and food were fully satisfactory. Prisoners were especially troubled by the question of being sent to the Soviet Union. "A return to their homeland" was particularly not wanted by a great majority.

The English military had the idea of training a special unit made up of prisoners and to then mix them in with Allied armies fighting against the Germans in Europe. Their motives were clearly practical. The Allies had few ocean ships, which were needed for much more important work than that of transporting thousands of people from England to Murmansk. Besides that, the sea passage was fraught with great danger. German aircraft and submarines based in Norwegian fjords vigilantly sought out Allied ships bound for Murmansk and sunk them by the dozens. Did it make any sense to expose people to danger when they could have been used as workers on the Western Front?

The now departed G. E. Chaplin, who had joined the English Army during the war, in which he commanded a battalion (engineering corps), told me:

"Toward the end of July, 1944, I found myself with my battalion as part of the advanced guard of Allied armies advancing on Paris. It was hot. Our work was involved up to our throats with bridges damaged by the Germans, clearing mines and obstacles from fields, clearing and repairing roads leading to the front, stores of abandoned weapons and military supplies, and so on. All of a sudden, I got a telephone call from our corps staff headquarters telling me that the Main Office had sent an airplane for me and an order for me to turn over command of my battalion to my assistant and fly with all good speed to the Main Office to discuss important confidential matters.

"Several hours later I was at the main office and reported to the general on duty. The next morning, I was called to the staff offices. The general who met me told me of the decision of the Main Command to form a special unit from Russian prisoners of war. They wanted me to be the commander of the unit, since I was a former Russian officer. They would have to transfer me to that brigade and give me complete latitude in designating junior officers and establishing the units along the lines of Russian military rules. I naturally accepted the assignment.

"The general nonetheless told me that whether Russian units would be formed had not been completely decided, since the Soviet government categorically required the return of all Russian prisoners of war to the Soviet Union. How the English government would respond to this request was still unknown. After a day or two, I was again called by the staff and told that an order had reached them from London to put an end to any efforts in forming Russian units and to send all Russian prisoners to England. Obviously, with the goal of protecting good relations with Stalin, Churchill had decided to turn over Russian prisoners to the Soviets.

"I returned to my unit."

Transports for conveying people and about two dozen naval ships to escort the transports were gathered in Liverpool in the middle of October in 1944. The Russian prisoners were loaded onto two large ocean-going passenger ships, with about 5,000 people on each. The crowding was unbelievable. People had to sleep in the holds. Dining rooms were in corridors. Crowding became even worse when landing barges were put onto the empty decks: the English wanted to create the impression that they intended to make a landing in northern Norway. The transports traveled under the white flags of a military flotilla instead of commercial flags.

Such an expedition had to have aroused the special attention of the Germans and caused them to send out to sea their battleship, "Tirpitz," which had been hiding in the Norwegian fjords. The Germans made a furious attack on the English ships with airplanes and submarines. They released the Tirpitz from its hiding place.

Forced Repatriations from France, Italy, and England

Several German airplanes were brought down by fire from anti-aircraft guns and the Tirpitz was sunk. The English lost two minesweepers that were sunk, and two more were greatly damaged. The transports carrying the Russian prisoners came out of the battle without damage or losses.

Besides the English convoy, there were also Soviet officers on the transports who had been commandeered to accompany the expedition by the Soviet embassy in London. Nonetheless, they did not interfere at all in anything, did not enter into any intercourse with the prisoners, and stayed in their cabins almost without ever coming out.

During the journey, extending to almost three weeks, the Russians comported themselves impeccably. They humbly obeyed all orders from the English Command. They were fed well. They were dressed in good English uniforms. Among the convoy officers were two or three young Canadians of Russian extraction. They fulfilled the duties of interpreters. In the evenings of those times when not under German attack, the prisoners organized parties with choir and solo singing of Russian songs, dancing, and so forth.

The several problems that the English convoy had were caused strictly by the "Mongols" (by all signs, Turkestan and people of the Caucasus). They did not speak a word of Russian, only understanding commands made in German. There were about forty of them. They were truly savages, having no understanding of such elementary things as, for example, bathrooms or toilets.

There was not a single instance of suicide or its attempt among the prisoners. According to English newspapers, however, about thirty prisoners escaped while under convoy by rail to Liverpool. English authorities did not bother to try to stop or catch them.

The transports arrived in Murmansk on November 7, 1944. Prisoners were disembarked onto the shore and turned over to the authority of the Soviet government. Among the prisoners were four former officers of the Soviet Army who had been in the ranks of the German Army, also as officers. They were shot almost immediately on their arrival in Murmansk. Their execution was completely public, and in the presence of a large crowd of onlookers. English officers from the convoy were among the spectators.

The rest of the prisoners were separated into two large groups. Soldiers, officers, and all those capable of bearing arms were sent to the Northwestern Front in military punishment battalions to "pay for their guilt before the motherland." The elderly and invalids were loaded into boxcars and taken to concentration camps in Siberia. Naturally, those good English uniforms, underwear, and footwear were taken off the prisoners and replaced with Soviet rags ...

About the Cossacks who were turned over and members of Vlasov's army, of forced "repatriations" of former eastern workers and those freed from prisoner of war camps, of the tragic fate of Russian emigrants held in Italy in camps near Rimini, who were turned over through English deceit to Soviet executioners, much was written in Russian foreign presses in its time. An account of my history of the turnover of ten thousand Russian captives in Allied prisons in France has not to this time come to light.

Everything in this history is characteristic. Prisoners were officially told that if they voluntarily gave themselves up, they would be kept until the end of the war in the status of prisoners of war in agreement with the laws of the Geneva Convention. And I can attest that such formal and official announcements were made: I myself listened to a radio transmission in Russian, Polish, and German of the promise in the name of the Allied Command to units of the German Army found in Brest.

For the handover of ten thousand Russians to the Soviets, full responsibility must be born by the English government, especially its head, Churchill. The cancellation of the project by Allied forces to form special Russian units was ordered by him. It also needs to be noted that this handover was long before the disgraceful Yalta Agreement, when the English government had not yet been bound to the Soviets by some sort of formal obligations. Churchill, of course, knew full well how the Soviets would deal with these Russian people sent to Murmansk. He used them cynically as sacrifices to Communist arch-executioners.

It is curious to note that the English were not at all shy in risking the lives of Russian people in order to lure the German battleship from its hiding place. German reconnaissance aircraft could not have missed seeing the landing barges on the decks of ships flying under military flags, while the uncommonly large escort of naval ships must have infused in the Germans a belief that the English had decided to make a landing in Norway.

About the English giving Russians taken prisoner in France over to the Soviets, I had known for a long time. However, because many details of this handover were not known to me, I did not make this history public in print. A lucky chance had me bumping into a certain English officer (he is now strictly a state person) who had been the leader of the convoy command on one of the transports. He amiably shared with me facts spelled out by the state, but asked that I not reveal his name in print. Also, I gave my word that several details of strictly military interest would not be revealed.

London **A. Baikalov**

(From the newspaper, *Russian Thought*, May 19, 1959)

In the Hands of the Bolsheviks

In the Hands of the Bolsheviks

The Sufferings of Contemporary Martyrs
(Memoirs of Bezkaravainy)
—Excerpts—

On the morning of May 28, English soldiers and tanks approached. Interpreters came up and began to hurry us along in our preparations. To my question why there were tanks, they answered me:

"To protect you from SS partisans."

"Unnecessary!" I said. "Even if there are German partisans out there, they are not about to attack us."

"I don't know," the interpreter answered. "It is what was ordered."

The regiment started to stretch itself out into a column along the road. With the commander of the regiment, I helped to seat people not having any manner of conveyance. By 8:30, the column started. I rode with the remainder of my company at the tail, followed by the tanks. At 10 o'clock, we came upon a settlement with a huge sawmill. Many curious residents came out of their homes to look at us. They brought us water and gave Cossacks things to eat. Beyond that settlement stood the camp of the Hungarian Corps.

I was surprised and asked a Hungarian officer:

"Aren't you going to Italy?" (Before we left the place we were staying, the English had told us that we were being transferred to Italy.)

"No! We are returning to Hungary," the Hungarian answered.

"But the Soviet Army is there."

"They are supposed to leave soon and then we will go back."

Here, the Cossacks set up their campfires and burned their documents and papers. The English exchanged good "kubankas" for cigarettes. Others were out trotting on Cossack horses.

I gathered my people together, arranged them, then went looking for the temporary commander of the regiment. This was a very tall lieutenant, and he could always be found with one glance, but right then, no matter how I looked, I could not find him. Going ahead, I saw a formless man, but recognized that it was the lieutenant by his clothing. He was sitting on his things, head held down to his knees. He no longer had his kubanka on his head and gray hairs had thickly spread over his head. He raised his face, which was twisted from suffering, and looked at me. I started to calm him:

"What is it with you? What has happened?" I asked. He started to cry.

"Understand—when you left from Novorossisk in 1919, I was left ill with typhus. I had to suffer so much. How they hounded me! Look at me—at my hands. These are the marks of the GPU. Somehow, I got rid of them. What awaits me now is even more terrible."

Having calmed the lieutenant somewhat, I went over to my own group in a depressed mood, where I was similarly pelted with various questions and suggestions.

At this time, English convoys were continually taking people somewhere by the hundreds and returning for the next group. My turn came up. They led us into one of the yards that was enclosed with barbed wire. In the distance, we could see the shed where the previous groups had been led. We waited in line. Two Cossack constables stood at the gate. I walked over and asked:

"What are you doing here?"

"We were sent here to help, but we aren't doing a thing but watching how they are sending people off."

"Where?" I asked.

"Where else—to the Soviets."

"Is it really to the Soviets?"

"Youngsters are crying. No, I don't know, but that's what I think."

I was summoned, and I led some people, carrying a list of the people and belongings. An interpreter and an English officer came out to meet me.

"What is that you have?"

"A list of people."

The officer took it and started to look through it. My people went into the shed. Having checked the list, the officer returned it to me, and I went into the shed.

It was semi-dark inside. The dust inside stood in pillars. Here the English made thorough searches, taking away knives, razors, forks—all those things with which we might commit suicide. After that, we were lead along a narrow path fenced in by barbed wire, into a place enclosed by three rows of barbed wire and surrounded by tanks and machine guns.

Finding myself in this trap. I started to shout and called for the interpreter. A Jewish interpreter showed up.

"What do you need?"

"Take me to your officer."

"Why?"

"I need to talk to him. I do not fall under those for repatriation, for I'm an old emigrant."

The interpreter shrugged his shoulders and said:

"We do not involve ourselves in politics." And he left.

I did not stop shouting. Another interpreter came up to me.

"What do you want?"

"I want to speak with your officer."

"He's not here. He left. Why?"

"These people and I are old emigrants, while these six people are Montenegrins."

He interrupted me:

"So, then you do not wish to go to Italy?"

I think—You are a lying scoundrel!

"I want to speak with the officer!"

"Excellent, but he is not here. Find a separate place for your group here, and tomorrow morning, the officer will be here."

I felt like something was definitely wrong. I put on a clean shirt and began to prepare for death, I was ashamed to feel like a chicken about to be plucked,

They called for the Polish citizens and took them away. It became clear as day. Cossacks tore off their trouser stripes, ripped up their kubankas, and tied their heads with handkerchiefs.

It did not save them. I have mentally gone through my memories of all my suffering. What will become of the children? They are still small and need help. This tortured me. Dawn found me in these kinds of reflections. I woke up. People were being taken out singly to somewhere or other. We sat and waited. Soldiers with automatic weapons came up to us and made us go through a narrow opening. We came out on the road. There were about 300 trucks standing there. They seated us about 30 to a vehicle. The vehicles were supplied with a box of German crackers per person and canned meat—a carton for every 6 people—and forms we were ordered to fill out: rank, name, nationality, family, and which unit we had been in.

"You will need these in order to board ship in Italy," we were told. Across from us sat a soldier with an automatic weapon. It had not yet become completely light when the column started.

Thus, early in the morning of May 28, we were put into trucks and taken in an unknown direction. I asked the English soldier with the automatic weapon:

"Where are they taking us?" He shrugged his shoulders and said: "I don't know."

In the Hands of the Bolsheviks

We did not feel very well and were afraid to say the frightening word.

We went through a place that indicated the direction to Graz. We turned off to the left.

"Thank God! There are Bolsheviks in Graz. But where are they taking us? We are going to Judenburg. But who is there?"

Then we went through a place where everything became clear: the road was littered with trouser stripes, weapons, letters, photographs, and such … Our predecessors had destroyed and thrown out everything that was dangerous to keep on themselves. My throat was choking with pain. There was no way out; we were going to slaughter. I again asked the man with the automatic where we were being taken. I got the same answer.

There was a chain of soldiers and machine guns on both sides of the road. Every 200-600 meters, there was a tank. Resistance was futile.

There was dead silence in the vehicles. Pale faces with wide, saddened eyes waited for something frightening from people like themselves, of one and the same tribe.

In Judenburg, the chains of soldier were tighter. A tank stood on the corner. We quickly rode out onto the bridge and stopped. A shudder went through me. On each side stood Soviets with automatic weapons. The trucks stood in two rows. Soviet officers arrived with the words:

"You have fought enough!"

I stayed seated, but one of the Cossack answered:

"We did not fight enough."

"Look at that hero! I bet you killed not a few of our brothers!"

"Yes! They all got it, whoever I could get!"

I gave the Cossack a tug. "Be quiet. Why anger them!" I whispered.

"And what about you? Are you expecting mercy from these bastards? We will all be shot anyway."

"Yes. I know, but so that they not torture us."

"It's now all the same," the Cossack answered.

Ahead of us, they were unloading. I looked toward an Englishman and signaled to him with a hand across my throat. The Englishman waved his arm—Don't worry.

This was when I saw how Cossacks coming off the vehicles were cursed while Red Army men beat them with clubs. I nodded to the Englishman—Look!

Our turn came. The Englishman sprang out, cut off the Red Army men and we got off quietly.

They herded us toward the wall of a factory. Red Army men stood almost everywhere. We bunched together. Scenes from the past flew through our minds like lightening: family, children … Now they would set up the machine guns and it would be the end.

Outraged grumbles came from the mouths of thousands of Cossack against those who gave us away. Neither reassurances nor threats from the NKVD helped.

This is when some sort of Soviet military man arrived and clapped his hands. Everything became quiet.

"We will now shout out a letter and those with names beginning with that letter will step out," he ordered.

They shouted out the letters "S" and "T." I was lost in my thoughts and did not expect mercy.

Absorbed in my thoughts, I did not hear when they shouted out the letter "B." Bastrich nudged me: "Let's go! That's our letter!" We went. They took us someplace that was covered with glass. There were many tables with letters on them. The letter "B" was at the first table. Other tables went of to the right, inside. To the left were several doors and a hallway to an exit, through which those already registered exited.

I stood in line at table "B" and looked around the place. Suddenly, I hear a whisper: "General Krasnov …" Everyone turned to look to the left and I turned and saw the general through an open door, sitting on a chair and speaking to someone, although I could not see who it was. The door closed. I felt calmer in spirit. I was no longer tortured by hope for justice and freedom. If General Krasnov had been betrayed, then what hope or pretensions could I have—an ordinary emigrant ...?

My turn came up:

"Last name, first name, nationality, place and date of birth? Where were you living until 1939?"

I named a city in the Balkans. He stopped writing and looked at me:

"Then you are an emigrant? You do not come under repatriation. Stalin made no claims on old emigrants. Why are you here?"

"I was fooled into being turned over. I was never a Soviet citizen. I'm a Bulgarian citizen." I had to lie. A hope for saving myself sparked up, but after the following words, it died out.

"You do not come under repatriation, but once you're here, you will not go back from here. I myself was a laborer in Germany, but now, against my wishes, I am being returned."

My registration was complete. I turned to go out the exit. I saw General Shkuro being led by a Soviet officer. I wanted to salute him from habit, but thought better of it and continued toward the exit. I went out into the yard. Again, tables. But it was here that the favorite pastime of all representatives of the Soviet Union was being carried out—"search," or rather—theft. People were stripped naked. They checked for anything that might be hidden inside of you, took away everything sharp, especially what was expensive or valuable. I walked up to a table. A skinny NKVD-ist came running up:

"Are you an officer?" he asked.

"No."

"That can't be!"

"I am telling you that I am not."

"I don't believe you. Have you any money?"

"Yes."

"Give it here, except for any Soviet money."

"Soviet money I do not have."

I took out my wallet and held it out to him. He did not take it, saying:

"Empty it and put it into the basket."

He held it out to me. It was full of all manner of currencies.

I took out my money, dropped it into the basket, closed my wallet, and looked at the NKVD-ist. My wallet was new, soft leather, beautiful. Was he going to take it?

He asked: "Is that all?"

"Yes."

"Put your wallet in your pocket." I smiled and said, "Thank you!"

I walked up to a table that had a different representative of the NKVD, untied my things, and gave them to him.

Beyond my expectations, the attitude toward me was different from the others.

The NKVD-ist pushed back my things and said:

"Do you have knives or razors? Give them to me."

I took out my razor and penknife and gave them to him. He very affably said to me: "Just take out the blades and throw them on the table, but keep the razor. It will come in handy."

I took out the blade and, taking back the razor, thanked him, then stretched out my overcoat, and raised my arms for a search. Nail scissors, without which I could not get along, were in one of the pockets, and I thought that if he found them, I would ask if I could keep them. He looked at me and said:

"Go. Your search is over,"

I picked up my untouched things, in which there were still many photographs and scenes of Vienna, Nuremberg, and Beirut, where I had been laid up in an infirmary, then I went out the door indicated to me to a damaged factory.*

The dust inside stood in pillars. People were putting their things away and getting dressed after being searched. I went over to

---

* Note: Bezkaravainy, throughout all his remembrances, repeatedly tells of the friendly attitude representatives of the NKVD had toward him, as in Austrian territory, so on the way to Siberia and its concentration camps. However, he does not explain why. I could not find any explanation for it from reading his entire work. [Besskaravainy (spelled with a "c" instead of a "з") mentioned in an earlier item by Naumenko is most likely this same person.]

the door opposite to where the guard stood and made myself a place there, gathering all the emigrants: Abolin, Ivanov, Grigoriev, Lakeyev, Shishkin, Berezov, another captain from the 3rd Regiment whose name I do not remember, Bastrich and his two brothers, Marko Petrovich and his son, and the wounded Brazho. Conversation started about how who was searched. It turned out that I alone had come through well. To what this should be credited, I have no idea, but what I write further will convince you that Soviet leaders and citizens kept me in their full view and selection [*взгляд и выбор*].

About two hours later, the families arrived, mainly women from Lienz. The women crowded around me with questions: Have you seen my husband and such.

The voice of an NKVD-ist woke me in the middle of the night. He was walking through the factory and calling out certain names ... This took place for about an hour. Someone who was hiding, decided in the end that it was no use to hide, and answered from some two paces from me.

The NKVD-ist ran up and began to kick him while he was still lying down, saying:

"For two hours I've been wearing out my throat looking for you and you've been hiding. Get up! Let's go!" and he took him away. He did not come back. This is when the examinations and inquisitions began.

People were sent east twice a day from the factory. First, they sent off women and families, who arrived daily. People were sent off in groups of 700-800. They clamored to leave; everyone wanted to know their fate as soon as possible. Uncertainty was agonizing. As I had been hoping, I was not among those to go. Our nearness to the English made me feel safer, for I thought that they would be too ashamed to shoot us there, out of deference to the English. I so wanted to live.

I chose not to go to the east right away. I wanted to wait a few more days. I had fallen, like a stupid bird, into a pit trap and now I wanted those in my regiment to leave before me and myself go instead with strangers.

A bathroom of sorts had been put up up against the wall across from the factory door, its walls made of wooden boards about a meter and a half in height. Those who needed, both men and women, went there together while a guard kept watch. On my second day there, I had a need to use the facility. It felt shameful, but there was nothing else to be done. Everyone there could see everything and be seen by others.

Then a tall, naked figure of a Cossack suddenly arrived there. walking very slowly. One of the very many NKVD officers who were there took notice of him in passing.

As he walked among us, he looked only at our faces.

"Hey!" the NKVD-ist shouted. "What an outrage! Why is he naked?"

The Cossack slowly turned to the officer and asked him:

"Are you Russian?" The officer answered: "Yes."

"And we are Russian," said the Cossack. "Kill Stalin and we will have a good life."

"Take this madman!" the NKVD-ist shouted. They took him away. I don't now what happened to him, but I think it was the same thing that happened to those who were called out in the middle of the night and never returned.

What could I do? The NKVD let the Montenegrins be turned over to Tito. My friends were gone. That was when I decided to leave, too.

About 4 o'clock in the afternoon, someone from the NKVD shouted:

"Form up to be sent away!"

We made up two columns. They counted out 50 and herded them off. We were counted out, too, and taken out the door. A convoy took us and, with bayonets at the ready, forced us almost at a run into a train station. Many people were already sitting in freight cars.

Others were being loaded 50 at a time. I stood in my line. My thoughts were on my family.

A Red Army soldier came up to me. Without a word, he began to unstrap my kettle as if it was his own. One of the Cossacks standing in the row said:

"Why are you taking that? What is he going to eat from?"

"He no longer needs it," the Red Army soldier said.

We sat down in the freight car. Soon there was a whistle and the train started. I stood up, took off my cap and, crossing myself, pronounced:

"Well, brothers! We are with God in His keeping!"

Everyone jumped up as if on a spring, crossed themselves, and whispered something.

The train stopped just short of some station. The guards disconnected the cars and began opening them up,

"Step out, all those who want to do what you need!"

People had to take care of their needs in front of the eyes of workers in the Austrian settlement. The guards hurried them along. People returned quickly. Neighboring cars being closed up could be heard. They closed ours, too, but soon reopened it. Three Red Army soldiers climbed into the car and began to check people out.

"Here he is!" one of them said, indicating a grownup Cossack.

They came up to him:

"Take off your boots!"

The Cossack stubbornly answered: "I will not give them to you!" The people in the car came to his support. They made noise.

Voices were heard outside.

"He's not giving them up?" a voice could be heard outside, cursing blasphemously. "Climb out! I'll teach you how!"

The Red Army soldiers climbed out and closed the door. It opened up again partially and the sentry asked:

"Who did they want to take the boots from?"

"From me," the Cossack answered.

"Okay. Come here."

The Cossack squatted by the partially opened door with his back to me. Struck by something blunt and bloodied, he fell backwards onto my knees. The door slammed shut and the lock clicked. Everyone jumped to their feet. The Cossack spit out blood. A blow from a rifle butt had knocked out several of his teeth. His lips and eyes were very swollen. Blood poured from his nose and mouth. Several people shouted out:

"Damn them! It would have been better to have given them up." Then they began to rip the boots to ruin them.

By dark, we were in Graz. The train did not stop at the station, but somewhat beyond it in the direction of Vienna. They started to open up the cars.

"Climb out and sit on the ground wherever you find room!" They counted off 100. A convoy then chased us almost at a run with their bayonets down a dark road to a predetermined location in the direction of Graz. Soon, we saw blinding electrical lights and headed for them. We were sweaty and breathless when we got there. They straightened us out in line and shouted:

"Sit!"

We sat down and looked about at our surroundings. A large parade ground lit up by electric lights. Mass numbers of tables. People sitting at them and writing. New arrivals coming up to them. A place fenced in by barbed wire with sentry towers can be seen not too far away. This was the main transfer point. The work at the tables continued well into the night. We were forbidden to stand. People asked to take care of their natural needs. Sentries allowed them to crawl away 4-5 paces from the sitting group and take care of themselves without rising.

Just about dawn, people arrived at the tables and began to register our group. Soon, they came to me. The same procedure as at Judenburg. The same forms with questions and the same surprise:

"An emigrant! You do not come under repatriation, but since you are here, you are not going back!"

Having registered, I returned to my place and sat down. Someone tall, big-bellied, and in the uniform of an officer watched the registration and chatted people up. As soon as he came to our group, he began to parrot his memorized speech:

"Comrades! What made you take up arms and fight against us?"

Someone answered: "Hunger!" Another: "Our side abandoned us and the Germans took us prisoner. Being imprisoned was very bad."

"That is what you all say, but you had a way out. Emigrants sought what was spineless. You comrades have done something bad, and now you are asking what will happen to you for that. I know nothing. Here, I only have a transfer point—I take so many heads and send them off so many. There, you will understand. Don't worry. You will not be killed there …"

I sat on the edge of the fifth row. After saying that, the pot belly did not take his eyes off me, but on finishing his memorized speech, turned to me:

"You there, comrade!" I stood up.

"Come here!" I went up.

"You're going to be in charge of your group." Turning to those sitting, he said:

"Comrades! This is your leader. If you need something, go to him, for he will have access to the head of the camp. Understood?"

They brought bread and soup. The big-bellied personage told me:

"Serve your people their meal!"

It was almost 9 o'clock in the morning. I gave out bread to the group, while the cook poured the soup. After we had eaten, the big belly said:

"Now take your people to the camp. Right into the baths."

I commanded: "Get up! Follow me and march!" And, surrounded by a convoy, we went to the camp's gate. They counted us again and let us through the gates.

Big belly turned out to be in charge of the transit camp.

Once in the camp, we headed to the baths. We undressed, and barely had time to warm up from the cold water before they searched us carefully, taking away everything, even toothpaste, shoe polish, and, of course, valuables. Many already knew this routine and had brought their things into the bath with them. My things were untouched. I was told to observe the searches so that nothing other than what was not allowed in the camp was taken, but I had no idea what was not allowed, and those conducting the searches took whatever struck their fancy.

After the bath, the head of the camp (a sergeant-major) took us to a huge barrack, *No 37*. Based on the size of that facility, they gave me another group of 60 people.

My duties did not change: report the number of people to the commandant of the camp in the morning, lead people to the dining area twice a day, and name a squad, if such was needed, to keep order.

After settling into four large rooms with bunk beds, we went out to look the camp over. It was full. I took the last unoccupied space. New arrivals appeared at the door.

What caught my attention first was the massive size of the tents. A woman in a red blouse was depicted on one of them—with wild hair and arms outstretched—with the caption, "Come back, our native one, from Fascist bondage!" On another tent, there was a country road through grain the height of a man. An old man with a white beard stands on the road beside a little one—a girl—looking off into the distance with her hand shading her eyes from the sun. The caption to that one was, "We are waiting for you, our native one, from Fascist bondage."

At every tent, people crowded around and laughed, saying:

"Well, we're going to get it when we return to the homeland. Who did they paste this up for? They can't fool us. We know very well, that such demagoguery is for those who don't know and still believe the [Soviet] Union. They are masters of smoke and dust for this, but idiots beyond their borders still believe them!"

Suddenly, everyone began to fuss. Suicide? Who? Where? In the baths.

People rushed to the baths. I went, too. The guards chased off the crowd that had gathered. I asked the head of the camp:

"What happened?"

"Newly arrived ethnics (from the Caucasus) went into the baths, and two of them stabbed themselves in the heart with an awl or maybe a knitting needle. I don't know, but they are dead. Probably they had been given great punishment and were afraid."

These "dreaders," as the camp head called them, turned out to be quite a few. There were successful suicides almost every day. One Chechen figured out how to bring a small-caliber revolver with him. He also shot himself in the baths.

A new group came after two days. The newcomers had to find places to sleep outside in the fresh air around the barrack.

(What follows in the original is a description of serial searches, which turned out to be nothing more than thefts of what had not already been stolen in initial searches. Editor.)

At this time, a shot rang out from a sentry at a nearby tower and the heart-breaking shout of a woman was heard. People ran in a wave toward the shout. The crowd blocked from sight what was happening ahead. I heard a shout from the sentry on the tower, warning the crowd not to come nearer and saw a machine gun aimed at it. The crowd stepped back with grumbling and indignation.

"They are killing children," was heard from indignant voices.

Later, we learned what the problem had been. Our camp was enclosed in tall and wide barbed wire, and sentry towers stood on the corners and in gaps. On the side facing the camp from the fences, there was wire one meter high with boards hung from it that had "Forbidden Zone" written on them to denote, at a distance from which it was obvious, a line it was forbidden to cross. Anyone walking past the wire would be shot by the sentries. So this is what had happened: in view of there not being enough bathrooms in the camp, when one boy of about 7-8 years old needed to go, his mother took off his pants and the boy crawled under the wire and started to do his duty. A sentry saw him, aimed, and shot him without any warning. The child fell to the ground, dead. A guard came running out after the gunshot, dragged the child out of the "Forbidden Zone," and lectured the distraught woman for having let the child relieve himself in the "Forbidden Zone." They took the child away to bury him but did not allow the parents to be present at his burial.

Our people in camp wanted somehow to forget themselves. They lived one day at a time and feared the next, not knowing what it might bring.

Every morning, military men came to the camp and posed one and the same question that they had to have learned by rote:

"Comrades! What is it that made you raise arms against the Union?" and so forth. There was also bickering.

Still, during one such conversations, a Cossack came forward and, addressing the Soviet soldiers, asked:

"But why are you wearing epaulets? You are not Communists!"

"No, we are Communists. This is our uniform."

"Well, now ... Your uniforms!" With these words, the Cossack took off his shirt and said:

"Look! They shot those who wore epaulets, cut epaulets off shoulders. See these scars—they are from Communists cutting epaulets off my shoulders. And now you have put on epaulets. You are not Communists!"

"Then, who are we, in your opinion?"

The Cossack answered heatedly:

"You are Stalin's puppets!"

The half-stifled laughter that followed embarrassed the Soviet officers. They left, but soon, the Cossack disappeared, too,

There was a priest or a monk among us who was called "Grisha" for some reason. He soothed us with sermons about God, but he soon disappeared without a trace and no one dared to take an interest in his fate.

One morning I rose earlier than normal. I washed with the sunrise, and went out for a walk to the dining area.

There was a free space in the middle of the camp and during the war a bomb shelter had been built there. A sentry stood at its entrance. From the day I came to the camp, I knew that the place was restricted, but what was saved there, none of us knew. Just before coming to the bomb shelter, I saw some blood along the road, but none any farther. There was blood in several places in front of the entrance to the bomb shelter. It was obvious that, either someone had gone bloodied into the bomb shelter, or someone was taken out of there onto the road, and into an automobile, sounds of which we had heard during the night, but without any idea why it had visited the camp at night. What it meant, I realized, was that this was where people wound up who had disappeared and their corpses were taken out at night. I started to look for marks from automobile tires along the road in support of my assumption. Tracks from an automobile were clearly visible in one place not far from the blood marks, where they would not have still been in the daytime due to all the foot traffic that passed by. All was now clear to me. A truck had come in by way of a rear entrance. Corpses where loaded into it and it left through the camp's exit. The tracks indicated the path of the truck. But could they have hauled something other than my assumed corpses? I returned. I wanted to make certain, to find something else in support of my hypothesis. Before reaching the bloody marks, I saw an officer of the NKVD coming out of the bomb shelter with a folder of papers in his hand. He dragged himself along as if sleepy or out of sleeplessness, looked around, and probably noticed the traces, of blood right away, he shouted into the bomb shelter, from which two Red Army soldiers hopped out. He said something to them and indicated the bloody marks. The Red Army soldiers started to quickly rub them away with their feet, while on the road, they threw handfuls of soil and rubbed it in with their feet. There was no longer any doubt! Gunshots could not be heard from under the ground. I quickly made a wide circle in returning to my barrack to tell my friends of my discovery ... The monk who some called Grisha had disappeared there, as had the Cossack who had had his epaulets cut off, killed by executioners.

It started to become cool just before evening and all those locked up came out of the barracks to breathe some fresh air. I came out with A. I. Shmelev. Coming to the commandant's barrack, we saw a group of people talking with a Kalmyk who had a rank of Captain in the NKVD. We walked up and overheard the following conversation:

"How can you praise Hitler!" the Kalmyk shouted. A Cossack quietly answered:

"Well, with him, everything was fine, orderly, clean, and precise, and Germans are the same kind of people, not like those in the Union who only say things and write in the papers. When have such good rations ever been given out in the Union? With Hitler, we were even given toothpaste and toothbrushes ..."

"How can you praise him when the entire world was against him and reviled him?"

The Cossack just as quietly answered:

"Well, and Jesus Christ came and could not satisfy everyone and He was crucified."

"Take this crazy person away!" the Kalmyk shouted.

Red Army soldiers took him off and people dispersed, no one daring to object. Gone was another honest, fearless son of the motherland ...

The next morning, I came out of the barrack. I was met by the head of Barrack *No 8*, a huge Georgian. All of the Caucasus people were with him: Circassians, Kabardin, Chechen and a small number of Ossetians. He greeted me on seeing me and said:

"Come, let us find out what our place in line is for being sent back."

These words were offensive for me to hear, but what could I say?

"Let's go. Let's see what they have to say."

In the Hands of the Bolsheviks

Before we came to the entry gate, we met an officer with a folder in his hand. The Georgian knew him. He was the head NKVD-ist. Without any greeting, the Georgian asked:

"Comrade Chief! When are we being sent?"

The officer gave him a ferocious look and said in a malicious croak:

"What! Are you in a hurry? Come on, I will send you on your way."

The frightened Georgian followed him and was never seen again in the barracks. His things were divided up by his countrymen. When I returned, I told those waiting for an answer what had happened and said:

"Those who want to leave right away, let them go find out themselves when. I am no longer going."

And then, on one beautiful day, some long-awaited guests arrived—six clerks who started to fill out the very same forms as before. Once they finished them they put them in envelopes on which they wrote: "Sent according to order in line. Group leader N. I. Bezkaravainy."

Two or three days later, they led us out of the camp to a place fenced in with barbed wire. There was supposed to be a thorough search carried out there, and we would be loaded after being taken to the railroad. We stayed in that place a day or two, as if in quarantine. Such was the regime. We were given very little water. We were there for a whole day in quarantine.

We were called at night, ordered into formation, searched, and were about to be sent to be loaded into freight cars, but it was then decided to put that off until morning. We did not sleep well that night. Various thoughts disturbed our tired organisms. We cherished our hopes for an international commission on the Rumanian-Soviet border. That was our only hope for salvation, but we feared that we might not be allowed to approach this commission and in some manner or other would be secretly sent to the Union. In such a half dream we met the morning.

By midday, we had been sent to the railroad and began to load. They were plain freight cars. Windows were tightly barred with barbed wire, and one door was nailed shut. A hole of about 20-25 centimeters was cut through the floor and a tin oval attached to it at about 60 degrees. This served as a toilet, but one needed to be allowed to relieve oneself by standing and one was only allowed to stand while the train was moving. A rusty metal bucket for drinking water stood alongside it. The freight car fit 54-56 people and the door was locked. A small platform was built in each wagon to fit two people, guards armed with Tommy guns or automatic rifles. When the train stopped, the guards got off and posted themselves, one on each side of the car.

The worst was at night, when the guards knocked along the sides of the entire car with large, wooden hammers, testing whether a board had been weakened for escape. This was done at every stop. Sometimes the train stopped several times during the course of a night and inspectors, laughing and using all their strength, beat against the cars, where, out of crowding, people slept half-sitting against a wall of the car and a the hammer's blow landed sometimes on the other side of one's head or back. Groans and curses followed, while idiotic laughter poured from the self-satisfied guards outside.

We, too, were chased to the freight cars.

"Leader, climb in and seat people!"

I climbed into the car, took a place in one corner and began seating people like sardines in a barrel. All sat themselves tightly together, leaning against the walls of the car, but many of them did not have room against walls and had to sit inside the car, almost against the legs of the others. In the corner next to me were placed the emigrants' psalm reader with his two sons and some others. Every group leader had to get food, distribute it, and communicate with the head of the guards.

It was June 28, 1945, when we left Graz. We went at night and our first stop was in Budapest. After crossing a newly repaired bridge, we were put on a track reserved for trains headed for the Soviet border. On seeing one of these trains and what they were loaded with, I began to feel ashamed for these Soviet bastards. They were carrying trash that even gypsies would not have taken: old, rusty, tin stoves and pipes filled the entire train. Those in our car were outraged and laughed at these trophies of the Soviet Union.

Our second stop was in Rumania. I don't remember the name of the city. The leaders went in to get a bag of bread each. We were fed tolerably. Galushki were prepared from American canned meat. There was drinking water in abundance. The attitude of the border NKVD accompanying us, it can be said, was tolerable, even if its head was Jewish.

The third stop was in Plaesti. The Rumanian residents treated us with sympathy. We let them know through signals that we were bring taken to certain death, while they reassured us that it would not happen. In the evening, we arrived at the Rumanian-Soviet border.

This is where our suffering began, with our humiliation over having fallen entirely under the authority of the NKVD.

They brought us to the Rumanian-Soviet border in the morning, some 4-5 days after we had disembarked from Graz. There was a huge camp. We unloaded and were taken across a huge square, where we were arranged in columns of 50 people each, with two paces separating one column from another. Across from us was a formation of three columns of German prisoners of war, also with 50 per column and at the same distance from one another as we were. Some NKVD-ist announced to us:

"The first column will join with the third, the second with the second, and the third with the first. Your friends are going to search you. All three columns, march!"

I, with the first column, came up to the Germans. We took off our things and the Germans, following orders given by their victors, proceeded with the search. Untying my pack, I suggested that he look for what he was ordered to. The German simulated going through my things and asked in German if I had a knife or fork or anything else made of metal which might be lethal. I answered that everything had been taken away before we were handed over, and in the frequent searches that followed they took not only metal, but anything they liked.

"Comrade!" said the German. "And how are they treating you?"

"So far, so good," I answered. "But when they bring us back to their homeland, then it will be unpleasant."

"Listen friend," I asked, "is there an international commission here?"

"There is nothing," the German answered. "We ourselves do not know what is to happen to us. They say that we will be sent to the Union. We are afraid of that."

A command was given. It was "Onward," of course. We stood and went onward.

The columns were changed to 10 men. As we passed through, we received but bread and a bucket of uncooked, raw peas in water. Farther, we stopped in a field to eat. That was our meal. We threw away the peas. It was impossible to bite through them, but we ate the bread. We quickly finished the meal, if one can call a piece of black bread a meal, and were led onward for disinfection, They took away our things in the disinfection chamber and took them into the chamber, while we were taken to the baths next to it.

Germans stood there with electric clippers and sheared everyone anywhere they might have any hair. I started to behave stubbornly, but the Germans were firm, saying that that was the order, and that "if we let even one person pass, then we will be grilled—they don't fool around here!" They sheared me everywhere and I headed for the baths. This was a huge shed. In the middle of it stood a giant trough with water piped above it. The water was cold, the soap like ointment—wash as much as you like! We washed our hands and faces and walked out naked through another door into the street. Two Germans at the door poured some sort of liquid on the heads of those going through. Right in front of me the liquid got into some unfortunate's eyes and he screamed. Out of fear, the Germans dropped the liquid and started to wash his eyes out with water.

I went out on the street naked, following a chain of naked people. We walked in a circle and went into a place that had our things, dressed, and went into a room. They brought out the first group's things—almost half had been lost.

At about 3 o'clock that day, we were taken out onto the square by the railroad tracks, formed up into columns of 300-400 people, each column 10 meters apart, in accord with NKVD rules, and told to sit where we were standing. We sat. Guards with automatic weapons stood behind and to our sides. Not too far off into the distance a huge consist of Pullman cars could be seen. We all sat quietly wondering why we were in our formation. Military people appeared from the left flank. They stopped at every column, saying something for about five minutes before going on to the next.

Our column's turn came up. A tall, fairly portly sort, a colonel in rank, came up wearing black trousers that hung out, a white tunic without a belt, and a Soviet cap. Accompanying him was a short captain wearing the cap of the Don Host, which, to my mind, he had apparently just taken from some Cossack.

Walking up to us gravely, putting an arm behind his back, his belly hanging out, this Soviet colonel said:

"Comrades! I came from Moscow from the Highest Administration of the NKVD for your issue." Everyone pricked up their ears. What was he going to say?

"Comrades! I will hide nothing," continued the pot-bellied NKVD-ist. "You are all needed in the Urals." I could not keep myself from shouting:

"Say it more plainly—to Siberia!" A. I. Shmelev pulled me back: "Be quiet! Don't do this."

The pot belly looked at me and said:

"Siberia is also in the Soviet Union. So, you are needed there. We do not want to separate you from your families. When you get to your designated place, write to your families to come to you, and we will try to get them there quickly."

Again, I could not hold back and, still being held by A. I., I said, although not so loudly:

"It is idiocy to call for families who will disappear in Siberia."

The pot belly looked at me questioningly, apparently not having heard my words. I stood and said:

"Allow me to ask a question."

"If you please," the big belly answered. This unexpected occurrence interested not only our column, but also the neighboring one.

"What is the situation for people who do not come under repatriation but got here in error?" I asked.

A snide smile played across his face and he asked:

"Are you an emigrant?"

"Yes," I answered. A ray of hope sparked up in me that this could be my salvation, that these bastards had a sense of justice.

"Yes. I am an emigrant and a Bulgarian citizen."

With a smiling glance at me, the Soviet lickspittle said:

"One way or another, you fought against us and must, like all prisoners of war, have to serve out your sentence, but we will return you after that, if the Bulgarian government requests it."

"And how is the Bulgarian government to know that I am here?"

He looked askance at me, shrugged his shoulders, and walked on without saying anything.

My blood was boiling. I let pass some curses. A. I. Shmelev pulled on my coat: "Sit!" I stood and realized that only by escaping could I save myself. There were no laws or justice here. If I am not executed immediately, I decided I would slip away and not be like some bull awaiting my turn for slaughter.

Thinking about such things, I heard one of the convoy guards ask with amazement of a sitting Cossack: "He's a white emigrant?" The Cossack answered: "Yes!"

I looked around, gave the guard a disgusted look, and sat down. I was very angry and continued to complain while sitting, but the guard's amazement and that he did not react to me according to NKVD protocol to shout, "Sit down!" had me fascinated.

I later came to understand that the entire population of the Soviet Union, with the exception of its leadership, looked with sympathy and respect at the White Army emigration. The Soviets could not convince everyone that we were animals and killers, and even those who did believe them changed their ideas about us after coming upon emigrants, saying then that they had been tricked and convinced that we emigrants were evil people. They recognized us emigrants instantly, they said, by the way we spoke. Whoever I talked to would tell me:

"You, I bet, are not local, but a foreigner. You don't talk like a local, for "local" speech—foul language and Soviet terminology, not Chinese or Mongolian—have ruined the Russian language."

The NKVD-ist finished his inspection of the columns. I had no interest in learning his name, which I now regret.

They stood us up and took us to the boxcars. Loading began as follows: 93-94 people per car and, right off, each loaded car was locked. Those sitting on the floor were in the dark, since the only light came through small spaces in the upper rows of boards, near where I set myself up with some 22 others. At first, no one felt any shortage of air, but later, everyone was gasping.

The train started toward evening. Tired from a day of Soviet disinfection, disappointed that no kind of international commission had appeared at the Rumanian-Soviet border, and rocked by the motion of the train, I fell asleep. In the morning, I was told that we had gone through the Fastov station, meaning that we were in the Kievan Province. We spent the day on the steppe, then started again toward evening. We did not stop at any populated points. Clearly, the Soviets were avoiding them ...

Swept away far from reality by my thoughts, I turned to smile at A. I. Shmelev, but, seeing that he was praying and afraid to disturb him, I turned away. He prayed, raising his tearful face to the ceiling of the car and whispering something as he pressed a photograph of his daughter to his face. I pretended to sleep so as not to disturb his fervent prayers and actually did fall asleep. Awakened by conversation, I turned to A. I. He sat quietly, and as always, smiled at me. From that time on, he was silent.

Soon, though, we changed roles and he began to calm me:

"You can't go on like this, N. I. Take yourself into your own hands. What do you think you look like? ..."

For food, we were given salted fish and crackers. On first receiving fish, I remembered that I had once read that NKVD-ists gave prisoners salted fish and no water. I feared for that happening to us and refused to eat the salted fish. All the others zealously ate every serving of salted fish. There was not enough water. We received 4-5 pails for 94 people and poured them into a rusty metal barrel. The water immediately took on a brown color. I stood at the barrel and measured out two German-military-issued cups in sequence to everyone. Those receiving them drank the water immediately and then drank more from what was left of the water, now thick with rust, which I allowed them to get themselves.

That caused a melee. Everyone tried to scoop out a little more of the red liquid. After that, they picked up the barrel and meticulously decanted it. Still, they could not quench their thirst.

These were the conditions under which we came to our first partially inhabited stop, the Akhtyrka station in Kharkov Province. This was a well-used station. Many people traveled through it. There, through the car's barbed-wire window, I saw a small, half-demolished building on which "Akhtyrka" was written. There were several earthen dwellings along the railroad's route that had rags hung on clotheslines. They were small, low dwellings, some two or two-and-a-half meters in height, from which weeping women in rags looked at us. Unable to approach our NKVD-guarded column any closer, they started to cry out:

"Are any of our loved ones among you?" And they called off family names. Two raggedy Belarussian boys, probably brothers, came up to our freight car in torn, white linen clothes. The bare belly of one was visible, while the other had one leg naked from hip to foot. Approaching the car, they begged, "Give us a piece of bread, Uncle!"

And yet, there are scoundrels who write in newspapers and broadcast on radio that all Soviet citizens live very well, with more than they can eat—but what a different reality! Just look …

After the Akhtyrka station, we stopped by a field. Lacking enough water, they gave us some from the train's boiler. On one such stop, there turned out to be not enough water for the train to haul its cargo. Disconnecting from the cars, the engine went off to get water without leaving even a drop for us. It left at 10 o'clock in the morning. We got no water on this day. The day before, we had been given only a cup each. People sat with their mouths open and breathing hard due to unbearable thirst and not enough water. Drops of sweat poured down naked skin. Tongues swelled and became leathery. There was not enough room in mouths for tongues to move around. Everyone took on a frightening, inhuman look and stood shouting, "**Water!**"

Then, suddenly, as if by signal, everyone jumped up and started using cups and pots to drum on the walls of the car, shouting:

"Water! Why are we being tortured? …"

Dear compatriots and comrades-in-arms! Imagine for yourself the chaos that ensued. Four thousand, five hundred or more people in 50 freight cars drumming and shouting, "**Water!**"

Out of fright, all the guards surrounded the train, set up machine guns and automatic rifles, and shouted something threatening, but no one heard a thing; there was just the incredible noise and the shouts for "**Water!**" Thirst had destroyed people's reasoning.

Their single want was water, or to die faster. I breathed rapidly, inhaling the hot, humid-from-sweat air. No better were all of the others who sat at the car's windows. It got darker within the car, because the windows were blocked by the heads of people needing water. Those below propped up those above who were trying to climb to a window, breathe some clean air, and shout:

"Water! Air!"

Acrid, salty sweat in abundance caused eyes to burn. People were infuriated almost to madness. Others tried to rip the barbed wire from the windows. Several managed to get their heads through to the outside.

Demyanovsky, a Kuban Cossack, got to a window and stuck his head through to the outside to begin greedily inhaling fresh air. On being threatened by an NKVD guard, he answered:

"Shoot!" and cursed him. A shot rang out. Demyanovsky slipped like a sheaf of straw back into the car, He had a bullet in his head. There were several other rifle shots and a burst of machine-gun fire, then everything became quiet.

People became still and stared with pupils widened in horror at the almost motionless Demyanovsky.

A terrible uproar disturbed the peace:

"Torture! Murder!" And, again, it was with hatred and curses that we laid the blame for our misfortune on the English.

I never once heard the Americans—or any of the other allies—being cursed. All the hatred, anger, and threats were directed at the English.

From the inside, we could hear the noises of the emboldened animal tamers of the NKVD. We could hear them opening cars, firing off shots, and closing them again. It was obvious that they had shot somebody. Who it could be went through my mind. Probably, they were shooting the heads of each car for being unable to tame the people ...

Having heard noise in our car, the 46th in line, they opened it and shouted:

"Head of car. Right here, right now!"

I went to the door. How I looked at that moment, I had no idea, but I was calm. The car door rumbled rumbled aside. I stood in the front. A dozen rifles and automatic weapons were aimed at the door of the boxcar.

The Jew in charge of the convoy, with a shaved head and a pistol [наган, a trade name] in his hand, stood in the semicircle of guards. I expected the order, "Climb down," and I looked each one of them in the face—which would shoot me? The guards were all Russians, even some Don Cossacks, but at their head was a Jew.

He asked coarsely, "Is he dead?"
"No, still alive," I answered.
"Bring him here!"
I shouted, "Fellows! Bring Demyanovsky here."
Four men brought the half-dead Cossack to the door. He sobbed weakly through his mouth.

Their leader told the NKVD-ists:
"Get him and lay him down here!"
He indicated across from the car, some 4-5 meters from the railroad tracks, and ordered one of the NKVD to "Finish him off!"

A young NKVD-ist walked up, stuck the barrel of his rifle against the Cossack's head, and fired. Demyanovsky was dead.

Everyone was disturbed by what they had seen. Many dropped their heads and stared silently at the floor of the car. I looked at the executioners and saw that not all of them were of a same mind with the order: "Kill your brother!" Several turned away when the Cossack was shot.

But what could one do? The ruthless Soviets ruled over all the Russian nation.

After that, the leader turned to the boxcar and, threatening us with his pistol, said:

"This can happen to you all. Only the head of your car can talk to me or ask for anything! Understand?" After those words, he ordered the car shut.

My God! All their hatred and maliciousness fell on me. Ninety-three pairs of eyes never took their gaze from me as they groaned:

"Leader, I need water!"

No exhortations of any kind from me helped. I knew that there was no water and that to ask for more was useless, but something had to be done to calm people who had already lost a day to tortuous thirst. I shouted through the window to a guard, "Call the head of the guards!"

Everyone quieted down in trembling expectation. All cherished hope for receiving a drop of water. For the first time, I was required to pronounce the foul word, "comrade." I usually used the words, "lads" or "bothers." It was only with the leadership that I used the unavoidable, "comrade."

Comrade Jew came to the window. I expected him to be coarse, but he was very polite.

"Comrade chief!" I greeted him. "The people are in a terrible situation. They need at least a small amount of water."

"I understand," the chief said, "but we ourselves have not a drop of water." On this, he lied.

"We are waiting for the steam engine to return. Yesterday it went off to get water and for some reason has not yet returned. Probably it will be back soon."

"I understand," I said, "but people are already ill and unconscious."

"I will give an order to send them to infirmary right away," the chief said.

I thanked him and he left. NKVD-ists appeared and took away the ill.

Not only those in my car were ill. Among the 4,500 people, there were a lot who were ill. That meant that dozens of Pullman cars were needed for the infirmary, but the NKVD-ists cleverly contrived to put all the sick into one car at the end of the train. It is not surprising that after a few days I was told that the people from my car had died in the infirmary. But to my question of how they died, I received the following answer:

"One had a serious ear infection, another died of a heart attack, a third of heat stroke." Whether that was true or not, I don't know, but I never saw any of them again.

I could hear groans coming from the car: "Leader! I need water!" No exhortations of any kind helped. Distraught people were yelling, "**Water!**"

I was no better off myself. My tongue became wooden, dried out. My throat was constricted. I couldn't get enough air. But I understood that we would only get any water when we get it and when the NKVD-ists decided in their own sweet time to give it to us.

It was hard for me to assure people that we would get water within a half hour or hour to quench our thirst. I started to lose hope myself that we would ever get water and began to think that the "Father of All Nations" had decided to torture us to death with thirst.

But then, unexpectedly, a Russian saying was confirmed: "God is not without mercy!" Clouds gathered. There was a peal of thunder. Everyone in the car settled down, faces beaming with joy. A heavy rain began to fall.

Everyone rose up like a whirlwind with cups and pots, ran to the windows, and pressed against each another. Everyone tried to push their dish outside to get at least a few drops of water to moisten their dry mouths and throats. A thousand arms stretched outside to collect just a few drops of water, They cut themselves on the barbs of the wire but felt neither pain nor noticed the bleeding.

The guards stood by in silence. There were no orders or warnings to "Get Back!" The guards smiled as they looked at what was happening. I don't know if they were smiling because God had shown mercy on us or because they were enjoying seeing our suffering.

In the general melee, I got no chance to get anything. I and A. I. Shmelev were pressed against a window by the crowd of people. A few drops of rain fell on my face and my bare chest. What bliss I felt at that moment. The pleasant touch of raindrops on my hot flesh made me forget all my troubles and those that were still coming to me, and I wished for nothing more than to have these cool, refreshing drops fall continually on me. But alas! A new wave of arrivals pushed me and A. I., who was sucking on his dirty hands, from the window. He returned my smile and said:

"It is nothing, N. I. We find ourselves in the Soviet paradise and we have to be satisfied with that. But how pleasant it would be to have a little more, even in this way."

But our minute of good luck ended. The rain stopped, although it became fresher and cooler, so that many of us fell right asleep. The engine arrived at about four in the afternoon. They gave each car two buckets of water. The buckets held 10 liters when filled to the top, which was good. We divided 18 liters among 90 people and quenched our thirst at least a little.

Almost over the entire course of our two-moth trip, we were on similar water rations.

This seems almost comical and intolerable, but in the Soviet Union, everything is possible.

After we were given water, the train continued. What stations we went through, I don't remember, but about 8-9 in the evening, we went over a small, newly repaired bridge over the Donets River. The larger, semi-circular bridge had been blown up in several places. The smaller bridge was guarded by women sentries.

Don Cossacks threw themselves at the windows, looking at the river with sadness and loudly proclaiming, "Donets! Donets, and the Don, too, will be up ahead!"

Every time, as soon as we came to a stop, there would begin the favorite Soviet pastime: a search. They would chase people into one end of a car without their things and the NKVD would begin to shake them down. In my presence, they found something on three or four men, beat them viciously, and took away all their things down to threads.

After such searches I always became indignant about how the authorities could allow such robbery, but a Kuban Red partisan told me with a smile:

"Ha! Allow? They are themselves thieves. They require such thievery then split the proceeds afterwards. When you get to the place assigned to you and are left with only the shirt on your back, you should feel yourself lucky …"

A few days later, the foreman came and, seeing how utterly weak I had become, ordered me to have someone replace me while I went to the infirmary.

I really did not feel at all well from lack of water and fresh air. I kept hearing, "Leader, I need water!" Without question, I needed to rest and calm my nerves.

I took my coat and climbed out of the car with difficulty. I had no strength left. My legs gave out from having crouched for over a month. I had already forgotten how to walk. Following the foreman's recommendation, I trudged over to the rear car that they called an infirmary. The foreman opened the door, called over the medic, and said:

"Let him into the senior car."

With the help of the medic and the foreman, I climbed into the car and the foreman closed the door.

I imagined that I would be in the kind of infirmary typical of medical cars, but alas! There were bare pallets on both sides. There were the same kinds of openings in the walls and tin buckets serving as toilets; a tank with a lid holding one-and-half-to-two buckets of water, windows covered with barbed wire, and a single medic having no medical skills,

The one thing good about it was that there were very few people in it, which struck me as being strange, and more air.

The medic in the infirmary had been in the Cossack Corps. There were 7-8 patients.

"Do you have any bromine?" I asked the medic.

He smiled and answered:

"They put me here as a medic without giving me any medical aids or skills. I can help those who are ill only with what I kept from when I was with the Cossack Corps and what I received from the Germans. A lot of patients come here. Many die. The head of the guards comes here and makes up a report: died in the infirmary, given medical treatment, but it did not help. Then they make me sign it."

He gave me a cup of water.

"Drink up!"

I drank the water greedily. Draining another cup, I laid down on my back and closed my eyes. The fresh air made me tipsy. I wanted to sleep.

When the train started up again, I sampled all the benefits of the "infirmary." The car threw you from one side to the other. I was afraid it was going to fly off the rails. It shook so terribly that by resting ten days in this infirmary, a healthy man might lose his mind, even die.

The next day, on the first stop, I said to the chief of the train:

"I am returning to my own car. A day of fresh air has invigorated me."

Our train began to stop more frequently at stations to let other trains pass through.

They labeled us as: "Vlasovites," "traitors to the homeland," and "enemies of the people." Through this, the Soviets avoided reminding people that Cossacks, the entire northern Caucasus, and all the Russian nations were enemies, but not enemies of the homeland, enemies, rather, of Communism.

In the Union, it was made known only that A. A. Valsov, with an unspecified number of people (three million) became "traitors." No mention was made of any others.

After many stops and minor adventures, we arrived in the city of Kuibyshev on the Volga (formerly Saratov). Our train stopped past the railroad station, not far from the city.

We waited a whole day in Kuibyshev. We received up to ten buckets per wagon, but we no longer had the same thirst we had before, because it was cool there and even so cold at night that we all put on shirts and pants.

Food did not get any better. We were all half-starved and wanted to get to our assigned place, hoping it would be better there.

Thus, on the morning of August 10, 1945, we arrived at our place of assignment: the city of Osinniki, Kemerov Province (Central Siberia), "Kuzbass," the Kuznetsk Basin—the "Molotov Coal" Trust.

This city was founded during a nightmarish episode of Soviet achievement: dekulakization. Unfortunate Russian families who fell under the label of "Kulak" were brought here in the winter to an aspen forest.

More than half of them died before the arrival of the Siberian spring due to lack of inhabitants and construction tools, along with insufficient food and clothing. Those who were still alive made use of the goods of those who died and, regaining their health, set out to erect homes for themselves, logging the forest for that purpose, so that the Soviet Union in this way could create a new city and trumpet it as their accomplishment.

Baghdad

N. Bezkaravainy

On the Way from Graz to a Concentration Camp in Siberia

Prisoners of war and "osters" captured by the Western Allies in German territory in Austria at the end of World War Two and given over by the Allies to the Bolsheviks, as were other compatriots of ours who had been carried off by the Germans, along with escapees from areas in western Russia occupied by the Germans, were sent by the Soviet Command by way of Graz and Hungary to Rumania and from there to Siberia.

From Graz, the majority of people captured by the Bolsheviks were sent by train farther east. Some were moved to Rumania in trucks, while some experienced parts of this circuitous route [*крестного пути* could also be translated as Via Dolorosa, the Way of Sorrows or the Way of the Cross] on foot.

On their return to the west from the USSR after finishing their prison term, people sometimes mentioned a castle in Feldbach.

Most trains were held up there for various periods of time as they went from Judenburg to Graz during the first turnovers.

We had only bits and pieces about Feldbach from witnesses, but now we have written details not only about Feldbach, but also about life locked up in it.

The May and June issues of the San Francisco newspaper, *Russian Life,* have portions of the memoirs of N. Kozorez, who was turned over at Lienz, spent a ten-year term in a Siberian concentration camp, and now lives in Europe.

His remembrances complete the details of the circuitous path [*крестного пути*] from Lienz to Siberian concentration camps.

Excerpts from them are given below.

V. N.

I don't remember the number of days, but we did not travel for an especially long time, one or two nights, it seems, before we arrived somewhere.

The door to the car was opened and the usual command given:

"Come out like bullets!"

Our consist did indeed fly out straight off the platform and out of the car. It was a good thing that the platform was not too high off the ground. All these commands came equipped with curses and urgings from clubs. We climbed out, or more accurately, flew out, and found ourselves in a shallow ditch.

Before we could even look around, there was another command:

"Sit!"

We sat. We sat in the ditch, while above us stood the VOKhRA (to translate into normal language, vokhra is the contraction of two words—armed guards) [*Вооруженная ОХРАна*].

We sat for a while, not more than half an hour, during which time more teams of guards approached with a dog and the following command:

"Get up! Choose up by fives!"

We climbed out of the canal and organized ourselves into groups of five. We were surrounded by automatic weapons. The vokhra with the dog stood behind the formation. The head of the convoy read us the "prayer."

"Attention! A step to the right; a step to the left will count as an escape! The convoy will use weapons without any warning! Guides, march!"

We went. A highway in terrible condition led us to a small village. We walked through the village. There was garbage and filth everywhere. Everything was covered with a layer of dust, and there was not a single resident who was not in the military. There were lots of "ZiS" vehicles, shabby and also dirty. On almost every machine there was a portrait attached to the roof of a mustached face that was "sweet" and "cherished" by all Russians. The portraits were decorated with wreaths of flowers or red ribbons and all were covered in dust.

The civilian populace, as throughout the land, was absent, but there were masses of soldiers and soldierettes—I don't know how else to call them—in blouses and khaki skirts. The "b.u." blouses (that's what the things were called, formerly) were fading and dirty. On every house wall there was written in chalk:

"Cleared of mines, Lieutenant Petroff," "Ivanov household," and the like.

We went through the city and came out on a paved road planted with huge, centuries-old trees. Barbed wire was stretched over low stakes on both side on the road. There were boards attached to the stakes on which there was written in pencil:

"Attention! Mine Field."

Thoughts that this field was obviously our future work arose in me and many of my neighbors, or that maybe we would simply be march into the field and that would be the end.

During my time spent in the Lubyanka, yes, and in other lush places of which we had more than enough of in our "Homeland," I often remembered this field and regretted that they had not chased us out onto it. A person can stand situations that not a single, even the strongest of animals can't, but there are limits to it.

It was the rarest of warm and sunny summer days. We spent the night in the train. It was obvious that the sun had taken pity on us here and spared us from any foul weather, in light of our clearly sorrowful situation.

So, we went off on this road for a while, not more that five kilometers; we reached a turnoff to the left, where a directional sign pointed to "Feldbach."

We turned off on this road and came to slatted, steel gates gates and a sentry station in which there sat a guard. The gates were opened and we went into Feldbach.

Beyond the gates there was an ancient, four-cornered castle-fortress with tall bell towers. Along its walls was a wide moat, across which there was a drawbridge to the castle gate.

Our column was led along all the walls of the castle and brought to a large meadow. The meadow, the castle, and the land around it were fenced in with barbed wire. There were also sentry towers with guards sitting inside of them.

Here, on the meadow, as soon as it came in, each group sat on the ground to undergo a "shmon" (shmon is prison-talk for a search), even though there was little left to shmon. Here, I was separated from my boots, which I had only managed to keep during my journey because they did not fit anyone in our convoy, who had all swapped their footwear for our boots in the freight cars. Here, the matter was put on a more rational footing.

The "shmonner," seeing my boots, simply said:

"Well, peasant. Take off your boots."

After I took them off, he pulled out some old German military boots from his sack and, in addition, hideous blue laces, which he also awarded to me, while my own boots went into his bag.

After the shmon, they led us into the castle. On the right side of the entrance, there was a marble plaque with an inscription in Arabic letters, which mountain people, when they also were brought there, later translated for me. What was written on the plaque was that a certain Moor, Omar or Mohammad, in the N-th year (the year was written in the Mohammadan chronology) captured this castle, married its mistress, and remained there, where he died in such-and-such a year and was buried.

The castle made a perfect square. There were living quarters on the second floor, while below them, on the first, there were various services. Along all the inside walls, there was a covered balcony, by way of which heat from the ovens reached into the rooms, and which was the only way to go into those rooms. This way, the outside walls of the rooms were the same as those of the castle.

The burial vault of the Moor and mistress was to the left and even with the central part of the Catholic church and its bell tower. In the middle of the rather large, quadrangular yard, there was a basin with a fountain (no longer working) and the grave of a Red Army soldier that had a red stake at its head on which there was a star that had been cut out from a tin can. A photograph in a frame was attached to the stake, on which the deceased's full name and date of death were written with pencil.

When we were led into the courtyard, we were all ordered to stand against the wall and take off all our clothes. We undressed and an entire gang of MGB soldiers began to carry out the most thorough of searches. They took away all our papers, down to the very smallest scrap, and everything they took was stuffed into a sack.

One of us asked naively:

"What are you doing to those papers and documents you are talking? There, in that sack, they are all mixed up and might be lost."

"Never mind! They will not get lost. They will follow you," was the answer.

These papers taken from us are following us still, although they have yet to reach us.

After being searched, we were ordered to make places for ourselves in the lower, basement-like room. There had been artillery caponiers, embrasures, and cut-outs for cannons on this level in its time, while, in even older days, it was where cattle were sheltered.

When we went into our allotted place, we found remnants of straw. Judging from the hints we found, it had to have cloistered prisoners of war before us.

It took us little time to settle in. Where to lie down for a person who has nothing is a matter of complete indifference—one place on the floor is no different from another.

Having settled in, that is, having looked at our future abode, I went out the door and wandered around the castle.

There were an awful lot of rooms, and almost all were in a different style. There were rooms in Chinese style, Moorish, Indian, Japanese, etc. It was obvious that even the furniture had been in an appropriate style, but that could only be judged by the two pieces which by some miracle had been preserved until then. As can be understood, furnishings were no longer in existence. There were only ancient portraits left in wide gold frames, which were lying around all over the balconies near the ovens. On the ladies at their ancient toilets in the portraits, without fail, there were mustaches sketched on with ink. The corridor or balcony which led to the gate had a window which had obviously been installed later, and all the walls in it were hung with horns and tusks, apparently hunting trophies of the master or guests who had come to visit and hunt in the area.

In previous times, there had been a Jesuit College there and probably a grand library. Now, for some reason, all those books were dumped into a single pile at the bathrooms. The bathrooms were piled to the ceiling with books. What unique people had been here! Bindings made of pigskin, books in almost every language. Some had been written by hand, and I need not mention all the books there from the XVI-XIX centuries.

I went into the church. It had been emptied and desecrated. No altar, no crosses—there was nothing left. Scraps of material lay on the floor, pieces of broken crosses, and gonfalons.

There was a door on the left side of the church which led to the burial vault of the Moor and the mistress of the castle. The vault was very tall, with lancet windows. In the middle of the vault there were two sarcophagi made of white marble. The Moor's sarcophagus was covered with Arabic writing. His wife's appeared to be an exact copy of the Moor's, but without all the various inscriptions.

At the head stood a statue of the Madonna with the Child in her arms. I don't know why, but both were black, that is, carved having Negro features, with dark, coffee-colored skin and brightly colored, turned out lips. Both the sarcophagi and statue stood on a small platform. When the mountain people arrived, they told me that the inscriptions on the Moor's sarcophagus were sayings from the Koran.

On the wall to the left of the sarcophagi there was a sun dial, obviously as old as the castle, by which we oriented ourselves temporally. The clocks of later origin on the bells no longer worked.

The entire castle was situated on a place that was as level as a table, at a distance from the mountains.

Before I had a chance to examine the entire castle, I heard, not a command, but a wild cry:

"All of you! Come out like bullets and work! Like bullets!"

We were pioneers and, judging from the preparations, the camp was expected to accommodate a large number of residents. Several vehicles arrived with steel containers of oil and kerosene underneath them. All of them had their bottoms knocked out and our task was to scorch them out and wash them in a stream that flowed past. In the open air, we built posts with old bricks from a damaged barn and set the burnt-out and washed containers on them. These made the most primitive of hearths. It turned out that the work was none too difficult, but how much time we wasted in vain until we managed to set all those hearths into one straight line.

In the end, the containers were washed, set up on posts, and, most importantly, put into one straight line. We used the containers to bring water from the stream where we had washed them, and the command was given to light these primitive stoves. The wood was moist and in no way wanted to catch fire. Then the person in charge of all these kitchens, giving parade commands, a huge babe in a tunic with stripes and two strips sewn on, gave the command to haul books over with which to start the fires. We brought over books and set them on fire beneath all the containers. Everything went into one pot to be cooked for dinner.

And so, after long and stubborn effort, the water in the containers began to boil, as did our dinner—balanda [a thin soup, possibly named after a Russian river.]

Our commander took a taste, approved, and gave a new command:

"Everybody come out to dinner."

They came out, but no one had either a bowl or a spoon, for you see, based on the sworn promise of Major Davies and the other Englishmen, we were supposed to have been returned to Lienz in less than two hours, so that we didn't even bring overcoats with us, let alone bowls, spoons, knives, and other such things.

We stood in a long queue. Our parade commander beauty stood on a stool. One of us waiting in line (silly us, we waited in line without our weapons, that is, without bowls or spoons) asked:

"And where do you expect us to take the balanda?" In truth. he said "goulash [кулеш]"—"balanda" came into general use for it later.

Here, my beauty let loose such a string of curses, that my mouth fell open. She invoked all the saints, relatives back for ten generations, the weather, the earth, and the sky and mixed all of that together to finish with:

"Next you will be asking me to hold you by the hand while you sh-- [ср..., the equivalent of a common four-letter Anglo Saxon word that, quite truthfully, even burly Cossacks are timid about using in mixed company or putting into print].

Yes! Boatswains on old Russian fleets were probably turning over with envy in their graves. This had been my first experience with women commanders. How artfully she cursed!

It was necessary to leave the queue and go collect suitable material from which something could be improvised with which we could eat our meals. For spoons, everybody picked up twigs and sticks, and we ate like the Chinese from the very same unbelievable relics in which we received the balanda.

After the meal, we separated into regiments. All of us (officers of the Cadet Corps) wound up in the second.

A day later, the succeeding parties of Cossacks began to arrive. They walked right past the kitchen, where we were making our preparations with the containers. They were all better off than we were: they still had their things with them.

Since reinforcements arrived every day, reorganization into regiments was done daily. We were moved through five or six regiments. Besides that, they kept moving us from one place to another.

I did not understand all the confusion and mix-ups at first— why they did not just leave the regiments that were already made up the way they were, then add regiments based on their order of arrival, did not make any sense to me until considerably later. It was only after several years of sitting in camps that I could understand the system: nothing was allowed to be done simply, things had to be so confused that no one would be able to figure them out. When everything was made to be so confusing and complicated that the devil himself could break a leg, only then could one show off the work, zeal, fire, effort, etc., but if everything went smoothly, then there was neither zeal nor fire and, more importantly, no one could be shown to be at fault, for in the presence of the "taverns [*kabaka*] that are systems of organization," there are always people to fault— right up to the devil's mother. Just pick one.

After the basement, our regiment was transferred to the second floor, and from there to the attic, where we kept changing places, wandering about the attic until we were taken away under guard.

By this time, there were several thousand of us gathered there. A commandant was named, a sergeant-major from one of the Terek Regiment's companies, I believe. He was given a suitably large staff. All orders, which he received from the Chekists, went through this commandant.

Once, I was called along with S. to the commandant's office, where we were given an order to make a survey of the camp and the territory adjacent to it. They gave each of us a sheet of paper and a pencil and off we went in the company of a guard to make a survey. The survey, of course, had to be made without compass or protractor. On our side, we used the opportunity to wander and amuse ourselves with the survey for four days, if not more. Then we finished it in our quarters, with the result that we came up with a suitably presentable sketch.

I had great success: while doing the survey, I found an old, bent, German spoon that was missing its handle. I fit a branch to it, tied it on with twine which I filched from a produce sack during unloading, and with such a luxury, I drew general envy.

Five or six days after our arrival, a magnificent black auto, a trophy Opel, came to the inner door of the castle and a colonel in an MGB uniform stepped out of it.

"Come closer," the brass announced. "Let's talk."

Cossacks poured out of every door and surrounded the car in a dense mass.

"Well, how are your young lives? Perhaps you have questions? Ask!" the brass announced pleasantly.

The most important and main question everyone asked was:

"What is to happen to us?"

"Yes!" the brass answered in a serious mien. "You, yourselves, understand what you have done. Your crimes are horrible. You turned against your Motherland, but the Russian people have big hearts. They have forgotten and forgiven all of your crimes. Soon you will be sent farther into your country. There, you will be examined and those who do not have any special crimes counted against you will be set free after the examination and will work, as is expected of honest Soviet citizens. Much has changed in Russia now."

After this, the brass kindly offered cigarettes to those nearest, got back into the auto, and portentously rolled off.

Yes, later I very often came to remember the artful song of this high brass about the changes in the USSR.

At the end of the second week of our stint in the castle, every place was fully occupied, so that arriving Cossacks had to settle along the ramparts. Improvising with available materials, they fashioned semblances of tents and huts. There were always small cook fires burning in front of the huts, boiling water in kettles. They transformed the entire area around the castle into a bazaar.

Then, one beautiful day, our regiment received the order to prepare for transport. The messenger bringing the order told us to prepare quickly for, within five minutes, we were to be beyond the gate.

We had nothing to gather together, if one does not count that, on the eve of transport, we were issued six old blankets and four worn, Hungarian greatcoats, of which one, by lot, had come my way. It was quite useful. I could lay half of it on the ground and cover myself with the other half.

We were ordered into formation. We formed up, but then the orders were set aside. A new convoy showed up, which the Chekists started to process. My good acquaintance, G., was in this convoy. We managed a conversation. Learning that I was being transported, he asked:

"But where are your things?"

"I am wearing all of my things," I answered, "but for holding in my hands this bob-tailed Hungarian coat."

"That's all?"

"Yes. All."

Right then, he tore his blanket into two and held out a half to me. In physical strength he was unmatched and in goodness unbelievable. This blanket, or rather, half a blanket with many patches, in truth already of late origin, I still have to this day.

Finally, there came the command:

"Rise! Group into fives."

We regrouped and formed up.

"In step. March!" And we were led out the castle gate. We crossed a highway and went out onto a huge field, where corn had obviously been grown the previous year. Here they spread us out at five paces and began the shmon, which was carried out by the guards who were convoying us. Everything made of metal was taken away. One of our old emigrants had a large, metal cross, which he always wore, with the intention that he would be buried with it.

"What are you ... a pope?"

"No, not a pope."

"Then why the cross?"

"I want to be buried with it."

"You're a lying bitch! Admit it! We will find out anyway and then you ... (an entire net of curses) we will rip everything inside out of you."

And the cross flew out into the field, thrown by the practiced hand of the "shmonalshik," a lad of about 25-26 with two ribbons on his stripes and a Komsomol badge on his chest. All this took place under the approving grumbles, laughter, and witticisms of the other convoy guards. Finally, the shmon ended, and the order was given:

"Form up by five!" We formed up.

"The first five, go off." After this five had walked five paces, the command followed:

"Second five, go off." After them went the third and so on.

One person who was obviously counting, stood at the transfer point [*сдающий*], and we walked past him. We were counted. Another person—the one accepting us—counted us on the way out in the same way.

Their numbers apparently agreed, since after the second count, there followed the "prayer:"

"Go over to the convoy that is to lead you. Any disobedience to this convoy, a step left or a step right, is to be considered an escape attempt. The guards will use their weapons without warning. Understood?"

The chorus answered: "Understood."

"Those being sent off, in step, march!"

The convoy and its dogs surrounded us and we walked again past the mined field to the station.

On the road, after we had gone approximately half way, a huge column appeared before us. It was being led under convoy to the camp.

Our guards became as concerned as mother hens with their chicks. A series of commands were given:

"Put out your legs! Go right! Into the ditch! Sit! Do not look at the road! Turn your backs to the road!"

After we did this, the new group was led past behind us. The new group went by, but we remained sitting. Only after it was some fifty paces beyond us, did the guards let us up. There were the same commands and on we went.

We came to the station, where there was already a train made up of red cars, the windows of which were covered by barbed wire.

N. Kozorez

General Peter Nikolaevich Krasnov in the Hands of the Bolsheviks

The article below is drawn from the totally reliable testimony obtained from N. N. Krasnov, the grandnephew of Peter Nikolaevich, and from individuals who served time simultaneously with General Krasnov at the Lubyanka prison in Moscow, several times in the same room.

On being freed from Soviet prisons, Nikolai Nikolaevich had distant relatives in Switzerland sponsor his exit from Russia. He had been subjected to heavy physical labor while in prison awaiting passage to America.

He sent notes from Switzerland on his stay as a Soviet prisoner, excerpts from which that had to do with P. N. Krasnov have been included in this article.

Editor

[N. N. Krasnov's full account of his travails is available in English translation as *The Hidden Russia* (Henry Holt and Company, New York, 1960) at the HathiTrust's online digital library.]

After being called from Lienz to Spittal for a conference by the English on May 28, 1945, among the officers there of the Cossachi Stan, three other Krasnovs could be found in one room with

Peter Nikolaevich: Major General Semyon Nikolaevich and Colonel Nikolai Nikolaevich, with his son, also Nikolai Nikolaevich.

Besides them, General Domanov and Colonel Butlerov were also in the room.

All of them were in military uniform, with epaulets. P. N. Krasnov had a Russian cap and wore a German jacket with the Russian epaulets of a cavalry general and a St. George medal on his chest. There were no German insignia on him at all.

In the evening, the English commandant of the Spittal camp called for Generals Domanov and Tikhotsky. He told them that all the officers would be given over to the Bolsheviks on the next day, May 29.

Even though many of them had anticipated being turned over, the reality affected all the officers.

Peter Nikolaevich Krasnov took the news cheerfully, even though he, too, was struck by it.

What was really killing him was the "word of honor" given by English officers and the conduct of the English General Alexander.

What he said, almost word-for-word, was:

"They will turn us over to the Bolsheviks, but there is no reason to smear our faces in the dirt. Death awaits us and we should meet it proudly and directly, not with grovelling."

Then he voiced his surprise that Field Ataman Domanov was not able to put the matter under reconnaissance so that we might know, even partially, what awaited us.

"I pity our Cossacks and their families," he added, "left without officers; but I believe that all of them will not fall into the hands of the Bolsheviks and that the world will learn the truth."

Domanov seemed depressed to passersby. Ignoring the words that P. N. Krasnov had just addressed to us, he took off his epaulets.

That night, General Peter Nikolaevich wrote a letter in French petitioning the English King. In it, he said that if England counted him and his direct colleagues and relatives as war criminals, then we were all prepared to accept the order to be turned over, but he asked that the rest of the people be spared from death, as they were innocent.

Of course, he did not receive any answer to the petition.

On the morning of May 29, we were forced into vehicles. I still have a scar from an English bayonet on the back of my hand.

My father and I helped Peter Nikolaevich into a bus, in which he took a place on the right side next to a window. Next to him was Semyon Krasnov, while my father and I sat behind them.

As well as I can remember, other than those already mentioned, Shkuro, Solamakhin, Domanov, Golovko, Voronin, Vassiliev, Morgunov, Zimin, Butlerov, Markov (from Zagreb), and several other men were on the bus.

Three English soldiers with automatic weapons took places at the back of the bus.

I remember very well how Peter Nikolaevich, sitting in the bus, crossed himself very solemnly and said:

"Lord! End our misery!"

We rode at the front of the convoy. Passing through Villach, we stopped for a five-minute halt and got out of the vehicles. I almost got left behind, but when the vehicle started to move, someone called me. It stopped and I got on.

They took us to Judenburg, where we arrived after mealtime.

***

The bridge across the Mur. On one side were English guards; on the other, Soviet.

Our vehicle crossed the bridge and stopped. We started to get out. An NKVD colonel met us.

Before anything else, he asked if General Krasnov was with us, and, receiving an affirmative answer, inquired about the other Krasnovs, generals, and regional atamans.

No one talked with us there.

Then they led us into the office of a factory. There, in a large hall with machinery, we saw officers from the XV Cossack Cavalry Corps.

At a table for registration, behind which sat officers of the NKVD, our first and last name, nationality, date of birth, the unit in which we served, and our rank were taken down.

From some of us, such as myself, Red Army soldiers managed to remove our watches, done so in a way that did not let any officers see.

Usually, soldiers walked right up and asked:

"Have a watch? Give it. They'll be plunked [шлепнут] anyway."

No one struck us, although the officers smiled angrily and the soldiers laughed and cursed. No one was searched.

After questioning, they put P. N. Krasnov in a small room in which General von Pannwitz and his ordinance officer were already, along with the other three Krasnovs, Shkuro, Domanov, Golovko Vassiliev, Morgunov, and several other men.

They brought canned English food, but no one touched it.

They brought a trestle bed and a straw mattress for Peter Nikolaevich, but me and Morgunov were sent to a large room (hall) where the officers of the Cossachi Stan were, so that we could bring enough for all of us to use as bedding for the night from the many greatcoats lying around there.

We were forbidden to speak with the officers of the Corps.

After some time, P. N. Krasnov and Shkuro were called.

On returning, they said that they had been called by a commander of military groups in the Ukraine and asked about events from 1918-1920 during the Civil War.

Toward evening, a general in the NKVD, a Don Cossack by descent, came into the room. Peter Nikolaevich was lying on the bed. He had the chills.

He wanted to get up on when the Soviet general entered, but the general stopped him with the words:

"Mr. General. Stay in bed! Don't trouble yourself to get up. I simply came to see about your welfare."

"I thank you," Peter Nikolaevich answered. "So far, so good, even though I am an old man."

"I wanted to ask you," continued the Soviet general, "what your feelings are about returning to the homeland! You must truly fear it!"

"I am too old for fear," Peter Nikolaevich answered, "and I count myself as a soldier, for whom fear is a serious taboo. Aside from that, if a person considers himself in the right, then he can have no fear. And, to my mind, your question has no place. There is an old saying: Grief is for the vanquished. It would be better if you, as the victor, not put such questions to me."

"What do you mean, Mr. General?" the Soviet general asked, as if startled. "I did not mean to offend you with my question. I only wanted to know, not as a Soviet officer, but man-to-man: Do you believe in a great future for the Soviet Union?"

"I believe in the future of Russia," answered P. N. Krasnov. "Neros have come and gone. The Russian people are strong. They stood up to the Mongols. And I will answer you this, man-to-man: The Russian future is great. I am sorry that I will not see it, but then, neither might you see it."

The Soviet general smiled, opened his arms, and turned to us.

"Are there any Soviet citizens among you?"

Domanov and Golovko answered, "Yes."

The Red general looked at Domanov and said:

"You are Domanov?" and, not waiting for an answer, he said. "Well, then! When General Krasnov began in 1941 to fight against us, we understood. He was and remains a White officer. But you? I would not have done what you did, if I had been in your place. After all, you were raised with Soviet bread. However—there will be a conversation with you in Moscow."

That is how we found out that we were going "home."

Over the course of the night, General Shkuro was "sociable" almost without interruption, chatting with Soviet officers and soldiers who came into our room. They listened with interest to his stories about the Civil War of 1918-1920. Older Soviet officers tried to contradict him, but Shkuro said to them:

"I beat you so bad that only fuzz and feather were left."

This brought about a burst of laughter from the soldiers and awkward smiles on the faces of the officers.

As is well known, Shkuro did not need to search his pockets for words. He joked, but by watching him carefully, it was obvious that his jokes and the laughter they earned were only to ease the pain in his soul. We all understood very well the sorrow he felt for himself and all of us, although he did not want to appear like a young bride [*молодушным*] in the eyes of the Reds.

On the morning of May 30, we were all taken outside. It was completely empty. There was not a single person anywhere. Lots of clothing, stripes, medals, notebooks, pads of paper, satchels, and such lay on the ground.

Two trucks were waiting, one of which had an armchair for Peter Nikolaevich.

Then, a senior lieutenant of the NKVD came out to us and said:

"Before you get into the vehicle, Mr. Generals, I ask that you remember what will happen to you if you attempt to escape."

We could see two soldiers with automatic weapons bringing out General von Pannwitz's ordinance officer, a German senior lieutenant.

"This fascist tried to escape last night. In the name of the Soviet Union, I order that he be executed for attempted escape. Fire at the fascist bastard!"

Struck by bullets, the senior lieutenant fell, but he was still alive. The Red lieutenant personally finished him off with a pistol.

***

All of the above-mentioned people and General von Pannwitz rode in one single vehicle to Graz. The rest went in the other. Among those being transported as a group to Graz, besides General Krasnov, there were 12 Cossack generals.

We arrived in Graz in the evening. They led us to a prison, where they searched us thoroughly. This was where we first heard, to

In the Hands of the Bolsheviks

our regret, profanity not just from Soviet soldiers, but also several Germans.

The four Krasnovs and Morgushin [probably previously identified as Morgunov] were put together in room *No 23*, on the second floor of the prison. No force of any kind was used. We were treated very correctly. They brought us a good meal, by its looks from the officer's table.

We slept peacefully that night. In the morning, before leaving the prison, we met a column of our officers. They had apparently been brought from Judenburg to Graz by train.

Two trucks waited for us. First, we drove into the outskirts of Graz, where a good breakfast was prepared for us at one of the villas. P. N. Krasnov said we were being fed as if we'd been condemned to death.

Back in the vehicle (a three-ton truck), we rode to Baden, near Vienna. That was where the center for counterintelligence. "Smersh," was located.

They put us all into five basement rooms in one of the villas. We slept in beds. There was no impediment to communication with one another, but we were not allowed out of the basement. Again, there was another search. They took away knives and spurs.

Before the search, everyone was told to sign a paper attesting that they were "temporarily detained on Soviet territory until identity was determined." To my question of what kind of nonsense this was and that I had been turned over, not detained, they answered:

"This is a simple formality for a visa to Moscow." (I obtained a visa to return only after ten years.)

In Baden, we were all photographed as a group. Anyone who no longer still had their epaulets, was provided epaulets that matched the person's rank from NKVD stores for the photo. (There were only 3-4 such men.) They took those epaulets away after the photography. Those who still had epaulets on their shoulders had them taken away in Moscow.

In Baden, we were questioned over the course of two nights. Nobody was beaten. We were treated very correctly, even more so than necessary, which troubled us most of all.

On June 3, in the morning, the first party to be flown to Moscow was taken away: Domanov, S. N. Krasnov, Sultan Kelich-Ghirey, and some others.

On June 4, at 7 o'clock in the morning, Peter Nikolaevich Krasnov, Shkuro. Vassiliev, my father and me, and some others were loaded onto a passenger airplane, a "Douglas." We were accompanied on it by an NKVD officer and a soldier with an automatic weapon.

This is where the Russian newspaper, *Pravda*. first came into our hands.

Only Shkuro had motion sickness. P. N. Krasnov and the others held up very well during the flight.

At 14:30 hours, we flew over the Smolensk-Moscow Highway, the Kremlin, and the Central Airport ...

A prison auto, a "Black Raven," was waiting for us. Peter Nikolaevich had a small sedan waiting for him.

They took us to the Lubyanka (Dzerzhinksy Square, *No 2*).

They separated us right away there. The first room was a "box [*бокс*, a transliteration of the English word]." This was a small place holding only one person, no bigger in area than a telephone booth, and without a window. All one could do in it was sit. Stretching one's legs or standing up was impossible. Right above your head there was a bright 500-watt light. It was terribly stuffy in it. You felt cut off from the entire world, beyond time and space. There was no way of knowing how long one had been sitting there. One time, a soul-wrenching scream reached me from one of the other boxes.

How long I sat in it—I have no idea, maybe a whole day. Then they called me out for a search. I was accompanied by two unarmed guards. It was as silent as a tomb. We walked without saying a word. The guards communicated with each other using signs.

After the search, a shower.

On the fifth of June, they brought me by his request to help Peter Nikolaevich with his bath. This allowed the opportunity for a prolonged conversation. Peter Nikolaevich spoke of his past life and asked me, should I somehow manage to free myself, to tell others everything I knew.

"I am dying," he said, "with the feeling that I have discharged my debt to the motherland in full."

I tried anew to calm him, but he answered that he was not a child, that he understood his situation well, and he advised me on what to do to stay alive and get out of the current situation. He had concerns for his wife, Lydia Fyodorovna, who would be left by herself, and how she would live without him. He expressed a wish for his manuscript, "The Dying Caucasus," [*Погибельный Кавказ*. translated as *Fatal Caucasus* in *The Hidden Russia*] to be published by the emigré press.

"Remember, Kolyunok," he said in farewell, "Russia will remain! Remain," he repeated. "Everything will change, but for this, suffering is necessary. I believe that the Lord God will return Russia to its people. Perhaps we are the last to see its death, but after death, there will come a day. I believe that there is nothing on earth that is permanent and that Russia will be resurrected."

After the bath, I helped him to dress. His coat no longer had epaulets or his Georgian Cross. They were removed during his search.

Peter Nikolaevich embraced me, kissed me, and parted from me forever ...

Soon after, Peter Nikolaevich fell ill with inflammation of his kidneys, running a temperature of 39 degrees, and was sent to the infirmary of the Butyrka Prison, where he lay for more than a year, until September, 1946, when he was returned to the Lubyanka. There, he was put on the 5th floor in Room *No 7* with two other men.

One of those who was with him for some time in that room relates that he was able to converse quite a bit with Peter Nikolaevich and to observe his moods.

General Krasnov told him that he was cared for well in the infirmary, but that the food was bad, even though they did once give him port wine to fortify him. The food there was incomparably worse than that in his prison room in the Lubyanka.

Peter Nikolaevich's moral was good. He said that he expected nothing good for himself, but, nonetheless, he did not think that he would be executed.

He thought that his execution would not be useful to the Bolsheviks, as it would make a martyr of him and cause unwanted comment from the West, where he was famous as a writer, given that his works had been translated into 17 languages. General Krasnov suggested that, since he was old and did not have long to live, they would allow him some sort of small house someplace or other in the Urals, where he could live out the rest of his days.

He wore prison clothing: a green tunic and matching trousers. In light of his feet having swollen from disease, his shoes were cut open in the infirmary, and he was then given high boots with a leather foot and a sheepskin top. These boots were fitted by his personal interrogator Colonel Morozov, who himself took off P. N.'s boots and replaced them with the others, since it was difficult for the general to do so on his own, given that his right leg was stiff from a wound received during World War I and did not bend.

His personal clothing, a tunic with epaulets that signified a general and trousers with stripes, were ironed and kept in the storehouse of the Lubyanka prison. Rumor has it that when he was on trial, he was dressed in his personal general's uniform.

I personally only saw this uniform when they brought it to him from the prison storeroom to show him how it looked. Then they took it away again. Peter Nikolaevich generally went around in his prison tunic and trousers. To go outdoors to walk, he was given a black prison coat with ties in the front instead of buttons, and a cap in the fall, while in the winter, a gray, soldier-type of papakha.

The prison gave him two pairs of socks and, every ten days, clean clothes in the baths: shirt, drawers, towel, bed sheets, and pillow case.

He had two mattresses on his bed, so that it would be softer. When he was undergoing interrogation, they put a leather pillow on his chair, to make it softer to sit on.

He had his prince-nez and his cane, which he used for support.

During his time in prison, either in the infirmary or in his room, where he was with me, Peter Nikolaevich wrote absolutely nothing. I generally doubt that he could write anything even later, since those under investigation had neither paper nor pen, nor were they given even a pencil.

At any rate, if Peter Nikolaevich did write his memoirs, which I little believe, it could only have been in that period after I left on December 25, 1946, and up to his execution in the second half of January, 1947.

Peter Nikolaevich spent his time in the Lubyanka prison, where we all served along with him, as follows:

At 7:30-8:00 AM, he woke up, since that was when they brought bread to the room. Then, about 8:30, we went to the bathroom, to which I carried the bucket, in order to wash it in the bathroom, while Peter Nikolaevich walked to it with the help of his cane and carrying a glass "duck" in one hand, for, unable to bend his leg, he could not use the bucket.

He washed the duck himself, and once a week, a nurse took it to give it a thorough cleaning.

When Krasnov went to the bathroom and on his return, an officer on duty held him up from the side, since one time just after his return to the prison from the infirmary, he had stumbled and fallen, breaking his nose.

Following a physician's directions, we did not hurry him in the bathroom. Even though the bathroom interval for everyone was 12 minutes, we often stayed some 20-25 minutes.

At 9:30 AM, we were brought breakfast, barley coffee and sugar.

After breakfast, at 10 AM, Peter Nikolaevich typically lay down to sleep and slept until 11:30, when they again let him alone go to the bathroom.

From 12:00-13:00, we had lunch.

From 13:30-14:00, they typically called him for questioning.

From 17:30-18:00, he returned and dinner was brought, after which he read for a little while and we had many conversations. He obtained books to read from the prison library, which was suitably well stocked at the Lubyanka. It even had foreign language books in addition to those in Russian.

In the evening, we were once more led to the bathroom, but at 22:00, it was lights out and we went to sleep.

Peter Nikolaevich received a special, what we called a "general's" diet, which was brought separately to him from the officer's canteen.

He received: 1 kilogram, 200 g of white bread (I received 700 g of black, or 500 g of black and 200 g of white, which was called a supplementary diet, while the typical diet was 600 g of black bread) and 9 lumps of sugar (a typical ration was 2 lumps). For breakfast, we had either rice kasha or an egg. For lunch, we had a good soup or borscht, a piece of fried meat, and 200 g of sweet fruit preserve compote (the typical ration was: fish soup and some kind of kasha; 50 g of meat was given only for supplementary portions).

For dinner, Peter Nikolaevich received some sort of kasha or pureed potatoes with pieces of herring (the typical ration was shchi).

He was treated kindly. His interrogator used his name and patronymic and referred to him in the formal, plural, second person ["*Вы*"]. All the others were called by their last names and addressed in the familiar, singular, second person ["*ты*"].

We spoke with each other quite a bit every day from September 2nd up to December 25th of 1946. He told me about his past life and about his wife, often asking me to sing her favorite love song, "Northern Star." (At one time, I hand sung on the stage.) He told about his trip in escorting the Russian mission in Abyssinia, trips with his wife to Manchuria, work as a war correspondent in the years

1900-5, cavalry officer's school, his service in the Tsar's Army, World War I, his writing, the content of his novels, his visit with Grand Duke Nikolai Nikolaevich, the Civil War, being Ataman, meeting Skoropadsky, Dennikin, and others, his letter to Kaiser Wilhelm (which he identified as the reason that the English turned him over to the Soviets), the work of the Cossacks in World War II, his betrayal by the English to the Bolsheviks—all the deceptions that had been made. He talked about all this in much detail, for the room had no eavesdropping devices of any kind, and, after all, Peter Nikolaevich had nothing to hide. In his own words, he and other generals were called for a meeting with an English general. He and his colleagues believed it and went, but instead of that, they were betrayed to the Bolsheviks.

The four months that we were with Krasnov, he was called out for questioning every day the first two months, aside from Sundays, and then only once or twice a week. Interrogations were held only in the daytime, since he told his investigator that his vision was poor at night and he could not walk.

They asked him about his actions as Ataman in 1917-19, about his time as an emigré, and about Cossack organizations during World War II.

He was accused. first of all, of violating the terms of his release from prison in Bikhov,which were that he would not fight against the Bolsheviks. Peter Nikolaevich answered that he did not consider himself obligated to abide by his word as given to the Bolsheviks, and secondly, of anti-Bolshevik attacks during 1917-19. He was also accused of supporting the Brothers of Russian Truth and leading the Cossacks in World War II.

V. Naumenko

Memoriam of a Singer to the Double-headed Eagle

General-of-Cavalry P. N. Krasnov

> We can not see Krasnov's grave
> Can not hold a memorial service over it—
> To eternity went the white word
> Of our casual refugee days.
>> The Cossacks do not see their ataman
>> The falcon has flown his last
>> He will no longer write a novel
>> To grab you by heart and soul.
> At his unknown grave
> Somewhere there far from Moscow
> At least the wind will cry sadly,
> Yes, and the weeds will bow their heads
>
> **V. Petrushevsky**

Unforgettable. 1945-1956. — N. N. Krasnov

The author of the book, *Unforgettable*, Nikolai Nikolaevich Krasnov, the younger, was the son of the General Staff's Colonel Nikolai Nikolaevich, the brother of General Semyon Nikolaevich Krasnov. These brothers were distant relatives of the famous General Peter Nikolaevich Krasnov, former Don Cossack Ataman and author of a number of novels based mainly on military life and written in emigration.

The author of the book, *Unforgettable*, was designated "the younger" to distinguish him from his father. He was Peter Nikolaevich's grandnephew.

Of these four Krasnovs, Peter Nikolaevich and Semyon Nikolaevich were executed in Moscow, Nikolai Nikolaevich, the elder, died in exile, while Nikolai Nikolaevich, the younger, was released after serving a 10-year prison sentence in Siberia. After a brief time with distant relatives in Sweden, he moved with his wife to Argentina, where he died unexpectedly amid suspicions that he had been poisoned.

In 1957, his memoirs were published in Russian in San Francisco by the publishers of the newspaper, *Russian Life*.

In the Hands of the Bolsheviks

The author of the memoirs wrote in sequence about what he lived through and saw while in the hands of the Bolsheviks.

This work differs from memoirs published earlier, in which the attention of the reader is mainly drawn to descriptions of the physical suffering of prisoners. It instead draws attention to the spiritual suffering of the author and his analysis of it.

The book is written without affectation, simply, clearly, without guile, and truthfully. It is easy to read and gives a full picture of the tragedy that the victims of the betrayal suffered.

Unforgettable is a book that everyone should read and treasure as a document that touches on the contemporary morality of mankind.

Several lines from this book having to do with N. N. Krasnov and his son being called to the room of the Head of State Security, General Merkulov, in the Lubyanka Prison in Moscow are reprinted below.

First, though, it must be noted that Merkulov himself spent time in this prison in 1954 and was subsequently hung there.

Prior to his conversation with the Krasnovs, Merkulov ordered that they be given tea, appetizers, and cigarettes ...

V. N.

***

"Why are you not smoking, Krasnov, not drinking your tea? To my mind, you are not very talkative or friendly! I think that by this silence you are trying to cover up your concerns ... fears ... but you have no reason to be concerned. At least, not in this room. When you are called before the investigator, than I advise that you tell only the truth and find an answer to every question, or else ... we are capable of hangings." Merkulov laughed quietly. "Do you know how that is done? At first, it is quiet, easy ... painless, even, but then ... Hasn't Ataman Krasnov written in his books about similar methods?"

I felt fingers walking all over me. My pulse beat out a raging "tom tom" on my temples. My heart beat so loudly that Merkulov must have heard it as he sat by his desk at a distance of some ten meters away.

My father kept quiet. His face was pale, but quietly focused. I envied him.

"… you will not find freedom," the General continued. "After all, you are no child! Nonetheless, if you do not resist, you will easily pass through all the formalities, sign something, spend a few years in the ITL [*ИТЛ, Исправи́тельно-Трудово́й Ла́герь*, Correctional Labor Camp] where you will become used to our way of life and … find its better features … Then, possibly, we may release you. You will live."

Again, there was a pause.

"… So, Colonel Krasnov, make a choice between truth and life, or resistance and death. Don't think that I am just trying to frighten you. Quite the opposite! After all, Peter Nikolaevich, Semyon Nikolaevich, and you are old acquaintances of ours. In 1920, you managed to slip from our hands into the bushes, but now—you have no cards left. You are not getting away! 'There are no [*Нэма*] others,' as they say in the Ukraine …"

… Several steps back and forth. The General keeps his hands behind his back. He crosses his fingers together. I can't help noticing that there is a shiny ring on one.

"… So, Colonel, have we come to an agreement?"

"There is nothing I can agree to with you," my father said sharply.

"What do you mean, 'nothing?'" the Chekist laughed quietly.

"Agreement is dearer than money, Krasnov. Your past does not interest us. We know all about you. But … there are clearly small details about your actions in recent times that it would do no harm to hear from you."

"I have nothing to tell you! I don't understand what all of this paperwork is all about. Let's be done with this right now. A bullet to the back of the head and …"

"Eh-eh-eh, no, 'Mister' Krasnov!" With a crooked grin on his face, Merkulov eased into a chair. "That just is not done. Think about it. A bullet to the back of the head and that's it? No-no-no-s [*Дудки-с*, the appended final "s," an abbreviation for *сударь*, "sir," is a relic of former times, when appending it to a word marked either respect or subservience to the one being addressed], Your Honor! You need to work! There will always be time to play in a casket. There is plenty of manure with which to improve the soil. But you can at first work for the glory of Russia. A little timbering, a little mining up to your waist in water. Spend some time, smart guy, on the 70th parallel. After all, it is all so interesting. 'You will get to live!' as we say.

"You don't know how to speak 'our' language. You don't know any of the camp expressions born there in the polar regions. You will hear them! You will become 'thin, ring hollow, and be invisible but for ears like hatchets!' You will walk with 'macaroni' legs!" the General laughed. "You will work! Hunger will force you!"

We sat in silence. My head was spinning. My palms were sweaty from helpless rage.

"We need to build, Colonel Krasnov! And where will we get the labor? We no longer get any use from exiles and 'malcontents [*жмуриков*].' Times have changed. Executions are rare. We need labor, free labor. We have waited for twenty-five years for this happy meeting with you. You've wagged your tongue for too long in exile and knocked our youth off the one true path …"

Merkulov was a bit winded from his monologue. A vein was bulging on his forehead! His eyes stung out at us with hatred.

"… Frightened? … Why? Afraid of work? … On the contrary … What is there to say? Neither you of me or I of you believe a word the other says. To me, you are White bandits, while to you, I am Red scum! Still, the victory is on our side, for the Reds. Both in 1920 and now. Strength is on our side. We do not flatter ourselves with hopes that we will be able to re-educate a Krasnov and make him into an obedient Soviet lamb. You will never have any love for us, but we can force you to work for Communism, in the building of it, and this will give us the very highest moral satisfaction."

Merkulov stopped talking, expectantly staring with his eyes at father.

"Why such a long introduction?" my father answered wearily. "I understand you perfectly without any explanation, Mister General.

The hopelessness of our situation is clear to me. My son and I are soldiers. We both have been in battle. Both have stared into the eyes of death. We don't care on what parallel it is, 70th or the hundredth, she will swing her sickle ... I curse myself only about one thing—why I believed the English. In either case, I have removed my own head ..."

"Ach! If only it was death!" Merkulov grinned. "Drop your loud words of a 'soldier's death.' That's just simple balderdash! Death passed by without noticing you! But that of believing the English was definitely stupid. They are, after all, nothing but a bunch of merchants historically!"

...... (pp. 76. 77, 78, and 79)

[I have translated these pages independently of *The Hidden Russia*, although I did peek in a few places in the book: there were differences, one of which I made use of.]

N. N. Krasnov

Capital Punishment in Moscow in 1947

The end of the Second World War brought the Russian anti-Communist emigration of Europe to great tragedy: the turnover of a significant part of it to reprisals by the Bolsheviks.

This fate fell on both those who escaped from under the "Iron Curtain" during the last war, as well as those who left the borders of their homeland back in 1920, that is, back when there was no curtain and there had never been Soviet citizens.

The old emigration, as it has become accepted to call the emigration of 1920, had spent many years outside of the homeland, settling everywhere in the world. Parts of it settled in the United States of America, Canada, countries in South America, and even Australia, although a significant part settled in Europe. Those who lived in the western and central parts of Europe, especially in the Balkans, found themselves within the spheres of influence of two warring sides at the very beginning of the war.

The emigration that had previously crossed the ocean was more estranged from it both physically and morally because of its distance from the homeland than that which had remained in Europe.

The overseas emigration, from the beginning to the end of the war, remained outside of Russia's immediate influence, knew about it only from what was printed, and its attitude toward it was made up under the influence of global conditions and information from newspapers. Taking as an example those who then lived in the United States of America, we know that they did not suffer from the war: they were not exposed to continuous aerial bombardment from opposing sides, did not experience shortages of items of absolute necessity, did not have to change where they lived, and, related to this, did not lose the belongings they had worked hard all their lives for. Neither were they subject to being captured by the Bolsheviks.

Succumbing to the general attitude of the countries in alliance with the Bolsheviks, they began to forget the inhumanity of the Bolsheviks, and there were even instances, rare, it is true, when they came to the aid of the oppressors of our Motherland.

The situation of the emigration in Europe, especially in countries happening to be in the thick of the war, was much different.

We must not forget that Europe, especially the Balkans, was where the Bolsheviks carried out their continual efforts to bias the local populace against Russian emigrants. This was felt especially so by our emigrants in Yugoslavia. The soil there had been meticulously prepared by the Bolsheviks, so that the entire Russian emigration was considered a German "Fifth Column" by the local populace.

The killing of Russian emigrants began with the first days of the war. Several priests were killed, two Kuban Cossacks among them: Father Danil Novosiltsev and Father Baev, along with a host of other Russians.

The situation became very difficult, especially in remote areas, and Russian people, abandoning what they had earned through years of hard work, began to be pulled into the big cities, Belgrade, especially.

Almost the same thing was happening in Bulgaria.

The continual instigation of hatred in the local populace toward Russians by the Bolsheviks, which was reinforced by unemployment and the approach of Red Army forces, in addition to circumstances of the war already mentioned above, put the Russian emigration into a situation from which there was almost no way out.

It needs to be remembered, too, that Russian emigrants living in Europe felt more acutely and were more concerned over what was going on in our homeland than our compatriots who were separated by thousands of kilometers of ocean from it.

Our emigration in Europe, especially that in the west, lived with the thought of taking up arms and awaited the chance to be included in the battle to free their Motherland.

It saw this opportunity when war began between the Germans and the Bolsheviks. Those who could, took up arms.

Thus, the formation of the Russian Corps was promoted in Yugoslavia and Bulgaria with the German High Command's permission, in concert with the agreements of the governments of the countries named.

Into it went the Cossacks, forming the 1st Cossack Regiment under the command of General V. E. Zborovksy, who is now deceased.

Upon the retreat of the Germans from Balkan territories, a large number of Russians, who had lived there were allowed to follow the Germans north, and did so. Some went into the Russian Corps. Some left to work in Germany. Others left simply in hope of escaping the Reds.

All this led to tens of thousands and perhaps a hundred thousand old emigrants being found in territories of Germany and Austria which were then a part of the Reich.

As far as the new emigration is concerned, that is, the emigration from this last war, we know that they were made up mostly be Soviet prisoners of war, but there were also those who were impressed for labor in Germany and were called "osters." These made up a great number of the people who left for the west with the Germans.

From this core, mainly prisoners of war, General Vlasov proceeded to form the Russian Liberation Army, making significant progress toward the war's end.

About the Cossacks, we all know that, with the coming of German forces into Cossack lands, Don and Kuban Cossacks took up arms, then, as the Germans invaded farther into the southeast, Terek Cossacks and several of the mountain nationalities in the Caucasus did likewise.

They all jumped at the chance to continue their armed battle against Bolsheviks that had been broken off in 1920.

With the retreat of German forces, entire Cossack families and even stanitsas were pulled west along with them. They could no longer remain under Bolshevik power and went west in search of a quiet life under the protection of the Western Allies.

The war ended. That was when the high judges of mankind, Stalin, Churchill, and Roosevelt, met in Yalta to settle questions having to do with the end of the war. Among those questions was the fate of prisoners of war found on German territory and in the countries of western Europe.

They signed an agreement on repatriation, but it was made up of such ambiguous terms, that, subsequently, Stalin easily connived to have his friends and other like-minded people in the Allied Command take on the duty to repatriate, by force if necessary, all of those who did not want to return to behind the "Iron Curtain." The use of weapons by Allied forces to that end resulted in blood being shed not only by able-bodied men who did not wish to return, but also by the frail and elderly, women, and children,

We know where the forced repatriations took place: Austria, Germany, Italy, Switzerland, France, Denmark, Norway, and the United States of America.

At that time, convinced and unwavering anti-communists could not find anywhere or anybody to save them from the reach of the claws of Red Moscow.

In the years since, we have had many reliable accounts about the fate of Cossacks and other anti-Communists so betrayed.

The fate of the many thousands of people caught then by the Bolsheviks is not known to us, but we know from official Soviet documents of the execution in the main of Russian anti-Bolsheviks, among them the leaders of the Cossacks, who were given over by the "Western Allies" to their friend Stalin.

An official notice by the USSR, published in the Soviet newspaper *Pravada, No 15* (10406) on January 17 [here, the author obviously neglected to add the year (1947) in front of the abbreviation for year, *г*.], which we reproduce below, tells of the execution of Generals P. N. Krasnov, Shkuro, Sultan Kelitch-Ghirey, S. Krasnov, Domanov, and von Pannwitz. It says that the sentence was carried out, but not specifically when, so it must be assumed that all of the generals named were executed on the date of sentencing, that is, January 17.

Since they were turned over in May of 1945, they spent more than a year and a half agonized behind the walls of the NKVD. It is possible that the delay took place because of the prolonged stay of General P. N. Krasnov in the infirmary.

V. Naumenko

ANNOUNCEMENT

Supreme Court of the Military Collegium of the USSR

The Supreme Court of the Military Collegium of the USSR has examined the matter of the guilt of those arrested as agents of the German espionage service, the leader of armed White Guard units at the time of the Civil War, Ataman **Krasnov P. N.**, Lieutenant General of the White Army **Shkuro A. G.**, Commander of the "Native [usually pejoratively translated as "Wild"] Division—White Army Major General Prince **Sultan Kelitch-Ghirey**. White Army Major General **Krasnov S. N.**, and White Army Major General **Domanov T. I.**, along with German Army SS General, von **Pannwitz Helmuth**, that under assignment by the German espionage service during the period of the War of the Fatherland formed White Guard armed units to fight against the Soviet Union and carried out espionage, diversionary, and terrorist activities against the USSR.

All of the accused admitted to their guilt in the accusations given.

In accordance with Paragraph 1, of the Decree of the Supreme Presidium of the Soviet of the USSR of 19 April, 1943, the Supreme Court of the Military Collegium of the USSR sentences the accused **Krasnov P. N.**, **Shkuro A. G.**, **Sultan Kelitch-Ghirey**. **Krasnov S. N.**, **Domanov T. I.**, and von **Pannwitz** to death by hanging.

The sentence was carried out.

Pravda No 15 **(10406) from January 17, 1947**

Initial Place of Exile of Cossacks in Siberia

As indicated by those who returned from Soviet confinement, the first place of exile by the majority of those forcibly repatriated by the Western Allies, the Cossacks, was the Kemerovo Region [*Область*].

It is located in Western Siberia, south of the city of Tomsk, in what is known as the Kuznets Basin. It contains the following cities: Kemerov, Prokopyevsk, and Stalinsk (previously Staro-Kuznetsk [now Novo-Kuznetsk]), which is often referred to as Zinkovo and is a suburb of Prokopyevsk.

This region lies south of the Great Siberian Railroad route and is connected to it by a branch coming out of the Yurga Station (the westernmost railroad junction of the Taiga). This line goes to Prokopyevsk and farther to Stalinsk.

The basin is rich with brown hard coal, the mining of which occupies a great number of people who are imprisoned in the many concentration camps of the region.

As can be seen from a geographic atlas of the USSR published by the Main Geodesic and Cartographic Administration from the Council of Ministers of the USSR in 1949, the Kuznets Basin is the most densely populated part of Siberia. Conventional symbols that show the population density of cities show that in Kemerov, Prokopyevsk, and Stalinsk, there are from 100 to 500 thousand people in each.

The Kemerovo Region is bordered on the west by the Novosibirsk Region and the Altai Area, on the south by the Gorno-Altaisk and the Khakassk Autonomous Regions, and on the west by the Krasnoyarsk Area.

From Prokopyevsk to the Chinese border (the Mongolian Republic) is a distance of approximately 500 kilometers.

Ed.

List of Places of Imprisonment Mentioned by Returnees from Soviet Captivity

Kemerovo Region

Camp Zinkov [Зинкого, one of many on this list not found on other lists], near the station of the same name some 15-20 kilometers from Prokopyevsk.
Camp Tirgansky Slope—at Prokopyevsk
Camp Birch Grove—at Prokopyevsk.
Camp Abagur—within 10 kilometers of Stalinsk.
Camp Baidayevka—near the town of the same name on the River Tom.
Camp *No 10*—within 3-4 kilometers of Kuznetska.
Transit Camp near Kuznetska.
Transit Camp in Novosibirsk.
Central Camp near Stalinsk.
Novosibirsk Camp.
Central Infirmary near Stalinsk.

Kazakh SSR.

Central Prison in Petropavlosk on the Ishim River.
Camp Kengir for 7-8 thousand prisoners.

Camp Spassk—within 45 kilometers of Karaganda.
Special Camp in Karaganda created out of Camp Section *No 1*.
Camp Balkash.
Camp Dzheskazgan [tranlator's note: Джесказган, for which modern spelling is fluid].
Camp Churbai-Nura within 45 kilometers of Karaganda.
Sandy Camp in Karaganda.

Mordovia ASR [Autonomous Soviet Republic].
Camp Potma *2*.
Dubrov Camp *No 11*.

Irkutsk Region:
Camp Taishet *No 019*, *No 022*, and *No 038*.
Alexandrovsk Central Prison.

Komi ASSR:
Camp Abes [*Абес,* which stumped me], Inta Region (Abes *No 3* and Abes *No 4*).
Invalid House, Ukhta,

The above list of the names of places of imprisonment, of course, is far from complete, since the USSR has endless numbers of them on its territories,

Ed.

Forced Repatriation, In the Hands of the Bolsheviks, and Freedom from Soviet Confinement

On May 28, 1945, at around 13:00 hours, all the officers found in the Stan of Field Ataman Domanov, headed by General P. N, Krasnov and along with Domanov, himself, were put in automobiles covered with canvas. We were told that we were going to a "conference."

My wife brought me my coat, but an English officer who stood right there told her that we were returning after three or four hours, so that it would not be necessary to bring a coat, for the day was a hot one.

On leaving Lienz, approximately five kilometers from the place, leading up to Oberdrauburg, we saw motorcycles with side cars on which machine guns had been placed; farther ahead, there were tanks and English Gendarmes in red caps. Our column stopped and two English soldiers got into every car: one had an automatic weapon against his body, where we were sitting, the other was on the roof of the driver's cabin.

We all immediately understood that such accompaniment did not portend well for our going to a "conference." Several people suggested that they were taking us to an English camp to hold us there as prisoners of war, but no one thought that they might give us over to the Soviets.

In Spittal, they took us out of the vehicles and announced that we were being turned over to the Soviet Command, adding that, according to an agreement made, we would not be shot.

After this, before entering the barracks, we were asked to hand over our valuables, such as cigarette cases, watches, and the like. They also took away our pocket knives.

I was put in a barrack with General Krasnov and other generals, along with the head of Domanov's Stan. In the same room with me were Colonel Sklyarov, V. V. Lukyanko—Ataman of the Kuban stanitsas in Italy, Colonel F. [Ф, sometimes translated as Th, as in Theodore versus Fyodor]. P. Gridasov, Colonel Y. N. Bely, Colonel M. I. Zimin, and several others whose names I no longer remember.

A petition directed to English General Alexander was written in the room in which General Krasnov and other generals had been put, in which it was stated that turning us over to the Soviets constituted a gross violation of international law and asked that it be stopped. The petition was signed by all the officers in the barrack and turned over to an English officer with the request that it be taken to the person designated.

General Shkuro and his staff were put in a two-story, stone house across from us. At about 8 o'clock in the morning, English soldiers brought us a meal. All but two of us refused it.

The night of May 28-29 was anxious; almost nobody slept. Colonel Sklyarov and I walked in the yard next to the barrack. General Domanov came up to us at about two in the morning and condemned with outrage the actions of the English Command, saying:

"Had I known the intentions of the English some two days earlier, things would be different." But we were all convinced that he had been aware of preparations for turning us over.

During this conversation, we heard some sort of fuss near the bathroom and, walking nearer, saw three officers removing our Lieutenant Colonel Sutulov from a noose. They quickly informed the head of the English guards. He sent a stretcher and Sutulov was carried away to the infirmary. What happened to him later, I don't know. The rest of the evening went by peacefully.

Early in the morning on May 29, everyone gathered in the camp's yard, where the priests with us began a worship service.

At the end of the service, English soldiers appeared in the camp with rifles and automatic weapons. We all, as if on command, sat on the ground and decided not to enter the vehicles voluntarily. General Krasnov sat at the window of his room. The soldiers surrounded us and started to move us by force, beating us with gun stocks, kicking us, pulling us by the arms, and the like.

They wanted to pull General Krasnov by force from his window, but those close to him came up and carried him through the window. Then they sat him in the middle of a group of officers who protected him from the blows of the soldiers.

Realizing that their methods, that is, beatings, were not helping, the soldiers started grabbing us individually and throwing us forcibly into the vehicles that stood at the camp gate. In this way, loading dragged on for three-four hours.

General Shkuro and his staff were put into a separate vehicle.

Three soldiers sat on each vehicle. One sat in the cab, another, with a Tommy gun, was on top of the cabin. The other was in the body with us. A tanket was between every two vehicles, and the entire column was encircled by gendarmes in motorcycles equipped with machine guns.

Each vehicle had 35-40 men. In the vehicle going with me were: Generals Solamakhin, Tikhotsky, Yesaulov, Voronin; Colonels Sklyarov, Golubok, Lukyanenko, Zimin, Gridasov; Lieutenant Colonel Vinikov; and others whom I do not remember.

We reached Judenburg about 3 o'clock in the afternoon. Soviet soldiers wearing green shoulder straps with similarly colored crowns on their caps met us on a bridge. Later we learned that they were the border NKVD.

As we were being unloaded from the vehicles, two men threw themselves into the river. Since the bridge was a high one, they were smashed to death.

An English officer handed a list of those brought to be given over to a Soviet colonel. The latter, announcing us to the Soviet convoy at the door of a hundred-year-old factory, started to call off everyone on the list while he stood on the bridge.

At that time, we heard some sharp words being exchanged between General Shkuro and a Soviet officer and listened as General Shkuro, raising his voice, said:

"In order to speak to a general, one must first stand at attention and salute." Addressing a Soviet general standing there, he insisted that the impertinent Soviet officer be removed. The general ordered the officer to leave.

After this, all of our generals were led off to the place assigned to them.

We were all put into separate workshops of the factory, where masses of clothes and such had been thrown around. They said that these were from the ranks of the Cossack Corps of von Pannwitz, taken away to Graz from there a few hours before our arrival.

In the evening, the English provided biscuits and canned meats for us for our meal.

We spent the night lying on the bare ground of the factory's workshops. Soviet guards stood at the doors.

On the morning of May 30, we were assembled in the yard and under strict convoy, with machine guns and dogs, led to be loaded into freight cars that stood not too far from the factory.

Toward the evening of that day, at around 18:00 hours, we arrived in Graz. On exiting the freight cars, we were led to a prison. There, they made us all sit on the ground, and we were ordered not to stand up.

That was when questioning and searches began, for which we had to take off our clothes until naked and be inspected everywhere imaginable, have our clothes and footwear mangled, have all our valuables taken away, along with documents, good new underwear, footwear and such. From me personally, a watch, cigarette case, 2653 Italian lira, and close to a thousand German marks were given up at this search. Searches and questioning went on the whole night.

On the morning of the 31st, we were led into a prison and put into chambers, 15-20 men in each.

In the chamber with me were: Sklyarov, Zimin, Medinsky. Gridasov, Lukyanenko, Morozov, Mikhailov, Tchebunyaev, Lieutenant Colonel Vinikov, and Lieutenant Sosyka. I do not remember the others.

We spent 10-12 days in this prison. During this time, some of our men were taken away, No one knew where they were taken.

All of the generals at Graz were taken by airplane to Moscow.

About 13-14 of us were led out of the prison into its yard, checked off a list, and under strict convoy, led to the railroad station, where we were loaded 40-50 per car.

During loading, the following happened to me: I was still walking with crutches at that time, for my leg had not yet healed. While being loaded, some NKVD lieutenant tore the crutches from my hands and said:

"They are no longer needed by you." Trying to throw them away, he turned and fell. In his fall, one of his legs landed on a neighboring rail just as a train was passing over it. He gave a anguished cry. The passing train had cut off the lieutenant's leg.

The freight cars were so crowded that everybody had to sit. To lie down was impossible. In those wagons (we were being taken in cattle cars), primitive bathrooms had been contrived, consisting of an opening through a door with a tin gutter [жолоб, probably a typo] extending outside.

After we had been loaded, a sergeant walked into the car, to collect vouchers for any money or things that had been taken away, announcing that if anyone hid anything, they would be beaten to death. Everyone turned over the required documents.

From Graz, we were taken to Hungary, then Rumania. At Plaesti, the rail cars were moved onto wide Russian tracks.

Along the way, soldiers broke into the wagons, taking away things of any value that we still had left after the searches in Graz, such as: boots, outer clothing, or underwear. We were given all manner of rubbish in exchange. Those who protested were ruthlessness beaten.

We were fed very poorly in the wagons (a thin, soupy balanda and raw black bread). Water to drink was given out twice a day. Washing up was not deemed necessary.

All the convoy soldiers were equipped with wooden mallets with long handles, with which they knocked on the walls and roof of the wagon every half hour, not allowing us to fall asleep neither by night nor day.

Morning and evening inspections of each wagon were conducted as follow: three soldiers with hammers came into each wagon, while soldiers with rifles and automatic weapons stood next to it. The one in charge, usually a sergeant, chased everyone into one corner and began his count. Everyone counted was chased to the opposite corner of the wagon with a blow from a hammer struck anywhere they might, usually on the back. Sometimes such inspections were made at night, also.

They took us by way of Moscow, where we stayed four days, but could see nothing, for the wagons were covered. We went farther on to Sverdlovsk (Yekaterinburg). At Sverdlovsk, we were taken out of the wagons, and led to baths under guard. From Sverdlosk, it was straight to Novosibirsk, After a daylong stop at Novosibirsk, it was on to the Kemerovo Region.

On the 12th or 13th of July, we arrived at the Zinkovo Station. Here, they let us out and led us to a huge barbed-wire-enclosed camp, in which there were all of two barracks, a kitchen and a bathroom.

A single camp tent was issued to 20 people, who were then ordered to put it up and accommodate themselves in it. About two days later, they brought some forest materials for bunks. They gave us no bedding at all. We all slept in the bare bunks without taking our clothes off. The insects ate us up. Food in this camp was particularly unpleasant: a thin soup in the morning, oatmeal or barley cereal, while for lunch, as it was called, borscht from rotting sour cabbage and thin barley kasha, with the same as for breakfast for dinner. Sometimes they gave us salted fish, often rotten, and 400 grams of bread of the worst quality.

People fell ill, especially the Germans. Intestinal disorders began, especially dysentery—15-20 people died each day.

The following outrageous event took place in this camp: one of the prisoner-of-war nationalists stepped out of a tent with a kettle, intending to wash, and took about five paces toward the wire fence. At that moment a round from an automatic weapon rang out and the poor nationalist fell dead. It turned out that a drunken officer had climbed into the watchtower and, taking the weapon from a guard, killed a man for the fun of it.

About three days after our arrival in camp, we were taken to the baths and all of us were shaved without a single hair being left untouched, which at least gave us a chance to free ourselves of insects. All of our clothing was disinfected several times.

The following happened to me in this camp: my still-not-fully-healed leg, swollen greatly from stress, broke out in purple splotches, thanks to which I could not wear any shoes and walked around barefoot. I went to the dispensary. The head of the medical unit, a woman in her mid-twenties, announced after looking at the leg that she could see no swelling and could not help me. I indignantly began to protest, to which she answered:

"The more of you die, the more I am paid."

With the same leg, a few days later, I walked to a different camp, during which guards took away the pole I was using as a cane.

Some 20-25 days later, we were formed up in the yard of the camp and all those who were not officers were taken away. Among them, there happened to be a few officers who were hiding their rank.

They led us officers away from the camp zone and took us under strict guard across the city of Prokopyevsk, which was some 15-20 kilometers from Zinkovo, to a camp carrying the name of "Tirgansky Slope," where there were coal mining shafts. Having dragged myself with a bum leg to the new camp, which already had German prisoners of war, I went to a German physician who worked in the camp's infirmary and in this way obtained the necessary medications.

At Camp Tirgansky Slope, most of the prisoners of war worked in the mine shafts and construction in the city of Prokopyevsk, but several brigades were sent to kolhozes to work in the fields.

Professor Phillip Ivanovich Bednyagin worked with livestock in a solhoz, while agronomist Lukinov worked as an agronomist in an ancillary household of the camp. I and about two dozen Russians and Germans were sent to a kolhoz to help with the harvest. We worked from dawn to dusk. After a month, we were returned to the camp and assigned to other work. I wound up in a mine called Voroshilov in the city of Prokopyevsk, where I worked for about a year.

In January of 1946, all former Soviet citizens who had served in the German Army, then been with us, had their guards removed and were allowed to live in the city and work on their own recognizance, although they had to register every week at a special office.

Thus, we—old emigrants and prisoner-of-war Germans who had served in General von Pannwitz's corps—were the only ones remaining.

In the month of October of 1945, due to deep freezes making it impossible live in tents, we were moved to Camp "Birch Grove" in Prokopyevsk, where we were put into barracks that were suitably warm but incredibly dirty. Bedbugs ate us up. We had no manner of bedding at all. We slept on bare bunks without taking off our clothes.

All this was reflected in our work, so the mine administration decided to supply us with mattresses and blankets from its own resources.

We ourselves brought coal for heating up from the shafts, which was forbidden, although the camp leadership looked the other way at it, seeing in it a savings in heating costs.

There, in Birch Grove, we began to be questioned by special investigators who came just for that purpose. All the questioning took place at night. People were called out at 7-8 in the evening and held until 5 o'clock in the morning, which was the time that we had to get up. Returnees from questioning did not go back to bed, but had breakfast and went off to work in the shafts.

The entire winter passed that way. In the spring of 1946, we were once more returned to Camp Tirgansky Slope, where we worked until January of 1947. During this time, several barracks were constructed through the labor of the prisoners of war.

In the middle of January, a column of Germans arrived from Germany (about 2,500). They had been sentenced to various terms from 10 to 25 years.

Our entire contingent of prisoners of war were awakened, put into rail cars, and transported to the town of Abagur, 10 kilometers from Stalinsk. There, they worked in a lumber mill and in construction.

During my time at Camps Zinkovo, Tirgansky Slope, and Birch Grove, mortality among prisoners of war was very high, Dozens died daily.

The deceased were buried naked. Those assigned to burials were awakened at 2 o'clock at night, given shovels and picks, and made to carry frozen corpses on a stretcher over the snow for 2-3 kilometers at 30-35 degrees and sometimes even more. [The author must mean degrees below zero, at which temperature Fahrenheit and Celsius scales are almost identical.] On the way, frozen corpses would fall off the stretchers. There were up to three corpses on each stretcher, carried by 6 men in snow up to their knees. A tag with the number of his personnel file was tied onto a finger on the left leg of each of the deceased. Beginning in the middle of 1947, the deceased were buried in their dirty old underwear, and from 1951, they were buried in coffins made out of scraps of wood.

On getting to the cemetery (an place without a fence on a hill), one began to dig the grave. The ground was frozen to an almost one-and-a-half-to-two-meter depth—neither crowbar nor pick penetrated it. How many bitter difficulties we went through in order to dig a grave a half meter deep and several meters in length! Not until 3-4 o'clock did we finish the funeral, as we called it, and returned to the camp so that at 2 o'clock the next night we could repeat this penal servitude all over again. I was part of this brigade for about two months.

In Camp Abagur, I was made the accountant for productivity (recording the work of the entire camp).

Lieutenant Colonel Yeremenko was named the engineer for the lumber mill, at which he led construction work.

In March of 1947, we were transferred in marching order to Camp Baidaevka, which was 2 kilometers from a fair-sized village of the same name on the River Tom. We worked there in the shafts, a brick factory, and in the construction of mine shafts. There, too, I was made the accountant for labor productivity, but I was often torn away from my main work and sent to a mine in order to load and unload coal and construction materials, so that I had to do physical labor in the daytime and still put in 2-3 hours in the office at night.

The sick and injured, some from Prokopyevsk, some from Abagur, were sent for treatment to a central infirmary near the city of

Stalinsk. Among them were Colonel Gridasov, Lieutenant Colonel Smitchek, Lieutenant Colonel Georgii Avksentyevich, First Lieutenant Akimov, Lieutenant Alexei Popov, Lieutenant Pavel Kuznetsov, Lieutenant Colonel Plossky, and Major V. A. Zakharin. [The disagreement over Cossack ranks is a subject suitable for scholarly research. Mine are approximations of relative rank, at best, rather than exact equivalents.]

Many people died in the camps, starting at Zinkovo and ending in Baidaevka. A particularly large number of deaths occurred in Zinkovo and Birch Grove. In Zinkovo, the ill lay in a field without any medical help, in horrid sanitary conditions, but some did recover, even there. First Lieutenant Butenko, Colonel Hedbaevsky, and many others died there.

It was only after our second time in Camp Tirgansky Slope that the head of the medical unit arrived. He was a good physician and an energetic person with great freedom to act (not a party member, he was rumored to be a former prisoner). He set right to work, organizing an infirmary at the camp, bringing in German physicians (there were no Russian physicians among us), and setting up places for the infirm (at camp entrances), where he ministered to them as well as he could. He did not stay for long, however. He was replaced, the medical unit's autonomy was taken away, and a physician who was junior to him was named as its head. Regardless of that, he continued to treat prisoners of war and saved many lives.

As I have already mentioned, investigators showed up at Camp Birch Grove and began to call people out to be questioned. Forced to work by day, we were questioned at night. Almost the entire winter went by in this way.

I was first called for questioning at 18 hours and was held until 5 o'clock in the morning, after which I had to be in the shafts by 6 o'clock, where my production quota was 101%.

The investigator, a Lieutenant Colonel, met me with horrid profanities and threatened me with a revolver. I sat in silence as I listened to his abuse and threats. I was indifferent to everything at the time. We all were awaiting the end and praying to God to speed it along. I must have actually smiled at his verbal abuse, because he suddenly ended it and asked why I was smiling. I answered that I was amazed by the behavior of an officer who was wearing the shoulder straps of a staff officer.

"You should be hung instead of cursed," he answered me.

Questioning then began and continued until 5 o'clock in the morning, wearing me out to such a degree that I felt as if I was drunk and only recovered out in the cold.

I had to endure this kind of questioning dozens of times.

Many were taken by the NKVD to Prokopyevsk after questioning. Among them were: Colonel Sklyarov, Lieutenant Dakhin, Lieutenant Nevzorov, Colonel Somov, Colonel Medinsky, Lieutenant Sosyka, Lieutenant Colonel A. M. Protopopov, Colonel Kadushkin, Colonel Fetisov, Colonel Zimin, and Colonel Morozov.

There were some nights when the inquisitor called for you at 6-7 in the evening and sat you down on a stool across from him while he wrote or read something or other. You sat quietly, watching him. After an hour or two, he posed some sort of stupid question having nothing to do with the matter at hand, which was followed by another two-hour silence, but if you should happen to start falling asleep, you were in trouble: either a blow to some part of your physiognomy or being put out in the cold in only a jacket to—"refresh yourself," as they called it, until your teeth begin to chatter and your entire body shake from the cold.

Testimony given during questioning was checked in places. For example: on the question of what I was doing in Yugoslavia, I answered that I was serving in the government. Two months later, I was called again and told that everything I had revealed had been correct, but that I had hidden from them my having served in the position of secretary to the Governor [*бана*] of the Danubian Province. To this I answered:

"I answered the questions. I was asked what I did; I answered that I served. Had you asked what position I had held, then I would have told you that."

On the investigator's table, there were sheets of paper with typing on them. On the bottom, at the left side, I read "Belgrade," along with the dates. This caught my interest, so I asked the investigator where this information had been obtained. He smiled and gave me one of the sheets. Just about my entire life in Yugoslavia was written there. I could not make out the signature.

In 1948, at the end of August or the beginning of September, we were transferred from Camp Baidaevka to Camp *No 10*, which was some 3-4 kilometers from the city of Kuznetsk Station [treanslator's note: *Cm.*] (the place that Dostoevsky lived in exile. The walls of his house there still stood.) The German prisoners of war from this camp were sent home, to their homeland.

The living conditions and regimen were better, even though we had to work just as hard.

At that time, there were no more than 250 of us from Lienz left: some had been taken away by the NKVD, some had perished, while several others, due to their "exceptional service," were freed and resettled in various places in the Kemerovo Region. These were: R. N., Colonel P., and 2-3 others whose names I do not remember.

In this camp, we Russians, had our fingerprints [*оттиски польцев*], palm prints, and photographs taken. We interpreted this to mean that something serious was about to happen to us. To this end, a few days before we were sent to Camp Baidaevka, an NKVD prosecutor arrived (by then, they were no longer NKVD, but MVD) and read the indictment beneath the receipt [*под расписку*] to every one of us, accusing us according to paragraph 58 item 4 [*Cm. 58 n. 4*] (providing assistance to the international bourgeoisie). When this was read to me, I told the prosecutor that they, not I, should be held on this point, because, by their participation in the war, they had provided assistance to their allies, the English, Americans, and French, for which he cursed me soundly.

On October 13th by date, they called out 78 people from our emigrant group, took away our bedding and part of our clothing, and led us out the gates of the camp, where a huge convoy with dogs and motorcycles awaited. The sergeant in charge of the convoy announced how we should behave on route: not to look to the sides and not to talk. In concluding, he told us:

"A step to the right or a step to the left will be considered an escape attempt, and you will be shot without warning."

From this moment on, we heard these same words every time we were led by a convoy.

They led us through Kuznetsk Station, across the railroad tracks, and stopped us at a high fence. This was the transit prison. The gates opened and we were led into a corridor, then from there into a room, but such a small one that we could only stand in it. There was no room to sit.

We were taken one at a time from this room to the prison office at the same corridor and told that, by a special session, according to paragraph 58 item 4, we were sentenced to 25 years imprisonment in special camps [*спечлагерях*]. We were given a pile of papers for our signatures, which already had written on them: our last name, first name, country of origin, date of birth, length of sentence, and signature of the condemned. These sheets were 12-15 centimeters in length and 6-7 in width. There was no way they could be called judgments. After this procedure, by orders from above, we were all moved to a room with a concrete floor, without pallets or any bedding necessities at all. We all lay down side-by-side on the floor, putting under us whatever we had. Crowding, stuffiness, poor food, all of it affected us oppressively.

All of us easily accepted the news of our sentences. I even laughed on hearing that it was to be 25 years, and to the question posed to me by the officer making the announcement, I answered that such a sentence can only be laughed at.

They held us there, in the transit camp of Kuznetsk Station, for about ten days, after which we were taken away in special wagon cars for the transport of prisoners (shortened to "zak" [from the first syllable of *заключенных,* instead of "zek" as derived supposedly from the the abbreviation "z/k" for the same term, according to others]). The wagon had shutters and no windows on one side. Each compartment in these cars was intended for only 10-12 people, but they packed twenty of us into each. The crowding and stuffiness was horrible. A guard with a revolver walked along the corridor. You were allowed to go to the bathroom twice a day, morning and evening. Drinking water was supplied 2-3 times, no more. We lived on dry rations, consisting of 600 grams of bread and salted fish, which we tried not to eat, for we would be tortured by thirst afterwards, since the water allowance each time was one 300-gram cup.

In this way, we were taken to Novosibirsk, unloaded, and transferred to a transit prison, where we were held 3-4 days. We sat in our rooms. They led us out into a small yard for 10-15 minutes of exercise, making us walk in circles, one on the heels [*затылок*] of another. From Novosibirsk we went to Petropavlosk in the same wagons, where, upon being unloaded we were seated inside a "black raven" (an automobile specially adapted for the transport of prisoners) that had a capacity of 8 people. Twenty of us, however, were put into one, so that we were packed in side-by-side, neither sitting nor standing.

In Petropavlovsk, they placed us in various rooms for transport. I and the now-deceased Lieutenant Colonel Yefimenko wound up in a room in which there were mostly *urkas* (criminals)—especially of the castes of thieves and bandits—the dregs of Soviet society. They could be divided into two categories: thieves and bitches. Thieves were the upper layer of this caste. They kept themselves apart, feuding with the prison administration and doing no work. Bitches were former thieves who had gone over to the side of the administration. They had administrative duties in camps and enjoyed all privileges possible. They robbed political prisoners in prisons and camps, turning over the stolen things to supervisors, who took them out of the zones to sell them, then divided what they got with the bitches. There was great enmity between these two classes, murderous even. If one of them turned up in the camp of the enemy, he did not come out alive—stabbed to death. There was no mercy. The first and second carried on in freedom, living exclusively off theft and robbery, at which they separated themselves into categories: one took only money and valuable things, the other disdained nothing. This horrible evil of the camps and prisons continued until the beginning of 1954, when, by special order from Moscow, all the thieves and bitches were gathered and taken to the far north.

I have already mentioned that Lieutenant Colonel Yefimenko and I were put in a room with mostly urkas. On entering the room the elder of this category of people asked us what we had. We showed our things. Not finding anything suitable for himself, he left us in peace, leaving us a place on the floor, by the wall ... Generally in transit, there is no bedding of any kind and everyone sleeps on the floor.

That night, Yefimenko had his pocket cut and 15 rubles removed. He told me about it in the morning, when he noticed the theft. A man who looked to be 45-50 lay next to me on the other side. He never spoke to anyone and was left alone by the urkas. He looked quite rough. Hearing us talk about the missing money, he called over the elder of the room, an urka, and said:

"The money stolen from this old man better be returned within 10 minutes!" He hesitated some, but the order was followed. Before 10 minutes had passed, one of their company walked by us, tossed Yefimenko the money and said: "Forgive me, old man. I took it by mistake!" We later learned that the man sleeping next to me was a famous thief and the leader of one of the thieves' organizations.

We stayed 10 days in Petropavlovsk. A train was made up there out of freight cars, equipped with a stove. They took us on foot under strict convoy across the entire city to the railroad station. When they took us from the prison out onto the square, there was a mass of people waiting. Many of the women were in tears. The convoy militia dispersed the crowd.

Several men fell on the way to the station, worn down by poor nutrition. They were picked up by a car that followed the column to the railroad station. It was about 5 kilometers from the prison to the station. Four days later, we were in the city of Ingir, where there was a large camp made up of some 7-8 thousand men. Some 2000 of us arrived there on our train, all guilty of paragraph 58 (politicals). We were let into the camp after being checked and searched. That lasted for some 4 hours.

We learned that there had been a fight there between the thieves and bitches some two days before our arrival. It caused 30 deaths. The day before we arrived, those responsible were sent off, along with others, in an unknown direction.

After being placed into barracks, we were led to the baths. Our belongings were disinfected and everyone except those who had been photographed with beards were shaved. Not a hair was left anywhere. We were similarly shaved over our entire stay in the camp at every visit to the baths (every 10 days). The next day, they took us out to work. Thus began our lives in prison camps.

Several others in our group, among whom were Lieutenant Colonel Vinnikov, Major Lukinov. Major Andrei Kalyuzhny, Colonel Gridasov, Lieutenant A. Popov, and Captain Akimov, and I stayed at this camp until the beginning of June, 1949, when, in a party of about 2,000 men, we were once more loaded on a train at Karaganda, from where we were taken by vehicle on another day to Camp Spassk—45 kilometers from Karaganda.

The village of Spassk is a former monastery, to which delinquent clergy were sent until 1914. A copper smelting plant and the offices for it, which were liquidated in 1928, I believe, had also been there.

The barracks and a hospital were built on the steppe. With nothing but sand all around, there wasn't a settlement anywhere. The camp was surrounded by several rows of barbed wire. Intended for 8-10 thousand men, there were 10-12 thousand of us and close to 16,000 men in 1950. There was terrible crowding in the double bunks (plank), that were intended for 4 people, but that slept 6-8 of us. There were about 2,000 women in this camp, who were separated from us by a 5-meter wall topped with barbed wire.

In August and December of 1949, two more parties arrived. With them were the emigrants who had been left behind at Ingir, except for Lieutenant Colonel Yefimenko, the former [*б.*] lawyer, Dobovsky and the priest, Malashko.

We stayed in this camp until September 21, 1954, that is, until the release of the foreign citizens and those without a country of citizenship in the special camp organized in Karaganda from the former Camp Section *No 1*. Those in the infirmary were temporarily left in Spassk, along with other invalids.

I worked on construction in Camp Spassk, where they built the new settlement of "Spassk," in which our administrators and guards later lived.

Stone served for structural material. It was obtained there in the camp. Sand and clay were added to it at the site of construction. Wood was brought from Karaganda.

In August of 1949, we read a note in the local paper, "The Karaganda Socialist," that the village of Spassk had been built by the Komsomol of Karaganda. They were congratulated and so forth. Yet, aside from prisoners, from the chief engineer down to the lowliest laborer, there were none there who were in freedom except for supervisors, guards, or officers—those in charge of us in camp.

Here is how cities and villages that, judging from what is printed in the newspapers had been built by the Komsomol, were really built.

All labor was provided for free by prisoners. As encouragement for excellent work, 100-150 grams of kasha and 200 grams of bread were added to their ration. There were no other kinds of privileges.

I started work in the stone quarry. Then the brigade I was in was transferred to construction. There, I worked in digging clay, for which one person was normally given 10 stretchers, which had to be filled over the course of a day, meaning that about 4 ½ cubic meters of clay had to be removed from a hole that was 3-4 meters deep. Doing this work, I dropped to 48 kilograms in weight, this for someone who was 182 centimeters in height.

One day, the head of the camp's medical unit, Lieutenant Yermakov, walking past where I was working and seeing me naked to the waist in the hole, ordered me to climb out, get dressed, and follow him. Walking up to the head of the guards, he said that he was taking me with him back to the camp. There in the camp, he put me on a scale and, establishing that I weighed 48 kilograms, ordered that I be taken off of work, gave me dietary rations for two months and put me to work in the greenhouses, where the work was easier.

This had been the first and only indulgence toward me in all my time in the camps.

As soon as I got a little healthier, I was taken to work at a lime oven, where the work was run by an imprisoned engineer, V., from the village of Kuzminki, some 30 kilometers from the Otradnoy Stanitza of the Kuban.

There, I caught my breath a little. Even though I had to work in very high temperatures at the oven, it was nevertheless much easier on me. I did burn my eyes with lime dust and had to spend 5 months receiving ambulatory treatment by an eye doctor, who was also a prisoner. Not having any specific work, I helped the camp's bookkeeper, keeping track of the clothing allowances for the barracks, but mostly keeping the books of the so-called special section of prisoners.

During this period, something happened to me that characterized the attitude of the authorities toward us old emigrants.

Each barrack had what was called a cultural authority (cultorg) [*Культурный орган (культорг)*]. This was usually one of the invalid prisoners who oversaw the newspapers, books, and mail received by prisoners in his barrack. The cultorg of our barrack left when he finished his term, and the head of the barrack assigned me to replace him. A month later, a new head of the camp [*лагпункта*] arrived, who wished to meet with the barrack cultorgs. He called them in turn into his office and gave them suggestions and such. My turn came up. I went.

He asked, "What is your last name?"
I told him.
"What were you doing prior to 1914?"
"I was an officer," I answered. "Emigrant."
"You can go."

Before I could even get back to my barrack, I was removed from that duty.

In August of 1954, a prisoner who worked permanently in the special section asked me to help him in making lists of foreign prisoners and stateless people and told me that there were rumors that they were to be sent to a special camp. Almost all of the old emigrants wound up on these lists. In all, there were 168 foreigners in our camp.

On September 18, we were informed that all foreign citizens would be taken to a special camp in Karaganda on the 21st.

It was true. On that day, toward 7 o'clock, vehicles were provided, we were seated and by 11 o'clock, we were already in Karaganda in Camp *No 1*. They began to bring others there from camps in Kazakh USSR. Among the arrivals were: Lieutenant Colonel G. S. Rudenko, from Kingir, Colonel Golubov, from Balkhash, Major Vonifaty Rakov, from Ingir, Lieutenant Colonel Alexander Fomich Kalyuzhny, from Dzheskangan [probably a typographical error for Dzheskazgan], and many others …

When this camp turned out to be too small, they transferred us to Churubai-Nura—within 45 kilometers of Karaganda.

As soon as we arrived at Karaganda, we were required to fill out an affidavit in which we had to give or country of citizenship, whether we were prisoners of war or internees, where we had relatives, and where we wanted to go from the Soviet Union.

On November 7, at about 19 hours, 14 men, with me in that number, Cpt. I. I. Kiselev, P. I. Akimov, Lieutenant Colonel G. Y. Smichek, Lt. M. A. Nevzorov, Lieutenant N. V. Kovalenko. and several native Yugoslavs, were called by the head of the Special Administration of Sandy Camp (that is what the camp they were holding us in was called). Each of us filled out a form in which, aside from the usual questions, there were some like these: prisoner of war or internee; where, when, and under what circumstances were we captured or turned over; where we wished to go; and who among our relatives lived outside of Soviet borders.

On arrival at Churabai-Nura, I was designated as the bookkeeper in charge of construction materials at a large construction establishment for residential buildings. I worked there until February of 1955, that is, until the day that I was summoned and told that I should be prepared to leave on February 9th from Collection Camp Potma 2 and, following that, to Austria, which is where were I had in the fullness of time announced that I wanted to go.

On February 21, I arrived at Potma 2. They brought zaks under guard from Karaganda to Chelyabinsk, Kuibyshev (Samara), then Ruzayevka, and, finally, Potma 2. We sat around for several days at each transfer. Along with me, there were: Captain. I. I. Kiselev, P. I. Akimov, P. S. Telegin, and 21 Germans and Yugoslavs.

On leaving the livestock car, I realized that there were no longer any guards. We were met by a supervisor, who led us into the camp.

The conditions were much better in this camp. No work was required. People rested. We were fed better. We were allowed, in the company of a supervisor, to go into settlements to get produce. Mainly we looked for fat, although during my entire stay there (5 months) it had been impossible to find sugar or butter. Most of the produce was of low quality.

I was there until the 11th of June. That day, 25 of us: (5 Russians: myself, Colonel V. D. Belov, Nesterovsky, Lieutenant B. K Ganusovsky, and G. Kozorez), along with 20 Austrians and Yugoslavs, were notified that we would be leaving for Bykovo (a Moscow suburb) on the Moscow-Ryazan railroad.

On June 12th, at 2 o'clock, we were let out of the zone and, accompanied by an officer, went to the railroad station. For the first time in 10 years, we were free to sit in the restaurant in the hall of the station. All in all, although not quite completely, we felt relatively free.

We arrived in Bykovo on July 14th at 9 o'clock in the morning. They put us up in a villa in which the German General Paulus had stayed during his time as a prisoner.

On July 18th, we were awakened at 5 o'clock in the morning, put on a bus, and driven into Moscow. We drove around Moscow until 9 o'clock, sightseeing. Central Moscow definitely had been transformed, but its other parts seemed little changed. The university on the Sparrow [Воробьевых (Vorobyevy)] Hills looked beautiful. It could be seen many miles from Moscow.

At 9 o'clock in the morning, we arrived at the hall of the Kiev station and took seats on the Moscow-Vienna Express. Each of us was provided with a reserved place in the sleeping car, four to a compartment. We ate in the dining car; the food was good.

Along the way—indeed it caught my attention in Moscow, itself—many churches were being repaired. In the Moscow Woods there was Vassily the Blissful and the Uspensky Cathedral in the Kremlin. According to the NKVD officer accompanying us, repairs were continuing on the [St] Sophia Cathedral in Kiev, with even its cupola having its gold restored.

We got to Austria (Wiener Neustadt) without any adventures. We arrived there on July 21st at 8 o'clock in the morning. There, the Soviet officer accompanying us turned us over to the Austrian authorities.

I quickly went to Villach, met with Colonel Dubin and gave a full report on my arrival.

Here, in short, is my life and the lives of almost all of us who wound up in the Soviet Union in 1945.

It was our fate to suffer terrible hardship, deprivation, hunger, and mainly—the humiliation of mindless slave labor.

M. I. Kotzovsky

EXCERPTS from "Amnesty Decree," signed September 17, 1955, in Moscow by the Chairman of the Supreme Soviet of the USSR, K. Voroshilov, and his secretary, N. Pegov.

....

1 — To set free from their place of imprisonment and other measures of punishment those persons who were sentenced up to 10 years of inclusive loss of freedom for the commission of the crime

during the period of the Great Patriotic War in the years 1941-5 of giving aid to the enemy and other crimes as provided under paragraphs 58-1, 58-3, 58-4, 58-6, 58-10, and 58-12 of the Criminal Codes of the RSFSR and the corresponding statutes of the criminal codes of other republics.

2 — To shorten by half the punishment given by the court for sentences of more than 10 years and for crimes listed under the first paragraph of this decree.

3 — To set free from their place of imprisonment, regardless of length of sentence, those sentenced because of their service in the German Army, police, or special German formations.

To free from serving out the rest of their sentences those persons sent for these crimes into exile or deported.

4 — To not apply such amnesty to those being punished for the murder or torture of Soviet citizens.

5 — To stop the processing of matters under investigation, and matters not yet judged by the courts having to do with crimes committed during the period of the Great Patriotic War in the years 1941-5 under paragraphs 58-1, 58-3, 58-4, 58-6, 58-10, and 58-12 of the Criminal Codes of the RSFSR and the corresponding statutes of the criminal codes of other republics, with the exception of the matter of persons sentenced under the fourth paragraph of this decree.

6 — To remove the criminal record and disqualification from citizenship of those freed from punishment by this decree.

To remove the criminal record and disqualification from citizenship of those individuals having previously been found guilty and having been punished for crimes listed under the first paragraph of this decree.

7 — To free from blame those Soviet citizens found outside of its borders who during the period of the Great Patriotic War in the years 1941-5 who surrendered to the enemy or served in the German Army, police, or special German formations.

To free from blame also those Soviet citizens presently found outside its borders who took part during the war in leadership duties in organs of police, gendarmes, or propaganda created by the

Germans, including those involving anti-Soviet organizations in the post-war period, if they atoned for their guilt by later patriotic actions in the service of Russia and acknowledged that guilt.

....

For everyone who knows the essence of Bolshevik power and how matters stand in Russia, it is clear that the "amnesty" is nothing but a propaganda gimmick to catch the weak of spirit and rub the eyes of Europe and America.

We know that Russian national wisdom has created a whole slew of sayings having deep meaning. One of them is: **"A soft bed makes for hard sleep!"** This needs to be remembered on reading this decree by the Soviets of the Soviet **"amnesty."**

Ed.

LETTER FROM THE GERMAN OFFICER, SENIOR LIEUTENANT, GERHARD V. PETRI, formerly commander of a company of the 5th Don Regiment and then a division of the XV Cossack Cavalry Corps.

1 — **March 15, 1954, Marburg**

Having returned from imprisonment in Soviet Russia in October of last year, I very much wish to greet you. I learned your address from Mister Otto Manfred von Pannwitz (brother of General von Pannwitz, executed in Moscow). You probably do not know me. I served as Senior Lieutenant in the XV Cossack Corps and commanded a division until the end.

I was turned over along with the Cossacks to the English on May 28, 1945, and lived for 8 years in Siberia, in the city of Stalinsk, Kemerovo Region.

At the end of 1949, I was sentenced by a military tribunal for having served as an officer in the Cossack Corps.

You, of course, are interested mostly in the fate of the Cossacks. As early as the summer of 1945, a special commission from SHMERSH came from Moscow to our zone. Many Cossack officers were sentenced to 10-25 years. Some of them were sentenced to death. The rest were sent north and to the Far East, in Kolyma and Magadan. Some of the Cossacks were freed from guard [*расконвоированные*] in 1946-7. They live in Siberia. They were not allowed to return to their homeland. A small number of officers also had their guards removed in 1947-8, but then it seems that they were all rounded up once more in 1949, put on trial, and sentenced to 25 years.

Old emigrants who wound up with the Soviets were all sent off to parts unknown in the summer of 1949. I think that they are all imprisoned behind barbed wire.

Esteemed General, sir, I think that you will be able to read what I have written, I have forgotten much. I knew Russian much better. To my regret, I no longer speak it with anyone. That's nothing! I will learn quickly when we go to the Kuban and the Caucasus.

If you have any special questions concerning the Cossacks or officers, I remain your servant. Please accept my heart-felt greetings. Hale to our Cossackdom! And hale to the friendship of Cossacks and Germans on the front!

Sincerely yours,

Gerhard Petri, former Senior Lieutenant

2 — On submission of questions, he answered by letter on April 15, 1954.

Highly esteemed General, sir!

I received your letter 2 days ago and wanted to answer as soon as I could. I want to apologize for writing in such an uncultured manner (as they say in Russia), but you must understand that there is so much I want to tell you that I do not know how to begin.

(He begins his letter with a detailed list of the units of the corps and its command staff. Ed.) Then he continues:

When Colonel Renteln arrived with his regiment (from France), he was sent at the end of March 1945 by von Pannwitz to the English General Alexander, with whom he had been personally acquainted in 1919 in Russia.

Von Pannwitz was anxious to save the Cossacks. He sent him to ask the English to take them into the English colonial army, rather than taking them prisoners, but mostly, not to turn them over to the Reds.

As far as I know, the regiments of the corps surrendered their weapons in Volkermarkt, except for the 4th Kuban Regiment, which was being held prisoner by Totoists and was disarmed there.

After giving up their weapons, the corps's staff and the 3rd, 4th, 5th, 6th, and 8th stayed in the area of Althofen and Melbling. The 1st and 2nd Regiments and the 1st Division staff were at Feldkirchen.

There was not a parade on May 10th or 11th, but there was sort of review near Griffen-Feldkirchen. (He writes this in answer to the question posed to him whether it was true that there had been a parade by units of the corps that day, as had been reported by several Russian publications. Ed.)

After the surrender, I was an officer in the staff of General von Pannwitz and know that General von Pannwitz was arrested on May 26, 1945 (Saturday), at exactly 11 o'clock in the morning in the small village of Mühlen.

May 26th, on the morning that von Pannwitz was arrested, we received an order from the English that all Germans, at 14 hours on May 26, should gather near the road to Neumarkt to be sent to an English camp. Only the Cossacks were left, and there were rumors that they would be taken into the English Army.

We (around 600-700 Germans) were gathered together, surrounded, and locked behind barbed wire. Many Germans had escaped for home earlier, or after dinner on the 21st had run off into the woods with the Cossacks, not believing the English.

On May 28th, we were taken to Judenburg and turned over to the Reds.

On May 29th, we walked 6 kilometers back to the railroad station and spent the night under guard, while on May 30th, we were taken by train to Graz, to prison. We stayed there approximately 10 days.

The Bolsheviks treated the Cossacks the same way they treated us, calling us, "Vlasov traitors!" We were not beaten, but they took away almost everything we had.

On the train that took us to Siberia, there were 2,600 men, of whom 600-800 were Germans, while the rest were Cossacks, of whom most were officers of the 15th Corps, those with Domanov, men from the Caucasus, and emigrants.

It took us over a month to get to Siberia. We arrived in Zenkovo, close to Prokopyevsk, on July 12. In August, the entire camp was transferred to Tirgansky Slope near Prokopyevsk. There on the grass, we began constructing fences, tents, and so on.

Living conditions were worse than I can describe: 600 grams of wet bread and half a liter of balanda (cabbage leaves in water) twice daily. There was no medicine. Approximately 600 Cossacks (old emigrants) and 160-200 Germans died in 1945-7.

The regimen was very strict. We were not allowed to write. We were forced to work for 10 hours a day. It was very bad.

Rank-and-file Cossacks had their guards removed as early as 1946. The junior command staff and those officers who did not fall into SHMERSH courts were set free up to March 1947. Of course, they were not permitted to return to their homeland. They live there. They fit in well even.

During 1945-7, 90 Cossacks, of whom about 10 were caught, and 25 Germans, who were all returned, ran away from our camp. I personally escaped on July 19, 1946, but on the 4th day, Volga Germans turned me in. (Lieutenant Gerhard Petri is a real German from Germany who learned to speak and write in Russian. Ed.)

Toward the end of 1949, the Reds collectively sentenced all of the Germans and officers in the Cossack Corps to 25 years. Rank-and-file Germans were sent home.

In October of 1953, completely unexpectedly, we were all "amnestied," as the Bolsheviks called it, as a group and sent home.

With Cossack greetings, my sincere regards to you.

H. Petri

3 — Letter of June 17, 1954.

....
Now I very much want to give you a more precise account and answer your questions as much as I can.

The 4th Kuban Regiment was taken prisoner by the Titoists May 8-9, 1945. They had been in some sort of settlement in the woods of Styria when they turned in their weapons. It can be said that the Titoists treated them not too badly. They were released on English orders and returned to where the corps was residing near Althofen.

Which English units turned us over to the Bolsheviks, I can not tell for certain, either 34th or 46th. I know for certain that the tanks and other vehicles had insignias—an iron fist. I know this for certain.

On May 26-28, all German officers were in a former RAD (Reichsarbeitsdienst—labor force) camp in the village of Griffen. We were treated fairly, only having photographic apparatus, compasses and binoculars taken away. They fed us very well and guarded us carefully—with tanks and machine guns.

They took us by truck at 7 o'clock in the morning to Judenburg. Along the entire way, there stood tanks, machine guns, and armaments, so that no one would escape.

We were turned over to the MVD on the bridge and herded into a factory.

The prison in Graz might be described as a collection point to which the Bolsheviks brought all Cossacks and those Germans who served with them. Among them were the Cossacks from Lienz, but I did not know them.

I do not know who else they sent out from Graz, for we were closely guarded.

As we were told by the guards, Generals Krasnov, Shkuro, and Domanov were there somewhere.

They took us to Siberia by way of Budapest, Arad, Chernovitz, Kiev, Bryansk, Moscow, Kurgan, Omsk, Novosibirsk, and Belovo.

In Austria and Rumania we were fed sufficiently, but it became worse in the USSR, especially with regard to water. There were 44 men in a 20-ton car, so that not everyone was able to lie down.

In Sverdlovsk (Yekaterinburg) we were taken for disinfection. We were guarded strictly, not allowed off the car. The cars were wrapped in barbed wire.

There were 2,200 of us in the camp: of them, 1600 were Cossacks and 600 were Germans who served in the 15th Corps.

We were quarantined for the first month, although we were still forced to work in a collective.

On the second day after our arrival in camp, twelve Cossacks tried to escape over the fence, but the sentries spotted them, and they were all killed. One of them was Senior Lieutenant Sapirkin (he commanded a squad under me—a good officer).

If someone was caught trying to escape, he was beaten severely, thrown in the cooler, and then spent 3 months in the punitive platoon. There, the workday was 14 hours, under a strict regimen.

Those called under truncated guard [*расконвоированные*] lived in the area of Prokopyevsk, lived in camp, but in comparison with other civilians—poorly.

....

(Farther on, the letter's writer tells about conditions of life in Germany and attitudes there.)

… Now there is such a trend against war, against what had been. People are only interested in money—the more they can accumulate, the better.

I was a soldier from 1933 and an officer from April 1941, serving on all fronts. I was awarded 10 medals, but I am unable to understand today's people. They think that Bolsheviks are people the same as them. They don't want to understand what danger they pose.

I have fought enough, but against Communist Russians or Germans or any others, even though I love life, I would go fight even now.

We have the same enemy—Communism.

Our slogan: Fight Communism wherever it appears.

Yours, **Gerhard Petri**

Letter from the Interpreter on the Staff of General von Pannwitz

The letters presented here from the interpreter answer questions posed to him in connection with facts obtained from Lieutenant Petri, with the aim of making them more specific.

This interpreter, an old emigrant, was turned over by the English on May 28, 1945, and spent time in various places of imprisonment in Siberia until the end of 1949, after which he was freed and returned to his previous residence in Germany.

1-17 November 1954

As you yourself know, people's opinions on one or another thing often differ. Similarly, I am not entirely in agreement with Petri's facts. He knows much that I do not know, for I was not with him all the time, and even in those moments, it was difficult to learn much about events that took place even less than a few kilometers away. As much as I can remember, I will try to answer.

— The city of Stalinsk (formerly Staro-Kuznetsk) is located south of Novosibirsk in the Kuznetsk Basin, not far from the city of Kemerovo. There were many prisoner-of-war camps in the region.

We were often sent from one camp to another, but all were close to the city of Stalinsk.

— Colonel Renteln was turned over along with me on May 29, 1945. He spent (together with me) about half a year in our camp, after which he was taken away and his further fate is unknown (to me). There were rumors that he had been tried and sentenced and attempted to do away with himself afterwards.

Cossacks under truncated guard lived in the region of Stalinsk and Prokopyevsk (a city approximately 50 kilometers from Stanlinsk). As far as I know, they were put to work which they could not quit without permission, the same way that they were forbidden to leave the region. They lived the same way as the free inhabitants, which was plenty bad.

Under truncated guard—this means that they are no longer under guard and live like special settlers [спецпоселенцы].

That about an officer under truncated guard being arrested again after 40 years and sentenced, I have no knowledge of.

— Old emigrants, to my knowledge, had already been transferred to a different camp in 1948. Later than that, I do not know.

— Our first camp was Zenkovo (in a suburb of Prokopyevsk), after which we were moved to Prokopyevsk (between Stalinsk and Novosibirsk). The "Tirgansky Slope Zone"—was designated as the second camp (along the mines of "Tirgansky Slope"—close to the camp.)

— I did hear about negotiations being carried out with the English. I do not know who met with whom and what the results were. The rumors had it that the Cossacks would be taken to Australia or Canada, and also that they would be enlisted into the colonial forces, but it is hard to say if this was true or not.

— On May 10th or 11th, there had been something like a parade. It was hoped it would make a good impression on the English.

— We left Graz on June 9th and reached Zenkovo on the 12th of June.

— From Graz, we went by way of Vienna-Neustadt, Budapest, Ploesti, Foksani (where we were transferred to wider tracks), Kiev, Bryansk, Moscow, Sverdlovsk, Omsk, Novosibirsk, and Prokopyevsk.

— Most of the German officers were tried in December of 1949. Some of them, along with the rank and file, were released in November and December.

In November of 1949, besides the rank and file, although again not all, several officers were likewise released, myself among them.

In January of 1950, they again released some of the officers and the remaining rank and file.

— I, personally, in all my time in the camps, spent a long time in the cooler in 1948, for they wanted to hang much on me that I could not even understand. After that, they left me in peace. Then they released me completely unexpectedly and without any investigation, ignoring that in October of 1949, there had been a special commission sent from Moscow which took people away to send home and, likewise, to prison. Questioning by it took place night and day.

They let me go November 19, 1949. There had been a release at that time of approximately 300 rank and file soldiers and several officers and physicians.

---

2 — December 5, 1954 (second letter).

— On camp regimen.

Living conditions, especially at first (1945-47) were not easy. We were fed poorly: 600 grams of wet, gummy bread and soup consisting of individual cabbage leaves and water, without any fat. We were forced to work for 10 hours a day, sometimes longer. The death rate at first was very high, 5-6 per day. Something resembling dysentery and dystrophia (edema from starvation) raged about. In the winter of '47, out of a total of approximately 1200 men in camp, only 50 went out to work. All the others were ill.

After that, conditions started to improve. An 8-hour workday was instituted and rations were increased. Instead of soup alone, they started to serve a small portion of kasha once a day.

The attitude of the administration and guards varied. Sometimes it was all right, sometimes bad. It all depended on the people who had those duties.

A norm of work was required. If exceeded, you were given supplementary bread and, later, even money. Most of us never met our norms, for they became high, meant only for the strong.

Officially, we worked 6 days a week, but they found work for us within the zones on our days off: cleaning, or straightening out the barracks, or even in the camp's farm. Each camp grew its own potatoes and cabbage.

Conditions in punishment cells also varied. Sometimes you were given a normal ration, other times none. Other than in isolated cases, there were no beatings.

Guards and sentries were strict. Approaching the forbidden zone along the fence was not allowed. Several men were killed by guards for noncompliance.

....

Interpreter on the Staff of General von Pannwitz's Corps

Who I Happened to Meet ...

From the memoir of a former prisoner. ....

A. Protopopov, who had served in the Russian Corps and then the Cossachi Stan, from which he was invited on May 28, 1945, "to a conference" and farther to Siberia, published this memoir under the title above in the journal, *Freedom, No 6*, June, 1957.

Having served out a 10-year sentence in Soviet concentration camps, he was released from its borders in February, 1956.

What is printed below is only that part of his memoir that tells of the fate of several Russian Cossack old emigrants.

Toward the end, as far as I know, several old Russian emigrants were freed from Camp Potma. Some of them voluntarily remained in the Soviet Union, returning to relatives.

These include:

The famous pilot from the First World War, General Tkachev, and General Solamakhin—left for the Kuban.*

Colonel Yegorov, F. [*Ф.*, which can also be Th.], Lazarev, I., Mazanov, P. Shevyrev, and B. Sutulov—went to the Don.

General Rubashkin, Colonel Shmelev, Yasevich, Lieutenant Colonel Kudinov—awaited being sent to Bulgaria.

Igor Kravchenko, F. [as above] Vyatin, B. Dabizha, Petrovich-Stranich, Novak—supposed to have been sent to Yugoslavia.

Lamzaky, Borisenko, and Bara were sent to Rumania.

The old emigrant from Manchuria, Udachny, went to his sister's in Kazan. Naumov, father and son, stayed in Novosibirsk. The old Drozdovets [*Дроздовец*, a White unit created by Major General Drozdovsky in the Civil War], Mikhailov, having lived as an emigrant in Bulgaria, left for Saratov.

Many old emigrants wound up in the invalid house at Potma-Somov, Pogulsky, Telegin, Serin, Pisarev, and others.

According to information I have, the following number returned to Europe from the Soviet Union: to Germany, 11; Austria, 9; Belgium, 2; France, 6; Greece, 3.

Old emigrants who could not confirm their country of citizenship with evidence* are being held in the USSR.

A. Protopopov

What Cossacks Lived Through at Lienz, Graz, and on Their Way to Their Homeland

A Cossack of the Novominsky Stanitsa, Stepan Ivanovich T., who lived through the tragedy at Lienz, was captured by the

---

* **Note:** It is more believable that Generals Tkachev and Solamakhin were held in the USSR as stateless individuals.

Ed.

* **Note:** Of those individuals listed, several later went to various countries in Europe.

Ed.

Bolsheviks and sent to Graz. He escaped on the way to Budapest. He related the following to me about what had happened to him during that time:

When the fall of Germany became obvious, Stepan Ivanovich, as did many single Cossacks found in the territories of Germany and Austria, went to Italy to join the group of Field Ataman Domanov.

On April 24, 1945, ill and worn out, he arrived in Italy and stopped in Covazzo, in the Umanskoy Stanitsa. He stayed there for 3 days, then he was sent to the central invalid house in the village of Alesso, which had been renamed Novocherkassk by Don Cossacks. It had been subjected to bombardment by aircraft in the days immediately before his arrival, so it was decided to move the invalid house someplace else.

Thus, at the end of April, seven invalids and two Sisters of Mercy under the command of Major Lazarev, a Don Cossack, left for the city of Ovaro, where the Major had been ordered to set up a new invalid house. They made the trip on carts, going by way of Covazzo and Tolmezzo.

There was a hospital in Ovaro. It was also where a company that was led by Major Nazykov was stationed.

Before Lazarev's arrival, on approximately May 1st, Italian partisans had told Nazykov to give up his weapons. However, this brave officer instead fortified a school with 92 Cossacks and a German club (32 men). Some two kilometers beyond the village was a post, 21 men in strength.

When the invalids reached Ovaro, they were captured by partisans who prodded them along to the German club by shooting over their heads. When those of Nazykov's Cossacks saw the invalids, they shouted to them that they had machine guns behind their doors and that the invalids should break the window next to the door and climb through it. At the same time, they started to cover the partisans with hand grenades. One of the arriving invalids knocked out a window frame and all of them, including the nuns who were with with them, were pulled inside. This was about 2 o'clock the night of May 2nd. The partisans tried to attack the club and fired tracer bullets at the building the post was in. They managed to set it afire, but at 9 o'clock on May 2nd, it started to rain and put out the fire.

The partisans yelled to the Cossacks that the entire Domanov group had surrendered and that the regiments had put down their arms. This had been only subterfuge, because, while Lobisevich's regiment was still in Gemona, the Cossacks and mountain people had already left for the Austrian border with their weapons in their hands.

Master Sergeant Pyotr Abramovich Nelidov, a Don Cossack who was in charge of the Cossacks in the school, did not believe the partisans and all by himself went the several dozen paces to the German club, under heavy fire, in order to connect with Nazykov.

Nazykov's orders to him were:

"Do not believe anyone but me and your own heart! Shoot anyone who tries anything?!"

The partisans continued their attack. Nazykov warded them off [*отражал его*] with hand grenades, which destroyed one of the automobiles and killed 11 partisans. Their bodies were left where they fell.

At just that time, Cossack horsemen came to the rescue, and soon after, several groups of cadets arrived.

Seeing help approaching, Nazykov shouted, "Shoot the partisans ... !" Heavy rifle and machine gun fire was opened up on them [*ним*, him, so the author might have meant Nazykov], and grenades were thrown.

A group of cadets under the command of their heroic Sergeant Major Zelensky came running up the main street.

The partisans ran off in panic. Some of them were captured in the village by the cadets. Some were cut off by the horsemen. In all, close to 600 bandits were captured, along with a Cossack woman who had been taken [*уведеная ими*, untranslatable for me and unrecognizable as a typo] by them from the post.

The latter explained that, at approximately 12:30 at night, the partisans had gone to a windowless wall of the post and placed several mines under the building. Fourteen Cossacks were killed and several injured. These bandits had dragged them out onto the banks of a stream, shot them, then threw their bodies into the water. The woman had been with her baby in a neighboring house, from which the partisans took her.

Those bandits were led by two Catholic priests from the village. They were shot for that and the village was set on fire.

There were no losses from the school or the club. These 130 men, 7 invalids and 2 nuns, under the command of Nazykov, left the village and headed for the post, where they saw the corpses of the Cossack dead.

From there, they left for Austria with the Don stanitsa under the leadership of General Fetisov.

Stepan Ivanovich spoke glowingly about Fetisov, about his resourcefulness and his concern for his Cossacks, with whom he shared the entire trip on foot. He spoke as sincerely and flatteringly about Nazykov.

The following happened during the battle with the partisans. There were about 150 wounded in the hospital. The partisans did not bother them. The wife of one of the Cossacks who had been with Nazykov in the building of the German club happened to be one of the Sisters of Mercy. Husband and wife managed to communicate with each other through the attic windows using gestures. Afterwards, Lazarev's 8- or 9-year-old son was sent to make contact with Fetisov. He completed his mission successfully. Lazarev himself had been captured with his daughter by the bandits, who knocked his teeth out and harassed them, although they were not killed, because some women stepped in to protect them.

They went to Austria, as did all the Cossacks, by way of Paluzza, came out on the Drau at Oberdrauburg, then headed to Lienz.

Further, my companion described his suffering through the day of June 1st and the days that followed it. He managed to avoid being turned over during those days, but that did not end his misfortunes.

Residents of the Cossachi Stan continued to be taken away in the days that followed the forced handovers, after the resistance of the masses had been extinguished.

In T.'s words, it was peaceful in the area of the Cossachi Stan from May 7 to 12. Healthy Cossacks and their families gathered at Camp Peggetz.

Stepan Ivanovich T. further tells how, when Shelekhov was named the commander of Camp Peggetz, he put guards around the camp. Along with someone in an English uniform, he checked the documents of residents. Those who had been in Pannwitz's divisions or in other specific units were turned over. Those who claimed to be Serbian, he examined carefully. If one raised his suspicions, Shelekhov tested his knowledge of the Serbian language and the geography of Serbia. By these means, he caught more than a hundred, who were then sent to the "Russian Camp" at the railroad station several kilometers west of Lienz. That camp was surrounded by barbed wire and guarded by the Soviets.

That was where the "osters" who wanted to go home were sent. They were allowed to come and go from the camp freely. The others, those put there forcibly, were separated from the "osters" by barbed wire. The guards did not allow them outside of the barbed wire or to mix with the "osters." Still, through the application of some well-known energy, several managed to leave the camp by going under the barbed wire fence. Then there was the instance of a particular Red Army man, a Jew from Berdychiv, advising an old Cossack to leave the camp and teaching him how to take two food containers to put in the things he needed, roll up his sleeves, and, when he was standing guard, walk out of the camp as if he was going to do his laundry. The Cossack did just that and managed to avoid being forcibly repatriated.

About himself, my companion says that he was taken from the church at Camp Peggetz. He stayed behind barbed wire in the "Russian Camp" for 3 days before being sent to Graz.

The cars for that journey were all meant for freight. They were securely nailed shut and had up to 4 English sentries posted on

In the Hands of the Bolsheviks

their front and back platforms. There was a flatcar with two machine guns in the middle of the train, as was also true at its the front and rear.

Along the way, several people knocked out hatches, that is, the boarded-up windows, and jumped out. Three men managed to escape in that way, while 11 were killed by sentries.

They roused us to load from the "Russian Camp" at 11 o'clock in the morning. We left at half past two, arriving in Graz after dark.

On the way, apparently at the border of the Soviet zone, the train stopped after rifle shots and two whistles and waited for three minutes. It was obvious that this was where the English guards were replaced by Soviet ones. During the time we were stopped, 2 men attempted to escape, but they were wounded and thrown into the last car.

At about 10:30, the train stopped by a field at the camp at Graz.

Unloading took 5 minutes. The arrivals were quickly organized into columns by fours.

Some sort of commander, judging by the quality of his clothing, came up with two buckets and said, indicating the buckets:

"This is a safe for watches, while this is for wallets!"

By the time he had made his way through the entire column, one bucket was full of watches. There were few wallets in the other, however, because most of us had thrown them out along the way.

After this, Red Army soldiers assaulted the newly arrived and began to swap their clothing, taking away what was good and replacing it from their own torn clothes. So it went until the morning. Some had their clothing changed as many as five times. By morning, we were all stripped of our valuables and in rags. There had been many soldiers responsible. Particularly avaricious were new foreigners in the Red Army: Rumanians, Bulgarians, Latvians, and others, some of whom were young Russian soldiers.

We sat through the next day in 8 rows, the way we had been arranged in our echelons.

Those who had arrived there earlier also sat in such echelons. All around were Red Army soldiers who did not allow anyone to leave the place where they were sitting.

We sat in this way without eating and without moving from our places until 7 o'clock in the evening, when they gave us a kettle of some sort of broth for every two people. Everybody was divided into groups of fifty and each group was assigned a leader [*пятидесятники*]. We were given flour through them, but we were not allowed to start a fire. The flour was given to the kitchen. There, it was mixed with water. We were never given bread.

In order to take care of our bodily needs, we were told to go a few paces to the side.

Over the course of the day, some were called to somewhere from which they returned beaten up.

As the day went on, they brought two more echelons from the French zone, in total, about 3,000 people ... At around 10 o'clock in the evening, they brought about 13,000 who had been captured by Titoists.

Among the others brought there were several Cossacks from the 3rd Reserve Regiment of the Domanov group, along with the choir.

In this way, we spent 6 days without leaving our places.

Children up to 13 years of age who arrived were quickly taken away, with total disregard for the screams and despair of their mothers. They were put into first-class cars in which they were tended by nannies and nuns, treated to candies, and given toys and flowers, as they were being taken off to somewhere.

Over the course of the day, we did absolutely nothing other than have interrogations carried out,

All Cossacks and Vlasovites, and even others who served in military units, were separated out, **especially the 13th group, and taken away at night, as if to work, but the vehicles that took them always returned empty. One night, they used 96 vehicles with approximately 20 per each.**

According to several Red Army soldiers, they were all shot.

Those who returned from being interrogated often carried marks of a fight. During interrogations, needles were driven under nails. Interrogations took place either in a closed place or in the bushes. Screams could often be heard from them.

The narrator says that he himself heard one Cossack scream during interrogation:

"You might as well kill me, you bastards, but I am not changing my story. You've tortured millions of people … Go ahead and torture me, too …"

All the women had their hair removed. Several men rubbed in some sort of liquid from head to toe with a brush, after which all their hair fell out leaving clean, bald skin. After it, skin became cold and lost feeling.

There were about 900 people in the echelon with the narrator, including the old emigrant, Colonel Sivolobov, who was missing a leg, and Lieutenant Colonel Gavrish of the Kushchevskoy Stanitsa, who was also missing both arms. Gavrish, regardless of his infirmities, managed to jump from a moving freight, fell behind a stump or something, and, even though the English sentries fired their machine guns ferociously, he was unharmed.

Sivolobov was recognized in camp by stanishniks from Tishchenk who were in the Red Army. He was shot behind the bushes.

We were fed very poorly: 112 grams of flour and a kettle of some sort of broth for every two people. We were given water once a day.

During questioning, those who did not serve in military units and those who were not sent to the 13th group were moved for transport [*на этап*], that is, separated out their into their own group.

And my companion managed to be designated for transport, only because an in-law happened to be among the Red Army soldiers. He whispered to him which way he should go and then, without it being noticed, moved him to the transport group. That was where the psalm reader, K., of the Popovichevskoy Stanitsa had earlier wound up, along with a 13-year-old girl, Lenochka Shabanova, the daughter of a Cossack who had disappeared without a trace and whose mother had been clubbed to death by the English during a forced removal near Lienz.

The three of them formed a team that was inseparable until betters days arrived.

On the 6th day, new sentries were posted.

My companion remained in the camp in Graz for 8 days. All that time, the investigative commission was at work: needles under nails, beatings ...

Some of the prisoners helped the Red Army soldiers.

My companion tells that he saw Colonel Novikov and Captain Ovsyanikov through a window of one of the barracks in the camp.

According to what he was told by his in-law and individuals in the Red Army with whom my companion happened to exchange a few words, he concluded that a majority of the 1700 officers who were taken from Lienz "to a conference" in Graz had been executed.

On the 8th day, says N. S. T., a column of 12,000 was made up that included him and the psalm reader and Lenochka. The head of the guards told them that, due to the destruction of their route, they would have to walk 12 kilometers to get to their train.

They were led out of the city of Graz under heavy guard, but went farther freely with hardly any guard. The column dragged itself out considerably along the way. Several of the Red Army guards treated the prisoners well. Others would not allow anyone to stop, even out of necessity.

In spite of it being announced before leaving Graz that, after walking 12 kilometers, the column would take a train, it took more than a week to walk the distance, necessitating having to sleep under the open sky.

On the 7th day of the trip, a Soviet lieutenant among the guards spoke to T. and said that his two sons had also served in one of our units. When the Bolsheviks captured them, one had been taken somewhere, while the other had been executed in Graz. He said:

"Nothing good awaits you. At best, you will be sentenced to a long exile in which you will perish. At worst, you will be executed." He suggested leaving while it was still possible.

Following this advice, our trio (Cossack, psalm reader, and girl) took advantage of the column having to go through a sparse forest to leave it on the first night. On the advice of the Soviet lieutenant, they hid behind a bush until the column passed by, then went off to the side from the road. After going about 8 kilometers, they saw a light in a window. The psalm reader walked over and asked for water. A Magyar woman gave them water. They managed to communicate with her somehow. When she learned that they had escaped from the Reds, she gave them a block of cheese, some rolls, milk, sugar for the girl, a pack of cigarettes for each of the men, and showed them to a road.

They walked for the rest of the night and all the next day. The girl lost heart [подбилась] and started to cry because she was barefooted and had worn her feet raw. Her co-travelers then fashioned something resembling shoes out of her clothing and she felt better.

When night fell, they spent it under the roof of some sort of shed out in the woods. They slept soundly.

They walked for two days. Meeting the Magyar worked out very well for them.

Toward evening on the third day, they came to some sort of mill on a stream, sat down by it, and ignoring the need to take turns, all fell asleep at once. In the morning, one of them awoke on hearing water splashing. To his horror, when he looked around a corner, he saw three Red Army soldiers washing themselves at the mill's well.

He quietly woke the others, and they spent some time in an alarming situation before the Red Army soldiers left into the woods from where noises could be heard. Apparently, a Red Army unit had spent the night there.

As soon as the 3 soldiers left, our trio hid in a dense thicket until the evening. They very sparingly ate the bread and cheese that the woman had given them on their first day.

In the evening, an old man walked past them to the mill. The psalm reader went after him and soon returned with a hunk of bread, cheese, and tobacco leaves. The kind old man had provided them. He also sketched a route for them on a piece of paper and told them that the Red Army soldiers were leaving.

After spending the night in the thicket, they pressed on at 4 o'clock, following the route indicated to them by the old Hungarian. Their aim was to cross over a pass, then wait until the Red forces left.

After walking a few kilometers, they saw a small homestead. There was only one woman there and it turned out that they could not communicate with her, but then the old man they had become acquainted with showed up. He spoke a little Russian because he had been held prisoner by the Russians during the First World War.

They barely had a chance to talk things over with him when a Red Army field kitchen drove into the yard, and the cooks began to prepare a meal.

The mistress of the place hid the men in a closet in small shed and put a broom into the hands of the girl.

My narrator says that they were all terribly overwrought, and he even feared that the psalm reader might have lost his mind, for he spent all the time while standing in the closet by reciting the litany.

Toward evening the mistress opened the closet and gave them some wheat buns and sour milk.

By using her fingers, she showed them that the kitchen was leaving at 3 o'clock that night. They could not eat, though. The psalm reader complained that his insides were burning. All from worry. They drank some of the milk, but could not eat the buns.

At 3 at night, the mistress of the house, cheerful and pleased, opened the closet and released them, telling them that the kitchen was gone.

The poor girl had been very anxious. She could eat nothing the entire day and only drank water. Apparently, her face became swollen because of that.

In the morning, the Magyar woman fed them well. Then she led them along a sheer cliff path, warning them that going along the road was very dangerous, since the Red Army soldiers were leaving along it, while they had another 12 kilometers to go before they could get out of the Soviet zone.

Having led them out of the Russian zone, this woman suggested that they to go to Graz, to the English. They thanked her, but they did not take her suggestion. They went in a direction that would take them south of Graz, spending the night near a small stream in the woods. There, along with local women, they gathered berries and decided on a good rest. They went to sleep at 10 o'clock and got up the next day at half past three. A German woman brought them cheese and milk.

Going on past the city of Leoben, they wound up in the hands of the local police of one of the villages. There, they were locked in a basement and told that they would be sent to the Reds. However, a car with two Englishmen in it soon drove up to the police building. The prisoners could overhear that a long conversation was taking place, then that one of the Englishmen, apparently senior in rank, said, "Okay!" They were taken out of the basement and the other Englishman, who turned out to be a Russian old emigrant, an officer of the Cossack stanitsa of Spokoynoy, who had lived all the time since in Sweden, told them that they had nothing to fear, and should tell them everything exactly the way it happened.

Having listened to them, the Englishman gave an order to send them to the Russia Corps at Klein St. Paul. Even though he provided a pass for them, local Austrians held them up two times.

In view of Cossack families and Cossacks who had not been turned over from the Cossachi Stan being in the area of Lienz, all three headed there. However, Shelekhov did not allow them into the camp, so they found places for themselves among the half-destroyed buildings of the city, where many Cossacks and families were living.

They were sent to work from there, given ration cards, and paid 2 marks a day.

On about the 7th or 8th of August, my companion managed to get around Shelekhov's vigilance and settled in a camp. It was a Yugoslavian camp, but many Russians were living there.

On about the 19th or 20th of September, the Russians living in that camp were told that they would be sent to a camp in Kaffenburg. Because the Cossacks were unsettled by this, the English major in charge ordered that they be made to understand that none of them were being threatened with anything bad. To confirm that, he took off his cap, crossed himself, and offered to send several senior Cossacks there, who could see for themselves that what he was saying was the truth.

Walkabouts [ходики] were sent, but enraged Cossacks ran away from the camp that same night. Only 13 barrack commanders and a few other people were left.

Quickly, English sentry posts were set up in all directions, and since most of the Cossacks had left for Lienz, those were caught there and sent elsewhere. A group of 23 Kalmyks went into the hills at night, while 3 Cossack, my companion among them, went along the railroad tracks, successfully went around the sentry post at the nearest station, and headed in the direction of Salzburg. They reached the nearest station. A heavy snow was falling. They got into an open coal car and hid themselves in the coal, covering themselves with a tarp that they found there. They were soon covered with snow and were not noticed by the sentries who checked the train.

In this way, they got to Salzburg, staying there for 7 days. From there, with the help of German acquaintances, they got on a bus in Bavaria that was going to Munich. There, they were taken for work on the repair of the Deutsches Museum that had been undertaken by UNRRA. After working there for 51 days, our narrator moved to Füssen on December 4.

Lenochka Shabanova remained in Lienz with people from her stanitsa, Udobnints [Удобнинцев]. Vassily Abramovich, the psalm reader, also remained there.

Having finished his tale, Stepan Ivanovich T. spoke very warmly about Hungarians. They never refused his group a piece of bread or shelter. He said that they had saved his life and his co-travelers and he would never forget them for that.

As far as the Austrians were concerned, he spoke about them with some bitterness.

V. Naumenko

Documents and Materials having to do with Forced Repatriations

Documents and Materials having to do with Forced Repatriations

Documents Published in 1955 by the Government of the United States of America in a Book Entitled: *Foreign Relations of the United States: Diplomatic Papers, Conferences at Malta and Yalta, 1945*, and Several Other Documents

Correspondence about the exchange of prisoners of war between official representatives of the USA, the governments of the Western Allies, and the USSR began in 1944, that is, before the Yalta Conference.

Below are reprinted documents or excerpts from documents of interest to us through their connection to forced repatriations.

(All capital and bold [*курсив*, (italics) obviously in error] lettering have been added by us. Ed. Sb. [*Сб.*, collection])

[With some exceptions, the documents here are all available, although not always readily, in their original English version. I include in the entirety of what is excerpted here only some of those passages that the general chose to emphasize by the above-mentioned fonts. Given that by "several," the general apparently meant "many," I have given an index to all documents in the very useful compendium the general prepared, with a very brief synopsis or the general's comment, if any, for each item. Translating from the Russian translation of documents that are originally in English would just be a ludicrous demonstration of the pitfalls of translation.]

....
From a directive of the USA State Department Supreme Command of Expeditionary Forces. Washington, September 22, 1944.

[Items 10a-10c of the directive, a first listing of suggestions on how allied prisoners of war were to be dealt with.]

....
From a telegram of the Charge d'Affaires (Kennan) to the Secretary of State (Stettinius). Moscow, November 27, 1944.

[The excerpt concerns Molotov's suggestions for an agreement on repatriation of citizens of allied nations.]

....
From a telegram of the Secretary of State (Stettinius) to the Ambassador in the Soviet Union (Harriman). Washington, January 3, 1945—9 p. m. Secret

... Among the persons found fighting with the German troops are a few with Slavic names who disclaim Soviet nationality. Over 1100 Soviet nationals found fighting with German troops WERE TURNED OVER TO THE SOVIET AUTHORITIES AT A WEST COAST PORT LAST WEEK. A further report of the problems which have arisen in this connection will be sent to you for your information.

Documents and Materials having to do with Forced Repatriations

Note:

It must be said that these "Over 1100 Soviet nationals" were turned over on the request from the Soviets of November 27, 1944, which had been passed on to Mr. Stettinius by Mr. Harriman.

These people were sent off to the Soviet Union at the end of December, 1944, that is, before the Yalta Agreement on prisoners of war.

Ed.

From a telegram of the the Acting Secretary of State (Grew) to the Embassy in the United Kingdom. Washington, January 27, 1945—12 p. m. Secret

At this time the Soviets gave the governments of England and the USA a draft agreement on prisoners of war.

....

British Embassy has made available to Department series Foreign Office telegrams regarding proposed Soviet agreements with British and ourselves for treatment of American, British and Soviet prisoners of war and civilians liberated by our respective forces. One British message indicates SHAEF is working out combined British-American text of agreement to be submitted to Big Three meeting. SUGGESTED BRITISH TEXT OF THIS AGREEMENT IS AT CONSIDERABLE VARIANCE WITH PROPOSALS STATE, ARMY, NAVY COMMITTEE IS PROPOSING TO JOINT CHIEFS OF STAFF. Please inform American representatives working on SHAEF draft that Department considers it important that BEFORE MAKING ANY COMMITMENTS ON OUR BEHALF THEY AWAIT FURTHER INTSRUCTIONS which it is hoped will be sent through Joint Chiefs on January 29.

Note:

As will be seen from one of the documents that follows, there was no concern in Washington that nothing had been said about protections in the Geneva Convention and provisions on the rights prisoners of war who are political refugees in the text submitted to the English for the agreement.

367

Obviously, this situation even aroused Mr. Grew to ask the staff of the Supreme Command to not pass on the text of the agreement for examination by the Big Three before receiving instructions from Washington.

[For some reason, "STATE, ARMY, NAVY COMMITTEE" and "JOINT CHIEFS OF STAFF," above, were translated into Russian as "State Department Commission."]

....

Ed.

From the telegram of the Ambassador in the United Kingdom (Winant) to the Secretary of State. London, January 28, 1945—12 p. m. Secret

... [The first three paragraphs of the excerpt are omitted.] In October I sent back a draft directive on United Nations Prisoners of War, BASED ON THE LATEST AND MOST AUTHORITATIVE JCS POLICY PAPERS, THINKING THAT IT WOULD BE QUICKLY CLEARED FOR MY USE. ON DECEMBER 1 I SENT AN URGENT APPEAL FOR INSTRUCTIONS, AND WAS INFORMED THAT **THEY WERE HELD UP BY DISPUTES WITHIN THE WAR DEPARTMENT.** SINCE THEN I HAVE CABLED REPEATEDLY, TRYING TO GET SOME ACTION IN A MATTER WHICH HAS GREAT **HUMANITARIAN IMPORTANCE** and which may deeply affect our relations with our allies. Only yesterday I received a message from the department, sent on January 26, that it expected to transmit a statement of policy on prisoners of war "within a few days."

The Yalta Conference took place February 4-11, 1945, and all of the documents that follow below were contemporary with it.

From the letter of the British Foreign Secretary (Eden) to the Secretary of State (Stettinius). Yalta, February 5, 1946 [1945]. Secret

Documents and Materials having to do with Forced Repatriations

... [The first paragraph of the excerpt is omitted.] There is one further point, however, which I should like to mention. It is clear, as S.H.A.E.F. have already reported, that the only real solution to the problem of Soviet citizens who are likely to fall into British and American hands shortly is to REPATRIATE THEM AS SOON AS POSSIBLE. For this shipping is required and WE HAVE ALREADY SENT 10,000 BACK FROM THE UNITED KINGDOM ["(from England)" is added here in the Russian text] AND 7,500 FROM THE MEDITERRANEAN.

It seems to me that IT WOULD MATERIALLY HELP THE NEGOTIATIONS IF WE COULD INFORM THE RUSSIANS AT A SUITABLE MOMENT OF OUR PLANS TO REPATRIATE THEIR CITIZENS. From the British point of view I can say that we have found shipping to send back from the United Kingdom a further 7,000 of these men in the latter part of this month and it is hoped that we can provide further ships to take some 4,000 a month from the Mediterranean during March, April, and May, EVEN THOUGH THE SOVIET CITIZENS IN THE SOUTHERN PART OF FRANCE AND HALF OF THOSE LIBERATED IN ITALY ARE PRIMARILY THE RESPONSIBILITY OF THE UNITED STATES. I am however without any information on the United States plans on this. GENERAL EISENHOWER HAS RECENTLY PRESSED THE COMBINED CHIEFS OF STAFF ONCE AGAIN TO PROVIDE SHIPS TO TAKE 3,000 EACH FROM MARSEILLES UNTIL THE PRESENT LARGE NUMBERS HAVE BEEN CLEARED. No doubt your experts have been examining the position in the light of General Eisenhower's telegram, and I should be very glad if you could tell me whether you will be in a position to make any statement to the Russians about the United States plans.

Whilst it is clear that the discussions should not be delayed in order that a statement can be made on the shipping position, I would be very glad to KNOW AS SOON AS POSSIBLE whether you can give the Russians any information on the lines I hope to give him from the British point of view, since THE SOONER THIS INFORMATION CAN BE PROVIDED ["(to the Soviets)" is added here in the Russian text] THE BETTER ARE THE CHANCES OF REACHING AN AGREEMENT DURING THIS CONFERENCE.

    Sincerely yours,   Anthony Eden

Note:

  This document confirms that the English turned over 10,000 men, 7,500 from the Mediterranean, even before the decision of the Yalta Conference, and were preparing for more turnovers from Austria and ports of the Mediterranean Sea.

  From this document, we see in how much haste the Minister of Foreign Affairs of Great Britain was to turn over Russian prisoners of war to the Soviets and how he hurried the Americans to do the same.

                                Ed.

From the letter of the British Foreign Secretary (Eden) to the Soviet Foreign Commissar (Molotov).
Secret.   **Yalta February 5, 1945.**

  You will remember that during the Moscow conversations of last October, I discussed with you and with Marshall Stalin the question of caring for and repatriating Soviet citizens and British subjects liberated by Allied forces in the south and west and by the Soviet forces in the east of Europe.

  Since then our two Governments have exchanged Drafts and on 20th January our Embassy received from your Government a redraft on this matter. We have examined this redraft and, subject to what is stated below, I am glad to say that it is generally acceptable. I UNDERSTAND THAT A SIMILAR DRAFT WAS PUT TO THE UNITED STATES GOVERNMENT AT THE SAME TIME.

   ....

From the editor. — Further in this document, it is mentioned that the British Government (embassy) was given a redraft on January 20 by the Soviets of a proposed agreement between the USSR and Great Britain (England), concerning the liberation of Soviet citizens found on English territory, while in item 4 it is noted—NOT FOUND—

meaning that at this time Russian prisoners of war had already all been repatriated from England.

From the telegram from the Acting Secretary of State (Grew) to the Secretary of State.
Top Secret Washington, February 7 [8], 1945. (That is, 3 days before the agreement had been fully authorized by the signatures of the USA and the USSR.)

War Department has just made available message dated February 7 from Marshall that indicates JCS on February 7 approved WITH CERTAIN CHANGES British preliminary text of agreement with Soviet Union for exchange of prisoners of war and apparently also for liberated persons. (This is our message No. 27.) While it is not definitely clear what preliminary British text is referred to, if it is the preliminary text in JCS 1266, ["(This ... 1266" has been deleted from the original] THE AGREEMENT WOULD NOT APPEAR TO COVER THE FOLLOWING SPECIFIC POINTS which were incorporated in the United States counterproposals forwarded to JCS staff with you:

1. PROTECTION OF GENEVA CONVENTION WHICH WE HAVE INFORMED SOVIET GOVERNMENT WE WILL ACCORD THE SOVIET CITIZENS CAPTURED IN GERMAN UNIFORM WHO DEMAND SUCH PROTECTION.

2. SOVIET CITIZENS IN UNITED STATES NOT PRISONERS OF WAR WHOSE CASES ATTORNEY GENERAL FEELS SHOULD BE DEALT WITH ON BASIS OF TRADITIONAL **AMERICAN POLICY OF ASYLUM**.

3. Persons liberated by United States forces no longer in their custody.

4. Questions of the liberation and repatriation of other United Nations citizens.

5. Persons claimed as citizens by the Soviet authorities WHO WERE NOT SOVIET CITIZENS PRIOR TO OUTBREAK OF WAR AND DO NOT NOW CLAIM SOVIET CITIZENSHIP.

(Allstate Horseshoe) [Not in Russian text] IT IS FELT that these questions and others referred to in JCS 1266 and 1266/1 should be brought to your attention IN ORDER THAT CONSIDERATION MAY BE GIVEN TO THEM BEFORE FINAL AGREEMENT IS REACHED.

The telegram from the Secretary of State (Stettinius) to the Acting Secretary of State (Grew). [The Russian text has the men reversed.]

Top Secret

Argonaut. Crypto-War for Acting Secretary of State only from Secretary Stettinius. [The Russian text leaves off "from Secretary Stettinius" and gives a date, February 9, 1945.]

By this reply, Secretary of State Stettinius [See above two paragraphs.] DECISIVELY REJECTED THE ADDITION OF THE JOINT CHIEFS OF STAFF IN WASHINGTON WITH THE AIM OF EXCLUDING THE USE OF FORCED REPATRIATIONS.

The text referred to in your number 27, dated February 8, is the British redraft of the Soviet redraft to the British and American Governments on January 20. In origin, it is a SHAEF paper. The British have subsequently made a few changes in it which I feel WE CAN ACCEPT WITHOUT RESERVATION. The British are most anxious to present this draft to the Russians today for their consideration. JCS (American in Yalta with Stettinius) ARE IN FULL AGREEMENT. I CAN SEE NO OBJECTIONS TO THE REDRAFT AND HAVE AUTHORIZED, IN SO FAR AS WE ARE CONCERNED, **TRIPARTITE DISCUSSIONS BASED ON IT. IT DOES NOT COVER THE NUMBERED POINTS** in your reference telegram which were embodied in the Department's note of February 1 (underlined note in paragraph 758 point 3 in the Yalta document — "This note has as its subject the application of the Geneva Convention to certain prisoners of war of Russian origin who were wearing German uniforms at the moment of their capture by the armed forces of the United States) to the Soviet embassy. THE CONSENSUS HERE IS THAT IT WOULD BE UNWISE TO INCLUDE QUESTIONS RELATIVE TO THE PROTECTION (rights of prisoners of war) OF THE GENEVA CONVENTION AND TO SOVIET CITIZENS IN THE U.S. IN AN AGREEMENT WHICH DEALS PRIMARILY WITH THE EXCHANGE OF PRISONERS liberated by the Allied armies as they march into Germany. With respect to "claimants", (obviously they meant by this word individuals asserting their rights under the Geneva Convention — note made by the translator, — regardless of the dangerous treatment by the Germans (by their contacts with allied soldiers found with them as prisoners — noted by the translator), not withstanding the danger of German retaliation, we believe there will be serious delays in the release (by the Soviets — noted by the translator) of our prisoners of war unless we reach prompt agreement on this question.

[All parenthetical remarks in the above passage were added by the Russian translator for the original Russian version of this work, not the present translator, whose comments are always in brackets like these.]

Excerpt of the telegram from the Secretary (Early) to the President's Administrative Assistant (Daniels).

TOP SECRET [Yalta] 11 February 1945

Under these arrangements each ally will provide food, clothing, medical attention and other needs of the nationals of the others until transport is available for their repatriation. In caring for British subjects and American citizens the Soviet Government will be assisted by American and British officers. Soviet officers will assist British and American authorities in their task of caring for Soviet citizens liberated by the British and American forces during such time as they are on the continent of Europe or the United Kingdom, awaiting transport to take them home.

We are pledged to give every assistance consistent with operational requirements to help ensure that all these prisoners of war and civilians are SPEEDILY REPARIATED.

Agreement

Relating to Prisoners of War and Civilians Liberated by Forces Operating Under Soviet Command and Forces Operating Under United States of America Command; February 11, 1945.

The Government of the United States of America on the one hand and the Government of the Union of Soviet Socialist Republics on the other hand, wishing to make arrangements for the care and repatriation of United States citizens freed by forces operating under Soviet command and for Soviet citizens freed by forces operating under United States command, have agreed as follows:

Article 1. All Soviet citizens liberated by the forces operating under United States command and all United States citizens liberated by the forces operating under Soviet command will, without delay after their liberation, be separated from enemy prisoners of war and will be maintained separately from them in camps or points of concentration until they have been handed over to the Soviet or United States authorities, as the case may be, at places agreed upon between those authorities.

United States and Soviet military authorities will respectively take the necessary measures for protection of camps, and points of concentration from enemy bombing, artillery fire, etc.

Article 2. The contracting parties shall ensure that their military authorities shall without delay inform the competent authorities of the other party regarding citizens of the other contracting party found by them, and will at the same time take the necessary steps to implement the provisions of this agreement. Soviet and United States repatriation representatives will have the right of immediate access into the camps and points of concentration where their citizens are located and they will have the right to appoint the internal administration and set up the internal discipline and management in accordance with the military procedure and laws of their country.

Facilities will be given for the despatch or transfer of officers of their own nationality to camps or points of concentration where liberated members of the respective forces are located and there are insufficient officers. The outside protection of and access to and from the camps or points of concentration will be established in accordance with the instructions of the military commander in whose zone they are located, and the military commander shall also appoint a commandant, who shall have the final responsibility for the overall administration and discipline of the camp or point concerned.

The removal of camps as well as the transfer from one camp to another of liberated citizens will be effected by agreement with the competent Soviet or United States authorities. The removal of camps and transfer of liberated citizens may, in exceptional circumstances, also be effected without preliminary agreement provided the competent authorities are immediately notified of such removal or transfer with a statement of the reasons. Hostile propaganda directed against the contracting parties or against any of the United Nations will not be permitted.

Article 3. The competent United States and Soviet authorities will supply liberated citizens with adequate food, clothing, housing and medical attention both in camps or at points of concentration and en route, and with transport until they are handed over to the Soviet or United States authorities at places agreed upon between those authorities. The standards of such food, clothing, housing and medical attention shall, subject to the provisions of Article 8, be fixed on a basis for privates, non-commissioned officers and officers. The basis fixed for civilians shall as far as possible be the same as that fixed for privates.

The contracting parties will not demand compensation for these or other similar services which their authorities may supply respectively to liberated citizens of the other contracting party.

Article 4. Each of the contracting parties shall be at liberty to use in agreement with the other party such of its own means of transport as may be available for the repatriation of its citizens held by the other contracting party. Similarly each of the contracting parties shall be at liberty to use in agreement with the other party its own facilities for the delivery of supplies to its citizens held by the other contracting party.

Article 5. Soviet and United States military authorities shall make such advances on behalf of their respective governments to liberated citizens of the other contracting party as the competent Soviet and United States authorities shall agree upon beforehand.

Advances made in currency of any enemy territory or in currency of their occupation authorities shall not be liable to compensation.

In the case of advances made in currency of liberated non-enemy territory, the Soviet and United States Governments will effect, each for advances made to their citizens necessary settlements with the Governments of the territory concerned, who will be informed of the amount of their currency paid out for this purpose.

Article 6. Ex-prisoners of war and civilians of each of the contracting parties may, until their repatriation, be employed in the management, maintenance and administration of the camps or billets in which they are situated. They may also be employed on a voluntary basis on other work in the vicinity of their camps in furtherance of the common war effort in accordance with agreements to be reached between the competent Soviet and United States authorities. The question of payment and conditions of labour shall be determined by agreement between these authorities. It is understood that liberated members of the respective forces will be employed in accordance with military standards and procedure and under the supervision of their own officers.

Article 7. The contracting parties shall, wherever necessary, use all practicable means to ensure the evacuation to the rear of these liberated citizens. They also undertake to use all practicable means to transport liberated citizens to places to be agreed upon where they can be handed over to the Soviet or United States authorities respectively. The handing over of these liberated citizens shall in no way be delayed or impeded by the requirements of their temporary employment.

Article 8. The contracting parties will give the fullest possible effect to the foregoing provisions of this Agreement, subject only to the limitations in detail and from time to time of operational, supply and transport conditions in the several theatres.

Article 9. This Agreement shall come into force on signature.

Done at the Crimea in duplicate and in the English and Russian languages, both being equally authentic, this eleventh day of February, 1945.

For the Government of the United States of America: John R. Deane, Major General, U.S.A.

For the Government of the Union of Soviet Socialist Republics: Lieutenant General Gryzlov.

On the Attitudes of the Western Allies on the Question of Forced Repatriation

The documents presented above—or excerpts from them—in several ways allow an understanding of the questions concerning forced handovers, up to the Yalta Agreement and after its finalization.

If we are not yet able to name individuals who are the major perpetrators of this crime, then at least we can establish through these documents what the attitudes of the individual governments of the Western Allies were on forcible repatriations.

It must be admitted that the French did not play a decisive role in the matter. In fact, the Supreme Command of the Allied Armed Forces [probably should be Supreme Headquarters of Allied Expeditionary Forces] was in charge in France and carried out the forcible repatriations there.

As far as the Soviets were concerned, they of course appeared to be initiators of the betrayal of former Soviet citizens and did not let up on it no matter what.

As can be seen by the documents presented, they urged their allies to repatriate all former Soviet citizens who fell into their hands, and to do it quickly and without delay.

They prepared, then offered to their allies, the text of the agreement on the exchange of prisoners of war and other citizens of the affected countries.

In their draft agreement, this point is specified in item 6, which states the following:

"Both sides agree to use all means available to them to evacuate captured citizens and subjects of other countries to the rear, if it is deemed necessary, and in the quickest way possible, to repatriate these individuals—."

The Bolsheviks knew what they were doing when they said that "all available means" be used in the matter of repatriation. By this, they opened up the possibility of further forcible repatriations.

The English accepted the Soviet text with several changes, but item 6, stating that all possible means be used for rapid repatriation, actually entered into the agreement in item 7, which was written by the English in the stronger words that it was necessary to use all "possible" means for the evacuation to the rear and all "allowable" means to transport liberated citizens to those places where they could be turned over to the Soviets. [The word in the Yalta Agreement in both of the phrases at issue is "practicable," which is translated in item 7 of the Russian translation here as both *"возможные"* and *"допустные,"* in that order, and where in this paragraph I use "possible" and "allowable."]

This point was accepted, too, by the American Joint Chiefs of Staff with Secretary of State Stettinius at Yalta. **The attempt by the Joint Chiefs of Staff in Washington to protect individual freedoms was decidedly rejected by Stettinius** in his dispatches to various types of American representatives in Europe.

As can be seen in these documents, British Foreign Minister Eden urged the Americans in all ways he could to sign the agreement with the Bolsheviks, saying that the sooner it was done, the better would be the chances for progress on the agreement during the course of the conference. (This was traditional English politics of bartering with the heads of others.)

These documents show that Americans were far from from unanimous on the question of forced evacuations.

It is obvious that in America, the general consensus was against any use of force in the question of repatriation. This was expressed by the offer of the heads of state in Washington to protect the individual freedoms of prisoners of war.

With respect to American leadership circles in Europe, as can be seen by Stettinius's answer to Grew and from other documents, they were wholly under the influence of the Bolsheviks and their English supporters.

Subsequent to this situation, the Supreme Headquarters in April of 1945 accepted IN PRINCIPAL THE FORCED REPATRIATION OF SOVIET CITIZENS. The attempt of General Patch, who held to his own ideas, drowned in the general attitude of the American leadership circles in Europe.

The Bolsheviks won on the question of forcible repatriations, and into their hands fell millions of anti-Bolsheviks.

The reason for that was, it must be said, the same as that which made the allies AFTER A VICTORIOUS CONCLUSION TO THE WAR, GIVE ALL OF EASTERN EUROPE TO THE BOLSHEVIKS AS A GIFT.

V. Naumenko

"Betrayal at Yalta"

—Translation of excerpts from the brochure of John T. Flynn, published in 1955 in New York by "Future America."

Not everything about the deal was made public.

[This writer goes over (originally in English) the rumors and questions regarding why full details had not yet been released.]

The End of the Conference

[The writer describes what he calls the "orgy" at the conference's culmination.]

The Yalta Conference in the Letters of Sir Winston Churchill

This article is reprinted from *News of Russian National Unity in Great Britain No 11* (18), December 1, 1953.

It does not have an immediate relation to the betrayal of Cossacks, but it is characteristic of the attitude of one of the creators of the agreement and of his attitude toward Stalin.

[The author of the article, originally in English, is G. Bennigsen. The attitude suggested is one of appeasement toward Stalin.]

On the Responsibility for Forcible Repatriations

The horrible events in post-war times, when hundreds of thousands of people were forcibly turned over by the Western Allies and sent behind the "Iron Curtain," were felt with extreme pain in the hearts of Russian people.

Questions about it in Russian—most commonly in Cossack—presses had a great number of articles devoted to it. In the archives of editorials in our Collection there are 28 titles of newspapers and journals that responded to these horrible events. First among them was the newspaper, *Russia*, printed in New York and published in those days by the now deceased N. P. Rybakov, who put a lot of very valuable material into his sentences.

The first to bring up the tragedy of the Cossacks in the foreign press was the Dutch Professor, L. G. Grondis, who wrote an article under the title of "The Spittal Tragedy" in *The Telegraph, No 225*, December 1952. In it, he was the first to make known to Western society the tragic removal of the officers of the Cossachi Stan "to a conference" on May 28, 1945, and the subsequent forced repatriation of the population of the Cossachi Stan.

The question of handovers then began to have articles devoted to it in the foreign press and the individual books of other authors. First among them, it must be noted, are the Polish writer J. A. Maczkiewicz [*Мацкевича*, author of *Tragödy an der Drau* (never translated into English) who Jurgen Thorwald has as J. Mackewicz in the bibliography to his book, *The Illusion*], and the English writer, Huxley-Blythe, who repeatedly put into print his defense of the human rights that were trampled by the Western Allies. Other books have been published on the question.

Voices began to ring out in print that the Yalta Conference did not provide for the forcible handovers of anyone. Individual figures in America society began to press for an investigation of those responsible for the evil.

At present, the Yalta documents have come out in print, but far from completely, and the explanations that are in print do not give the comprehensive details that this painful question needs.

In any event, on the basis of what we have, it can certainly be said that forcible turnovers arose after the arbitrary explanations of the ideas of the Yalta Conference, and who it was who sent people to death and torture without even considering that those who did the actual turning over by all possible means made protests against such violence, which led to suicides.

In the ranks of those nationalities we know are taking an interest in questioning these forced turnovers are the English, Belgian, Dutch, German, and others.

One of them is an English journalist who is zealously gathering material on these horrible evils and putting some of them into a bulletin published in English and distributed mainly in England. In a letter to me on January 4, 1963, he wrote:

"On reading your collection, I asked one of my friends, who happens to be a member of our Parliament, to raise the question on January 25 of who gave the order for the turnover of Cossacks from Lienz, Spittal, and the Drau Valley. In this way, I hope to clear up who gave the order to Major Davies, Lt. Colonel Malcolm and General Musson."

But then, in his next letter, on February 11, he writes:

"The Member of Parliament about whom I wrote to you in my previous letter tried on January 25 to raise the question of the Prime Minister in order to establish once and for all who gave the order to turn over the Cossacks in Austria, but he was not allowed to do so, since the full, official 'history is currently being written, and according to a pronouncement by Churchill, is to be published next year.'"

The question was also raised in the USA. The newspaper, *Sonntagsblatt Staats-Zeitung und Herald*, published in New York in German, printed an article by journalist Julius Epstein with the title, "We Turned over 5 Millions DPs to Red Executioners." in which he confirms that the Yalta Agreement does not permit the forced repatriation of anyone at all and asks: "Who is guilty in this?"

Excerpts from this interesting piece are printed below.

V. Naumenko

"We Turned over 5 Millions DPs to Red Executioners"

Compulsory extradition of Soviet citizens by the Government of the USA. Julius Epstein.

The author of this article, which publicizes the investigation of mass murders in Katyn, brought about an investigation by Congress of this evil that also, as a result, shed some light on the turnover by English soldiers and individual citizens with the help of the US government. The author asks for new investigations by Congress to identify the government officials who must be considered as having assisted in this destruction of human rights.

Acheson's well known speech.

[Describes a speech given by Dean Acheson on October 24, 1952, having to do with the situation in Korea, the Geneva Convention, and the repatriation of prisoners of war.]

Conduct in Korea and in Germany.

[Compares the contradictory behavior of the Truman administration in Korea to that at the end of World War Two.]

Guilty Consciences are not Enough.

[The subtitle tells it all.]

Translated [feminine verb form] **N. V. N.**

Editor's note:

The words of Mr. Julius Epstein about "Guilty consciences" still have force to this time

Debates in the English Parliament on the Question of Forced Turnovers in Italy

Wednesday, May 21, 1947

Stokes asked the Secretary of State for Foreign Affairs whether he is aware that the forcible repatriation of some 185 Russians was attempted from camps Nos. 6 and 7 under British control at Rimini on 8th May; whether he will state the number of attempted suicides, the number of deaths and the number wounded now in hospital as a result of this action; and whether he is aware that this forced repatriation is contrary to promises made to this House.

Mayhew I have received a telegraphic account of the incident to which my Honorabl Friend refers. My information is that there were no suicides, nor attempts of suicide, nor woundings, nor admissions to hospital. From the party of 180 men, three were excluded before entrainment on medical grounds, and one died of pneumonia. Three men escaped. I am told there were no other incidents. The men repatriated fall within the categories of Soviet citizens who are serving members of the Soviet armed forces or who gave active assistance to the enemy, and who, under the instructions issued to the Allied Command in Italy by the British and American military authorities, fall to be repatriated under the Yalta Agreement on Repatriation. No undertaking has been given which would preclude the repatriation of men within these categories.

Stokes As there is evidently some varied evidence, will my Honorable Friend examine the evidence which I will lay before him —

Gallacher Why does not the Honorable Gentleman join the Honorable Member for Queen's University (Professor Savory)?

Stokes I can do without your advice. Is it not outrageous to expect to continue to carry out a policy laid down at Yalta, which clearly adumbrated that there should be a fair trial and return of these people, when there is now no fair trial; and is my Honorable Friend aware that these people were got into the train by being told that they were going to Scotland to help the miners?

Mr. Mayhew I will willingly examine any further evidence which the Honorable Member supplies. There is certainly a variation in the evidence, but possibly most of the variation is on the

Honorable Member's side. I cannot agree with his remarks on the Yalta Agreement, which it is our clear duty to carry out.

June 11, 1947

Mr. Stokes asked the Secretary of State for Foreign Affairs what information he has regarding the number of British and United States soldiers killed or wounded and the number of Soviet displaced persons from camps in Rimini and Pisa killed or wounded in course of forcible repatriation at Bologna on or about 10th May.

Mr. Bevin My information is that there were no British soldiers, no United States soldiers and no Soviet displaced persons either killed or wounded in the operation to which my Honorable Friend refers.

Mr. Stokes Does the term "displaced persons" in the answer include also ex-prisoners of war?

Mr. Bevin Yes, Sir.

Mr. Stokes Is my Right Honorable Friend aware that my information comes from a Reuters correspondent, who is usually very authentic? I will supply my Right Honorable Friend with details if he will look into them.

Mr. Bevin I shall be very glad to get details if they controvert the facts given to me. I understand that nothing happened in this case. I have great respect for Reuters, but I cannot accept the report my Honorable Friend has as final.

Mr. Nicholson Can the Right Honorable Gentleman tell the House how often these operations take place? Is he aware that the whole idea of repatriating people to any country against their will is foreign to this country?

Mr. Bevin It is abhorrent to this country. On the other hand, I cannot allow these people to exploit that fact. Really, we are carrying a very great burden. I am willing to give asylum to the utmost, but I cannot tolerate people exploiting it by being permanently on our backs.

Mr. Nicholson May I ask if the Right Honorable Gentleman would give us this amount of consolation—that we do not forcibly repatriate people who thus would be sent back to certain death?

Mr. Bevin I do not think we have done that. We have had cases where citizens of particular countries have committed suicide rather than go back. But on the basis of the Yalta Agreement my duty is quite clear.

In view of the very unsatisfactory situation, and of the fact that the Foreign Office do not seem to know the facts, I beg to give notice that I shall raise this matter on the Adjournment at the earliest possible moment.

....

Mr. Stokes asked the Secretary of State for Foreign Affairs whether he now has any statement to make regarding the incident at Bologna, on or about 10th May, when British soldiers and Soviet citizens were killed and wounded during the forcible repatriation of the latter.

Mr. Bevin I am not yet in a position to make the statement for which I have been asked. The material with which my Honorable Friend was good enough to supply me contained allegations which have necessitated detailed investigations, and these investigations are not yet complete. I can, however, state quite categorically that no British soldiers and no Soviet citizens were either killed or wounded in the course of this operation.

[Parenthetical notes have been added by the book's editor to show political affiliations as follows: Stokes, Member of Parliament, Labour Party, Deputy of Labour Party; Mayhew, Parliamentary Secretary, Minister of Foreign Relations; Gallacher, Communist, is reportedly Professor Savory, conservative, often speaks up in Parliament against Soviets in defense of political emigrants; Nicholson, Deputy of Conservative Party.]

Documents and Materials having to do with Forced Repatriations

***

Aha! Deputy Stokes raised the question in Parliament on May 21 of Minister of Foreign Affairs Bevin if he knew about the bloody incidents in Italy that took place 8 months before.

On receiveing a guarded answer, Stokes repeated the question on June 11, but once more failed to receive a satisfactory answer.

Enough time had passed for the English Government to obtain the most detailed and exhaustive data on everything that took place in Rimini and Bologna.

There is no sense that, in the time before Stokes's third question, Bevin had availed himself of anything like that, but he again avoided giving a straight answer and, cynically, categorically announced that **there were no bloody victims in the turnovers in Italy.**

To completely understand the cynicism of that answer, it must be remembered that Bevin, many years after the conclusion of the Civil War in Russia, boasted and represented himself as a great influence in the situation in which in his own time he stopped English assistance to Denikin.

One cannot disagree that he turned out to be a valuable servant to his fellow-thinking Bolsheviks.

V. Naumenko

A Question on Forced Turnovers before an American Conference

The *Daily News,* an American newspaper, published the following article by Mr. John O'Donnel on April 22, 1955.

[The article questions the role of the American government in repatriations after world War Two and reviews the politics surrounding the release of details, with annotations by Sergey Polyakov, who translated it into Russian.]

Resolution Presented to Congress by Mister Bosch

This resolution, presented by Mr. Bosch in January of 1957 has to this day not had any progress.

[The text of the resolution, H.R. 137, which follows is as given on pages 199-200 of *Operation Keelhaul* by Julius Epstein. Devon-Adair Company, Old Greenwich, Connecticut, 1973]

Creating a select committee to conduct an investigation and study of the forced repatriation program carried out by our military and civilian authorities in the years 1945-1947.

Whereas the forced repatriation to Soviet controlled countries of millions of anti-Communist prisoners of war and civilians by American military and civilian authorities in the years 1945-1947 in Germany and in other countries brought death and misery to untold thousands of these anti-Communists before Soviet firing squads, on Soviet gallows, and in the Siberian slave labor camps; and

Whereas this forced repatriation of prisoners of war and civilians cannot be justified by the agreement on prisoners of war signed at Yalta on February 11, 1945; and

Whereas this forced repatriation was in violation of the rulings in implementation of the Yalta agreement on prisoners of war, made public by the Department of State on March 8, 1946; and

Whereas the forced repatriation of prisoners of war who had enlisted in the enemy's army was in contradiction to the opinions of the Judge Advocate General of the Army, as expressed during the last forty years; and

Whereas the forced repatriation of millions of anti-Communist prisoners of war and civilians represents an indelible blot on the American tradition of ready asylum for political exiles; and

Whereas the forced repatriation and annihilation of millions of anti-Communist prisoners of war and civilians of Russian, Ukrainian, Polish, Hungarian, Baltic and other origin is still poisoning our spiritual relations with the vigorously and anti-

Communist people behind the Iron Curtain, and is therefor impeding our foreign policy: Therefore be it

Resolved, That there is hereby created a select committee to be composed of seven members of the House of Representative to be appointed by the Speaker, one of whom he shall designated as chairman. Any vacancy occurring in the membership of the committee shall be filled in the same manner in which the original appointment was made.

The committee is authorized and directed (1) to conduct a full and complete investigation and study of the facts, evidence, and extenuating circumstances of the forced repatriation program, carried out by our military and civilian authorities in Germany and other countries in the years 1945-1947, under which millions of anti-Communist prisoners of war and civilians were forcibly repatriated to Soviet controlled countries, and (2) to fix responsibility for such program.

The committee shall report to the House (or the Clerk of the House if the House is not in session) as soon as practicable during the present Congress the results of its investigation and study, together with such recommendations as it deems advisable.

For the purpose of carrying out this resolution the committee, or any subcommittee thereof authorized by the committee to hold hearings, is authorized to sit and act during the present Congress at such times and places within or outside the United States, its Territories, and possessions, whether the House is in session, has recessed, or has adjourned, to hold such hearing, and to require, by subpoena or otherwise, the attendance and testimony of such witnesses and the production of such books, records, correspondence, memoranda, papers, and documents, as it deems necessary. Subpoenas may be issued under the signature of the chairman of the committee or any member of the committee designated by him, and may be served by any person designated by such chairman or member.

About Questions Having to do with Determining Guilt in Forcible Repatriations

In determining the story of who is culpable for forcible turnovers, we can only gather facts concerning them and try to learn from them.

In his article, **"Lessons from Lienz,"** Mr. Akube Kubati speaks of who had culpability through their actions at the scene.

It is also understood that Bolsheviks and their fellow travelers took their part in the matter without ever putting a hand on anyone.

Aside from introducing their people into the ranks of the anti-Bolsheviks, they tried also to take the apparatus of UNRRA, on which the the Allied Governments had placed the care of DPs (displaced persons), into their own hands.

They tried and they succeeded to a significant extent at that.

It must be noted, however, before anything else, that M. A. Menshikov (later the Russian Ambassador to the USA) happened to obtain a leadership position in UNRRA.

He had been in America in 1943 as a member of the Soviet delegation to a conference on UNRRA in Atlantic City.

The Director-General of UNRRA, Herbert H. Lehman, named Menshikov as one of three Deputy Director Generals. He began his service in Washington, after which he assumed the duties of Director of the Bureau of Areas, which then became the Bureau of Services. He managed their divisions of welfare and health, and, in the end, their division of displaced persons (DPs). He also organized the territorial branches of UNRRA, managing the recruitment and establishment of its personnel.

As can be seen from these facts obtained from Menshivkov's official biography, he was presented with full capability of filling the ranks of UNRRA personnel with Bolsheviks and fellow travelers, who, as life showed, he used in full measure.

As an illustration of this, let's take a small cog in the Soviet machine in the apparatus of UNRRA.

On August 12, 1945, there was a forced handover carried out in the Russian camp in Kempton.

There, among the personnel of UNRRA having minor duties, was a certain de Sorby [*Сорбье*]. She was Russian by descent, and by her own account was the daughter of one of the governors and a lady in waiting to the Empress. Such a family was listed among the governors at that time and the highest ladies in waiting in the official directory of the Royal staff of 1913. She had been married to Prince G. [could be "H"], divorced him, then married the French Communist, de Sorby.

This personage demonstrated "special" energy and zeal in matters having to do with forced turnovers in Kempton. When those designated for turnover were led to the railroad station to be loaded into freight cars, she went there, too.

There, during loading, de Sorby watched attentively to make sure that none of those being brought tried to hide.

It must be noted that American soldiers tried not to notice runaways during the trip from the camp to the station and on loading; but she, on noting any such intent in anyone, called it to the attention of the soldiers, who could do nothing else but prevent the escapes.

The ranks of UNRRA were filled with such "de Sorbys" from top to bottom.

But, it would be unjust to raise accusations against all of UNRRA's personnel.

For example, on that day in Kempton, the inhabitants of the camp saw an UNRRA officer, a Negro named Washington, who on seeing the violent images of what was taking place, hid himself against the wall of the church corridor and cried like a baby.

Other such occurrences can also be noted taking place in Camp Füssen (Bavaria). Somehow, a rumor spread through the camp that that night, that the Soviets planned to make a raid on the camp with the aim of capturing several of its residents. Many abandoned the camp toward evening and left for the surrounding forests.

When the camp commandant, White, who was Jewish, was informed of the anticipated escapes, he spent the entire night sitting in the guard post at the camp's gate with the American sentries, ready to repel the Soviet raid.

It must be said that we will yet learn a few more details on the influence of Soviet provocateurs on UNRRA and their helpers.

As far as the actual forced turnovers are concerned, they were carried out mainly by the English and Americans. The methods used, however, were different. Americans openly used brute force, paying no attention to how the victims responded. The English, though, starting with the generals and reaching down to the junior officers, tried, above all, to lull the vigilance of the people marked for betrayal. Their main method was the use of lies. The generals lied, The officers lied. There were even instances in which priests lied. Often the lies were reinforced by the word of honor being given by an officer of the King's Army. They gave their oaths and didn't even stop at the cross in affirmation of their word.

We first became acquainted with their tactics in the tragedy of Lienz at the end of May and the beginning of June in 1945. They also applied them in turning over the ranks of the Cossack Corps. Only a few hours before the handovers on May 8, 1947, in the camps in Italy at Rimini, English officers swore oaths that gave assurances that no one would be turned over to the Soviets.

This tactic succeeded thanks to Russian officers having been trained in the spirit of military etiquette. They simply could not allow the thought that English officers might lie and then reinforce their lie by giving the word of honor of an officer.

Not only those putting the orders in effect lied, but it did not stop with them. Even higher dignitaries did. An example of such are the assurances of the English Foreign Minister Bevin in categorically denying to Parliament that any bloody events had transpired in the handovers of May 8, 1947, in Rimini.

That forced turnovers are illegal is supported by questions of national representatives posed in Parliaments of the United States and England—Albert Bosch and Henry Kirby—asked many years ago that have not been examined to this time.

V. Naumenko

From the Notes of a Soviet Dignitary on the Progress of Repatriations in 1945

In the newspaper, *Pravda*, *No 214* (9935), December 7, 1945, there is an article entitled ON THE PROGRESS OF REPATRIATIONS OF SOVIET CITIZENS. It is an interview by a correspondent from TASS with Colonel General Golikov, a fully authorized official of the USSR on the matter of repatriations.

From this interview, we learn from a Soviet official that from May 25 to September 1, 1945, that is, for the first three months after the end of the war, more than TWO MILLION prisoners of war and other Soviet citizens (and some who had never been such) who had fallen into the hands of the Allied Command had been exchanged.

It was said in this interview:

"The general number of Soviet citizens repatriated as of September 1 has reached 5,115,709.

"Of that general number of those repatriated, 2,886,157 people were freed by the Red Army, while **2,229,552 people were turned over to us by allied forces** from territories liberated by Allied Armies, in which number 1,855,910 people were exchanged directly across the lines of contact of Soviet forces with allied armies during the period of May 23 to September 1 of this year."

....

"It is necessary to note with appreciation the great help of our allies in returning to their native land those Soviet citizens they liberated from German imprisonment. **The numbers themselves tell the story—more than two million** Soviet citizens returned to us by the allies."

....

General Köstring

In one of the issues of the journal, *Ukrainian Review*, printed in English in London, there was an article printed by the Dutch journalist, Hans de Beed, about forced repatriation to the USSR of prisoners of war and refugees.

The presentation by the author of the words that General Köstring, who was in charge of the volunteer organizations of the German Army during the Second World War, gave in response to questions submitted to him by allied investigators, is significant.

[I here contradict my personal edict about not re-translating into English material that was originally in that language, but this is a short, simple piece, and it must already have gone through translation from German to English.]

"We Germans destroyed great 'capital' in battle with Bolsheviks when concluding the peace.*

"Right now, you probably will not understand me when I tell you that, over the course of the last few weeks, you have repeatedly destroyed this 'capital' and not just in the material sense, but also within the souls of those who had not been supported in their time in Germany and who had put all of their hopes on your help and understanding.

"It might be that, in the near future. you may call out in despair for that which you have destroyed."

A brief biographical resume of General Köstring

Born in Moscow to the family of a clerk on June 20, 1876. There, he completed the Russian-German Gymnasium of St. Petersburg.

---

* **Note:** By speaking of "capital," General Köstring implied the people who were forcibly repatriated to the Bolsheviks.

He served in one of the regiments of the Russian Guard Cavalry. He went into the war in 1914 at the rank of captain.

After the revolution of 1917, he served in 1918 under Hetman Skoropadsky. After that, he transferred to the German Army.

Attaining the rank of Major, he served as an adjutant under General Seeckt.

After that, he was with the German embassy in Moscow.

In the last years of the war, he led the volunteer forces in the German Army.

He died on November 20, 1958, and was buried in a cemetery in Bavaria.

A. P.

Preface of the Italian Senator Mr. Franz Turchi to the Notes of Prince Margani

In several issues of the Italian newspaper, *Il Secolo d'Italia* [*Secolo d'Italia* is the newspaper founded by Franz Turchi], in 1951, there was an article by Prince Margani, "Journey to Ternova," which tells of the turnover of Cossacks in 1945.

This extensive material, illustrated with many photographs, gives a frightening portrayal of the days of the Cossack tragedy.

To our regret, Prince Margani died without finishing his memoirs.

In light of the author having used information that was earlier published in this Collection that is well known to its readers, we print verbatim below only the preface for Prince Margani's notes by the editor of the newspaper, Senator Franz Turchi, showing that in our misfortune we have not been left alone, but that others painfully suffer with us and want to help in matters of investigating this evil perpetrated by the Western Allies and certain foreigners.

Ed.

The author of this sensational reportage, writes Senator Turchi, happens to be Prince Peter Margani, an Italian journalist known to our readers and the wider public as an irreconcilable anti-Communist through his many articles. A witness to one of the most tragic post-war dramas, he gives an account of those events. Truthfully, on the basis of official and eyewitness accounts of the horrible crimes, he writes without sparing those guilty of this unforgettable evil.

For a "free world," this reportage, illustrated with photographic documents, is unexpectedly frank. He tears off, in the end, the veil of hypocrisy and silence which the allies, most often the English, draped around this "final" Russian anti-Communist fight and its participants.

Touching pages, unknown by the world, open before the reader's eyes the desperate drama in all of its grim realism.

Pages, alas, full of suffering, blood, and immeasurable insult and grief; pages that call forth real indignation in the soul of any more or less civilized person for the bloody criminal acts that, without a doubt, had been thought out and prepared in advance by its perpetrators.

To the countless, serious consequences of the Yalta Agreement, we need today to add, too, this evil that extinguished the light of the resolute White Guards—in secret, in cold blood more appropriate to bringing cattle to slaughter—all for the benefit of their "ally," Stalin.

An entire army with its officers was turned over to the Soviet command for torture and death. Given up—without trial, without any formal basis. And nobody raised a voice in defense of the doomed!

Our newspaper became the first in Italy to shelter on our pages a narrative of the Cossack drama and the entire White movement that played itself out on the banks of the Drau in Lienz.

And we are proud of being able to publish this historical and humanitarian document.

The West today, having sampled the fruits of Soviet "coexistence," is trying now to strengthen ties with the Federal

Republic of Germany, with General Franco, with the obvious enemies of the Communist regime.

But, giving their due to the legions of Spanish nationals in the fight against Red tyranny, the world should not forget the sad fate of the Cossacks, Circassians, and other fighters in the White Movement, who were left by fate in foreign lands and there, fighting for that same shining ideal, tragically finished their earthly existence through a crime of honor by the English. This tragic epic is described on the pages of our newspaper by the Italian journalist and Russian patriot, Peter Margani.

Senator **Franz Turchi**

Still Hidden Secrets on the Operation of Forced Turnovers.

Mr. Huxley-Blythe is an English journalist specializing in Russian anti-Communist matters. He has written a number of articles for newspapers and journals that call for an investigation of the politics behind the forced repatriation of Russian anti-Communists in the years of 1944-1946. His book, *The East Came West*, which sheds light on the history of Cossackdom during the Second World War and the betrayal of the Cossacks and the soldiers of the R. O. A., will be coming out in the near future.

We can hope that the secrets that remain hidden about the operation of forced repatriations of Russians in the post-war period will eventually be revealed.

To this time, as long the American, British, and French governments refuse to open their archives concerning this gross violation of the Geneva Convention on prisoners of war; as long as they refuse to admit that the orders for repatriation were ignorant and criminal mistakes; that these orders were secretly made by Communist agents holding high positions in Allied governments—until then, the anti-Communist population of Russia will never believe that the West, and especially the United States, is their true friend, a friend that can be believed.

In 1954, I gave Captain Henry Kirby, a Member of British Parliament who was born in pre-Revolutionary Russia, details of the turnover of Cossacks at Lienz. In January of 1955, he attempted to get the British government to exoplain who it was who gave the orders on forced repatriation in the valley of the Drau River. He could not receive any information on this question.

On February 8, 1955, Congressman Albert H. Bosch (Republican, New York) called upon Congress in his House Resolution 137 to form a select committee to investigate all aspects of repatriation, but again, no decision was taken on the matter.

In May of 1958, a group of former Cossack officers, all old emigrants who were turned over in 1945 from southern Austria and have returned to the West after having spent many years in Soviet concentration camps, approached me with their request to obtain monetary compensation for their being illegally turned over to the Soviets. They sent me a petition, along with documents concerning the matter, and I conveyed them, along with a detailed analysis of the politics of forcible handovers, to British Prime Minister Harold MacMillan on September 4, 1958, requesting him to give the matter a go.

On October 7th of the same year, I received an answer from the Secretary of State, Mr. Lloyd, consistent with there being nothing that could be done about the matter.

All the details concerning this request, along with much new material, are published in my book, *The East Came West*, brought out by Caxton Printers, Caldwell, Idaho, in 1964.

Obviously, neither London nor Washington want this question investigated. The accumulation of lies and deliberate misrepresentations that surround this question hide the true facts as if by an iron curtain.

All this points to those in government who were involved in the matter having something to hide.

All this is understandable, of course. Individuals involved in the handovers must have long ago understood that by turning over the ranks of the XV Cossack Cavalry Corps, which comprised a unit of the German Wehrmacht, and the Russian Liberation Army of Vlasov, the West did more for the repression of anti-Communism inside of Russia than could the entire combined strengths of the CHEKA, OGPU, NKVD, and MVD.

From a clearly military point of view, this turnover of noble warriors, along with thousands of refugees, was a more serious crime than that committed by the Rosenberg couple as members of an American espionage organization who passed atomic bomb secrets to the Kremlin and were executed for it.

If the Cossack Corps and the ROA were in existence today as part of NATO (North Atlantic Alliance), made up of the younger generation of Russian emigrants, they could be the torch bearers of liberation to light a fire under Communism in the Kremlin and with that fire destroy it.

Regardless of the Berlin wall and the barbed wire fences that separate Eastern Europe from the West, Russian people of all ages would find the means to get to the West and reunite with their free compatriots.

Now, many in the West consider that we should forget the handovers. They admit their error, but since it all happened long ago, almost 20 years, they claim it has lost its significance.

They discount two very important issues.

First, Russian people in Russia, until they learn the truth about forcible repatriations, will never believe the West no matter how much they hate the Communist system.

Second, the continuing increased infiltration and capture of countries by Communism, as in Cuba, with a final goal of installing a red flag on the entire world, can be stopped only through the liberation of Russia from Communism and the other countries enslaved by it.

In order to win the Cold War against Communism, the West must have the Russian people on both sides of the Iron Curtain as their trustworthy and active allies. But Russians are deciding not to take on such a role at this time, not as long as the criminal actions of forcible repatriations are not being fully investigated and the guilty not being exposed.

Peter Huxley-Blythe

A Hole in the Curtain of Lies

The turnover of Cossacks by the Allies in 1945 to the Bolsheviks should, it would seem, have shaken the conscience of the free world. Nonetheless, this did not happen. To the contrary, few even knew about it and those who did were inclined to quickly justify the actions of the Allies, at best not even willing to give much significance to the events: 'This alleged episode of war, in truth, rather ugly, is something that happens often in war, but ... compared to Hitler's crimes ...." etc., etc.

I wrote a book on this theme in Polish entitled *Zbrodnia w doline rzeki Drawy*, and in German as *Tragoedie an der Drau oder die verratene Freiheit*, based mainly on the invaluable material collected over the years by General Naumenko. I call it "invaluable" not out of some sort of banal kindness, but in the sincere belief that he is drawing together historical documents exposing one of the most terrible pages in the history of human hypocrisy. Not just political, nor diplomatic, nor military, but universal hypocrisy.

What happened?

This is it: Over the course of six years, all the countries in the world that call themselves free democracies carried on one of the bloodiest of wars; one for which the general slogan and moral principle was not one of life, but of death, ostensibly tied to their love of freedom and their attempt to overthrow tyranny and free the enslaved. In a political sense, the issue was not the liberation of a certain country, but of all the people of Europe. Subsequently, the blame was placed on tyranny rather than on the political violations of the sovereignty of other nations and such, but more directly: for crimes against humanity. In the face of this global moral arousal, it logically seems that the fighters for the freedom of humanity should first have bowed before those who, not just in the course of six years, but for twenty-eight years now did not make peace with slavery, did not lose hope, but waited or, without putting down their arms, fought to free people against a not yet revealed, but fuller, more total, more shackling tyranny.

Thus it would seem when based on noble ideals of justice and conscience. But it turned out to be the opposite. When the war ended, those who suffered in bondage more than others, who fought for freedom incomparably longer than others, were the ones who were herded behind barbed wire, then given into the hands of executioners to their deaths, to imprisonment in concentration camps.

Were the lofty slogans about the higher aims of the war, then, nothing but lies? It seems so. And today, we know this. Otherwise, the result of this so-called war of "liberation," would not have been the giving away of half of Europe into the most ruthless slavery. But then, in the spring of 1945, many still believed in the word "liberation." And so, the betrayal of the Cossacks, hundreds of thousands of Russians, and other Eastern Europeans to certain death or imprisonment appeared as the first precursors of the sad reality.

The betrayal of Cossacks and other people to death was, in essence, an incomparable crime committed by those who, several months later, under the pretext of international justice, hung Hitler's generals and ministers for identical crimes. That is how it appears when looked at from a moral point of view based on moral quality, not numbers.

However, by borrowing deep into the analysis of these events, it is possible to come to the conclusion that, on a given specific scale, this betrayal appears as one of the highest of evils, since it did not come about due to military needs, nor can it be understood as some sort of political necessity. Thus, a bit simply and a bit too lightheartedly, it was all just to show kindness with regard to a compatriot:

"We will be pleased to do you that favor if you insist, so take them, shoot them, hang them, let them agonize in prisons ..." How many people? Tens of thousands? Yes, people ...

They object: Do not compare this crime by the Allies to the innumerable crimes committed by Hitler! ... But why not compare them? Comparison underlays everything on earth; without it, it is impossible to be fully objective; without it, there can be no single exact science. Only Communism does not allow for comparisons and subsequently does allow an objective evaluation of anything.

But it might be that the matter in this instance is without comparison. Somebody once said: "It is not a problem when the killer turns out to be a professional criminal. It is much worse when the professional judge turns out to be a cheap pickpocket."

Nonetheless, even this juxtaposition does not fit here, because at the very same time, as came out in the Nuremberg trials ... Things were very much the opposite: rather than a minor thief caught there, it was an accursed criminal, by orders of magnitude worse than those put on trial. In one instance, the Katyn Massacre, he blamed those on trial for the evil deed that had been done entirely with his own hands. Those in court knew well that it was so, that killers were brought to court but not charged. Nevertheless, the Tribunal considered it proper to sit in comradeship with professional killers and even to call the entire vulgar masquerade "Tribunals of International Law."

Such were the deeds at the beginning of the epoch we have lived through, an epoch of collective hypocrisy. And the preface to it was the betrayal of free people to certain death and suffering.

It is true that by clanging their sabers, Cossacks were blamed for turning to an inconvenient side of world politics, that is, against the criminal who repressed them since 1918, then made them go against that which threatened Great Britain and America in 1938 ...

Of course ... with complete objectivity, democratic morals, were soundly sinned against ... But couldn't the steppe farmers of the Don, Kuban, and Terek have found use for such political preparation for the "realpolitiks" of future days to let them know and foretell that in the 46th year of the Bolshevik infection, even the Pope would send the recipients of godless Chekist power a telegram greeting?

No! Predictions are difficult.

The Bolsheviks succeeded over the course of the Second World War and after to complete a reshuffled understanding, mainly to break the historical-objective evil that was Hitler, into something more like the absolute evil of the higher categories. Behind this curtain of world psychology, more successful than the "Iron Curtain," they managed to hide not only their basic evil, but because of the type and and number of outrages of Hitlerism, to threaten in the future the entire world. That succeeded only because this psychological curtain was used also by the allies to close off what was behind this facade—their hypocrisy.

The future establishment of a free world depends on whether this false facade is destroyed in the near future to show the truth,

General Naumenko, to my mind, belongs to those few who, as much as they are able, attempt to break through the curtain of lies.

Josef Maczkiewicz

•

Translator's Note

In his book, *Unforgettable*, the younger Krasnov writes of asking to have fried eggs with six eyes (yolks) waiting for him on his return (which never happened), instead of the six-egg omelet that a translation (not mine) has historians and others believing, a trivial detail, but one that points out a simple pitfall in translation: readability in another language can sometimes be easily achieved by changing facts. I bring this up here, because I have much had on my mind during this project Constance Garnett's translations of *War and Peace* and *Brothers Karamazov*, the former lauded for its readability, the latter, no less applauded for that, has also been criticized, however, for having smoothed out Dostoevsky's distinctive style to the detriment of its substance. Russian syntax, whose sentence structure depends on the case endings of its nouns more than on their position with respect to verbs—perfectly good sentences can be crafted in Russian without visible subject, verb, or preposition—can be brutally wearying to an English reader. As with the first volume of this compendium, I have struggled with the vagaries of Russian capitalization, syntax, lack of pronouns, punctuation, nuanced vocabulary, and other grammatical and editorial quirks, all exacerbated by having multiple authors. (I have especially enjoyed the endearing double negatives that Russians like to employ, and I have been especially bedeviled by the lack of any capitalization rules for names of organizations, especially when used as adjectives.) In that first volume, I may have erred in transliterating more than I should have. This time, I hope I have not erred too much on the side of readability. While it is true that I have taken apart many sentences syntactically and reconstructed them into ones more appropriate to English, I have also purposely left many others in their Russian syntax. In general, while translating writing that was essentially an analysis or a recapitulation of primary material from elsewhere, I have bent in the direction of readability, which did, at times, let a distinctive voice come through. When the material was evidentiary in nature, I stuck to the actual words used and their syntax as much as possible, even at the cost of readability. Sometimes the need for a very close translation usurps that of readability. I submit that the reader should know that Krasnov the Younger ate his fried eggs sunny-side up!

Additionally problematic in this volume is text, especially toward the end of this work, that was originally English but translated into Russian. (And also text that was originally in Russian then translated into English and back to Russian, only to have me translate it back again into English.) I used the original English when easily available, or referred the reader to it as best I could.

As with the first volume, illustrations have been omitted. I

Translator's Note

could find no simple, cheap way to reproduce in a suitable form the poor quality photographs available to me. This made translating the captions unnecessary. (They can be inferred from their images.) In addition, the extensive bibliographic material and the indices in this work, of use mainly to someone literate in Russian, have also been omitted.

     Finally, I have taken some liberties that might best be described as personally idiosyncratic, as with Cossack ranks. I have also substituted for the Germanic "Russian Korpus," used by many historians, the English "Russian Corps." As I have confessed in the first volume for things like "wire" or "barbed wire," "trucks" and "transports" and "convoys" and "echelons" and "trains" and "automobiles" of all sorts, I have used my own judgment on which of the equivalent terms, "forced" or "forcible," to use, as I have also with the several terms used by the authors that can be translated as "betrayal." Other than the word made use of in the title, I have translated them often as some variant of "return" or "turning over" or "handing over," instead of "turnover" or "handover." They are the closest words in English that describe the specific, simple physical action that took place. The morally judgmental term appropriately used in the title is, of course, historically defensible. Something similar may have entered my mind, although from current events, in my use "automatic weapon" over some probably more appropriate term.

     As a final treat for the reader, I have included a Table of Contents, at the end, very much in the Russian style, instead of the beginning of this book.

William Dritschilo
Proctor, Vermont
March 28, 2018

Table of Contents

Foreword—V. Naumenko 11
Cossachi Stan 18
How the Turnover of the Cossachi Stan was Carried Out by the
English Military Command—**O.D.R.** 19
From "The History of the 8th Argyll Sutherland Scottish Battalion.
1939-1947"— **A. D. Malcolm** 29
Which Military Units of the Western Allies Carried Out the
Forced Repatriation of Cossachi Stan—**A letter by V. Naumenko
and an answer from A. D. Malcolm** 33
Concerning Chekists Among Scottish Soldiers in Camp Peggetz
on the Day of June 1st 1945—**F. V.**...35
Churchill-Davies—**V. Naumenko** 36
Major Davies—**V. Naumenko** 38
Letter to the Prime Minister of the Kingdom of Great Britain,
Winston Churchill, and Its Answer 39
Preparation for Betrayal—**V. Naumenko** 41
The Psychological Preparation of Major Davies—**Peter Mar** 48
More on the English Psychological Preparation for the
Lienz Slaughter—**Translator R.** 50
Concerning the Article by Translator R., "More on the English
Psychological Preparation for the Lienz Slaughter"
—**V. Naumenko** 52
More on the Tragic Days at Lienz—**Archpriest Timothy Soin**.....52
From the Past of Camp Peggetz—Former Commandant, 10th Barrack 57
The Death of E.V. Tarrusky (E.V. Rishkov)—**Yu. T.** 60
Lienz (Poem)—**B. Burdarm** 62
By Reason Inconceivable—Professor **F. V. Verbitsky**..................64
More "On the Spittal Tragedy"—**V. Naumenko** 81
More on the 1st Cossack Regiment of Cossachi Stan
and on Cossack Horses—**S. E. B.** 83
The Lessons of Lienz—**Akube Kubati** 89
Betrayed Beliefs—**M. V.** 96
The Number of Inhabitants of Cossachi Stan Forcibly
Turned Over from Lienz and Its Surroundings—**V. Naumenko** 98

Table of Contents

The Final Housewarming—**G. Tuaev** 100
Letter from **Captain Tuaev**..111
Victims of Forcible Repatriation, Their Graves, Monuments,
and the Group Cemetery in Camp Peggetz Near Lienz
—**V. Naumenko** 113
The Painting, "Lienz Massacre, June 1, 1945," by S. G. Korolkoff
—**V. Naumenko** 127
Memorial, Victims of the Cossack Tragedy in Lienz in 1945
—**Gr. A. Ulitin** 128
Victims of the Cossack Tragedy in Lienz in 1945 (Poem) 129
15th Cossack Cavalry Corps 132
On the 15th Cossack Cavalry Corps and Its Commander,
General von Pannwitz—**Jurgen Thorvald** 133
Bezkaravayny's Memoir 140
The Arrest by the English Command of the 15th Cossack Cavalry
Corps's General Helmuth von Pannwitz, His Staff, and
Cossacks Found with Them—**V. Naumenko** 142
On the fate of Lieutenant-General von Pannwitz—**V. Naumenko** 143
A German with a Russian Heart—**A. Delianich** 147
The Last Days of the 15th Cossack Cavalry Corps—**A. Sukalo**.............148
More on the First Cossack Division—**V. Ostrovsky** 164
The End of the 360th Cossack Regiment— **V. N.** 178
From the Memoir of an Officer on the Staff of General
von Pannwitz's Corps—**V. K. G** 182
Total Number Turned Over from the Ranks of the 15th
Cossack Cavalry Corps—**V. Naumenko** 191
The Tragic End of the Noble Colonel Kulakov—**V. Naumenko** 191
Forced Repatriations from France, Italy, and England 195
Forced Handovers from France—**V. Naumenko** 197
Testimony by Kuban Official, **N. P. K.**, Pertaining to
Times of Handovers..200
The End of the 3rd Reserve Regiment—**V. Naumenko** 205
From the Letter of Kuban Cossack, **A. G. Denisenko** 214
Forced Turnovers of Russians to the Soviets 220
Preparations for the Handovers 221
The Operation Carried Out 223
Sequential Events 226
After the Rimini Handovers—**A. G. D** 228

407

On Handovers in Italy—From the book by **V. N.** 229
The Cessation of Forcible Handovers from Italy—**V. Naumenko** 232
A List of Those Turned Over from Rimini (Riccione).............................233
The 20th Century was Horrible—**B. S.** 233
Letter from Protopresbyter **Father Michael Polsky** 237
Why the English are Silent—**A. Baikalov** 240
In the Hands of the Bolsheviks 246
The Sufferings of Contemporary Martyrs—**N. Bezkaravainy** 247
On the Way from Graz to a Concentration Camp in
Siberia—**N. Kozorez** 281
General Peter Nikolaevich Krasnov in the Hands of the
Bolsheviks—**V. Naumenko** 293
Memoriam of a Singer to the Double-headed Eagle
General-of-Cavalry P. N. Krasnov (Poetry)—**V. Petrushevsky** 305
Unforgettable. 1945-1956. — **N. N. Krasnov** 306
Capital Punishment in Moscow in 1947—**V. Naumenko** 310
Announcement of the Supreme Court of the
Military Collegium of the USSR 314
Initial Place of Exile of Cossacks in Siberia 315
List of Places of Imprisonment Mentioned by
Returnees from Soviet Captivity 316
Forced Repatriation, In the Hands of the Bolsheviks, and
Freedom from Soviet Confinement— **M. I. Kotzovsky**..........................317
Excerpts from "Amnesty Decree," signed September17, 1955 338
Letter from the German officer, **Gerhard V, Petri** 340
Letter from the Interpreter on the Staff of General von Pannwitz 346
Who I Happened to Meet—**A. Protopopov** 349
What Cossacks Lived Through at Lienz, Graz, and on
Their Way to Their Homeland—**V. Naumenko** 350
**Documents and Materials having to do with
Forced Repatriation**s 364
Documents Published in 1955 by the Government of the United
States of America in a Book Entitled: *Foreign Relations of the
United States: Diplomatic Papers, Conferences at Malta and Yalta,
1945*, and Several Other Documents 365
Agreement Relating to Prisoners of War and Civilians Liberated
by Forces Operating Under Soviet Command and Forces
Operating Under United States of America Command;

Table of Contents

February 11, 1945 374
On the Attitudes of the Western Allies on the Question
of Forced Repatriation—**V. Naumenko** 377
"Betrayal at Yalta" 379
The Yalta Conference in the Letters of Sir Winston Churchill 380
On the Responsibility for Forcible Repatriations—**V. Naumenko** 380
"We Turned over 5 Millions DPs to Red Executioners" 382
Debates in the English Parliament on the Question of
Forced Turnovers in Italy 383
A Question on Forced Turnovers before an American Conference 387
Resolution Presented to Congress by Mister Bosch 388
About Questions Having to do with Determining Guilt
in Forcible Repatriations—**V. Naumenko** 390
From the Notes of a Soviet Dignitary on the Progress
of Repatriations in 1945 393
General Köstring 394
Preface of the Italian Senator Mr. **Franz Turchi** to the
Notes of Prince Margani 395
Still Hidden Secrets on the Operation of Forced Turnovers
—**Peter Huxley-Blythe** 397
A Hole in the Curtain of Lies—**Josef Maczkiewicz** 400
Translator's Note—**William Dritschilo** 403

Made in United States
Troutdale, OR
04/07/2025